GW01159012

LANGUAGE AND ENLIGHTENMENT

OXFORD HISTORICAL MONOGRAPHS

Editors

P. CLAVIN,
L. GOLDMAN, J. INNES, R. SERVICE
P. A. SLACK, B. WARD-PERKINS
J. L. WATTS

Language and Enlightenment

The Berlin Debates of the Eighteenth Century

AVI LIFSCHITZ

OXFORD
UNIVERSITY PRESS

OXFORD
UNIVERSITY PRESS

Great Clarendon Street, Oxford OX2 6DP
United Kingdom

Oxford University Press is a department of the University of Oxford.
It furthers the University's objective of excellence in research, scholarship,
and education by publishing worldwide. Oxford is a registered trade mark of
Oxford University Press in the UK and in certain other countries

© Avi Lifschitz 2012

The moral rights of the author have been asserted

First Edition published in 2012
Reprinted 2013

All rights reserved. No part of this publication may be reproduced, stored in
a retrieval system, or transmitted, in any form or by any means, without the
prior permission in writing of Oxford University Press, or as expressly permitted
by law, by licence or under terms agreed with the appropriate reprographics
rights organization. Enquiries concerning reproduction outside the scope of the
above should be sent to the Rights Department, Oxford University Press, at the
address above

You must not circulate this work in any other form
and you must impose this same condition on any acquirer

Published in the United States of America by Oxford University Press
198 Madison Avenue, New York, NY 10016, United States of America

British Library Cataloguing in Publication Data
Data available

Library of Congress Cataloging in Publication Data
Data available

ISBN 978-0-19-966166-4

לזכרם של
סבתי מרים ליפשיץ לבית ז'וכוביצקי
וסבי בצלאל שמאלי,
מוקירי המילה הכתובה.

Acknowledgements

This book started its long period of gestation as a DPhil project at the University of Oxford. Several scholarships enabled me to embark on this complex endeavour: an Overseas Research Scheme (ORS) Award granted by Universities UK (formerly the Council of Vice-Chancellors of British Universities), a Clarendon Fund Bursary from the University of Oxford, the Dan David Scholarship from Tel Aviv University, the Bryce Research Studentship at the Faculty of History, and a Senior Scholarship at Lincoln College, Oxford. The final stages of my work on the thesis were supported by the Royal Historical Society Marshall Fellowship at the Institute of Historical Research, University of London, a Hanadiv Fellowship from the Rothschild Foundation, and the William Golding Junior Research Fellowship in the Humanities at Brasenose College, Oxford. Research in Continental archives and libraries was assisted by a grant from the German Academic Exchange Service (DAAD) and a Scatcherd European Scholarship from the University of Oxford. The revision was partly conducted during research sojourns at the Zentrum für Literatur- und Kulturforschung in Berlin and at the Clark Library and the Center for 17th- and 18th-Century Studies at UCLA. I am grateful to these institutions and their directors at the time, Sigrid Weigel and Peter Reill, for the invitations. Most of the work on the book version was, however, done in London. I am particularly grateful to my friends and colleagues at the Department of History at University College London, who provided me with a most hospitable academic home (and two terms of research leave) for the completion of this project.

During my work on the thesis and its revision, I have incurred many academic and personal debts. The greatest of them is to John Robertson, who supervised this project at Oxford and has since migrated to Cambridge. His excellent advice, close reading, and erudite comments were all essential to the successful completion of this work. David Cram, my second supervisor at Oxford, contributed insightful remarks on various aspects of my research, and kindly assisted me in my first steps in the field of the history of linguistic ideas. In Germany, Gerda Haßler and Cordula Neis were exemplary hosts at the University of Potsdam. Further advice was generously provided by Wolfgang Knobloch, former director of the archive of the Berlin-Brandenburg Academy of Sciences. Back at Oxford I received invaluable comments on the thesis and helpful suggestions for its revision from my examiners, R. J. W. Evans and Anthony La Vopa.

Further helpful comments were provided in the review process for the Press.

Many thanks to the following colleagues and friends for their help and advice over the years: Hans Aarsleff, Monika Baár, Efrat Blumenfeld-Lieberthal, Richard Bourke, Christopher Brooke, Tristan Coignard, Michael Collins, Nicholas Cronk, David d'Avray, Hannah Dawson, Simon Dixon, Carmella Elan-Gaston, Holger Essler, Ilit Ferber, Gideon Freudenthal, Sean Gaston, Perry Gauci, Angus Gowland, Roni Harnik, Jens Häseler, Tim Hochstrasser, Istvan Hont, Julian Hoppit, Maurizio Isabella, Ben Kaplan, Axel Körner, Amélie Kuhrt, Neven Leddy, Jan Loop, Thomas Maissen, Nicola Miller, Sarah Mortimer, Matthew Niblett, Edward Nye, Fania Oz-Salzberger, Bernhard Rieger, Hartmut Rudolph, Peter Schröder, Quentin Skinner, Michael Sonenscher, Giora Sternberg, Adam Sutcliffe, Jürgen Trabant, Kate Tunstall, Martin van Gelderen, Margrit Vogt, Masatake Wasa, Joachim Whaley, and Richard Whatmore. Different parts of the book manuscript were read by Knud Haakonssen, Anthony La Vopa, Joseph Mali, John Robertson, and Alexander Schmidt, who were all very generous with their time and advice.

An earlier version of Chapter 6 was published as 'From the Corruption of French to the Cultural Distinctiveness of German: The Controversy over Prémontval's *Préservatif* (1759)', *SVEC* 2007:06, 265–90, and parts of Chapter 1 were included in 'The Enlightenment Revival of the Epicurean History of Language and Civilisation', in Neven Leddy and Avi Lifschitz (eds), *Epicurus in the Enlightenment* (Oxford: Voltaire Foundation, 2009), 207–26. I am grateful to the Voltaire Foundation and the *SVEC* series editor, Jonathan Mallinson, for the permission to use the material here.

Finally, my warmest thanks to my parents Anat and Oded, and to my sisters Inbal, Adi, and Ayelet, for their support and understanding over the years. Mirko Moroni accompanied my work in Oxford, London, and Berlin with much patience and forbearance. My grandmother Miriam Lifschitz (née Zhuchovitsky) and my grandfather Bezalel Smoly, both lovers of the written word, did not live to see the completion of this work: the book is dedicated to their memory with love and gratitude.

Table of Contents

Note on citations   xi

Introduction   1

1. The Mutual Emergence of Language, Mind, and Society: An Enlightenment Debate   16
    No Name-Givers: Ancient Epicureans on the Emergence of Language   17
    After the Deluge: How to Marry Epicurus and Genesis   21
    Between Nature and Artifice: The Trouble with Epicurus   27
    Passionate Speech: Reinterpreting Descartes on Language   29
    Signs of What? The Crisis of Sensualist Epistemology   33

2. Symbolic Cognition from Leibniz to the 1760s: Theology, Aesthetics, and History   39
    Leibniz, Wolff, and Pufendorf   40
       Leibniz on confused ideas and symbolic knowledge   40
       Leibniz on natural languages and the vernacular   43
       Wolff on signs and cognition   46
       Pufendorf and the role of natural law   48
    Halle, Göttingen, and Berlin   50
       Reason and language in the Wertheim Bible   50
       An aesthetic response to the rationalist challenge   52
       Siegmund Jacob Baumgarten: Pietism, history, and Wolffian philosophy   54
       Semler and Neology   57
       Academic history: the beginnings of the Göttingen School   59
       'Popular philosophers' probing language and method   61

3. The Evolution and Genius of Language: Debates in the Berlin Academy   65
    Institutional Preliminaries   66
    Debating Language   73
       La Mettrie's barren suggestion   73
       Maupertuis after Condillac   74
       Responses to Rousseau's conundrums   78
       The genius and politics of language   87
       The prize question for 1759   91

Table of Contents

4. **J. D. Michaelis on Language and Vowel Points: From Confessional Controversy to Naturalism** — 95
   - Prelude: In Defence of the Ancient Vowel Points — 96
   - Sacred Poetry without Vowels: English Encounters — 101
   - From Göttingen to Arabia: Research and Discovery — 104
   - Ancient Legislation: The Case of the Hebrews — 109
   - Natural Evolution: The Case of Hebrew — 114

5. **A Point of Convergence and New Departures: The 1759 Contest on Language and Opinions** — 119
   - Academic Arrangements and Expectations — 120
   - Origins versus Mutual Influence: Replies to the Prize Question — 122
   - Language as a Democracy: Michaelis's Prize Essay — 127
   - The Labyrinth of Language: Responses to the Prize Essay — 135

6. **Language and Cultural Identity: The Controversy over Prémontval's Préservatif** — 143
   - How to Germanize Oneself: Prémontval's *Préservatif* — 144
   - Freedom of the Press and Academic Manners — 150
   - Fatalism and Providence, Content and Form — 158
   - Group Identities between French and German — 160

7. **Tackling the Naturalistic Conundrum: Instincts and Conjectural History to 1771** — 165
   - Language, Method, and the Animal–Human Boundary — 166
   - Historical Evolution from Unknown Origins: Abbt, Herder and Sulzer — 171
   - Naturalism and Instincts in the 1771 Contest — 178

8. **Conclusion and a Glimpse into the Future** — 188

Bibliography — 196
Index — 225

Note on citations

Unless references to English editions are provided, translations from foreign languages are my own. In all citations, I follow the original spelling and punctuation.

Introduction

> No cities have been erected by the lyre of Amphion, no magic wand has converted deserts into gardens: but language, the grand assistant of man, has done these.[1]

This assertion, made in 1785 by Johann Gottfried Herder in his *Ideas for a Philosophy of the History of Humanity*, highlights a central tenet in the debates of the preceding decades about the interrelations between language, mind, and human civilization. Herder here takes it for granted that language stood not only at the origins of poetry, literature, the arts, and the sciences. It is thanks to words and speech that we can perform even the largely physical activities of building cities and cultivating gardens. To put it otherwise, linguistic signs enabled human beings to forge their entire material culture, as well as their intellectual endeavours. This book traces the intricate contours of a debate among authors who tended to take this view as their starting point, to the extent that by the late eighteenth century it had become almost a commonplace. Yet what were the roots and implications of the thesis that human beings could do nothing we recognize as distinctly human without language?

The first and clearest underlying assumption was that language plays an active role in our cognition, or that we cannot think in a properly human way without linguistic signs. Language does not communicate ideas we have formed in the mind independently of it: we simply cannot work mentally with such ideas without using signs. As Leibniz argued, most human thinking is inevitably symbolic in that it is executed by manipulating linguistic signs. This was a view with which various other thinkers, from Hobbes to Condillac to Herder, would readily agree (despite some significant differences). It was also an important transition from an older theory of language as 'encoding' or mirroring our thoughts. According to the traditional view, elaborated by different authors from Aristotle to Descartes, we express in words our already existing ideas. Language

---

[1] Herder, *Outlines of a Philosophy of the History of Man* (Part 2, Book IX), trans. T. Churchill (London: Luke Hansard for J. Johnson, 1803), i. 420; *Ideen zur Philosophie der Geschichte der Menschheit*, ed. Martin Bollacher (Frankfurt am Main: Deutscher Klassiker Verlag, 1989), 348.

functions, according to this 'encoding theory', mainly as a communicative means to render our ready-made thoughts intelligible to others (or to ourselves). If that is the case, we can certainly have pre-linguistic concepts. Equipped with the relevant non-verbal knowledge, we might even be able to build cities. This view of language was rejected by Enlightenment authors such as Condillac and Herder in their different and fascinating ways. Their main point was that language plays a major *constitutive* role in human cognition. In its more radical version, endorsed by Herder, even our simplest perception of the world involves some sort of linguistic performance. Condillac allowed human beings to have ideas about the world without language, but he too insisted that what makes us human is precisely our ability to manipulate our perceptions in a conscious way. And linguistic signs were, for Condillac, the prerequisite for acquiring such self-awareness. If we needed signs to gain control over the sea of perceptions and to act self-consciously, language was indeed the quintessential tool of human cognition and action. It did build cities.[2]

Secondly, if we asked what these peculiar signs are that enable us to barter and exchange, form governments, and convert deserts into gardens, virtually all Enlightenment authors would reply that such signs must be either *arbitrary* or *artificial*. These notions are not coterminous, for arbitrariness implies the absence or impenetrability of a cause, while artificiality suggests a conscious agent who is usually aware of her or his actions (if not of their ultimate goal). But the point was to distinguish the arbitrary or artificial signs of any human language from *natural* cries and gestures, shared by man and animal alike. Most Enlightenment authors agreed that only human languages had a complex structure and the unique ability to refer to abstract terms, general qualities, and non-present items. The diversity of human languages supported this assumption of the artificiality of words: it was all too clear that the English 'table' was not more naturally linked to a wooden piece of furniture than the German 'Tisch'. There were different ways to look at this issue, from complete arbitrariness in the imposition of names to fairly restricted human freedom in the creation of words.[3] However, all authors who defined human signs as arbitrary or artificial faced the same problem: how to account for the shift from animal-like expression by cries and gestures to the uniquely human use of self-made words.

[2] For a critical perspective on this distinction, see Michael Dummett, 'Language and Communication', in *The Seas of Language* (Oxford: Oxford University Press, 1996), 166–87. A different dating of the turn to 'constructivist' views of language is suggested in Tuska Benes, *In Babel's Shadow: Language, Philology, and the Nation in Nineteenth-Century Germany* (Detroit: Wayne State University Press, 2008), 34–63.

[3] Avi Lifschitz, 'The Arbitrariness of the Linguistic Sign: Variations on an Enlightenment Theme', *Journal of the History of Ideas* 73(4) (2012).

This challenge leads us to a third major aspect of the Enlightenment view of language as an instrument of thinking. If language was indeed the 'grand assistant of man', facilitating all our mental and material accomplishments, its origins could clarify the emergence of a whole range of exclusively human phenomena, especially our social and political institutions. And if language was a necessary tool of cognition, any inquiry into its origins was simultaneously a study of the evolution of the human mind and its achievements. This central role of artificial signs in the unfolding of human culture may explain the manifest preoccupation with language in eighteenth-century thought. The Enlightenment was arguably the heyday of investigations into the emergence and development of cultural phenomena, and these inquiries were usually cast as essays on the origins of different human skills and institutions. Some of the most renowned eighteenth-century works pondered the emergence of civil society, human customs, religious rituals, social inequality, and political power. Voltaire, Denis Diderot, Jean-Jacques Rousseau, Adam Smith, Adam Ferguson, and Johann Gottfried Herder (among others) tried to explain why and how eighteenth-century societies came to have their complex social, economic, and cultural forms of life. Their reply usually took the shape of a potential historical narrative; Dugald Stewart would later call such investigations 'conjectural histories'. (Indeed, he coined this term in reference to Adam Smith's essay on the emergence of language.[4]) In all these domains, from government and inequality to the arts and the sciences, a crucial transition was depicted from a rudimentary condition termed 'nature' to a man-made sphere of 'artifice'. In Stewart's words, 'It cannot fail to occur to us as an interesting question, by what gradual steps the transition has been made from the first simple efforts of an uncultivated nature, to a state of things so wonderfully artificial and complicated.'[5] The challenge was to clarify how such a *qualitative* change in all aspects of human existence could have occurred without supernatural intervention.

This last point was fundamental to Enlightenment conjectural histories. If earlier thinkers could answer the question of the origin of language

[4] Stewart, 'Account of the Life and Writings of Adam Smith, LL.D.' (1793), in Smith, *Essays on Philosophical Subjects*, W. P. D. Wightman and J. C. Bryce (eds) (Oxford: Oxford University Press, 1980), 292.
[5] Ibid. See also Hans Medick, *Naturzustand und Naturgeschichte der bürgerlichen Gesellschaft* (Göttingen: Vandenhoeck & Ruprecht, 1973), 13–29; Jean Dagen, *L'Histoire de l'esprit humain dans la pensée française de Fontenelle à Condorcet* (Paris: Klincksieck, 1977); Robert Wokler, 'Anthropology and Conjectural History in the Enlightenment', in Christopher Fox, Roy Porter, and Robert Wokler (eds), *Inventing Human Science: Eighteenth-Century Domains* (Berkeley: University of California Press, 1995), 31–52; Wolfgang Pross, 'Naturalism, Anthropology, Culture', in Mark Goldie and Robert Wokler (eds), *The Cambridge History of Eighteenth-Century Political Thought* (Cambridge: Cambridge University Press, 2006), 218–47.

by reference to God's will or the biblical account of Adam's speech, Enlightenment authors usually found this explanation insufficient. Most of them did believe in God's creation of the universe and in some form of divine providence. 'To be sure,' as Herder put it, 'creating Providence must have presided over the first moments of coming to conscious control—but it is not the job of philosophy to explain the miraculous aspect in these moments.' According to Herder, philosophical inquiry must look at the free activity of human beings—'and hence [it] explains these moments only in human terms.'[6] Rousseau made the similar point that while 'religion commands us to believe that God himself drew Men out of the state of Nature', a proper philosophical investigation would be 'based solely on the nature of man and of the Beings that surround him, about what Mankind might have become if it had remained abandoned to itself'.[7] The exhortation to leave God out of the philosophical picture, made by two believing authors (each in his own idiosyncratic way), emphasizes the naturalistic outlook of Enlightenment conjectural histories. The wish to explain the emergence of our social and intellectual world as naturally developed by human beings was a predominant feature of Enlightenment thought, irrespective of religious allegiance and conviction. Following the perceived success of Newtonian laws in explaining the workings of nature, God was usually seen as having created the universe, pre-programmed it or set it in motion; Herder and others also allowed God to maintain providential supervision of his creation. But this realm could and should be, for most Enlightenment authors, separated from what they saw as philosophical or, in our present-day terminology, scientific inquiry—and this conviction was shared by Enlightenment authors who have been labelled 'radical', 'moderate', and 'religious' alike.[8]

While it would go beyond the confines of my project to offer an all-encompassing definition of the Enlightenment, I would like to suggest

[6] Herder, 'Treatise on the Origin of Language', in *Philosophical Writings*, ed. Michael N. Forster (Cambridge: Cambridge University Press, 2002), 129; 'Abhandlung über den Ursprung der Sprache', in *Frühe Schriften 1764–1772*, ed. Ulrich Gaier (Frankfurt am Main: Deutscher Klassiker Verlag, 1985), 771.

[7] Rousseau, 'Discourse on the Origin and Foundations of Inequality among Men', in *The Discourses and Other Early Political Writings*, ed. Victor Gourevitch (Cambridge: Cambridge University Press, 1997), 132; *Œuvres complètes*, eds Bernard Gagnebin et al. (Paris: Gallimard, 1959–1995), iii. 133.

[8] For radicals and moderates, see Jonathan Israel, *Radical Enlightenment: Philosophy and the Making of Modernity 1650–1750* (Oxford: Oxford University Press, 2001), and *Enlightenment Contested: Philosophy, Modernity, and the Emancipation of Man, 1670–1752* (Oxford: Oxford University Press, 2006). On the more orthodox current, see David Sorkin, *The Religious Enlightenment: Protestants, Jews and Catholics from London to Vienna* (Princeton: Princeton University Press, 2008). See also Paolo Rossi, *The Dark Abyss of Time*, trans. Lydia G. Cochrane (Chicago: University of Chicago Press, 1984), and Helmut Zedelmaier, *Der Anfang der Geschichte: Studien zur Ursprungsdebatte im 18. Jahrhundert* (Hamburg: Meiner, 2003).

one common aspect to various currents of the Enlightenment or to different Enlightenments: naturalism in relation to the emergence of human skills and institutions. However counter-intuitive this may initially sound, the common endeavour of various eighteenth-century authors was to present human artifice as natural—or to explain how human beings have naturally crafted their cultural and material environments. This conception of eighteenth-century naturalism is based on the methodology explicitly endorsed by Rousseau, Herder, and their peers: the explanation of all the intellectual and social achievements of mankind without reference to supernatural agencies. Commitment to naturalism varied, unsurprisingly, in its extent and character. But as we shall see, even orthodox thinkers who advocated the Mosaic authorship of the Pentateuch—in this book, Johann David Michaelis and Moses Mendelssohn—came, at times, to view the emergence of human language and civilization in naturalistic terms, and adhered to most aspects of the ancient Epicurean narrative of their emergence over long ages of barbarism. Michaelis, Mendelssohn, and Herder joined a wide range of authors, from Vico and Warburton to Diderot and Condillac, who endorsed this naturalistic narrative of the evolution of language and society. It was not, however, all that easy to think in naturalistic terms about the emergence of such complex phenomena as language, the human mind, and civilization as a whole. Throughout this book we shall encounter time and again the conundrums that Enlightenment authors had to overcome if they wished to maintain their naturalistic stance. Far from claiming triumphantly the higher philosophical ground, even the most ardent naturalists could not ignore the challenges exposing some vulnerable knots in their narrative.

Enlightenment naturalism, as expressed in conjectural accounts of how human institutions could have emerged, further emphasized the use and the significance of historical methodology. Inquiries into origins were not, of course, historical projects in the manner of David Hume's *History of England* (1754–62) or Edward Gibbon's *History of the Decline and Fall of the Roman Empire* (1776–89). Yet as much as conjecture constituted a major aspect of essays on origins, contemporary authors did not arbitrarily pursue their historical fancy when tracing the emergence of language or political society. As Rousseau noted in his account of the origins of inequality, such works were better suited 'to elucidate the Nature of things than to show their genuine origins, and comparable to those our Physicists daily make regarding the formation of the World'.[9] Rousseau's link between conjectural history and theoretical physics is telling. Just as present-day physicists would not rule out the Big Bang theory of the

---

[9] Rousseau, *Discourses*, 132; *Œuvres complètes*, iii. 133.

origin of the universe only because it is hypothetical, Rousseau declared that his conjectures were well founded and methodologically probable. Even if one had access solely to the present condition of a certain phenomenon—be it the universe, human language, or political government—the Newtonian method enabled Enlightenment authors to apply the known to the unknown, and thereby to mount hypotheses supported by both logical procedures and the historical evidence (where available). Rousseau himself famously claimed that he started his investigation by 'setting aside all the facts', but any cursory look at the abundant notes to his *Discours sur l'inégalité* (*Discourse on Inequality*, 1755) would reveal the extent to which he employed facts to buttress his conjectural argument. Inquiries into the joint evolution of language and mind were even more closely related to questions of historical method and interpretation. After all, it was only by means of language that human beings could acquire a historical perspective on themselves through the transmission of documents, social customs, and oral traditions.

This widespread belief in the historicity and linguistic rootedness of all human forms of life, together with complex naturalism and the view of language as a tool of cognition, should lead to a thorough reassessment of Isaiah Berlin's notion of the Counter-Enlightenment. According to Berlin, this was a strong intellectual current emphasizing relativism and the irrational aspects of human nature; its champions included Vico and Herder. They were presented by Berlin as attacking an Enlightenment whose main tenets were 'universality, objectivity, rationality, and the capacity to provide permanent solutions to all genuine problems of life, and (not less important) accessibility of rational methods to any thinker armed with adequate powers of observation and logical thinking'.[10] Yet in the 1750s or 1760s it was difficult to identify mainstream philosophical belief in the all-encompassing sovereignty of reason or in the self-evident power of logic. In fact, the view of language as a necessary tool of thinking entailed quite the opposite. If language was a basic instrument of cognition, if we could not acquire self-consciousness without signs, the human mind and all its endeavours were sullied by the artificiality and contingency of linguistic signs. Universality was countered by the diversity of human tongues; and if we think in or through language, this linguistic diversity demolished the objectivity of human thought. As we shall see, the increasing awareness of the artificiality of human language, alongside the understanding that the human condition was linguistically embedded and historically adapted,

---

[10] Isaiah Berlin, 'The Counter-Enlightenment', in Berlin, *Against the Current: Essays in the History of Ideas*, ed. Henry Hardy (Princeton: Princeton University Press, 2001), 1–24, here 20. Note also that the new edition of Berlin's works on Vico, Hamann, and Herder is entitled *Three Critics of the Enlightenment* (Princeton: Princeton University Press, 2000).

led to a very different view of 'rationality' and 'logical thinking' than the one depicted by Berlin. What we shall encounter as the prominent view of language and civilization in the mid-eighteenth century was much closer to the frame of mind Berlin attributed to the Counter-Enlightenment. Subtle awareness of the limits of reason and the historical situatedness of human existence was common to Montesquieu, Diderot, Condillac, Hume, Michaelis, and Herder. Strong confidence in the authority of reason and logic was much more characteristic of seventeenth-century authors such as Descartes and Spinoza.[11] This frame of mind, however, did not entail extreme relativism or the renunciation of reason and rational debate. On the contrary, most mid-century authors argued that a finer awareness of the limits of reason would allow us to employ it more reliably and effectively. For example, if (according to Leibniz) we can perceive the Christian mysteries only through our symbolic cognition, we should not aim or claim to see them in clear and distinct light.

What was, then, common to different Enlightenment works on language, mind, and civilization? Was there anything linking authors traditionally regarded as radical (Diderot or Condillac) with those whom Berlin saw as champions of the Counter-Enlightenment (Vico, Herder)? Beyond the careful employment of different versions of naturalism, most authors writing on language and mind accepted the universality of human capacities. These capacities were increasingly seen through an anthropological lens, and on the basis of empirical evidence that tended to undermine the strict Cartesian distinction between body and mind. The universality of such capacities implied the historicity and linguistic nature of human life, not the uniformity of actual values and criteria of judgement. Each society was unique in its own cultural features precisely because all societies evolved on the basis of the same human instincts for environmentally conditioned self-development. The use of artificial signs was perhaps the most prominent among these organic dispositions. There was no need to resort to constant divine intervention, magic wands, or the lyre of Amphion: the peculiarly human capacity for linguistic representation could naturally construct our cultural and material worlds. Moreover, if one wished to let God in through the back door, one could always ask why human beings were the only species equipped with such a linguistic capacity or instinct. Yet as Rousseau and Herder argued, divine endowment was strictly out of bounds for philosophical inquiry, a realm firmly focused on natural human action.

---

[11] For the ongoing reassessment of Berlin's ideas, see Joseph Mali and Robert Wokler (eds), *Isaiah Berlin's Counter-Enlightenment* (Philadelphia: American Philosophical Society, 2003) and the exchange between Robert Norton and Steven Lestition in *Journal of the History of Ideas* 68 (2007), 635–81, and 69 (2008), 339–47.

To conclude this brief overview of the Enlightenment discussion of language and mind, I would like to highlight its common ground with attempts, over the last few decades, to emphasize the constitutive role of language—or the fact that it does not only describe our social world but goes a long way to form the very medium in which we live. This constitutive (rather than descriptive) aspect of language has been investigated with particular force by Charles Taylor and Quentin Skinner in the 1970s and 1980s.[12] Taylor argued that this theory of language originated with Herder and the Romantics; yet as we shall see, its foundations had been laid earlier.[13] The view that language moulds social reality has recently been carried forward (in a different direction) in John Searle's infrastructural analysis of human society. Beyond a few differences, the idea underlying Searle's book *Making the Social World* (2010) is remarkably similar to the main features of the Enlightenment theory: all peculiarly human institutions are created and maintained by linguistic representations. Unlike physical phenomena, the reality of marriage or private property is primarily linguistic. All such institutions are based on a series of declarative speech acts, or utterances that change a situation in the world to constitute what they depict.[14] As Searle argues, 'Language doesn't just describe; it creates, and partly constitutes, what it both describes and creates.'[15] Yet Searle holds a grudge against previous attempts to tackle this issue, arguing that most earlier authors did not explain adequately what language is. As correct as this observation may be—Enlightenment authors were less interested, for example, in the syntactic features of language—Searle does not do justice to the depth of the discussions we shall encounter. He claims that the 'worst offenders' were social contract theorists who assumed that human beings spoke in the state of nature, and then imagined how these speaking agents formed society. Searle's corrective is that once we have a fully fledged human language, we already have a functioning society and a social contract, since the evolution of

---

[12] Charles Taylor, 'Language and Human Nature', in *Human Agency and Language* (Cambridge: Cambridge University Press, 1985), 8–12, 215–47; Quentin Skinner, *The Foundations of Modern Political Thought* (Cambridge: Cambridge University Press, 1978), i, pp. xii–xiv, and the essays now collected as chapters 8–10 in *Visions of Politics*, i: *Regarding Method* (Cambridge: Cambridge University Press, 2002), 145–87.

[13] Taylor, *Human Agency and Language*, 227–34. Cf. Michel Foucault's similar emphasis on the end of the eighteenth century as the main watershed in attitudes to language, in *The Order of Things* (London: Routledge, 2002), 235–71.

[14] John R. Searle, *Making the Social World: The Structure of Human Civilization* (Oxford: Oxford University Press, 2010), 14. On speech acts or 'illocutionary acts', see J. L. Austin, *How to Do Things with Words* (Cambridge, Mass.: Harvard University Press, 1962) and Searle, *Speech Acts: An Essay in the Philosophy of Language* (Cambridge: Cambridge University Press, 1969).

[15] Searle, *Making the Social World*, 85.

language requires interpersonal commitments and obligations.[16] As we shall see, this very point was repeatedly made by eighteenth-century authors. Indeed, one of its most influential statements was made by a certain social contract theorist, Jean-Jacques Rousseau, in his own conjectural history of mankind.

CHRONOLOGICAL AND INSTITUTIONAL FRAMEWORK

Philosophers should perhaps not be taken to task on the historical front, which is admittedly marginal to their endeavour. This book is, however, an attempt to provide a historical account of eighteenth-century debates on language, the human mind, and their joint evolution. Except for a short introductory overview, what follows is centred on the period from the late seventeenth century to the 1770s, with a strong focus on the 1750s.[17] This temporal framework requires further fine-tuning, as the eighteenth-century debate on language and mind took place in a wide range of locations and contexts: from Edinburgh all the way to Königsberg and from Naples up to Riga. Though the debate has attracted the attention of literary scholars and linguists, a historical account requires its closer examination in particular settings. Here I have chosen to concentrate on the discussions in and around the Berlin Academy of Sciences and Belles-Lettres.[18]

---

[16] Ibid. 62.
[17] Among other wider-ranging accounts, see Arno Borst, *Der Turmbau von Babel: Geschichte der Meinungen über Ursprung und Vielfalt der Sprachen und Völker*, 4 vols. in 6 (Stuttgart: Hiersemann, 1957–63); Joachim Gessinger and Wolfert von Rahden (eds), *Theorien vom Ursprung der Sprache*, 2 vols. (Berlin: De Gruyter, 1989); Sylvain Auroux et al. (eds), *History of the Language Sciences*, 3 vols. (Berlin: De Gruyter, 2000–6); Jürgen Trabant, *Europäisches Sprachdenken: Von Platon bis Wittgenstein* (Munich: Beck, 2006).
[18] For differently focused accounts, see Alan Megill, 'The Enlightenment Debate on the Origins of Language and Its Historical Background', PhD dissertation, Columbia University, 1975; James Stam, *Inquiries into the Origins of Language: The Fate of a Question* (New York: Harper and Row, 1976); Daniel Droixhe, *La Linguistique et l'appel de l'histoire 1600–1800* (Geneva: Droz, 1976); Sylvain Auroux, *La Sémiotique des encyclopédistes* (Paris: Payot, 1979); Gerda Haßler, *Sprachtheorien der Aufklärung zur Rolle der Sprache im Erkenntnisprozess* (Berlin: Akademie Verlag, 1984); Lia Formigari, *Signs, Science and Politics: Philosophies of Language in Europe, 1700–1830*, trans. William Dodd (Amsterdam: John Benjamins, 1993); Ulrich Ricken, *Linguistics, Anthropology and Philosophy in the French Enlightenment*, trans. Robert Norton (London: Routledge, 1994); Nicholas Hudson, *Writing and European Thought, 1600–1830* (Cambridge: Cambridge University Press, 1994); Downing A. Thomas, *Music and the Origins of Language* (Cambridge: Cambridge University Press, 1995); Daniel Rosenberg, 'Making Time: Origin, History, and Language in Enlightenment France and Britain', PhD dissertation, UC Berkeley, 1996; Sophia Rosenfeld, *A Revolution in Language: The Problem of Signs in Late Eighteenth-Century France* (Stanford, Calif.: Stanford

Although Paris was in the 1740s the centre of debates on language and mind, by the mid-eighteenth century the Berlin Academy had become an important node in this cross-European web. From the 1750s to the 1770s it was arguably the most dynamic venue of the debate. The Academy was peculiar in its structure, combining a literary section and a class of speculative philosophy with the classes of mathematics and experimental philosophy. In London and Paris, the Royal Society and the Académie Royale des Sciences were confined to natural philosophy and mathematics, while their counterpart in Berlin retained Leibniz's original design for universal scholarship. Despite the troubled early history of the Berlin Academy and its internal tensions, the inclusion of these diverse classes under the aegis of a single institution led to significant cross-fertilization. Intellectual openness was also reinforced by the peculiar membership, comprised of recently arrived French émigrés, scholars from the Huguenot community in Berlin, Swiss authors, and local *Aufklärer*. The open prize contests sponsored by the Academy attracted submissions from all over Europe: from d'Alembert and Condillac in Paris to Michaelis in Göttingen and Herder in Riga. In the meantime, the topics of the contests and the Academy's decisions were vigorously discussed in pamphlets, books, and journals. As argued in Chapters 3 and 5, the Academy became a major centre of intellectual regeneration in Germany. Any study of the Berlin debates on language should therefore take into account contemporary developments in Halle, Göttingen, and Königsberg, for example (see Chapters 2, 4, and 7). Far from being unduly restrictive, the sharpened focus on the Berlin Academy should result in a clearer picture of wider intellectual currents in the German states and beyond.[19]

Debates on language at the Berlin Academy were the focus of an important 1974 essay by Hans Aarsleff, 'The Tradition of Condillac'.[20] Aarsleff challenged the then-dominant view that Herder's 1771 prize essay on the origin of language was a decisive break with all preceding inquires, which were usually presented as simplistic accounts of the human mind. As its title suggests, Aarsleff's essay stressed the significance

University Press, 2001); Matthew Lauzon, *Signs of Light: French and British Theories of Linguistic Communication, 1648–1789* (Ithaca, NY: Cornell University Press, 2010).

[19] On the contextualized study of related debates in different cultures, see John Robertson, *The Case for the Enlightenment: Scotland and Naples 1680–1760* (Cambridge: Cambridge University Press, 2005).

[20] Hans Aarsleff, 'The Tradition of Condillac: The Problem of the Origin of Language in the Eighteenth Century and the Debate in the Berlin Academy before Herder', in Dell Hymes (ed.), *Studies in the History of Linguistics: Traditions and Paradigms* (Bloomington, Ind.: Indiana University Press, 1974), 93–156; reprinted in Aarsleff, *From Locke to Saussure: Essays on the Study of Language and Intellectual History* (London: Athlone, 1982), 146–209.

of Condillac's *Essai sur l'origine des connoissances humaines* (*Essay on the Origin of Human Knowledge*, 1746) in the discussions that preceded Herder's renowned prize essay. This was a much-needed corrective, but Aarsleff's strong emphasis on Condillac's *Essai* may have downplayed the local underpinnings of the debate. While sharing the thrust of Aarsleff's attempt to put the 'big names' of the philosophical tradition back into their historical context, my work tries to balance the scales by exploring further the local intellectual circumstances. By extending the remit of my investigation to works written beyond the confines of the Academy and not necessarily for its contests, I shall argue that the language debates were central to the wider *Aufklärung* in Germany and that German authors were prominent contributors to these discussions. Particularly important in this respect were Leibniz's notion of symbolic cognition and Moses Mendelssohn's reinvigoration of the intellectual scene in his detailed reply to Rousseau's *Discours sur l'inégalité*, which he translated into German. My examination of a wide range of contemporary documents, from printed treatises and review journals to personal correspondence and official edicts, is aimed at the reconstruction of a broad intellectual context. These sources should allow us to perceive more clearly the particular perspectives through which the evolution of language and mind was discussed in Berlin of the mid-eighteenth century, as opposed to the resonances of the same theme in Enlightenment Paris or Edinburgh.[21]

As will soon become clear, the 1759 prize contest at the Berlin Academy constitutes the main focus of this book. Aarsleff has noted that the traditional concentration on 'big names' resulted in an impoverished perspective on the debates on language before Herder. Yet even he, among others, did not dedicate more than a brief discussion to the first competition in Berlin on language and mind. In summer 1757 the Academy announced that the topic of its 1759 contest would be the reciprocal influence of language on opinions (understood as human thought) and of opinions on language. This was an explicit invitation to scholars across Europe to join the fray and examine the methodological and philosophical foundations of the debate. However, the 1759 competition has been so completely overshadowed by the contest of 1771 on the origin of language that its topic has been dismissed as an 'ill-formed question'.[22] By

---

[21] On the reconstruction of past discourses in their contexts, see Skinner, *Visions of Politics*, i; Hans Erich Bödeker (ed.), *Begriffsgeschichte, Diskursgeschichte, Metapherngeschichte* (Göttingen: Wallstein, 2002); J. G. A. Pocock, *Political Thought and History: Essays on Theory and Method* (Cambridge: Cambridge University Press, 2008).

[22] Stam, *Inquiries*, 103. A thorough account of the 1771 contest can now be found in Cordula Neis, *Anthropologie im Sprachdenken des 18. Jahrhunderts: Die Berliner Preisfrage nach dem Ursprung der Sprache* (Berlin: De Gruyter, 2003).

focusing on the first Berlin contest on language and mind, I am trying to avoid such a teleological perspective. The 1759 competition deserves to be studied on its own terms rather than as a negligible event on a trajectory that leads inevitably to Herder's prize essay.

The present lack of attention to the first contest on language in Berlin may be attributed to scholars' initial emphasis on the specific question of the origin of language rather than the broader problem of language in the mind. This narrower focus on origins prioritizes from the outset the topic of the 1771 competition. By contrast, one of my main claims is that the origin of language was not, and could not be, clearly distinguished by contemporaries from the interrelations between language and mind. Authors of diachronic narratives of the evolution of language could not do without a synchronic account of the reciprocal relationship between linguistic signs and human cognition—for the latter included such seminal questions as the extent to which our thinking is moulded by language, and the impact of environmental factors on human speech. I would therefore suggest that the first two contests on language in Berlin, on the synchronic link between language and mind (1759) and on the diachronic emergence of language (1771), were manifestations of a single theoretical thread.

STRUCTURE

The following chapters zoom in on the Berlin scene after a more general opening. I begin with an overview of the European debate on language and mind before covering the pertinent developments in Germany. These introductory chapters are followed by discussions of the controversies in Berlin, the work of the 1759 laureate, and the subsequent development of the local debates.

The first chapter surveys the emergence of the cognitive and social aspects of language as a central intellectual problem from the late seventeenth century onwards. Having rediscovered an ancient naturalistic account of the emergence of language, the theory elaborated by Epicurus and Lucretius, contemporaries made cautious attempts to merge it with the biblical narrative. This synthesis usually included the postulation of long ages of barbarism and bestiality after the Deluge, and the downgrading of the status of Adam's allegedly perfect language. However, the revival of the Epicurean history of language and civilization involved serious difficulties. The most challenging problem was the assumed transition from natural sounds to artificial, man-made words. The incommensurability between these two categories persistently haunted Enlightenment thinkers such as Condillac, Rousseau, Mendelssohn, and Herder. Even when projected over a large span of time, the shift from the natural to the artificial seemed nearly inexplicable. This impasse was closely paralleled in social theory and ethics: in all these domains, the transition from barbarism to civilization challenged authors to reconcile the natural (or essential) with the historical (or contingent).

While the first chapter focuses on diachronic accounts of the emergence of language, Chapter 2 explores a more synchronic approach to the interrelations between language and mind, as expressed mainly by Gottfried Wilhelm Leibniz and Christian Wolff. Leibniz's attempt to rehabilitate the Christian mysteries incorporated an influential distinction: clear and distinct ideas corresponded to intuitive perception, whereas most of the ideas accessible to the human mind were clear but indistinct (or confused). Such ideas could be processed only by means of signs, resulting in symbolic knowledge. From the 1730s to the 1750s, prompted by fears of radical rationalism, Pietists and orthodox authors adopted this rehabilitation of symbolic thinking by means of clear but indistinct ideas. Any claim for a direct, unmediated understanding of reality—by either extreme rationalists or religious enthusiasts—was rejected as entailing dry abstraction from the myriad features of the universe. This Wolffian-Pietist synthesis was productively elaborated in new works on aesthetics by Alexander Baumgarten and Moses Mendelssohn. The aesthetic emphasis on the symbolic nature of human understanding converged with controversies over Wolff's mathematical method, new studies of history at Göttingen, and the practical focus of the so-called 'popular philosophers'. Together, they stressed the man-made character, or artificiality, of all social institutions and cultural phenomena. The indispensable role of signs in cognition made human accounts of the surrounding world contingent, properly expressed only in historical terms.

In Chapter 3 we reach Berlin. After an overview of the history of the Academy since its foundation in 1700, I outline the main questions raised in Berlin of the 1750s. Foremost among these issues was Rousseau's discussion of the emergence of language, mind, and society in his *Discours sur l'inégalité* of 1755. Far from being perceived only as a version of the Epicurean or Lucretian story, Rousseau's *Discours* served to undermine the entire naturalistic thesis. In fact, it spurred into action a divine party arguing that language could have never evolved exclusively by human means. This conviction stood at the basis of Süßmilch's critique of the Epicurean-sensualist hypothesis, a major reference point in subsequent discussions. Meanwhile, another member of the Academy, Prémontval, combined the cognitive aspects of the language debates with the 'genius of language' discourse, or the thesis that language reflected and conditioned the cultural outlook of its speakers. His synthesis led to the declaration of the topic of the 1759 contest: the reciprocal influence of language and opinions.

Chapter 4 is dedicated to the early career of the 1759 prize laureate, the Göttingen orientalist Johann David Michaelis. The main question is how Michaelis, born and bred in a family of Pietist scholars at Halle, came to write a naturalistic essay on language that would appeal to the Berlin Academy. In this context I trace his complete change of mind about the antiquity and special status of the Hebrew vowel points. In his first works Michaelis adhered to the traditional Protestant view, endorsed by his ancestors, that the diacritical signs marking Hebrew vowels were extremely ancient. Michaelis claimed they were already in use in Moses's time, and have since undergone remarkably little change. By the late 1750s Michaelis had revised this view and regarded all languages, Hebrew included, as naturally evolving along the lines of the naturalistic thesis. This prompted a public apology and the withdrawal of his initial views on Hebrew. Michaelis's confrontation with his own background, ancestral and academic, demonstrates that a naturalistic view of language could be developed through a distinctive synthesis of different impulses, none of which was necessarily radical or materialist.

Michaelis's naturalistic view of language and mind was manifest in the essay he composed for the 1759 contest on the reciprocal influence of language and opinions, the subject of Chapter 5. While most other contestants tried to answer the question by recasting it as a historical account of the evolution of language, Michaelis focused on the set topic, the constant impact of language and mind on one another. He did adhere to the contemporary notion that the evolution of language paralleled that of the human mind, while adding to it a panoramic survey of language as an ongoing project of a living community of speakers. Michaelis's principled objection to invented scientific idioms and his espousal of the common use of the vernacular had strong political overtones, which he did not try to conceal. He repeatedly compared language to political democracy and discussed several Epicurean themes in a delicate manner. The combined effect of the 1759 prize contest and the local discussions of Rousseau's conundrums led to what was commonly perceived as an insurmountable stalemate. The chapter ends with an overview of the new challenges elaborated by Formey, Mendelssohn, and Hamann. One of the by-products of this reassessment of the 1759 contest should be a different perspective on the work of Michaelis, who is remembered today mainly as an orientalist or a forefather of modern biblical criticism. Chapters 4 and 5 together emphasize his significant contribution to anthropological and philosophical discussions of language, mind, and the emergence of human civilization.

The following chapter turns its focus to the socio-cultural background of the language debates, mainly through a detailed exploration of a largely forgotten quarrel in Berlin of the late 1750s and early 1760s. At stake was an ostensibly harmless stylistic guide to writing in French, the journal *Préservatif contre la corruption de la langue françoise* (*Preservative against the Corruption of the French Language*) by Prémontval, the Academy member who had proposed the topic of the 1759 contest. Prémontval's periodical immediately attracted the attention of the Prussian authorities and an official threat to ban its publication. The ensuing affair exposed the social tensions and academic norms in mid-century Berlin, while highlighting the significance of language as a marker of distinctive cultural identity. Prémontval's ideas about the use of French in Berlin were taken up by German thinkers such as Michaelis and Herder, who wished to refashion linguistic and cultural values.

Chapter 7 traces the further stimulation of the language debates in the 1760s by new impulses such as the first publication of Leibniz's *Nouveaux essais sur l'entendement humain* (*New Essays on Human Understanding*), the 1763 prize contest on certainty in metaphysics, and investigations of animal instincts. At the end of the 1760s, despite some contemporaries' exasperation with the naturalistic thesis, the Academy announced its prize question for 1771. It required an explanation of how initially speechless human beings could have invented language on their own, thereby asking for a vindication of the natural emergence of language and mind. Though Michaelis did submit an entry, the prize went on this occasion to Johann Gottfried Herder. The chapter ends with an overview of the original way in which Herder's prize essay recast the question: this was an attempt to save the human origin of language from both its detractors and its inadequate defenders. Herder's engagement with the preceding debate should corroborate the recent reassessment of his significance as a central thinker of the Enlightenment rather than its enemy.[23] The book ends with a short glance into the 1780s and the further transformation of contemporary views on the role language plays in the mind and in society. By this stage it should be clear what Enlightenment authors meant when they argued that language could construct bustling cities and irrigate vast deserts.

---

[23] John H. Zammito, Karl Menges and Ernest A. Menze, 'Johann Gottfried Herder Revisited: The Revolution in Scholarship in the Last Quarter Century', *Journal of the History of Ideas* 71 (2010), 661–84.

1

The Mutual Emergence of Language, Mind, and Society

An Enlightenment Debate

The 1759 contest at the Berlin Academy drew on two parallel currents of thought about the interrelations of language, the human mind, and social institutions. This chapter provides an overview of the first axis, accounting for the gradual evolution of these phenomena over time. The next chapter focuses on the second axis, the synchronic and simultaneous impact of language and the mind on one another—or the indispensability of linguistic signs in human cognition. The longer Enlightenment authors pondered such questions, the more convinced they became that it was the conscious use of artificial signs that enabled human beings to develop all their higher mental capacities. Such signs were also seen as indispensable for the foundation of the first social institutions, the arts, and the sciences.[1] In this chapter I shall trace the development of the Enlightenment narrative of the emergence of language with no recourse to supernatural endowment or divine intervention. A readily available account could be found in the naturalistic thesis of Epicurus (in his *Letter to Herodotus*) and Lucretius (in Book V of *De rerum natura*). This was an ancient attempt to attribute a natural origin to words, a starting point that also explained their man-made conventionality or artificiality. Ernst Cassirer has briefly noted the similarity between the ancient Epicurean account and modern 'expressive' theories of language, which he ascribed to Vico, Hamann, and Herder. Yet in this book we shall witness the much wider influence of the Epicurean history of language, in both

---

[1] On the changing meanings of 'civilization' in the eighteenth century, see Jean Starobinski, 'The Word *Civilization*', in *Blessings in Disguise, or, the Morality of Evil*, trans. Arthur Goldhammer (Cambridge, Mass.: Harvard University Press, 1993), 1–35; Josef Niedermann, *Kultur: Werden und Wandlungen des Begriffs und seiner Ersatzbegriffe von Cicero bis Herder* (Florence: Bibliopolis, 1941); Norbert Elias, *The Civilizing Process*, trans. Edmund Jephcott (Oxford: Blackwell, 1994), 5–52; Michael Carhart, *The Science of Culture in Enlightenment Germany* (Cambridge, Mass.: Harvard University Press, 2007), 1–26.

The Mutual Emergence of Language, Mind, and Society

France and Germany.² Enlightenment authors could not, however, easily overcome the tension in ancient Epicureanism between nature and artifice. This problem was exacerbated by the combination of the ancient narrative with contemporary reappraisals of the biblical account of Adam, whose allegedly perfect language became the subject of original reinterpretations.

Attempting to cover an entire century, from Descartes to Condillac (after a preliminary foray into the ancient scene), this chapter remains necessarily selective. It is focused on authors and themes which will come to the fore in the debates over language, mind, and society in mid-eighteenth-century Berlin. I start with a summary of the Epicurean account of the origin of language, highlighting its problematic aspects that would resurface in Enlightenment theories. The second part surveys the early modern reassessment of the Genesis narrative, and especially of Adam's linguistic capacities, in light of the revival of the Epicurean account of human evolution. It is followed by an analysis of Condillac's theory of language and mind, and an overview of debates among Descartes's disciples over the social and cognitive roles of language. The chapter ends with an examination of the challenges faced by sensualist psychology in the middle of the eighteenth century. The empiricist reliance on sense impressions as the main (or sole) route to knowledge raised intractable problems, all particularly distilled when applied to language.

NO NAME-GIVERS: ANCIENT EPICUREANS ON THE EMERGENCE OF LANGUAGE

The aversion of some Enlightenment thinkers to direct divine intervention in human affairs, or to a supernatural *fiat* at the beginning of history, had its parallel in the ancient world. Epicurus of Samos rewrote existing accounts of the origins of natural phenomena and human institutions, seeking to limit the inexplicable and the extraordinary. Unnatural rational agencies were denied a constitutive role in the evolution of civilization; myths of miraculous creation were traced back to simple causes, such as

---

² Cassirer, *The Philosophy of Symbolic Forms*, i: *Language*, trans. Ralph Manheim (New Haven: Yale University Press, 1953), 147–8. Cf. Stefano Gensini, 'Epicureanism and Naturalism in the Philosophy of Language from Humanism to the Enlightenment', in Peter Schmitter (ed.), *Sprachtheorien der Neuzeit*, i (*Geschichte der Sprachtheorie* IV) (Tübingen: Gunter Narr, 1999), 44–92; Avi Lifschitz, 'The Enlightenment Revival of the Epicurean History of Language and Civilisation', in Neven Leddy and Avi Lifschitz (eds), *Epicurus in the Enlightenment* (Oxford: Voltaire Foundation, 2009), 207–26.

natural effects and instinctive reactions, gradually developed over time into more complex phenomena, customs, and institutions.[3]

On the question of the genesis of language, Epicurus confronted Plato, or what was widely perceived as the latter's view of language. Several of the crucial problems tackled by Enlightenment thinkers had already been discussed in detail in Plato's dialogue *Cratylus*, which concentrated on the extent to which language represented reality. As in other Platonic dialogues, in *Cratylus* Socrates promoted a compromise between his interlocutors by examining their initial stances. To Hermogenes' theory of the complete arbitrariness of words (signs having no natural link to the things they denote), Socrates retorted that this would have rendered communication impossible. But the Socratic reply was more nuanced in the case of Cratylus' thesis that words actually reflected the nature of things. Socrates pointed out that some sounds could have had natural meanings, but it would be difficult to generalize from such examples because sound patterns were inconsistent. Though words might naturally correspond to reality, as they could have initially done, Socrates unwillingly admitted that convention did play a role in the daily function of language.[4]

To account for the desirable congruence between words and things, Plato put forward the idea of name-givers, superior craftsmen who might have set the basic rules and first vocabularies of languages. Just as laws had to be drafted by knowledgeable legislators, language and naming were a specialized craft to be mastered only by the wise and the skilful.[5] Each language might have had at its origin a legendary name-giver who directly perceived reality and coined names correspondingly. Subsequent historical evolution introduced convention and arbitrariness into the history of language, until it reached its present unsatisfactory condition.

Though Cratylus' vision of a perfect correlation between words and things was found impracticable, in the ideal Platonic language words would indeed reflect the essence of things, as preconceived wisely by a name-giver. Demonstrating Plato's general distinction between corrupt earthly imitations and perfect heavenly forms, his *Cratylus* contrasted

---

[3] On the relationship between Epicureanism and other ancient attitudes to language and civilization, see Thomas Cole, *Democritus and the Sources of Greek Anthropology* (Cleveland: Western Reserve University Press, 1967); Deborah Levine Gera, *Ancient Greek Ideas on Speech, Language and Civilization* (Oxford: Oxford University Press, 2003), 112–81; Alexander Verlinsky, 'Epicurus and his Predecessors on the Origin of Language', in Dorothea Frede and Brian Inwood (eds), *Language and Learning: Philosophy of Language in the Hellenistic Age* (Cambridge: Cambridge University Press, 2005), 56–100.

[4] 'I myself prefer the view that names should be as much like things as possible, but I fear that defending this view is like hauling a ship up a sticky ramp, as Hermogenes suggested, and that we have to make use of this worthless thing, convention, in the correctness of names' (Plato, *Cratylus*, trans. C. D. C. Reeve (Indianapolis: Hackett, 1999), 435c, 87).

[5] Ibid. 388e–389a, 11.

daily language, full of 'this worthless thing, convention', with a perfect language correctly reflecting the essence of things, a real instrument of knowledge devised by a mythical figure.[6] Aristotle, on the contrary, was not so disturbed by the conventional features of language. In part II of *On Interpretation*, he went as far as arguing that names signified only by convention: there were no such things as natural meanings directly linking words and things.[7]

The ancient Epicureans found both views wanting. The Aristotelian theory, they argued, did not explain the emergence of language: how could there be any mutual accord about the meaning of words if language had not already existed to enable such an agreement? The alternative account of mythical name-giving made no sense within the Epicurean framework, where civilization gradually emerged over time. In Epicurus' *Letter to Herodotus*, language originated in a two-pronged process: an animal-like expression of emotions and impressions was followed by the conscious modification of these initial sounds. Further processing of the initially natural sounds was required to distinguish between different objects, to clarify references, and eventually to denote abstract entities. In this account, the first signs differed among human tribes or races according to their particular circumstances and environments. The same tree would have been denoted by different sounds if it had been first encountered in the desert, next to a waterfall, surrounded by sheep, or in the midst of a thunderstorm. After some time and due to social interaction, human beings grew used to such sounds as names for the corresponding objects. Only later was convention introduced into this process: after knowledge had been gradually accumulated, language became enriched by analogy, abstract terms, and additional categories (such as pronouns or prepositions).

> Thus names too did not originally come into being by coining, but men's own natures underwent feelings and received impressions which varied particularly from tribe to tribe, and each of the individual feelings and impressions caused them to exhale breath peculiarly, according also to the racial

---

[6] I am following most early modern readers, who saw Plato's dialogue as endorsing a natural link between words and things. Recent interpretations have questioned this traditional reading: see Bernard Williams, 'Cratylus' Theory of Names and its Refutation', in Malcolm Schofield and Martha Nussbaum (eds), *Language and Logos* (Cambridge: Cambridge University Press, 1982), 83–93, and David Sedley, *Plato's Cratylus* (Cambridge: Cambridge University Press, 2003).

[7] 'We have already said that a noun signifies this or that by convention. No sound is by nature a noun: it becomes one, becoming a symbol. Inarticulate sounds mean something—for instance, those made by brute beasts. But no noises of this kind are nouns.' (Aristotle, *The Organon*, i: *The Categories, On Interpretation, Prior Analytics*, trans. Harold Cooke and Hugh Tredennick (Cambridge, Mass.: Harvard University Press, 1938), 117.)

differences from place to place. Later, particular coinings were made by consensus within the individual races, so as to make the designations less ambiguous and more concisely expressed.[8]

Though substantially different from Plato and Aristotle's accounts, Epicurus' history of language also combined central features from both. The Cratylian advocates of a natural link between words and things could be placated by Epicurus' view that words did not emerge arbitrarily; initially, sounds did have natural meanings.[9] However, human artifice played a major role in the Epicurean account beyond the level of quasi-bestial communication, and there was no room for name-givers, rule-setters, or legendary legislators. This became the crux of Lucretius' argument in *De rerum natura*, Book V.

> Therefore to suppose that someone then distributed names amongst things, and that from him men learnt their first words, is folly. For why should he have been able to mark all things with titles and to utter the various sounds of the tongue, and at the same time others not be thought able to have done it? Besides, if others had not also used these terms in their intercourse, whence was that foreknowledge of usefulness implanted in him, and whence did he first gain such power, as to know what he wanted to do and to see it in his mind's eye?[10]

Lucretius highlighted here the paradoxical implications of the invention of language by a name-giver. In order for such a figure to communicate with human beings, some rudimentary form of language must have already existed. But if this had been the case, there would have been no need for language to be miraculously invented. Moreover, if necessity had been at stake, each and every one of the primitive human beings could have equally invented language.

The Epicurean theory of the origin of language made room for both human artifice and an initially natural link between words and things, while simultaneously accounting for the diversity of languages. Unlike early modern Hermeticists, Cabbalists, and Paracelsians who tried to recover a single perfect language, the ancient Epicureans believed there was

---

[8] Epicurus, 'Letter to Herodotus', in *The Hellenistic Philosophers*, trans. A. A. Long and D. N. Sedley (Cambridge: Cambridge University Press, 1987), i. 97.

[9] On the different senses of naturalism in relation to language, see John E. Joseph, *Limiting the Arbitrary: Linguistic Naturalism and Its Opponents in Plato's* Cratylus *and Modern Theories of Language* (Amsterdam: John Benjamins, 2000), and 'The Natural: Its Meanings and Functions in the History of Linguistic Thought', in Douglas A. Kibbee (ed.), *History of Linguistics 2005* (Amsterdam: John Benjamins, 2007), 1–23.

[10] Book V, lines 1041–55 in Titus Lucretius Carus, *De rerum natura*, trans. W. H. D. Rouse, ed. Martin Ferguson Smith (Cambridge, Mass.: Harvard University Press, 1982), 459–61. See also the Epicurean inscription of Diogenes of Oenoanda in Long and Sedley, *Hellenistic Philosophers*, i. 98.

a natural connection between reality and language in all human tongues. Due to environmental and physical differences between tribes, their impressions were likely to prompt distinct sounds in various contexts. Therefore, simple nouns and verbs enjoyed a natural meaning in each language, even if over time this natural meaning receded from view under layers of metaphorical and abstract senses. It was particularly the historical perspective added by Epicurus and Lucretius to a theory of natural origin that allowed for a measure of contingency to emerge in the further evolution of language. This creative hypothesis, a third way between complete linguistic conventionality and a supernatural congruence between words and things, re-emerged in the early modern period in attempts to reconcile a natural history of language with the biblical account of Adamic name-giving.[11]

AFTER THE DELUGE: HOW TO MARRY EPICURUS AND GENESIS

The evolution of language was a central component of the Epicurean account of a natural history of mankind, in which human beings emerged accidentally from the earth but managed to develop language and civilization on their own. It seems there could not have been a greater contrast between such an account and the biblical one, where man is supernaturally created, commanding a language that reflects the real essence of things. A perfect man at the starting point of history seemed to contradict early modern observations of nature and man; if one wished to claim allegiance to the Genesis narrative, the imperative was to relativize the significance and wisdom of Adam. Such a downgrading of Adam's mental capacities entailed the questioning of the status of his language, in which he allegedly called the beasts according to their nature (Genesis 2: 19–20).[12]

---

[11] On broader issues in the Epicurean theory of language, see C. W. Chilton, 'The Epicurean Theory of the Origin of Language', *American Journal of Philology* 83 (1962), 159–67; Stephen Everson, 'Epicurus on Mind and Language', in Stephen Everson (ed.), *Companions to Ancient Thought*, iii: *Language* (Cambridge: Cambridge University Press, 1994), 74–108; Jonathan Barnes, 'Epicurus: Meaning and Thinking', in Gabriele Giannantoni and Marcello Gigante (eds), *Epicureismo greco e romano* (Naples: Bibliopolis, 1996), i. 197–220; Gordon Campbell, *Lucretius on Creation and Evolution* (Oxford: Oxford University Press, 2003); Tobias Reinhardt, 'Epicurus and Lucretius on the Origins of Language', *The Classical Quarterly* 58 (2008), 127–40.
[12] Hans Aarsleff, 'The Rise and Decline of Adam and his *Ursprache*', in Allison Coudert (ed.), *The Language of Adam—Die Sprache Adams* (Wiesbaden: Harrassowitz, 1999), 277–95; David Katz, 'The Language of Adam in Seventeenth-Century England', in Hugh Lloyd-Jones, Valerie Pearl and Blair Worden (eds), *History and Imagination: Essays in Honour of H. R. Trevor-Roper* (London: Duckworth, 1981), 132–45.

For Thomas Hobbes, man's characteristic faculties were acquired over time, gradually laying the foundations for culture, science, and social interaction. By seeing language as an artificial construct, naturally developed by human beings, Hobbes implicitly criticized in *Leviathan* (1651) contemporary views of Adam's perfect idiom. Though he paid tribute to Genesis in his account of the origin of language, Adam appeared there as God's problematic pupil rather than a wise name-giver.

> The first author of Speech was *God* himself, that instructed *Adam* how to name such creatures as he presented to his sight; For the Scripture goeth no further in this matter. But this was sufficient to direct him to add more names, as the experience and use of the creatures should give him occasion; and to join them in such manner by degrees, as to make himself understood; and so by succession of time, so much language might be gotten, as he had found use for; though not so copious, as an Orator or Philosopher has need of. For I do not find any thing in the Scripture, out of which, directly or by consequence can be gathered, that Adam was taught the names of all Figures, Numbers, Measures, Colours, Sounds, Fancies, Relations [...].[13]

Hobbes's reading of Genesis allowed him to implant within the biblical narrative an account of the gradual evolution of language by human beings: from simple objects named according to need and utility all the way to a philosophical vocabulary. God was still the 'author of speech', but creation endowed Adam only with rudimentary potential capacities, to be perfected over a long time.[14]

A similar argument was made by Samuel Pufendorf in *De jure naturae et gentium* (*On the Law of Nature and Nations*, 1672). Conceding that Adam might have named animals and things according to their essences, Pufendorf suggested that the basic elements of Adam's own words were arbitrary.[15] In all languages, Pufendorf observed, 'things allied by nature are usually allied by name,' but this did not mean that their names were perfect or natural. In line with his emphasis on the conventional and even contractual origin of language, Pufendorf explicitly espoused a version of Hermogenes' view of the arbitrariness of the sign in Plato's *Cratylus*. This

---

[13] Thomas Hobbes, *Leviathan*, ed. Richard Tuck (Cambridge: Cambridge University Press, 1996), 24–5. In *De homine* (1658) Hobbes argued that after the confusion of tongues at Babel, names never reflected the nature of things. (Hobbes, *Man and Citizen*, trans. C. T. Wood, T. S. K. Scott-Craig, and B. Gert (Indianapolis: Hackett, 1991), 38–9.)

[14] On language in Hobbes, see Michael Isermann, *Die Sprachtheorie im Werk von Thomas Hobbes* (Münster: Nodus, 1991); Quentin Skinner, *Reason and Rhetoric in the Philosophy of Hobbes* (Cambridge: Cambridge University Press, 1996); Philip Pettit, *Made of Words: Hobbes on Language, Mind, and Politics* (Princeton: Princeton University Press, 2008).

[15] Samuel Pufendorf, *Of the Law of Nature and Nations*, trans. Basil Kennett (Oxford: A. and J. Churchill, 1710), 4.1. 249.

entailed a clear rejection of the invention of language by either God or a human name-giver.

Richard Simon too suggested that the biblical account of Adam's language could be read in a naturalistic way. In his *Histoire critique du Vieux Testament* (*Critical History of the Old Testament*, 1678) Simon quoted Epicurus, Lucretius, Diodorus of Sicily, and Gregory of Nyssa against the divine origin of language. Equating nature and human reason, Simon explained that God created things, not words to denote them; all languages arose from 'reasonable nature'. His assault on supernatural agencies at the origin of language was completed by interpreting Plato's name-givers as metaphorical images of human reason. Like Pufendorf, Simon infused Genesis with ancient naturalism in order to claim there was no contradiction between the biblical account and a natural emergence of language.[16]

John Locke bowed before the biblical account of the origin of language not as a disguise for a naturalistic narrative of its emergence, but rather as an introduction to his examination of the operations of language. At the beginning of Book III ('Of Words') of his *Essay Concerning Human Understanding* (1689) Locke briefly noted that man was created speaking and sociable, endowed by God with a capacity for language. This endowment was similar to the very basic instrument depicted by Hobbes: God did not give human beings actual words and ideas.[17] There is no detailed account in the *Essay* of the unfolding of language throughout history, as Locke's aim differed from that of eighteenth-century followers of his psychology, particularly in France. Wishing to combat contemporary beliefs in a perfect accord between words and things, Locke emphasized the arbitrariness of signs, demonstrating the dependence of words on ideas formed in an individual's mind rather than on any correct taxonomy of nature.[18]

A contemporary of Locke tackling the same problem was Gottfried Wilhelm Leibniz, who rejected the strict dichotomy between naturalness and human artifice in relation to language. Like others who wished to overcome this ancient tension, Leibniz followed Epicurus' lead. He argued that human beings created words according to sense impressions,

---

[16] Simon, *Histoire critique du Vieux Testament* (Amsterdam: Elzevir, 1680), i. 92–101. For other ancient accounts of a natural emergence of language, see Diodorus of Sicily, *Bibliotheca historica*, 1.8; Vitruvius, *De architectura*, 2.1.1; Cicero, *De inventione*, 1.2–3 and *De re publica*, 3.2.3; Lactantius, *Divinarum institutionum libri VII*, 6.10.13; Gregory of Nyssa, *Contra Eunomium* 2.387–444.

[17] Locke, *An Essay Concerning Human Understanding*, ed. Peter H. Nidditch (Oxford, 1979), 3.1§1, 402.

[18] Hans Aarsleff, *From Locke to Saussure*, 42–83; Hannah Dawson, *Locke, Language and Early Modern Philosophy* (Cambridge: Cambridge University Press, 2007), 214–38.

employing an analogy between the acoustic properties of objects and the sounds used to denote them. The psychological and environmental circumstances of this act of naming introduced a contingent element into the natural process. Leibniz's Epicurean theory thus allowed languages to retain natural residues while accounting for the different names an object could have in different idioms. Since similar circumstances were likely to yield the same responses among the first human beings, some original roots might still be recovered from under the ages of evolution and change.[19]

Bernard Mandeville in *The Fable of the Bees* (two volumes, 1723 and 1729) did not even try to clothe his Epicurean account of the origin of language with the biblical narrative. Without mentioning Adam, the Deluge, or the Tower of Babel, Mandeville projected his history of language onto a large temporal canvas, where emotive cries and gestures gradually turned into articulate speech. As in Lucretius and Hobbes, this process must have occurred naturally.[20] Though the main goal of the invention of speech in Mandeville's treatise was deception and domination rather than social cooperation, his *Fable* contributed to the propagation of the Epicurean account of the origin of language in eighteenth-century Britain and France (it was translated into French in 1740 and immediately banned).[21]

Giambattista Vico, on a very different intellectual terrain, attempted in his own manner to reconcile Scripture and a naturalistic account of the emergence of civilization. In his *Scienza nuova* (*New Science*, three editions: 1725, 1730, 1748) he placed the long ages of transition from barbarism to culture after the Deluge, in order not to compromise Adam's wisdom and perfect language. The uniqueness of revealed history was also preserved by the exclusion of the ancient Hebrews from the general dispersion and descent into bestial existence. For all other nations, the postdiluvian condition was the starting point of a quasi-Epicurean evolution. Human beings with an elementary understanding imagined their gods

---

[19] Louis Couturat (ed.), *Opuscules et fragments inédits de Leibniz* (Paris: Alcan, 1903), 151–2; Marcelo Dascal, *Leibniz: Language, Signs and Thought* (Amsterdam: John Benjamins, 1987), 189; Stefano Gensini, 'De linguis in universum': On Leibniz's Ideas on Languages (Münster: Nodus, 2000), 43–96.

[20] 'Horatio: But if the old Stock would never either be able or willing to acquire Speech, it is impossible they could teach it their Children: Then which way could any Language come into the World from two Savages? Cleomenes: By slow degrees, as all other Arts and Sciences have done, and length of time; Agriculture, Physick, Astronomy, Architecture, Painting, &c.', Mandeville, *The Fable of the Bees, or Private Vices, Publick Benefits*, ed. F. B. Kaye (Oxford: Oxford University Press, d), ii. 287. See also E. J. Hundert, 'The Thread of Language and the Web of Dominion: Mandeville to Rousseau and Back', *Eighteenth-Century Studies* 21 (1988), 169–91.

[21] Kaye, Introduction to Mandeville, *Fable*, i, p. cxvi.

and simultaneously created language, ascribing divinely animate names to the most striking phenomena. Vico's emphasis on gentile humanity maintained his distinction between the biblical account of Jewish history and the Epicurean emergence of all other nations. According to Vico, only Hebrew resembled Adam's perfect language, bearing no traces of the polytheistic imagination and mythical thinking.[22]

Beyond Mandeville's *Fable of the Bees*, another English essay exerting profound influence in eighteenth-century Europe was (perhaps serendipitously) *The Divine Legation of Moses* by William Warburton (two volumes, 1738 and 1741). Condillac, Rousseau, Voltaire, and authors of various articles in the *Encyclopédie* all referred to Warburton's work, exalting its account of the origin of language and the evolution of writing systems. Unfortunately, it was almost the only aspect of the work with which they were acquainted through the partial translation by Marc Antoine Léonard des Malpeines, published in 1744. Though *The Divine Legation* was conceived as a refutation of Spinoza and Toland, or a vindication of the exceptionality of Hebraic history, its French version was focused on Book IV of Warburton's work. This was where Warburton sought to refute the hypothesis that the ancient Egyptians concealed esoteric wisdom in their hieroglyphs; the French title was, accordingly, *Essai sur les hiéroglyphes des Égyptiens* (*Essay on the Egyptians' Hieroglyphs*). Divorced from its theological context, *The Divine Legation* could be read as one amongst other Enlightenment essays on the natural transition from barbarism to civilization.

According to Warburton, Egyptian hieroglyphs were not at all sources of recondite knowledge; they constituted a primitive form of writing by images, intended for popular use and arising out of necessity. Warburton outlined a natural history of language and thought, where the shift from a lively 'speech by action' (gesture and mime) to articulate sounds corresponded to the modification of written forms from images (hieroglyphs) to analogy (Chinese characters), and later convention (phonetic alphabets).[23] The first human beings used concrete images as their symbols just as they spoke in fables before moving on to similes and metaphors. This process was prompted by nature, custom, and practice. Only later,

---

[22] Vico, *The New Science*, trans. Thomas Bergin and Max Fisch (Ithaca, NY: Cornell University Press, 1984), 127–8. On language in Vico see Jürgen Trabant, *Vico's New Science of Ancient Signs: A Study of Sematology*, trans. Sean Ward (London: Routledge, 2004), and for Vico's Epicurean account of human nature, Robertson, *The Case for the Enlightenment*, 238–55.

[23] William Warburton, *The Divine Legation of Moses*, 2nd edn. (London: For the Executor of Mr Fletcher Gyles, 1742), ii. 82–3. See also the influential French translation: William Warburthon [sic], *Essai sur les hiéroglyphes des Égyptiens*, trans. Marc Antoine Léonard des Malpeines (Paris: Hippolyte-Louis Guerin, 1744), i. 48–52.

following the development of a phonetic alphabet, did Egyptian priests appropriate the old hieroglyphic script and attribute to it secret truths in order to dominate the people. In a somewhat cumbersome manner, Warburton's refutation of the uniqueness of Egyptian religion was supposed to emphasize the workings of providence in the history of the ancient Jews. Warburton combined his view of Egypt with an acknowledgement that the Old Testament lacked a system of future rewards and punishments, usually deemed a pivotal tenet of all political societies. This feature of ancient Judaism allegedly proved the providential exception of God's chosen people. In France, however, *The Divine Legation* was received as an attempt to reconcile the biblical narrative with the Epicurean history of language in the tradition of Thomas Hobbes and Richard Simon.[24]

One particularly striking use of Warburton's *Divine Legation* in this manner was Étienne Bonnot de Condillac's *Essai sur l'origine des connoissances humaines* (*Essay on the Origin of Human Knowledge*, 1746). Like Vico, Condillac situated the starting point of his naturalistic account of human evolution after the Deluge, referring to Vitruvius, Diodorus of Sicily, Richard Simon and (at length) to William Warburton as his authorities. Praising Warburton for his intellectual acumen, Condillac added that 'if I suppose two children under the necessity of imagining even the first signs of language, it is because I do not think it was enough for a philosopher to say that something had been achieved by special means, but that it was his duty to think how it could have come about by natural means.'[25] This disclaimer is very similar to the ones issued by Rousseau and Herder when approaching the same risky question. Condillac went on to explain that there was no harm in accounting for the origin of language and mind in the following manner.

> Adam and Eve did not owe the exercise of the operations of their soul to experience. As they came from the hands of God, they were able, by special assistance, to reflect and communicate their thoughts to each other. But I am assuming that two children, one of either sex, sometime after the deluge, had gotten lost in the desert before they would have known of any sign. The fact I have just stated gives me the right to make this assumption.[26]

---

[24] Arthur William Evans, *Warburton and the Warburtonians* (Oxford: Oxford University Press, 1932); Clifton Cherpack, 'Warburton and the Encyclopédie', *Comparative Literature* 7 (1955), 226–39; B. W. Young, *Religion and Enlightenment in Eighteenth-Century England* (Oxford: Clarendon Press, 1998), 167–212.

[25] Condillac, *Essay on the Origin of Human Knowledge*, ed. Hans Aarsleff (Cambridge: Cambridge University Press, 2001), 113–14; 'Essai sur l'origine des connoissances humaines' in *Œuvres philosophiques de Condillac*, ed. Georges Le Roy (Paris: PUF, 1947–51), i. 60.

[26] Condillac, *Essay*, 113; *Œuvres* i. 60.

Condillac's *Essai* exemplified the contemporary device of maintaining an apparent reverence of the biblical narrative while simultaneously circumventing it. The status of Adam's language no longer bothered Condillac; it became irrelevant through a nonchalant reference to the Deluge as the starting point of the real (or Epicurean) history of civilization. Jean-Jacques Rousseau argued along similar lines in his *Essai sur l'origine des langues* (*Essay on the Origin of Languages*, 1756–61; published posthumously in 1781). Rousseau noted that, although Adam and Noah possessed language, the relevant beginning of human history was the ages of savagery following the Deluge. According to Rousseau, this combination of the Epicuro-Lucretian narrative with the biblical version was the only way to reconcile Scriptural authority with 'the monuments of antiquity'.[27] In this manner, the conflicting accounts of human history in Epicurus and Genesis seemed to have been successfully merged by the mid-eighteenth century. But neither Rousseau nor Condillac could resolve another serious problem raised by the revival of the Epicurean history of language and civilization: the transition from the natural to the artificial.

BETWEEN NATURE AND ARTIFICE: THE TROUBLE WITH EPICURUS

In Condillac's *Essai* language was not only a human achievement emerging through a slow civilizing process; it was the very prerequisite for the evolution of the mind, social life, and all forms of culture. Through the mutual evolution of language and the mind, human society acquired a historical perspective on itself, as language allowed experience to be accumulated and transmitted to posterity. At the heart of this account stood, however, a serious problem harking back to the Epicurean response to Plato's *Cratylus*: the combination of naturalism with a diachronic viewpoint. Historical evolution gave rise to a measure of contingency, whereas a natural origin of language entailed an initial connection between words and things beyond arbitrariness or convention.

Condillac was, apparently, well aware of this tension between natural origins and historical development. In the *Essai* he distinguished between

---

[27] Rousseau, *Discourses*, 270–1; *Œuvres complètes*, v. 398–9. On the Deluge in early modern thought, see Don Cameron Allen, *The Legend of Noah* (Urbana, Ill.: University of Illinois Press, 1949); Claudine Poulouin, *Le Temps des origines: l'Eden, le Déluge et 'les temps reculés'. De Pascal à l'Encyclopédie* (Paris: Champion, 1998); Maria Susana Seguin, *Science et religion dans la pensée française du XVIIIe siècle: le mythe du Déluge universel* (Paris: Champion, 2001); Martin Mulsow and Jan Assmann (eds), *Sintflut und Gedächtnis: Erinnern und Vergessen des Ursprungs* (Munich: Fink, 2006).

three kinds of signs: natural signs instinctively expressing emotions such as joy and pain (they ceased to be natural once deliberately used); accidental signs reviving unconsciously some ideas under particular circumstances; and instituted signs having 'an arbitrary relation to our ideas'.[28] The first instituted (or arbitrary) signs were introduced on the basis of a gestural 'language of action', the original means of communication through cries, gestures, and other expressive signs. Here too, the same object could be denoted in various ways by different peoples according to the circumstances under which it had been first encountered. All languages thus exhibited an initial relation between signs and things, which was subsequently lost under layers of human convention.

Already in the *Essai* of 1746 Condillac identified the transition from natural to instituted signs as a potential paradox: how could human beings use conventional signs if they had no command of the required mental capacities—which, in turn, depended on the use of conventional signs?[29] Condillac's solution was to be found in time and habituation. Frequent repetition made the use of natural signs a habit even in the absence of the objects and circumstances that had initially accompanied them. Subsequently, human beings came to do by reflection what they had initially done by instinct.[30] However, instead of clarifying the shift from natural signs to arbitrary ones, Condillac could be seen as merely projecting this transition onto a large temporal sweep.

Another attempt to explain this transition was made in Condillac's *Grammaire* (*Grammar*, 1775), an instalment in his series of textbooks for the Prince of Parma. Here Condillac found it necessary to rechristen conventional signs as 'artificial'. The modification of such signs from 'arbitrary' (in 1746) to 'artificial' (in 1775) was meant to address the apparent incommensurability between natural sounds on the one hand, and manmade, instituted signs on the other. Condillac argued that complete arbitrariness was impossible in language, since words had to be understood by the primitive users of natural signs. Because of our step-by-step mental progression, human intelligence did not tolerate pure chance in this domain.[31]

This distinction between 'arbitrary' and 'artificial' was made after three decades of intense debate over the Epicurean account of the history of language and civilization. The main objections did not concern the reconciliation of Genesis with *De rerum natura*, or of Adam's perfect language with the initial silence of Lucretian brutes. As we shall see in Chapter 3, critics across Europe levelled their attack at what they perceived as the

---

[28] Condillac, *Essay*, 36; *Œuvres*, i. 19.
[30] *Essay*, 114–15; *Œuvres*, i. 60–3.
[29] *Essay*, 41; *Œuvres*, i. 22.
[31] 'Grammaire', in *Œuvres*, i. 429, 432–3.

most vulnerable point of the naturalistic thesis: the supposedly smooth transition between two dissimilar categories. No projection over time could merge together incommensurable signs, the objection went, for at some point a *qualitative* leap must be assumed from the natural to the artificial.

PASSIONATE SPEECH: REINTERPRETING DESCARTES ON LANGUAGE

The difficult transition from speechless beasts to articulate human beings was not the only tension accompanying the revival of the Epicurean account of human evolution. Condillac and his readers in Berlin assumed that signs had a constitutive role in human cognition, but this was the conclusion of a long re-evaluation of the Cartesian view of language and mind. René Descartes distinguished pure intellection, an activity of the mind wholly independent of the senses, from the cognitive faculties of passion and imagination, engendered by the body.[32] In his *Discours de la méthode* (*Discourse on the Method*, 1637) Descartes referred to human language as one of the strongest proofs of this strict distinction between body and mind. Following the traditional theory of language as mirroring or merely representing mental ideas, Descartes saw signs as tools for the communication of already formed concepts. For Descartes, our creative use of language demonstrated that the immaterial mind directed the exercise of material signs, unlike the same operation in animals-automatons.[33]

The intellect's freedom from the intervention of signs was also emphasized in the debate over Descartes's *Meditations*. Replying to Descartes, Hobbes suggested that reasoning was the linking of names to each other by means of the copula. The implication was that we know nothing about the nature of things but merely about the labels we apply to objects in the world. According to Hobbes, reasoning depended on names; names, in turn, originated in the recollection of sense data by the imagination, a faculty consisting in physical motions within the brain.[34] In his response to Hobbes's objection, Descartes asserted that human beings could directly perceive things through their mental acts, requiring no mediating representations. In Descartes's framework, this immediate perception did not involve linguistic signs. The distinction between immaterial ideas and

---

[32] Descartes, *Œuvres et lettres*, ed. André Bridoux (Paris: Gallimard, 1953), 695–795.
[33] Ibid. 164–6.
[34] Thomas Hobbes, Third set of objections to Descartes's *Meditations*, ibid. 399–420 (esp. 404–6).

physical symbols was crucial for his dualism, which was allegedly further demonstrated by the diversity of languages. Bestial cries and interjections occurred everywhere in the same way, Descartes argued, while only human beings spoke in different languages and had various names for the same object—a testimony of their free will.[35]

This point highlights an important caesura between the Epicurean account of the evolution of language and Cartesian dualism. For Descartes, the human mind was uniquely able, thanks to its immaterial nature, to combine in language an intellectual act (mental perception) with its physical representation (sounds, characters) in stark contrast to all forms of animal communication. In the Epicurean narrative, however, human language evolved from the same rudimentary beginnings as animal language, initially differing very little from bestial communication. The similarity between human and animal language was emphasized by Lucretius, who treated the origin of human language as a natural, species-specific emanation of voices parallel to the neighing of horses or birds' chirping.[36]

Yet Descartes's view of speech, accompanied by his claim that the difference between human and animal language was qualitative and thus independent of physiology, was conditioned by the dualism it strove to prove—as pointed out by Descartes's sensualist opponents, from Hobbes to La Mettrie. Such critics tended to focus their attack on the unbridgeable gap between Descartes's materialist physics and his dualist metaphysics. The strict separation between body and mind was, however, a difficult challenge also for authors who did agree with the main tenets of Descartes's philosophy. Such thinkers as Antoine Arnauld, Blaise Pascal, and Bernard Lamy all contributed to a reassessment of the role of the passions and the imagination in human cognition.

Pascal distinguished in his *De l'esprit géometrique* (*On the Geometric Mind*, 1658) between nominal definitions, which are man-made, arbitrary, and cannot be contradicted (as in geometry), and real definitions, aspiring to convey the essence of things and liable to contradiction. According to Pascal, it was a natural human mistake to opt for real definitions and believe one could directly perceive the nature of things. This was the reason that at the level of practical communication, nominal definitions were not sufficient. In matters of daily life, truth was more accessible through an appeal

---

[35] On human and bestial communication, see Richard Serjeantson, 'The Passions and Animal Language, 1540–1700', *Journal of the History of Ideas* 62 (2001), 425–44; Lauzon, *Signs of Light*, 13–66.

[36] *De rerum natura* V, lines 1056–86. Note the tension between this view of language as an innate idiom and the accompanying account of its communal development by initially speechless human beings. This issue will be raised by critics of the naturalistic thesis, as discussed in Chapters 3 and 7.

to the unstable passions rather than to an innate and universal reason.[37] Such considerable attention to the pragmatic aspects of discourse differed from Descartes's own focus. Although he ascribed part of the uniqueness of human language to its free and creative usage, Descartes recognized no distinct levels of discourse. For Descartes, language reflected the mind's ideas in such a manner that there could be no difference between logical and verbal structures. Pascal, however, distinguished between the two and tried to employ this observation to the benefit of his art of persuasion.[38]

Antoine Arnauld and Pierre Nicole's *Logique, ou l'art de penser* (*Logic, or the Art of Thinking*, 1662) began with a reiteration of Descartes's arguments against Hobbes and Gassendi, reasserting the clear and distinct nature of immaterial ideas. In their *Grammaire générale et raisonnée* (*General and Rational Grammar*, 1660) Arnauld and Claude Lancelot had already postulated a parallel between the innate order of thinking and a natural order of language, presumably present in all languages and ruling their individual grammars. But whereas in the *Grammaire* practical deviations from the logical order were considered as violations of a universal grammar, in the *Logique* the pragmatic aspects of language received a more positive appraisal. In the latter work, such practical devices were seen as necessary elements of speech.[39] Arnauld carried on the rehabilitation of the sense-oriented faculty of the imagination in his controversy with Malebranche, particularly in *Réflexions sur l'éloquence des prédicateurs* (*Reflections on Preachers' Eloquence*, 1685).[40] In general, Cartesian authors wishing to revive strands of classical rhetoric tended to assign increasing importance to the imaginative use of language, focusing on the act of speaking. Logical attitudes to language and mind placed greater emphasis on the structural similarity between the two, tending to treat both language and logic as a system.[41]

---

[37] Pascal, *Œuvres complètes*, ed. Jacques Chevalier (Paris: Gallimard, 1954), 595.
[38] Ibid. 592–602. A rare reference to linguistic practice can be found in Descartes's view, in a letter of 1629 to Mersenne, that a universal language would not prove practical mainly due to difficulties in its pronunciation (*Œuvres et lettres*, 911–15).
[39] Antoine Arnauld and Claude Lancelot, *Grammaire générale et raisonnée*, ed. Michel Foucault (Paris: Paulet, 1969), 106–8; Arnauld and Pierre Nicole, *La Logique ou l'art de penser* (Paris: Charles Savreux, 1662), 115–17. Noam Chomsky traced the roots of his own generative grammar back to such early modern theories correlating linguistic, logical, and mental structures in *Cartesian Linguistics* (Lanham, Md.: University Press of America, 1966). Cf. Jean Miel, 'Pascal, Port-Royal, and Cartesian Linguistics', *Journal of the History of Ideas* 30 (1969), 261–71, and Aarsleff, *From Locke to Saussure*, 101–19.
[40] Arnauld, *Réflexions sur l'éloquence des prédicateurs*, ed. Thomas M. Carr (Geneva: Droz, 1992).
[41] Richard Waswo, 'Theories of Language', and John Monfasani, 'The Ciceronian Controversy' in Glyn P. Norton (ed.), *The Cambridge History of Literary Criticism*, iii: *The Renaissance* (Cambridge: Cambridge University Press, 1999), 25–35 and 395–401; Dawson, *Locke*, 13–87.

Another post-Cartesian reinterpretation of language was Bernard Lamy's *La Rhétorique ou l'art de parler* (*Rhetoric or the Art of Speaking*, 1675). Like Arnauld and Pascal, Lamy distinguished between the intellectual and physical aspects of language, while seeing the sensually orientated imagination as an indispensable tool for the successful transmission of ideas. Yet he went even further than the Port Royal authors, seeing metaphors as natural and necessary for the enrichment of language. Lamy also rejected another Cartesian commonplace, the view that word order should reflect innate human reason. While praising the perspicuity of modern French, Lamy pointed out that Greek and Latin enabled ancient writers to express themselves more freely and forcefully.[42] Lamy's contention was later taken up by Jean Baptiste Dubos in his *Réflexions critiques sur la poésie et sur la peinture* (*Critical Reflections on Poetry and Painting*, 1719), where Latin was similarly exalted as more expressive than French due to its free word order.[43]

At first glance it might seem rather unlikely that such views on passionate speech and the lack of congruence between logical thinking and its expression should coexist with professed adherence to the tenets of Cartesian philosophy. Yet as Ulrich Ricken has argued, the authors who revised the Cartesian approach to language built on the inherent tensions in the strict distinction between body and mind.[44] Since language belonged to both sides of the dualist divide, the physical and the intellectual, it attracted novel interpretations and presented Cartesians with difficult problems. If for Descartes physical signs could not partake in immaterial cognitive processes, Arnauld and his colleagues at Port Royal downplayed the powers of reason after the Fall and reassessed the role of the imagination and the passions in human communication. John Locke became well acquainted with contemporary French works on eloquence, logic, and rhetoric during his sojourn in France from 1675 to 1679, and he continued to follow these discussions from England.[45] The eighteenth-century reception of Locke's sensualist psychology in France amplified the already significant impact of the post-Cartesian reassessment of language

---

[42] Bernard Lamy, *La Rhétorique ou l'art de parler* (Paris: André Pralard, 1688), 49–52.

[43] Jean Baptiste Dubos, *Réflexions critiques sur la poésie et sur la peinture* (Paris: Pierre-Jean Mariette, 1733), i. 296–339. This was the most frequently cited work in Condillac's *Essai* in relation to expressive communication (Aarsleff, Introduction to Condillac, *Essay*, pp. xxxiii–xxxiv).

[44] Ricken, *Linguistics, Anthropology, and Philosophy*, 56–60. See also George Berkeley's emphasis on the pragmatic, non-representative function of language in the introduction (§XX) to his *Treatise Concerning the Principles of Human Knowledge* (1710), in *The Works of George Berkeley*, ed. G. N. Wright (London: Thomas Tegg, 1843), i. 83.

[45] John Lough, 'Locke's Reading during His Stay in France (1675–9)', *Transactions of the Bibliographical Society* 8 (1953), 229–58.

in the mind. The modification of Descartes's strict dualism was not, however, a perfect solution to the question of the role played by language in human cognition, and how the two evolved over time. As much as this issue troubled avowed Cartesians, it continued to haunt authors who subscribed to thorough sensualism.

SIGNS OF WHAT?
THE CRISIS OF SENSUALIST EPISTEMOLOGY

In mid-eighteenth-century sensualist epistemology, language and signs acquired an ever increasing cognitive role. Condillac's *Essai* was extensively used in the *Encyclopédie* (for example, in Diderot's *Discours préliminaire* and Jaucourt's entry *Langage*). Outside the Cartesian framework, the dependence of thought on signs did not sound too alarming, but doubts about the viability of sensualist representation—in both language and epistemology—surfaced in the 1750s, simultaneously with its alleged triumph. Since the sensualist edifice had been erected on a view of the mind as 'transformed sensation', as Condillac called it, questions arose about the reliability of sensation as a guide to external reality. Descartes's *cogito*, ensconced in self-consciousness, could not be refuted demonstratively, whereas the senses might be proven wrong on a daily basis—from optical illusions to the mismatch between sound and vision.

At the opposite ends of sensualist epistemology stood materialism and subjective idealism. If one were to trust sensations, the building blocks of language and mind, then our thinking might be reduced to physical occurrences in the body. On the other hand, since one had no adequate way to penetrate the link between sensations and the objects prompting them, one could not possibly know anything beyond one's own perceptions: the objective existence of external reality should therefore be questioned. As George Berkeley argued, if physical objects were real, their existence had to depend on a mind greater than our own.[46] There was surely a wide range of options for intellectual manoeuvre between Julien Offray de La Mettrie and George Berkeley, but both authors employed sensualist epistemology. Since the evolution of language was seen as reflecting the history of the human mind, such epistemological doubts bore directly on the nature and function of language.

One of the main issues disquieting contemporary authors was the fissure between the human perception of reality and its representation in

---

[46] George Berkeley, 'Three Dialogues between Hylas and Philonous' (1713) in *Philosophical Works*, ed. Michael Ayers (London: Everyman, 2000), 155–252, here 220.

language. Sensations were deemed instantaneous and immediate: we see a picture or feel extreme heat in their entirety and all at once. Yet if we want to give ourselves an account, mental or verbal, of these instantaneous sensations, we have to proceed in a linear manner. We cannot describe the various features and aspects of a picture all at once. In this respect, the gestural language of action was the best manner of representation, for its vitality and immediacy supposedly captured entire scenes. A single gesture, sometimes accompanied by emotive cries, could represent an agent's throbbing pain or terrifying fear, as witnessed in drama, pantomime, dance, and opera. Though sufficiently linear for intellectual endeavours, Greek and Latin were thought to be closer to this primordial means of representation as they could convey the meaning of an entire French sentence in a single inflected word. French and its distinctly linear sentences suddenly seemed very distant from the original language of action.

This view of ancient and modern languages delivered a final *coup de grâce* to the belief in the particular compatibility of French with the structure of the human mind. This view, sometimes called the theory of 'natural order', had its origin in the Aristotelian hierarchy of logical categories and its modification in the Middle Ages into a system of grammatical and ontological parallels: the subject reflected substance, and was therefore prior to accidents such as verbs, adverbs, and objects.[47] This hierarchy was regarded as part of the innate reason common to all human minds. The reassessment of the role of the imagination in cognition had already cast doubt on this medieval theory and its modern versions (Cartesian General Grammar), but sensualist epistemology combined with a historical perspective on the emergence of language demolished its foundations.

In his *Lettre sur les sourds et muets* (*Letter on the Deaf and Mute*, 1751), Diderot turned this traditional distinction on its head, arguing that the so-called natural order was much closer to the primordial language of action rather than to modern French. Diderot warned that the modern linearity of discourse had been achieved at the expense of the emotional immediacy and pictorial wholeness of our perception.

> Our mental state is one thing, our analysis of it quite another. [...] Our mind is a moving scene, which we are perpetually copying. We spend a great deal of time in rendering it faithfully; but the original exists as a complete whole, for the mind does not proceed step by step, like expression.[48]

---

[47] G. L. Bursill-Hall, *Speculative Grammars of the Middle Ages: The Doctrine of Partes orationis of the Modistae* (The Hague: Mouton, 1971), 35–42; Vivian Law, *The History of Linguistics in Europe from Plato to 1600* (Cambridge: Cambridge University Press, 2003), 112–89.

[48] *Diderot's Early Philosophical Works*, trans. Margaret Jourdain (Chicago: Open Court, 1916), 187; Diderot, *Œuvres complètes*, eds Yvon Belaval et al. (Paris: Hermann, 1978), iv. 161.

As a result of this disjunction between mental states and their linguistic description, Diderot aspired to revive a 'poetic hieroglyph', a hiatus of meaning that cannot be reduced to analytic terms.[49] The shattered correspondence between immediate perception and linear language paralleled another concern, namely that language represented only one's own perception, endowing its users with no direct path either to external reality or to the minds of others. The epistemological and linguistic implications of Berkeley's subjective immaterialism received increasing attention in France in the 1740s and the 1750s. Diderot alerted Condillac to the idealistic or solipsistic ramifications of reducing all reflection to 'transformed sensation', declaring Condillac to be a Berkeleian immaterialist *malgré lui*.[50] Diderot took Berkeley's observations on human sight to their farthest logical consequences, which cost him an incarceration in Vincennes. In *Lettre sur les aveugles* (*Letter on the Blind*, 1749), Diderot argued that our thinking was modelled after contingent manners of perception, which implied the relativity of all human consciousness—from the extent of fellow-feeling to ethical and religious notions.[51] Language played an important role here as well: only through social interaction and mutual instruction did human beings learn how to perceive objects the way they do. Language could neither reconstruct the immediacy of perception nor adequately represent external reality, but Diderot still deemed it indispensable for human cognition and action.

No longer capable of representing the nature of things, language could also not be trusted to represent mental processes adequately. Condillac's awareness of the increasing distance between modern idioms and the primordial language of action, alongside Diderot's worries about the linearity of human language, were taken seriously by Jean-Jacques Rousseau. Rousseau's *Discours sur l'inégalité* and his *Essai sur l'origine des langues* seemed to lament the loss of an early, innocent immersion in the senses. This loss was brought about, to a considerable extent, by the emergence of language as described in the Epicurean tradition, especially by the superimposition of analytic discourse over the first natural meanings. Criticizing Condillac for assuming social contact among the first human beings, Rousseau imagined man in the earliest ages as self-sufficient and solitary, hearing directly the voice of nature that spurred in

---

[49] Diderot, *Œuvres complètes*, iv. 169, 176–7. See also Edward Nye, *Literary and Linguistic Theories in Eighteenth-Century France: From Nuances to Impertinence* (Oxford: Oxford University Press, 2000), 153–7.
[50] Diderot, *Œuvres complètes*, iv. 44–5.
[51] See Kate E. Tunstall, 'The Judgement of Experience: Seeing and Reading in Diderot's *Lettre sur les aveugles*', *French Studies* 42 (2008), 404–16, and 'Pré-histoire d'un emblème des Lumières: l'aveugle-né de Montaigne à Diderot', in Isabelle Moreau (ed.), *Les Lumières en mouvement: la circulation des idées au XVIIIe siècle* (Lyon: ENS, 2009), 173–97.

him spontaneous feelings of self-love and pity. By placing an arbitrary language between nature and himself, man became deaf to nature and to moral sentiments, therefore in need of conventions and contracts.[52] Influenced by Mandeville's account of language as a means of dissimulation and control, Rousseau described how modern languages lost their vivid inflections, how melody became dominated by harmony, and how a golden age of social cohesion fell victim to fraud and deceit. In the *Discours sur l'inégalité* the first individual to speak publicly was a usurper defending his illegitimate private property; the *Essai sur l'origine des langues* traced the subsequent abuse of language.[53] For Rousseau, modern languages were artificial devices that carried human beings away from a blissful condition.

While regretting the loss of the language of action and noting the shortcomings of analytic language, Condillac and Diderot identified certain advantages in the march of civilization. Artificial signs enabled human beings to control and expand their cognitive faculties, and language was the instrument with which they constructed their material and intellectual culture. For Rousseau, however, the evolution of language triggered a double loss. Parallel to the sensualist problems of representation—an uncertain access to reality and the mistrusted reflection of mental states—language generated both external domination and an internal lack of authenticity.

* * *

The intrinsic tensions within the Enlightenment revival of the Epicurean account of human evolution stimulated a rich variety of reflections while simultaneously exposing the contradictions involved in the civilizing process. The artificial signs that crowned the transition from bestiality to culture were perceived as threatening the vestiges of direct perception and primordial creativity. Warburton and Condillac's language of action, Diderot's hieroglyph, Vico's mythical thinking—all were deemed so irrevocably lost that modern authors could only reconstruct them archeologically in conjectural histories.

Yet despite such longing for the past, most Enlightenment theories of the mutual emergence of language, mind, and society also exuded a sense

---

[52] Jean Starobinski, 'Rousseau and the Origin of Languages', in *Jean-Jacques Rousseau: Transparency and Obstruction*, trans. Arthur Goldhammer (Chicago: University of Chicago Press, 1988), 304–22; Robert Wokler, *Rousseau on Society, Politics, Music and Language* (New York: Garland Publishing, 1987).

[53] Rousseau, *Discourses*, 298–9; *Œuvres complètes*, v. 428. For different lines of argumentation in these works, see Marian Hobson, ' "Nexus effectivus" and "nexus finalis": Causality in Rousseau's *Discours sur l'inégalité* and in the *Essai sur l'origine des langues*', in Marian Hobson, J. T. A. Leigh, and Robert Wokler (eds), *Rousseau and the Eighteenth Century: Essays in Memory of R. A. Leigh* (Oxford: Voltaire Foundation, 1992), 225–50.

of confidence in human achievements. The history of language could be the torch of humanity in the search for its lost origins, as Turgot suggested.[54] The impressive complexity of the human mind, social institutions, and linguistic discourse was regarded as man-made and historically evolved. The first human beings came to be seen as categorically different from modern man, intellectually resembling children, feral men, and savages.[55] The biblical account of human origins was usually set aside as a foreword to the Epicurean narrative. Even the critics of this ancient view of human evolution subscribed to some of its main tenets: a natural emergence of language, the origin of artificial signification in universal capacities differently stimulated by sense impressions, and the mutual development of language and culture over time. We shall, however, see in later chapters how some of these convictions were seriously undermined from the mid-1750s onwards.

The naturalistic-Epicurean account of the emergence of language also rendered projects for the creation of universal languages obsolete.[56] A popular endeavour among seventeenth-century philosophers, in the middle of the following century such schemes were seen as static utopias, or as attempts to pre-empt the further evolution of language, the human mind, and national character. Suggestions for the improvement of human communication did abound in the late eighteenth century, especially during the French Revolution, and such proposals were recently linked by Sophia Rosenfeld to the mid-century discussion of the origin of language. Yet despite the manifest interest of later reformers in Condillac, it is not clear whether one could project their Revolutionary preoccupations on to the 1750s, or regard Condillac, Diderot, and Rousseau as espousing redemption via transparent idioms.[57] Within a historically orientated framework of an ongoing evolution, fixed universal idioms might actually forestall future progress instead of enhancing

---

[54] 'Plan du second Discours sur le progrès de l'esprit humain' (1751) and 'Étymologie' (1756) in *Œuvres de Turgot et documents le concernant*, ed. Gustave Schelle (Paris: Alcan, 1913–23), i. 289–323 and 473–538.

[55] Julia Douthwaite, *The Wild Girl, Natural Man and the Monster: Dangerous Experiments in the Age of Enlightenment* (Chicago: University of Chicago Press, 2002); David B. Paxman, *Voyage into Language: Space and the Linguistic Encounter, 1500–1800* (Aldershot: Ashgate, 2003); Lauzon, *Signs of Light*, 69–131.

[56] On these projects, see James Knowlson, *Universal Language Schemes in England and France, 1600–1800* (Toronto: University of Toronto Press, 1975); Paolo Rossi, *Logic and the Art of Memory: The Quest for a Universal Language*, trans. Stephen Clucas (Chicago: University of Chicago Press, 2000); Jaap Maat, *Philosophical Languages in the Seventeenth Century* (Dordrecht: Kluwer 2004); Rhodri Lewis, *Language, Mind and Nature: Artificial Languages in England from Bacon to Locke* (Cambridge: Cambridge University Press, 2007).

[57] Rosenfeld, *A Revolution in Language*, 36–56.

it. This particular point was forcefully made by Johann David Michaelis in his 1759 prize essay.

The authors discussing language in Berlin of the 1750s were well acquainted with the contemporary French scene. Their own contributions were, however, firmly grounded in a local context that emphasized the second axis of the debate: the synchronic, ongoing interrelations between linguistic signs and the human mind. The next chapter will present an overview of the complex German discourse on symbolic thinking in the first half of the eighteenth century.

2

Symbolic Cognition from Leibniz to the 1760s

Theology, Aesthetics, and History

Long before the invigorating encounter with French conjectural histories, promoted by the renewed Academy in Berlin, German thinkers were pondering the multifaceted links between cognition, language, and human sociability. Authors from Leibniz to Mendelssohn built upon plenty of local stimuli, originating mostly in debates over the credibility of the Christian mysteries and the proper balance between reason and faith. This intellectual constellation coloured the *Aufklärer*'s views on language and mind, contributing to their distinctive interpretations of French ideas from the 1750s onwards.

At the centre of early eighteenth-century German theories of language, mind, and the imagination stood Leibniz's rehabilitation of clear but indistinct or confused ideas. This defence was carried out on two levels: the status of these confused ideas as comprehensible concepts in the mind (alongside clear and distinct ideas), and the related epistemic act, called by Leibniz 'symbolic cognition' (as opposed to intuitive perception). I shall follow the development of this notion from its conception by Leibniz as a defence of the Christian mysteries to its later appropriation by authors who emphasized the irreducibility of human experience, especially of art and poetry, to logical analysis. Such thinkers were influenced by an uneasy compromise between Pietism and Wolffian philosophy that tried to encircle both reason and faith within distinct spheres, protecting them from their own claims for overarching jurisdiction over one another.

Significant figures such as Johann Franz Buddeus, Johann Lorenz von Mosheim, and Andreas Rüdiger receive here less than their due, as the focus remains firmly on intellectual currents pertinent to the 1759 contest in Berlin. Hence also the possible overemphasis on events and authors in Halle, Michaelis's home town and alma mater, and in Göttingen, where he spent most of his academic career. In all the examined domains I shall highlight the crucial significance of language for both creative self-expression and the understanding of past human experience.

LEIBNIZ, WOLFF, AND PUFENDORF

Leibniz on confused ideas and symbolic knowledge

Though fully elaborated in the *Théodicée* (*Theodicy*) of 1710, Leibniz's lifelong interest in the defence of the Christian mysteries began early in his career, in Mainz, where he served as a legal adviser in the local court and as an assistant to the former state minister Johann Christian von Boineburg. Boineburg introduced the young Leibniz to theological controversies in French and English, particularly over the Catholic notion of transubstantiation in the Eucharist. It was in these years that Leibniz started writing on several subjects he would repeatedly address throughout his life: projects for the foundation of scientific academies, a metaphysical system based on a new conception of substance, and attempts to reconcile all Christian confessions. Both his irenic and metaphysical endeavours may have been related to his firm resolve in the same years to defend the credibility of the Christian mysteries. Unlike some of his contemporaries, Leibniz did not wish to do away with elements of the traditional Christian dogma. He rejected the objections of deists and Socinians who tried to downplay the significance of the mysteries or explain them away on the basis of reason, while taking a different path from the one trodden by Newton and Clarke.[1]

Ever since the Augsburg Confession (1530), the Lutheran view of the mass had remained closer to the Catholic doctrine than its Calvinist or Zwinglian versions, admitting the real presence of Christ in the sacrament. Though in the seventeenth century an increasing number of authors came to interpret transubstantiation allegorically, understanding Jesus' words 'this is my body' as 'this signifies my body', Leibniz was convinced that the espousal of reason and the mechanist worldview should not attenuate one's belief in the Christian dogma. While sharing to a considerable extent the deists' conviction that the essence of Christianity lay in its ethics, Leibniz did not wish to reduce religion to that aspect alone. He recognized that 'love thy neighbour' and similar precepts might be found in other religions as well, and thus believed it was precisely the mysterious elements in Chris-

---

[1] Maria Rosa Antognazza, *Leibniz: An Intellectual Biography* (Cambridge: Cambridge University Press, 2009), 79–138. On the subversive potential of Socinianism see Sarah Mortimer, *Reason and Religion in the English Revolution: The Challenge of Socinianism* (Cambridge: Cambridge University Press, 2010).

tianity that endowed it with its distinctive character. Moreover, Christianity's claim for a continuous chain of transmission, oral or written, would be seriously jeopardized if central tenets of this tradition were abandoned following the rise of the new natural philosophy.[2]

Leibniz employed several strategies in his defence of the mysteries. A 'positive' approach was aimed at demonstrating that transubstantiation is possible by means of a new conception of substance. Though Leibniz's metaphysics was to change throughout the years, he held fast to the conviction that substance did not consist in extension—by contrast to Descartes's view—but rather in immaterial entities. The ensuing chasm between immaterial substance and material appearances rendered the mysteries at least theoretically possible: different external phenomena could have the same substance. By postulating an underlying spiritual substance behind the physical world, Leibniz could counter arguments against Christianity drawn from mechanist philosophy, showing that there was no immanent contradiction between the two. Another, 'negative' strategy was the employment of the traditional apparatus of disputation to turn the arguments of Leibniz's opponents upside down, shifting the burden of proof from defenders of the mysteries to their detractors. Leibniz held that the mysteries should be regarded as possible and true as long as no argument to the contrary could be conclusively demonstrated.[3] The relative ease with which he was able to sweep aside various syllogisms was rooted in the very nature of the mysteries. Their necessary obscurity, which the critics sought to dispel, afforded Leibniz sufficient room for logical manoeuvre, where he could redefine premisses and conclusions.

A different approach was required, however, to confront the threat to the mysteries posed by Baruch Spinoza's *Tractatus theologico-politicus* (*Theological-Political Treatise*, 1670). To critics of the mysteries who tried to prove their impossibility either according to mechanist philosophy or by logical syllogisms, Leibniz responded by appealing to his metaphysical notion of substance or by exploiting the obscure character of the mysteries. Spinoza, by contrast, criticized all calls to believe in inaccessible truths that went beyond simple and practical principles.

---

[2] Antognazza, 'The Defence of the Mysteries of the Trinity and the Incarnation: An Example of Leibniz's "Other" Reason', *British Journal for the History of Philosophy* 9 (2001), 283–309, and *Leibniz on the Trinity and the Incarnation: Reason and Revelation in the Seventeenth Century*, trans. Gerald Parks (New Haven: Yale University Press, 2007); Ursula Goldenbaum, 'Spinoza's Parrot, Socinian Syllogisms, and Leibniz's Metaphysics: Leibniz's Three Strategies for Defending Christian Mysteries', *American Catholic Philosophical Quarterly* 76 (2002), 551–75.

[3] Leibniz, *Sämtliche Schriften und Briefe*, eds Paul Ritter et al. (Berlin: Akademie Verlag, 1923–), VI.4.C, 2789–90 (indicating series, volume, and part, followed by page numbers); *The Art of Controversies*, trans. Marcelo Dascal et al. (Dordrecht: Springer, 2006), 86–7.

Now if anyone says that, while there is no need to understand God's attributes, there is a duty to believe in them straightforwardly without proof, he is plainly talking nonsense. In the case of things invisible which are objects only of the mind, proofs are the only eyes by which they can be seen; therefore those who do not have such proofs can see nothing at all of these things. So when they merely repeat what they have heard of such matters, this is no more relevant to or indicative of their mind than the words of a parrot or a puppet speaking without meaning or sense.[4]

Since human beings lacked the appropriate criteria to assess the credibility of biblical miracles and traditional mysteries, Spinoza suggested they should espouse only comprehensible religious elements such as ethical directives. Leibniz, who sensed that nothing historically unique in Christianity would survive its reduction to a mere natural religion, had now to limit the vagueness of the mysteries instead of drawing on their ambiguity. It was here that Leibniz resorted to clear but confused ideas, notions constituting a sort of knowledge while not being susceptible to full analysis. In a short essay written between 1669 and 1671, *Commentatiuncula de judice controversiarum* (*Little Commentary on the Judge of Controversies*), Leibniz addressed the question of faith and its content, arguing that human beings should indeed not believe in propositions they did not understand. Leibniz elaborated in the *Commentatiuncula* a new theory of interpretation, probably aiming to counter Spinoza's accusation that belief in incomprehensible mysteries amounted to the inconsequential prattling of parrots and puppets.[5] In this case, Leibniz's main difficulty was the transition from mere words, available to parrots and human beings alike, to the signified objects and their meanings in the mind.

The connection between words and things continued to occupy Leibniz in many of his subsequent writings, but a solution to this problem had to be found in relation to the Christian mysteries. In this case, Leibniz argued, partial understanding would not only be sufficient but actually desirable, since the complete analysis of the mysteries would diminish their special status.[6] Some visualized images or a general reliance on Scripture would suffice in such matters, according to Leibniz, even without the complete under-

---

[4] Spinoza, 'Theological-Political Treatise', in *Complete Works*, trans. Samuel Shirley, ed. Michael L. Morgan (Indianapolis: Hackett, 2002), ch. 13, 512.
[5] Leibniz, *Sämtliche Schriften* VI.1, 548–59; *Art of Controversies*, 8–24. On this text as a reply to Spinoza, see Ursula Goldenbaum, 'Die *Commentatiuncula de judice* als Leibnizens erste philosophische Auseinandersetzung mit Spinoza nebst der Mitteilung über ein neuaufgefundenes Leibnizstück', in Martin Fontius, Hartmut Rudolph, and Gary Smith (eds), *Labora diligenter* (Stuttgart: Steiner, 1999), 61–107.
[6] Leibniz, *Sämtliche Schriften* VI.1, 550; *Art of Controversies*, 11. See also Marcelo Dascal, 'Reason and the Mysteries of Faith: Leibniz on the Meaning of Religious Discourse', in *Leibniz: Language, Signs and Thought* (Amsterdam: John Benjamins, 1987), 93–124; Antognazza, *Leibniz on the Trinity*, 50–9.

standing of the concepts. Leibniz argued that most human knowledge never attained an adequate degree of certainty, not even in natural philosophy, where terms such as cause and finality were employed without clear and distinct definitions.[7] Whenever we can distinguish a thing from another, Leibniz argued, we have a clear idea of it, but such knowledge remains indistinct or confused as long as we are not able to analyse the idea into its basic elements. Leibniz returned to the notion of clear but confused ideas in an article published in *Acta Eruditorum* in 1684, in the context of the controversy between Arnaud and Malebranche over the nature of ideas. In his *Meditationes de cognitione, veritate et ideis* (*Meditations on Knowledge, Truth, and Ideas*) Leibniz referred again to Spinoza's parrot argument, while appealing to aesthetic experience as an example of clear but confused perception.

> Similarly, we see that painters and other artists correctly know what is done properly and what is done poorly, though they are often unable to explain their judgments and reply to questioning by saying that the things that displease them lack an unknown something. [...] Furthermore, what some maintain, that we cannot say anything about a thing and understand what we say unless we have an idea of it, is either false or at least ambiguous. For, often, we do understand in one way or another the words in question individually or remember that we understood them previously.[8]

Clear and distinct ideas were suitable for the intuitive perception (*cognitio intuitiva*) of God, who could directly penetrate the essence of things. But in their perception of most ideas human beings made use of blind or symbolic cognition (*cognitio caeca/symbolica*), except for situations of acute sensations such as pain. Intuitive cognition did not require any mediation through signs, while only reasoning by means of signs allowed human beings to overcome the shortcomings of their perception. Among Leibniz's examples were such terms as 'the fastest motion': we understand what this term means even if we do not possess a clear and distinct idea of it.[9]

Leibniz on natural languages and the vernacular

Unlike Descartes, who had attributed to language the role of communicating already formed ideas, Leibniz ascribed here to signs a constitutive role

---

[7] Leibniz, *Sämtliche Schriften* VI.1, 551–2; *Art of Controversies*, 12–13.
[8] Leibniz, *Philosophical Essays*, eds Roger Ariew and Daniel Garber (Indianapolis: Hackett, 1989), 24–5; *Sämtliche Schriften* IV.4.A, 586–8. See also 'Discours de métaphysique', §24, in *Sämtliche Schriften* VI.4, 1567–9.
[9] Leibniz, *Sämtliche Schriften* VI.4.A, 588–9. George Berkeley made a similar argument about the comprehensibility of the mysteries in the seventh dialogue of his *Alciphron* (1732); see *The Works*, i. 493–508. Berkeley tended, however, to see language as an obstacle to human knowledge.

in the cognitive process. In this respect Leibniz's theory resembled Hobbes's objection to Descartes's *Meditations*, the suggestion that all reasoning consisted in the combination of signs. Leibniz wished to emphasize, however, that the dependence of human thinking on linguistic signs did not involve arbitrariness.[10] Like ancient and modern adherents of the Epicurean history of language, Leibniz believed that all human idioms contained some natural, non-conventional elements. If the first speakers perceived objects in a striking way and adopted the accompanying sounds as their names, such words could not be considered completely arbitrary. Even if some of these natural meanings were later transformed metaphorically into abstract ones, they still included a residue of their original natural meanings. In Leibniz's eyes, the main motor of linguistic change was not the deliberate imposition of new meanings on words by consciously scheming individuals. In relation to the evolution of language, individuals were portrayed as entangled within large-scale social trends and movements.[11]

These linguistic transformations were the focus of Leibniz's etymological studies and his essays on his mother tongue. In *Ermahnung an die Teutsche, ihren Verstand und Sprache beßer zu üben* (*An Exhortation to the Germans to Improve the Use of Their Understanding and Language*, 1679) Leibniz lamented the lack of a single cultural centre in Germany and observed the scarcity of scientific books in the vernacular, which made German inferior to both Latin and French.[12] The German language could be improved only if serious writers respected it, discussing in the vernacular the most taxing subjects. As a proof of the suitability of the German language for complex endeavours, Leibniz pointed out that Luther's version of the Bible sounded better than most other translations. He lamented the unnecessary use of foreign words where German terms were available, proclaiming that it was better to be 'an original of a German rather than a copy of a Frenchman'.[13]

In another essay on the desired recovery of German, *Unvorgreiffliche Gedancken, betreffend die Ausübung und Verbesserung der deutschen*

---

[10] Leibniz, *New Essays on Human Understanding*, trans. Peter Remnant and Jonathan Bennett (Cambridge: Cambridge University Press, 1996), III.ii.§1, 278; *Philosophische Schriften* VI.6, 278.

[11] This point is elaborated in Lifschitz, 'The Arbitrariness of the Linguistic Sign'. For the differences between the Adamic thesis and Leibniz's keen awareness of the historicity of languages, see Klaus D. Dutz, ' "Lingua Adamica nobis certe ignota est": Die Sprachursprungsdebatte und Gottfried Wilhelm Leibniz', in Gessinger and von Rahden (eds), *Theorien vom Ursprung*, i. 204–40; Gensini, *'De linguis in universum'*, 60–5, and Sigrid von der Schulenburg, *Leibniz als Sprachforscher*, ed. Kurt Müller (Frankfurt am Main: Klostermann, 1973), 3–5.

[12] Leibniz, *Sämtliche Schriften* IV.3, 795–820.

[13] 'Beßer ist ein Original von einem Teütschen, als eine Copey von einem Franzosen seyn.' (Ibid. 818.)

Sprache (*Unprejudiced Thoughts on the Use and Improvement of the German Language*, composed between 1697 and 1712), Leibniz tackled the mutual influence of language and thought. He began by asserting that language is the mirror of the mind, and advocated the extension of local vocabulary by delving into the riches of Old German.[14] The vernacular had been in a relatively healthy condition at the time of the Reformation, but the recurring wars of the sixteenth and seventeenth centuries left it vulnerable to linguistic incursions. In this essay Leibniz criticized the drive to purge German of all foreign words, as this would deprive the language of its vitality, but he did observe the lack of philosophical, legal, and political terms in the vernacular. He envisaged a German Society enriching the vernacular by archiving its manifold dialects and investigating its history, for historical inquiries might provide essential clues towards the reconstruction of original, lost meanings.[15]

Leibniz's exhortation to the Germans to cultivate their own language may be compared to the contemporary stance taken by Christian Thomasius, who pioneered teaching in German at the University of Leipzig and later in Halle. When announcing in 1687 his lectures on Balthasar Gracián, Thomasius addressed his future students in a short prospectus entitled *Welcher Gestalt man denen Frantzosen in gemeinem Leben und Wandel nachahmen solle?* (*In What Way Should One Imitate the French in Ordinary Life and Action?*) Like Leibniz, Thomasius complained about the neglect of the vernacular in educated circles. Yet he also questioned the widespread critique of French in German universities (*Alamode-Kritik*) which contrasted an ideal, Tacitean image of Germanic virtue with the allegedly emasculating French manners. Arguing that the ancient Germanic tribes should not serve as an eternal model because human customs were subject to constant change, Thomasius espoused the moderate imitation of some French virtues—particularly *honnêteté*, *bel esprit*, and *galanterie*. Thomasius wished to challenge an unchanging ideal of virtue, immutable throughout history, while promoting his own concept of philosophy as a discipline concerned with civic engagement and worldly praxis.[16] His academic activities, from lecturing and publishing in German to founding a *Collegium styli* for law students, suggest that his espousal of the imitation of French concerned social change and the relevance

---

[14] Leibniz, *Sämtliche Schriften* IV.6, 528–65.

[15] Ibid. 545. See also Andreas Gardt, *Sprachreflexion in Barock und Frühaufklärung* (Berlin: De Gruyter, 1994), 348–67.

[16] Christian Thomasius, *Von Nachahmung der Franzosen*, ed. August Sauer (Stuttgart: Göschen, 1894).

of scholarship rather than the thoughtless copying of representational court culture.[17]

Wolff on signs and cognition

When Christian Wolff set out to write his German cycle of philosophical works in the first decade of the eighteenth century, Leibniz's main works were not yet available in print. From 1704 onwards Wolff corresponded with Leibniz, who facilitated his appointment as professor of mathematics at Halle and referred him to some of the concepts developed in his unpublished *Nouveaux essais*. Yet in addition to Leibniz's manifest influence, Wolff's philosophy included elements garnered from other systems.[18] Wolff's earliest work on language, *Disquisitio philosophica de loquela* (*A Philosophical Inquiry into Speech*, 1703), was written under strong Cartesian influence, before Wolff was introduced to Leibniz's philosophy.[19] Though reiterating Descartes's dualist depiction of language as an instrument for the transmission of immaterial ideas, Wolff followed the reassessment of Cartesianism by referring to Bernard Lamy's treatise on rhetoric. In his major works, however, Wolff presented a new theory of signs in thought, drawing mainly on Leibniz but also on Locke and the post-Cartesian currents. As in Locke and Leibniz, one of the main tenets of Wolff's theory of signification was grounded in the formation of general terms. Wolff held that general ideas emerged in a process of abstraction with the aid of signs, though not all ideas were formed from sensual input. The mind could develop them through the combination of already available ideas, as in the mental transformation of the concept of a triangle into the idea of a square or another polygon. According to Wolff, non-sensual notions could be formed through the combination of ideas by means of signs.[20]

---

[17] See also Eric A. Blackall, *The Emergence of German as a Literary Language 1700–1775*, second edn (Ithaca, NY: Cornell University Press, 1978), 12–26, and Olav Krämer, '"Welcher Gestalt man denen Frantzosen nachahmen solle": Stationen einer Jahrhundertdebatte', in Jens Häseler, Albert Meier, and Olaf Koch (eds), *Gallophobie im 18. Jahrhundert* (Berlin: Berliner Wissenschaftsverlag, 2005), 61–88.

[18] Charles A. Corr, 'Christian Wolff and Leibniz', *Journal of the History of Ideas* 36 (1975), 241–62; Jean École, 'En quel sens peut-on dire que Wolff est rationaliste?', *Studia Leibnitiana* 11 (1979), 45–61; Hans Werner Arndt, 'Rationalismus und Empirismus in der Erkenntnislehre Christian Wolffs', in Werner Schneiders (ed.), *Christian Wolff 1679–1754: Interpretationen zu seiner Philosophie und deren Wirkung* (Hamburg: Meiner, 1983), 31–47.

[19] In *Meletemata mathematico-philosophica*, II.3, 244–67, reprinted in Wolff's *Gesammelte Werke*, ed. Jean École (Hildesheim: Olms, 1974), xxxv.

[20] Wolff referred favourably to Locke in the preface to the 1712 *Deutsche Logik*, or *Venünfftige Gedancken von den Kräften des menschlichen Verstandes und ihrem richtigen Gebrauche in Erkänntniß der Wahrheit* (Halle: Rengerische Buchhandlung, 1754), 4ᵛ. See also Ulrich Ricken, *Leibniz, Wolff, und einige sprachtheoretischen Entwicklungen in der deutschen Aufklärung* (Berlin: Akademie Verlag, 1989), 38–9.

In the *Deutsche Metaphysik* (*German Metaphysics*), Wolff distinguished between natural signs, whose meaning did not depend on human beings, and artificial ones crafted by the mind.[21] The two classes of signs reflected different levels of understanding: *cognitio intuitiva*, the unmediated vision of a whole concept, and *cognitio symbolica*, indistinct knowledge aided by signs. Borrowing these Leibnizian terms, Wolff presented them in his German works as *anschauende Erkenntnis* and *figürliche Erkenntnis*.[22] He argued that most of our notions were not intuitive but 'clear and indistinct', so that signs must serve to distinguish between different ideas on the level of our symbolic understanding.

Wolff's account of the symbolic understanding implied that thinking depended on signs, since human beings had limited access to intuitive knowledge. Higher mental operations were set in motion by means of symbolic cognition, and signs enabled the mind to distinguish between initially unclear ideas.[23] In both his *Deutsche Metaphysik* and *Psychologia rationalis* (*Rational Psychology*), Wolff attempted to demonstrate the dependence of thought on signs by reference to feral children and deaf-mutes. He mentioned reports on a child, reared by wolves, who could not act intelligibly when reintroduced into human society due to his lack of language. Another example was a deaf-mute who eventually acquired language, claiming he had possessed no idea of God as long as he could not speak.[24]

Christian Wolff's account of the synchronic interrelations between language and mind was, therefore, similar to both Leibniz's view and Condillac's theory. Leibniz, Wolff, and Condillac all ascribed to signs a *constitutive* role in cognitive processes, seeing language as the tool enabling human beings to reverse their initial immersion in sense data.[25] Indeed, Condillac admitted the influence of Wolff in his *Essai* of 1746. He took up Wolff's examples of the feral child and the deaf-mute to illustrate the indispensability of artificial signs in human cognition, while claiming that Wolff had not adequately explained this phenomenon. Condillac credited Wolff with understanding the operations of the mind better than the followers

---

[21] Wolff, *Vernünfftige Gedancken von Gott, der Welt und der Seele des Menschen, auch allen Dingen überhaupt* (Halle: Rengerische Buchhandlung, 1751), 160–1.
[22] Ibid. 173–4; 519. See also Gerold Ungeheuer, 'Sprache und symbolische Erkenntnis bei Wolff', in Schneiders (ed.), *Wolff*, 89–112.
[23] Wolff, *Gedancken von Gott, der Welt und der Seele*, 536–7.
[24] Ibid. 537; *Psychologia rationalis* (Frankfurt and Leipzig: Rengerische Buchhandlung, 1734), 376–81.
[25] Aldo Scaglione, 'Direct vs. Inverted Order: Wolff and Condillac on the Necessity of the Sign and the Interrelationship of Language and Thinking', *Romance Philology* 33 (1980), 496–501; Gianni Paganini, 'Signes, imagination et mémoire: de la psychologie de Wolff à l'*Essai* de Condillac', *Revue des sciences philosophiques et théologiques* 72 (1988), 287–300.

of Descartes and Malebranche, while accusing him of not having recognized the 'absolute necessity of signs'.[26] Though writing in a different philosophical tradition, Condillac probably read in the 1730s and the early 1740s at least five of Wolff's works, including the latter's discussions of human psychology.[27] Condillac followed both Wolff and Locke in moving beyond the Cartesian theory of language and ascribing an important cognitive function to signs. Moreover, like Wolff, Condillac called for the development of scientific vocabulary in the vernacular as a way of advancing knowledge, while recognizing the creative role of the imagination in human cognition. These similarities may, however, be contrasted with their different ways of conceptualizing the link between signs and thought. While Condillac emphasized the joint evolution of language and the human mind, Wolff focused on their synchronic interrelations.

Pufendorf and the role of natural law

The aspect missing in Wolff's theory of language and mind—a historical perspective on their common evolution—was evidently present in Leibniz's etymological inquiries, even if not in his more theoretical essays. A parallel perspective on the creation of human language might be located in another German tradition: late seventeenth-century natural law, as elaborated mainly by Pufendorf and Thomasius. Despite later criticism of their approach to history (by authors such as Johann Jacob Schmauß and Jean-Jacques Rousseau), recent research on the early Enlightenment has uncovered the significant role played by eclecticism and voluntarist natural law in Germany before Wolffian philosophy rose to prominence in the universities.[28] In the early eighteenth century Leibniz represented a conservative approach to ethics and politics in comparison to Pufendorf and Thomasius. In addition to his rehabilitation of the Christian mysteries, Leibniz also condemned Hobbes and Pufendorf's attempts to demon-

---

[26] Condillac, 'Essai', I.4.II.§27, in *Œuvres*, i. 48.
[27] Condillac, 'Traité des systèmes', in *Œuvres*, i. 151; Laurence Bongie, Introduction to Condillac, *Les Monades* (Oxford: Voltaire Foundation, 1980), 36–49.
[28] Michael Albrecht, *Eklektik: Eine Begriffsgeschichte mit Hinweisen auf die Philosophie- und Wissenschaftsgeschichte* (Stuttgart-Bad Cannstatt: Frommann-Holzboog, 1994);. T. J. Hochstrasser, *Natural Law Theories in the Early Enlightenment* (Cambridge: Cambridge University Press, 2000); Ian Hunter, *Rival Enlightenments: Civil and Metaphysical Philosophy in Early Modern Germany* (Cambridge: Cambridge University Press, 2001) and *The Secularization of the Confessional State: The Political Thought of Christian Thomasius* (Cambridge: Cambridge University Press, 2007); Martin Mulsow, *Moderne aus dem Untergrund: Radikale Frühaufklärung in Deutschland 1680–1720* (Hamburg: Meiner, 2002); Thomas Ahnert, *Religion and the Origins of the German Enlightenment: Faith and the Reform of Learning in the Thought of Christian Thomasius* (Rochester, NY: University of Rochester Press, 2006).

strate that moral precepts could have been created by human beings without recourse to eternally existing logical concepts and relations.[29]

The importance of signs in individual thinking and social interaction was particularly highlighted by Pufendorf, who demonstrated that any second-order knowledge—of moral norms and duties, for example—was acquired only through the social construct of language. For the creation of artificial phenomena such as social associations and commercial contracts, human beings had to impose their own meanings on the external world, while at the same time affirming their consensus regarding the created conventional senses. This was emphasized in the first chapter of Book IV of *De jure naturae et gentium* (1672), 'Of Speech and the Obligation which attends it'. Pufendorf argued here that the genesis of language, like that of society, required two initial contracts: one for their actual establishment and another for safeguarding their effective operation by binding individuals to the honest fulfilment of the first contract. By contrast to the dominant eighteenth-century view of the emergence of language, as expressed by Leibniz and the Epicurean tradition, Pufendorf did not pay much heed to the environmental constraints on the act of naming. For him, the first human beings had absolute freedom in the imposition of names, except for natural sounds such as cries and simple gestures.[30]

Pufendorf not only emphasized, like Hobbes and Leibniz, the importance of articulate speech for all peculiarly human endeavours. He also viewed human language (and the double contract it required) as an archetype for the creation of other social or cultural phenomena.[31] The notion that human knowledge was mediated and conditioned by language was an important element of French conjectural histories, as argued in the previous chapter. The German reception of French theories of language from the 1750s onwards contained, therefore, several home-made ingredients: Leibniz's views on the emergence of language, his notion of

[29] Leibniz, 'Opinion on the Principles of Pufendorf' in *Political Writings*, trans. Patrick Riley (Cambridge: Cambridge University Press, 1988), 64–75; 'Jugement d'un Anonyme [Leibniz] sur l'Original de cet Abregé, avec des Réflexions du Traducteur', in Pufendorf, *Les Devoirs de l'homme et du citoyen*, trans. Jean Barbeyrac (Trévoux: L'imprimerie de S. Altesse Serenissime, 1741), ii. 193–280.
[30] Pufendorf, *Of the Law of Nature and Nations*, trans. Basil Kennett (London: Bonwicke et al., 1749), IV.i.§5, 318; *De jure naturae et gentium*, ed. Frank Böhling, in *Gesammelte Werke*, ed. Wilhelm Schmidt-Biggemann, iv (Berlin: Akademie Verlag, 1998), 310. See more in Lifschitz, 'The Arbitrariness of the Linguistic Sign'.
[31] Hochstrasser, *Natural Law*, 86–95; Knud Haakonssen, 'Protestant Natural Law Theory: A General Interpretation', in Natalie Brender and Larry Krasnoff (eds), *New Essays on the History of Autonomy: A Collection Honoring J. B. Schneewind* (Cambridge: Cambridge University Press, 2004), 92–109; Dawson, *Locke*, 151–3. On Pufendorf's contribution to conjectural history, see Medick, *Naturzustand*, and Istvan Hont, *Jealousy of Trade: International Competition and the Nation State in Historical Perspective* (Cambridge, Mass.: Harvard University Press, 2005), 159–84.

symbolic cognition (as further elaborated by Wolff), and Pufendorf's link between the emergence of language and other social institutions. By the mid-eighteenth century, however, it was the Wolffian theory of symbolic cognition that had dug the deepest roots in German universities, substantially aided by the intellectual developments at Halle.

HALLE, GÖTTINGEN, AND BERLIN

Reason and language in the Wertheim Bible

Some of these ideas about language and mind made their way into a controversial and influential translation of the Pentateuch. Johann Lorenz Schmidt, tutor to the Dukes of Löwenstein-Wertheim, published in 1735 the first part of *Die göttlichen Schriften vor den Zeiten des Messie Jesus* (*The Divine Writings before the Times of Jesus the Messiah*), publicly known as the Wertheim Bible after its place of publication. The subtitle announced that the translation was free in some respects yet at the same time 'explained and corroborated' by annotation. In a rigorous introduction, Schmidt presented the project as an attempt to defend the Bible against deist criticism.[32]

Though partly drawing on Leibnizian and Wolffian concepts, Schmidt parted ways with Leibniz in regard to the Christian mysteries: his project was informed by a firm aspiration to subject all religious mysteries to scientific and rational examination.[33] For Schmidt, who had been exposed to Wolffian philosophy at Jena and Halle, inner coherence and logical possibility were the only conditions for the reality of facts as related in historical texts, including the Bible. Unlike Leibniz, Schmidt wished to present a rational elucidation of the mysteries and thus to base Christianity on reason, uncovering a natural religion within Scripture. In this vein, miracles and other supernatural occurrences were explained according to the latest scientific theories in the accompanying notes. Schmidt also tried to minimize the references to a personal God, substituting for it a philosophical notion of divinity as the free, self-sufficient first cause of the universe. The word 'God' was therefore replaced on various occasions by 'divine will' or 'the autonomous entity' (*selbständiges Wesen*).[34] Unlike

---

[32] Johann Lorenz Schmidt, 'Vorrede', in *Die göttlichen Schriften vor den Zeiten des Messie Jesus: Der erste Theil worinnen Die Gesetze der Israelen enthalten sind nach einer freyen Übersetzung welche durch und durch mit Anmerkungen erläutert und bestätigt wird* (Wertheim: Johann Georg Nehr, 1735), 5.

[33] Ibid. 14–15.

[34] See, for example, the Wolffian terminology in the exposition of the concept of divinity in Schmidt's 'Vorrede', 12–13.

traditional editions of the Old Testament, the Wertheim Bible eschewed all references to Christ and his future incarnation. Schmidt's call for a scientific treatment of the text was defended by a radical interpretation of the Protestant *sola scriptura* principle: one should accept as God's word only what was explicitly mentioned in Scripture, thereby excluding the typological view of the Pentateuch as announcing Christ.

Other controversial editorial decisions were the transcription of proper names (persons, rivers, or towns) according to contemporary Hebrew pronunciation rather than the traditional German notation. On the other hand, Schmidt announced his desire to render biblical language as comprehensible to modern German readers as it had been to the ancient Jews. This was not particularly problematic in the case of physical objects, but metaphors presented Schmidt with a challenge. He acknowledged that in various periods and environments people had different motivations for naming things (*Gründe der Bennenung*), depending on diverse associations of ideas. Moreover, all languages were subject to daily changes through usage; abstract terms were denoted by metaphors (*verblümte Wörter*) that increased the differences between languages. Upon translating, one had to transmit into the target language the ideas and their associations in the source language, while paying attention to the circumstances under which the text was written, the state of the source language at the time, and the author's intentions. All these considerations called for a free translation into modern German, Schmidt argued: outdated vocabulary and ancient metaphors had to make way for the precise rendering of meaning. Practically applied, these principles led Schmidt to transform metaphors into unequivocal expressions. He was fully aware of the ensuing loss of the poetic nature of the text, as a 'land of milk and honey' became a simple 'land of abundance', and God's arm was transformed into his power or grace. The frequent and pedantic notes (around 1,600 in number), analysing even common and self-evident notions, contributed to the alienating effect Schmidt's translation had on readers familiar with more traditional versions of the Bible.

Though Schmidt professed his orthodoxy and claimed he merely wished to protect the historical and ethical truths of Christianity against its detractors, the Wertheim Bible was quickly singled out for vehement criticism by churchmen, academic theologians, and journalists who regarded it as a deist work stripping the Bible of its unique language and character. The clarion call was sounded by Joachim Lange, the influential leader of Halle Pietism who had spearheaded in 1723 the campaign for Christian Wolff's expulsion from Halle. In a short essay entitled *Der philosophische Religionsspötter* (*The Philosophical Religion-Mocker*, 1735) Lange drew attention to the lack of references to the Trinity and Christ in the Wertheim Bible, linking it firmly to his adversary Wolff.[35] Lange and other critics, even those more positively inclined towards Wolff's philosophy, capitalized on the stylistic aspects of Schmidt's translation which reduced all figurative language into prosaic descriptions. Pietists and other defenders of the Christian mysteries sensed that this might be the weakest link in rationalist interpretations of the Bible.[36]

An aesthetic response to the rationalist challenge

In 1735, the year in which the fierce controversy over the Wertheim Bible broke out, Alexander Gottlieb Baumgarten published his first work, *Meditationes philosophicae de nonnullis ad poema pertinentibus* (*Philosophical Reflections on Several Issues Concerning Poetry*), based on his amateur poetic experience. This work, like his later *Aesthetica* (two volumes, 1750 and 1758), was an attempt to legitimize not only artistic expression as such, but the whole realm of sensual experience. Baumgarten tried to subject the senses to the same rigorous examination Leibniz and Wolff applied to higher mental faculties by employing their notion of clear but indistinct ideas.[37]

Baumgarten adhered to Leibniz's classification of sensually based knowledge as inferior to intuitive or fully adequate forms of perception. Nevertheless, he strove to demonstrate that clear but confused ideas had some unique qualities that made pure reason redundant for their understanding. In the case of sense experience, complete structural analysis was not simply impossible but also undesirable. Just as the basic elements of light were irrelevant to the appreciation of a painting, aesthetics had to examine appearances without going beyond them in search for ultimate causes. Further analysis, a requisite step in geometry and mathematics, would not explain sensual experience but rather dissolve it altogether. According to Baumgarten, poetry and literature should not be completely

---

[35] Ursula Goldenbaum, 'Der Skandal der *Wertheimer Bibel*', in *Appell an das Publikum: Die öffentliche Debatte in der deutschen Aufklärung 1687–1796*, ed. Ursula Goldenbaum (Berlin: Akademie Verlag, 2004), i. 234–8.

[36] The controversy over the Wertheim Bible lasted several years, leading to its official ban in the Holy Roman Empire. On the tumultuous debate, see 'Wertheimische Bibel' in Johann Heinrich Zedler and Carl Günther Ludovici (eds), *Großes vollständiges Universal-Lexikon aller Wissenschaften und Künste* (Halle and Leipzig: Zedler, 1732–54), lv. 595–662; Paul S. Spalding, *Seize the Book, Jail the Author: Johann Lorenz Schmidt and Censorship in Eighteenth-Century Germany* (West Lafayette, Ind.: Purdue University Press, 1998); Goldenbaum, 'Der Skandal'; Israel, *Radical Enlightenment*, 552–5, and *Enlightenment Contested*, 188–93.

[37] Alexander Gottlieb Baumgarten, *Reflections on Poetry—Meditationes philosophicae de nonnullis ad poema pertinentibus*, eds Karl Aschenbrenner and William B. Holther (Berkeley: University of California Press, 1954).

analysed into their constituents, a stance resembling Leibniz's argument about the religious mysteries. Logical analysis of sensual perception dissolved beauty, while the uniquely human symbolic cognition allowed for richness and chaos. 'What does abstraction mean apart from loss,' wondered Baumgarten in his *Aesthetica*.[38]

Parallel to the publication of Baumgarten's aesthetic works, Moses Mendelssohn elaborated a similar view in his *Briefe über die Empfindungen* (*Letters on the Sentiments*, 1755), arguing that a creature more perfect than man would have broader access to the causes of external appearances. Like Leibniz and Baumgarten, Mendelssohn related man's symbolic knowledge to the limitations of his mind. It was this epistemological imperfection that granted human beings the experience of beauty, which was so characteristic of their sense-related faculties.[39]

What did this mean in practice, for writers and readers of poetry and fiction? Unlike the Cartesian view of words as mere coins for communication, Baumgarten's sense-based knowledge could not operate without signs as its medium. The sensual experience of poetry required clear but confused ideas in the guise of metaphor, synecdoche, and figurative speech, or as Baumgarten called them, 'improper terms' referring indirectly to their objects.[40] Yet precisely these aspects of biblical poetry had been proscribed by Schmidt in his translation of the Old Testament: miracles were explained scientifically, and ordinary language replaced the metaphors that allegedly suited only the ancient Jews. Baumgarten's positioning of sensual experience within an autonomous sphere may thus be seen as a response to the untamed claims of reason among Wolffian radicals. His view that full logical analysis was unsuitable for the confused notions of sense experience could be applied to the Old Testament as a poetic masterpiece. Such a view of the Bible would, however, require its further contextualization within history as a man-made artefact.

---

[38] Baumgarten, *Aesthetica* (Frankfurt an der Oder: Johann Christian Kleyb, 1750), 363; Hans Rudolf Schweizer, *Ästhetik als Philosophie der sinnlichen Erkenntnis: Eine Interpretation der 'Aesthetica' A. G. Baumgartens* (Basel: Schwabe, 1973), 241–3; Robert E. Norton, *The Beautiful Soul: Aesthetic Morality in the Eighteenth Century* (Ithaca, NY: Cornell University Press, 1995), 56–71.

[39] Mendelssohn, *Gesammelte Schriften—Jubiläumsausgabe*, eds F. Bamberger et al. (Berlin: Akademie Verlag, and Stuttgart: Frommann-Holzboog, 1929–), i. 58–61 (henceforth *JubA*). On the Leibnizian roots of mid-century aesthetics, see Johannes Schmidt, *Leibnitz und Baumgarten: Ein Beitrag zur Geschichte der deutschen Ästhetik* (Halle: Niemeyer, 1875); Hans Adler, *Die Prägnanz des Dunklen: Gnoseologie—Ästhetik—Geschichtsphilosophie bei Johann Gottfried Herder* (Hamburg: Meiner, 1990), 1–48; Frederick Beiser, *Diotima's Children: German Aesthetic Rationalism from Leibniz to Lessing* (Oxford: Oxford University Press, 2009).

[40] Baumgarten, *Reflections on Poetry*, 67–8.

Siegmund Jacob Baumgarten: Pietism, history, and Wolffian philosophy

Writing in Halle from the 1730s onwards, Alexander Gottlieb Baumgarten must have been aware of the relevance of his enterprise to contemporary theology not only due to the controversy over the Wertheim Bible. His elder brother, Siegmund Jacob Baumgarten, became the subject of a Pietist attack at Halle. In 1736, two years after his promotion to the rank of *ordinarius* professor at the University, complaints to the Prussian king about the older Baumgarten's suspected heterodoxy were filed by Joachim Lange, the arch-rival of Wolff and Schmidt. Baumgarten was accused of employing the mathematical method within the theology faculty, and importing Wolffian ideas into his lectures on ethics and religious dogma.[41] Interrogated by university and government officials for neglecting his duty to submit publications to faculty inspection, he was eventually found innocent.[42] After Lange's death Siegmund Jacob Baumgarten became director of the theological seminar (1744), pro-rector of the University (1748–9), and member of the reformed Berlin Academy (1748). This academic confrontation reflected the waning dominance of the old Pietist guard, led by Lange and Gotthilf August Francke (son of August Hermann Francke, the founder of the theology faculty and other institutions in Halle). Moderate and reforming theologians in Berlin, such as Johann Gustav Reinbeck, began to turn from the late 1730s to Wolff's philosophy as a possible means of renewal for both Pietism and orthodox Lutheranism, steering a middle course between excessive religious enthusiasm and rationalist deism.[43]

Though in 1735 Baumgarten joined the choir of condemnation of the Wertheim Bible, after the controversy abated he criticized what he saw as the wild persecution of Schmidt.[44] The debate over Schmidt's translation of the Old Testament, the legacy of Christian Wolff's career at Halle, and his own confrontation with the Pietists may have prompted Baumgarten to reconcile ardent Pietism with Wolffian philosophy. Baumgarten never abandoned Pietism, emphasizing like the founders of his faculty the personal union with God. But Baumgarten also wished to combine a devout

---

[41] Martin Schloemann, *Siegmund Jacob Baumgarten: System und Geschichte in der Theologie des Übergangs zum Neuprotestantismus* (Göttingen: Vandenhoeck & Ruprecht, 1974), 39–50.

[42] This outcome was guaranteed to a large extent by Baumgarten's colleagues Johann Heinrich Michaelis (the oldest member of the faculty) and his nephew, Christian Benedict Michaelis (Schloemann, *Baumgarten*, 43–4).

[43] For Baumgarten's place within larger latitudinarian currents, see Sorkin, *Religious Enlightenment*, 113–63.

[44] Goldenbaum, *Appell an das Publikum*, i. 69.

inner subjectivity with Wolff's philosophical method. Influenced by Reinbeck and Wolff, Baumgarten's exegesis was practically orientated, by contrast to the confessional speculation still common in contemporary theological faculties.[45]

While focusing on the ethical and salvific effects of Scripture, Baumgarten began to employ in his exegesis principles resembling some of Johann Lorenz Schmidt's ideas, especially in *Unterricht von Auslegung der Heiligen Schrift* (*Lesson on the Interpretation of the Holy Scripture*, 1742). Like Schmidt, Baumgarten required interpreters of the Old Testament to make detailed inquiries into the meanings of words in their historical contexts. Departing from the Pietist emphasis on the emotional effects of the text and from the traditional Lutheran view of the Bible as directly inspired by God, Baumgarten wished to attain certainty (*Gewissheit*) regarding Christian history through the application of reason and philology to its study. Following his view that the Bible was divinely inspired but composed by human authors, Baumgarten used the principle of accommodation in its interpretation. Apparent errors and inconsistencies had to be traced back to God's adjustment of his message to the circumstances of its deliverance and the mindset of his audience. Other inaccuracies were set apart from the ethical core of Scripture by reference to Leibniz and Wolff's distinction between truths necessary for salvation, for which the Bible was an unerring guide, and truths addressing less crucial domains such as ceremonies.

After Wolff's return to the philosophy faculty at Halle (1740), Baumgarten shifted his focus to history. Wolff regarded history as the uncertain study of contingent facts, unlike philosophy and mathematics where abstract deduction could be applied.[46] Baumgarten, by contrast, found much to admire in history while employing Wolff's own notion of *Zusammenhang*, the mutual connection and agreement of facts that wove them into a harmonious whole. His main aim was to transform history into a mediating link between human experience and divine revelation, partly as a reaction to what he considered as the abuse of history by deists and

---

[45] Siegmund Jacob Baumgarten, *Evangelische Glaubenslehre*, ed. Johann Salomo Semler (Halle: Gebauer, 1759–60), i. 6; Walter Sparn, 'Vernünftiges Christentum: Über die geschichtliche Aufgabe der theologischen Aufklärung im 18. Jahrhundert in Deutschland', in Rudolf Vierhaus (ed.), *Wissenschaften im Zeitalter der Aufklärung* (Göttingen: Vandenhoeck & Ruprecht, 1985), 35–6, and 'Auf dem Wege zur theologischen Aufklärung in Halle: Von Johann Franz Budde zu Siegmund Jakob Baumgarten', in Norbert Hinske (ed.), *Zentren der Aufklärung*, i: *Halle* (Heidelberg: Schneider, 1989), 71–89; Schloemann, 'Wegbereiter wider Willen: Siegmund Jacob Baumgarten und die historisch-kritische Bibelforschung', in Henning Graf Reventlow et al. (eds), *Historische Kritik und biblischer Kanon in der deutschen Aufklärung* (Wiesbaden: Harrassowitz, 1988), 149–55.

[46] Wolff, *Discursus praeliminaris de philosophia in genere*, eds Günter Gawlick and Lothar Kreimdahl (Stuttgart-Bad Cannstatt: Frommann-Holzboog, 1996), 18–19.

religious enthusiasts alike.[47] In the 1740s and 1750s Baumgarten wrote, edited, prefaced, and translated an abundance of publications on world history and on church history. Wishing to demonstrate that deism and atheism could be countered by profound historical research, Baumgarten reviewed in detail the works of English deists (Anthony Collins, John Toland, Matthew Tindal) and apologists (William Whiston, Samuel Clarke) in the journals he edited.[48] He also edited and extensively annotated the multi-volume English Universal History (originally published from 1736 to 1744), calling for a positive re-evaluation of mere probability as a criterion of truth instead of clear and distinct analysis.[49] This publishing venture was a great success; at the end of the century it was regarded a milestone in the emergence of a new historical understanding.[50]

Baumgarten's motivation in his historical studies was primarily apologetic, seeing Christianity as a historical religion whose truths might be fortified through a minute reconstruction of the past. In this framework history was not only meant to corroborate Scripture. It constituted a field in which the devout Pietist subject could verify his divine capacity for reason and objectivity by inquiring into the past and assessing the reliability of available documents. What aesthetics was for Alexander Gottlieb Baumgarten, history and biblical criticism may have been for his brother Siegmund Jacob: a systematic endeavour that could be employed as a measured defence of Christianity against its critics. As in the aesthetic works of the younger Baumgarten, an acute sense of language in its various manifestations was central to the elder brother's historical hermeneutics. His application of linguistic and philological tools to the history of the Christian dogma had a wide-ranging impact upon subsequent generations. Among his students were conservatives such as the future Prussian minister Johann Christoph Wöllner and Lessing's opponent Johann Melchior Goeze, but also the scholars Anton Friedrich Büsching, Fried-

---

[47] Schloemann, *Baumgarten*, 135–56.
[48] *Nachrichten von einer hallischen Bibliothek* (1748–51) and *Nachrichten von merkwürdigen Büchern* (1752–8). On Baumgarten's paradoxical role in the introduction of English deism into Germany see Christoph Voigt, *Der englische Deismus in Deutschland* (Tübingen: Mohr Siebeck, 2003), 149–73.
[49] Baumgarten, *Übersetzung der Algemeinen Welthistorie die in Engeland durch eine Gesellschaft von Gelehrten ausgefertiget worden* (Halle: Gebauer, 1744), 10.
[50] Johann Gottfried Eichhorn wrote in 1791 that Baumgarten's Universal History was a 'historical sensation' paving the way for a new generation of historical researchers. (Eichhorn, 'Johann David Michaelis', *Allgemeine Bibliothek der biblischen Litteratur*, iii/5 (Leipzig: Weidmannsche Buchhandlung, 1791), 839.) On this project, see Guido Abbattista, 'The English *Universal History*: Publishing, Authorship, and Historiography in a European Project (1736–1790)', *Storia della Storiografia* 39 (2001), 103–8; Zedelmaier, *Anfang der Geschichte*, 143–83; Monika Baár, 'From General History to National History', in Stefanie Stockhorst (ed.), *Cultural Transfer through Translation* (Amsterdam: Rodopi, 2010), 63–82.

rich Germanus Lüdke, and Johann August Nösselt. Two of Baumgarten's students in particular were to exert great influence on German hermeneutics from the 1750s onwards: Johann David Michaelis at Göttingen and Johann Salomo Semler at Halle.

Semler and Neology

Teaching at the theology faculty of the University of Halle for nearly forty years (from 1752 until his death), Semler was one of the main propagators of the application of historical and philological scholarship to Scripture. Drawing on Baumgarten's principle of accommodation, Semler further underscored the priority of historical exegesis over dogma. However, in Semler's writings the apologetic motive withdrew to the background, substituted by a rigorous scholarly ethos and a distinction between the form and content of the Bible. This dichotomy was mirrored in Semler's work by the separation of what he saw as theology from religion, and in his distinction between human spirit and its historical circumstances.[51]

The tendency to strip Scripture from allegedly irrelevant, time- and place-bound circumstances was relatively limited in scope in Baumgarten's own works, but it became much more pronounced in Semler's writings. The goal of overcoming both rigid orthodoxy and radical rationalism was to be attained through the vindication of the divine core of Christianity and its extraction from merely human forms of transmission. As different parts of the Bible were written for various ancient audiences, Semler argued that the tenets of Christian ethics were not present in them to the same extent.[52] He therefore found greater or lesser amounts of divine substance in different books according to their potential as ethical guides. Only sparsely could modern-day Christians find 'useful eternal truths' in the Old Testament, in Semler's eyes. When compared to the ethical core of religion, the Old Testament was found wanting, restrictively moulded by its temporal and geographical circumstances. By contrast to Michaelis, who found in the Bible's alien metaphors and customs a testimony to the liveliness of God's message, Semler attempted time and again to separate divine content from irrelevant stories, arguing that a healthy extract from

---

[51] Semler's most renowned works were *Vorbereitung zur theologischen Hermeneutik* (1760–9) and *Abhandlung von freier Untersuchung des Canon* (1771–5). In the 1750s and the early 1760s he edited Baumgarten's posthumous works, taking up the editorship of the German version of the English *Universal History*. For the distinction between theology as an interpretive endeavour and religion as a core of eternally divine truths, see Semler's *Lebensbeschreibung von ihm selbst abgefasst* (Halle, n.p., 1781–2), i. 96.

[52] Semler, *Abhandlung von freier Untersuchung des Canon*, 2nd edn (Halle: Carl Hermann Hemmerde, 1776), i. 58–9.

the Pentateuch would convey more eternal truths than its books read in their entirety.[53]

In some cases Semler compared the biblical style to the sounds and letters of language, arguing that external linguistic manifestations could never convey the immutable truths of religion.[54] By exploring the messianic movements in Herod's Judaea, Semler tried to demonstrate that Christ was steeped in the Jewish mentality of the time. Therefore, his message must have been encoded in contemporary linguistic and intellectual devices; for Semler, the unfolding of the truths of Christianity must have taken place ever since antiquity in a constant, infinite process.[55] This acknowledgement of the historical context of all religious expressions made Semler advance the thesis that religion itself, as a basic human drive, was changing along with human consciousness, addressing different spiritual challenges and needs in every age.

Semler's emphasis on the moral precepts in the Bible could perhaps be ascribed to the persistence of the Pietist notion of the primacy of personal ethics over dogma at Halle.[56] However, echoes of the Pietist tradition were combined in his works with the strong influence of Richard Simon's view of the Bible as a historically evolved human artefact and the Wolffian notion of *Zusammenhang*, the interconnection of all events and facts. Semler's emphasis on the original audience of the biblical books—their circumstances, language, and pragmatic orientation—also mirrored the shift in contemporary aesthetics from rules of composition to the sensory perception of spectators or readers. In both domains, symbolic cognition was crucial in the mediation of clear but indistinct ideas.

Semler has been alternately regarded as a harbinger or the leader of the hermeneutic school of Neology, whose adherents discarded the notion of the Bible as directly inspired by God and distinguished the ethical core of Christianity from its changing contexts. The main representatives of the school have sometimes been identified as Siegmund Jacob Baumgarten's collaborators and students, such as Ernesti in Leipzig, Michaelis in

---

[53] Semler, 'Antwort auf einige Recensionen', in *Abhandlung*, iii. 381. For different versions of this argument from Spinoza to the mid-eighteenth century, see Adam Sutcliffe, *Judaism and Enlightenment* (Cambridge: Cambridge University Press, 2003), esp. chs. 7 and 12.

[54] Semler, 'Antwort', 342–3. This argument seems to beg the question of the criteria used for distinguishing divine meanings from their linguistic manifestations: in Semler's view, divine and ethically relevant truths were self-evident.

[55] Peter Hanns Reill, *The German Enlightenment and the Rise of Historicism* (Berkeley: University of California Press, 1975), 169–72.

[56] For the Pietist impulse in Neological exegesis see Karl Aner, *Die Theologie der Lessingzeit* (Halle: Max Niemeyer, 1929), 150–2; more specifically on Halle, see Ulrich Barth, 'Hallesche Hermeneutik im 18. Jahrhundert', in Manfred Beetz and Giuseppe Cacciatore (eds), *Hermeneutik im Zeitalter der Aufklärung* (Cologne: Böhlau, 2000), 69–98.

Göttingen, and Semler in Halle.[57] Their fusion of Wolffian epistemology with inquiries into the contingent past stood at the centre of a parallel development in German universities, the advent of history as a central preoccupation within faculties of theology and philosophy.

Academic history: the beginnings of the Göttingen School

The rise of Neology corresponded to a more general trend in mid-century Germany, the increasing recognition of the historical character of the physical world, social institutions, and human nature. The waning of the Wolffian vogue from the 1750s onwards enabled eclectic currents and the legacy of Pufendorf and Thomasius to resurface in the universities and merge with strong impulses from France, especially the first works of Condillac, Buffon, and Diderot. As Reinhart Koselleck has argued, in this period the growing awareness of the temporal malleability of all things human led to the birth of the German word for history, *Geschichte*, in its modern sense of a collective singular and an objectified phenomenon. This was a major semantic shift from its earlier usage in the plural, *Geschichten*, as 'accounts' or 'stories'. The new meaning of *Geschichte* expressed an awareness of historical change as an independent phenomenon, a field of inquiry requiring a language of its own.[58]

The new interest in the complex web of links between historical events may be seen as a reaction to a mechanist model of causal explanation on the one hand, and on the other to seventeenth-century polyhistors or speculative historians such as Gottfried Arnold.[59] The *Aufklärung*'s rising interest in both universal history and local traditions was largely moulded by the Leibnizian notion of a system as a matrix of interconnected events. Within this matrix each period, region, and event served as a unique vantage point, conveying a particular view of the whole. The significant

---

[57] Karl Aner excluded Semler from the Neologist camp by reference to his change of heart from 1779 onwards (*Theologie der Lessingzeit*, 4, 98–111). Peter Reill, however, sees Neology as an earlier and less radical movement whose main practitioners were Mosheim, Ernesti, Michaelis, and Semler (*German Enlightenment*, 162).

[58] Reinhart Koselleck, *Futures Past: On the Semantics of Historical Time*, trans. Keith Tribe (New York: Columbia University Press, 2004), 32–4. See S. J. Baumgarten's use of the plural *Geschichten* in 1744 in his introduction to the Universal History (*Übersetzung der Algemeinen Welthistorie*, 9); Reill, 'Die Geschichtswissenschaft um die Mitte des 18. Jahrhunderts', in Vierhaus (ed.), *Wissenschaften*, 163–93; Alexandre Escudier, 'Theory and Methodology of History from Chladenius to Droysen: A Historiographical Essay', in Christopher Ligota and Jean-Louis Quantin (eds), *History of Scholarship* (Oxford: Oxford University Press, 2006), 437–86.

[59] Anthony Grafton, 'The World of the Polyhistors: Humanism and Encyclopedism', *Central European History* 18 (1985), 31–47, and 'Polyhistor into Philolog: Notes on the Transformation of German Classical Scholarship, 1780–1850', *History of Universities* 3 (1983), 159–92.

notion of a historical point of view (*Sehepunkt*), as elaborated by Johann Martin Chladenius, referred not only to the impact of mental and physical factors on historical agents but also to the inevitable immersion of historians in the contemporary contexts of their own writing. In his *Einleitung zur richtigen Auslegung vernünfftiger Reden und Schriften* (*Introduction to the Correct Interpretation of Wise Discourses and Writings*, 1742) and in *Allgemeine Geschichtswissenschaft* (*General Historiography*, 1752), Chladenius argued that no historical narrative could constitute a totally objective account of events. Drawing on Leibniz's monadology, Chladenius argued that a single episode might be mirrored in different narratives, all of them true and valid despite their inherent partiality. Each individual had a unique point of view, and the historian's task was to assemble a viable picture of the past by merging analytically the accounts given in different documents and testimonies.[60]

In a similar manner to the efforts of Alexander Gottlieb Baumgarten and Moses Mendelssohn to rehabilitate imperfect symbolic knowledge, Chladenius wished to counter Pyrrhonist critiques of historiography by highlighting the fragmented nature of human perception. By contrast to the high standard of perspicuity required in geometry, history—whose main concern was human affairs—required another explanatory apparatus to express the 'fused' or the 'con-fused' (*verwirrt*) interrelations of events. Chladenius traced the uncertainty of historical affairs back to their human agents, whose voluntary actions usually preceded rational deliberation.[61] Chladenius's use of the Leibnizian terms 'confused ideas' and 'intuitive judgment' may reveal the affinity between his own historical enterprise, contemporary aesthetics, and Neology. He too was trying to combine a grasp of the universal *nexus rerum*, the analysis of irrational human behaviour, and an emphasis on symbolic cognition.[62]

Johann Christoph Gatterer espoused a similar notion of the inadequacy of strict deduction for history in the myriad projects he undertook after his appointment as professor of history at Göttingen in 1759. These included universal histories, documentary compendia, textbooks, and historical journals. According to Gatterer, historians should use and address the powers of the mind (*Seelenkräfte*) in order to convey a lively

---

[60] Johann Martin Chladenius, 'Allgemeine Geschichtswissenschaft', in Horst Walter Blanke and Dirk Fleischer (eds), *Theoretiker der deutschen Aufklärungshistorie* (Stuttgart: Frommann-Holzboog, 1990), 226–74, here 241–2.
[61] Ibid. 272.
[62] See also Reill, *German Enlightenment*, 105–12, and Michael Ermarth, 'Hermeneutics and History: The Fork in Hermes' Path through the 18th Century', in Hans Erich Bödeker, Georg G. Iggers, Jonathan B. Knudsen, and Peter Reill (eds), *Aufklärung und Geschichte* (Göttingen: Vandenhoeck & Ruprecht, 1986), 191–221.

representation of the past.⁶³ Among the powers required for such a task were *Einbildungskraft* (reminiscence and re-experience of earlier events), *Dichtungskraft* (active representation of the past), and creative genius. In the anti-Cartesian vein of mid-century philosophy, Gatterer turned to ancient rhetoric and rehabilitated style as a prerequisite for historical exposition, not merely an ornament to be parachuted over historical facts. Symbolic cognition forced the historian to employ stylistic devices for popular transmission. Such notions were later applied by Gatterer's colleagues and successors at Göttingen to various projects, from the legal history of the Holy Roman Empire to interpretations of the Old Testament.⁶⁴

'Popular philosophers' probing language and method

The striving for the holistic representation of a contextual interrelationship, however much influenced by Leibniz and Wolff, was accompanied by a decisive move against Wolff's own method of geometrical demonstration. The opposition to this method was not new in itself; it had been manifest in seventeenth-century reactions to Descartes and Spinoza. Yet from the 1730s onwards, thinkers of different persuasions criticized Wolff's geometrical method not least because of the radical rationalist works that laid bare its potential theological implications. By denying the validity of mathematical certainty in human affairs, such authors raised the question of language and method in metaphysics, ethics, and theology.

Adolf Friedrich Hoffmann and his student Christian August Crusius provided some initial ammunition by reiterating seventeenth-century charges against Descartes.⁶⁵ They traced the distinctive certainty of the geometrical method to its objects of inquiry: mathematics owed its infallibility to its man-made imaginary objects, whereas philosophy dealt with real things outside the human mind. Crusius pointed out that in mathematics definitions could be deduced from a single example, while physics

---

⁶³ Gatterer, 'Von der Evidenz in der Geschichtskunde' (1767), in *Theoretiker der deutschen Aufklärungshistorie*, ii. 468.

⁶⁴ Reill, 'History and Hermeneutics in the *Aufklärung*: The Thought of Johann Christoph Gatterer', *Journal of Modern History* 45 (1973), 24–51. On subsequent developments in Göttingen see Carhart, *Science of Culture*, and Hans Erich Bödeker et al. (eds), *Die Wissenschaft vom Menschen in Göttingen um 1800* (Göttingen: Vandenhoeck & Ruprecht, 2008).

⁶⁵ Adolf Friedrich Hoffmann, *Vernunft-Lehre* (Leipzig: n.p., 1737); Christian August Crusius, *Entwurf der nothwendigen Vernunft-Wahrheiten* (Leipzig: Gleditsch, 1745) and *Weg zur Gewißheit und Zuverläßigkeit der menschlichen Erkenntniß* (Leipzig: Gleditsch, 1747).

and philosophy required more substantial verification.[66] Crusius' attack on Wolff's procedure had other motives, such as the vindication of free will and its primacy over reason, but discontent with the mathematical method was widespread also among Wolff's own disciples. A well-known popularizer of Wolff's system, Jean Henri Samuel Formey, the Perpetual Secretary of the Berlin Academy, argued in 1747 that geometricians would get lost in the labyrinth of actual things if they proceeded from their imaginary objects to physics and metaphysics.[67] The Academy's President, Pierre Louis Moreau de Maupertuis, was more resolute in his attack on Wolff's method. Following Fontenelle and Buffon's distinction between the mathematical and physical sciences, Maupertuis criticized Wolff in his *Essai de cosmologie* (*Essay on Cosmology*, 1751) for allegedly believing that the mathematical method possessed certainty regardless of its objects.[68] Another member of the Academy, André Pierre Le Guay de Prémontval, caused considerable stir in Berlin of the 1750s with his vehement attacks on Wolff and his method. Apart from generally targeting Wolffian ethics and metaphysics, in his various works of the 1750s Prémontval referred disapprovingly to Wolff's language and method. The concern with philosophical method at the Berlin Academy found its expression in 1761 with the announcement of the topic for the 1763 prize contest: the certainty of metaphysical evidence in comparison to mathematics.[69]

Wolff's method was also the subject of widespread discussion in Berlin beyond the Academy, among the authors collectively known as *Popularphilosophen* ('popular philosophers'). The so-called 'popularity' of their endeavour consisted in its orientation towards a well-educated segment of society, and in employing philosophy in the service a new civic culture. This emphasis on both praxis and broad learning was consciously set against academic philosophy. As a response to the consolidation of Wolf-

[66] Crusius, *Weg zur Gewißheit*, 17–21; Giorgio Tonelli, 'Der Streit über die mathematische Methode in der Philosophie in der ersten Hälfte des 18. Jahrhunderts und die Entstehung von Kants Schrift über die "Deutlichkeit"', *Archiv für Philosophie* 9 (1959), 37–66; Carlos Spoerhase, 'Die "Mittelstrasse" zwischen Skeptizismus und Dogmatismus', in Carlos Spoerhase et al. (eds), *Unsicheres Wissen: Skeptizismus und Wahrscheinlichkeit 1550–1850* (Berlin: De Gruyter, 2009), 269–300.
[67] Formey, 'Recherches sur les élemens de la matière' (1747), in *Mélanges philosophiques* (Leiden: Elie Luzac, 1754), i. 258.
[68] Maupertuis, 'Essai de cosmologie', in *Œuvres de Mr de Maupertuis* (Lyon: Bruyset, 1756), i. 21–2. See also his 'Examen philosophique de la preuve de l'existence de Dieu employée dans l'essai de cosmologie', in *Histoire de l'Académie royale des sciences et belles lettres, année 1756* (Berlin: Haude & Spener, 1758), 391–3.
[69] Hans-Jürgen Engfer, *Philosophie als Analysis: Studien zur Entwicklung philosophischer Analysiskonzeptionen unter dem Einfluß mathematischer Methodenmodelle im 17. und frühen 18. Jahrhundert* (Stuttgart-Bad Cannstatt: Frommann-Holzboog, 1982), 26–67. See also Chapter 6 below on Prémontval's works, and Chapter 7 for the 1763 contest.

fian philosophy in the universities, the *Popularphilosophen* heralded 'philosophy for the world' (*Philosophie für die Welt*), or at least for the emerging public sphere. While contrasting a vision of engaged and engaging scholars with a supposedly irrelevant sect ensconced in the universities, the *Popularphilosophen* shared Wolff's belief in the capacity of human reason to recognize the tenets of natural religion. Their espousal of natural theology was accompanied by a strong dose of Thomasian eclecticism and British and French empiricism, though these stimuli varied in their extent among different authors.[70]

The genetic and observational methods were accompanied in the *Popularphilosophen*'s works by a special concern with language. This preoccupation cannot be explained only by reference to the reception of French theories through the Berlin Academy, since the relationship between words, things, and human cognition was essential to the practical impact the *Popularphilosophen* sought to achieve. The question of the reliability of language was embedded within their view of 'philosophy for the world' as a means for the transmission of Enlightenment thought.[71] In this context, the crisis of sensualist representation constituted a considerable threat to their enterprise. Various *Popularphilosophen* wrestled in Berlin with Berkeleian and Humean themes, trying to maintain a firm belief in external reality and the reliability of its representation in human perception and language.[72]

* * *

German discussions of language and cognition in the first half of the eighteenth century tended to focus on several key notions, first among them Leibniz's rehabilitation of clear but indistinct ideas. The significance of such ideas was elaborated in aesthetics, historical scholarship, and biblical criticism into an intricate scheme mediating between abstract analysis and concrete sense experience. In all these domains, the interpreter's aspiration was to approximate intuitive knowledge (*anschauende Erkenntnis*),

---

[70] Frederick Beiser, *The Fate of Reason: German Philosophy from Kant to Fichte* (Cambridge, Mass.: Harvard University Press, 1987), 165–9; Edoardo Tortarolo, *La ragione sulla Sprea: coscienza storica e cultura politica nell'illuminismo berlinese* (Bologna: Mulino, 1989); Johan van der Zande, 'In the Image of Cicero: German Philosophy between Wolff and Kant', *Journal of the History of Ideas* 56 (1995), 419–42; John H. Zammito, *Kant, Herder, and the Birth of Anthropology* (Chicago: University of Chicago Press, 2002), 28–41.

[71] Bödeker, 'Aufklärung als Kommunikationsprozeß', in Rudolf Vierhaus (ed.), *Aufklärung als Prozeß* (Hamburg: Meiner, 1987), 89–111.

[72] John Christian Laursen, 'Swiss Anti-Skeptics in Berlin', in Martin Fontius and Helmut Holzhey (eds), *Schweizer im Berlin des 18. Jahrhunderts* (Berlin: Akademie Verlag, 1996), 261–82; Laursen and Richard H. Popkin, 'Hume in the Prussian Academy: Jean Bernard Merian's "On the Phenomenalism of David Hume"', *Hume Studies* 23 (1997), 153–91.

yet in most cases one had to do with the symbolic cognition characteristic of the human mind. Within this framework both language and history gained a prominent position. Contemporary authors were, therefore, well aware of the implications of the ideas that language was a social construct and that society was a linguistic construct.

The wide-ranging focus on language among theologians, historians, and aestheticians reflected the recognition that all cultural phenomena were, like language itself, man-made. Religions, social institutions, and ethical norms were seen as emerging through the human imposition of artificial meanings on the world, if only because all such phenomena had to be mediated through signs. Various mid-century authors believed that if human beings had been able to analyse nature down to its basic elements, approximating God's instantaneous gaze, they would have lost their capacity to perceive beauty. Our material and intellectual culture could be properly observed only in linguistic, symbolic, and historical terms. While this vision was influenced by Leibnizian and Wolffian concepts, it also entailed the rejection of Wolff's geometrical method of argumentation. In no other German venue were these issues as passionately debated in the 1750s as in the Berlin Academy.

3

The Evolution and Genius of Language

Debates in the Berlin Academy

In the 1750s Berlin was an intellectual melting pot, bringing together the different communities of local *Aufklärer*, immigrant or itinerant French *philosophes*, and local Huguenots (residing in the city since the late seventeenth century). As the main universities of Brandenburg-Prussia were located in Halle, Frankfurt on the Oder, and Königsberg, there was no corporate scholarly culture in Berlin. In fact, it may have been the absence of such a traditional academic centre that made the Prussian capital into a lively intellectual node in the Republic of Letters. This situation facilitated the emergence of various institutions such as literary societies, independent journals, and new cultural venues. The main catalysing agent of many of these activities was the Royal Academy of Sciences and Belles-Lettres, successor of the almost defunct Society of Sciences founded in 1700 by Leibniz. The central position of the Berlin Academy in European intellectual life from the 1750s to the 1780s may be largely attributed to its reform in the 1740s by Frederick II, who was aided by Maupertuis, the first President of the renewed Academy. This reform included the introduction of international prize contests, open to any willing participant, which generated heated debates and genuine fascination across the Continent.

This chapter reconstructs different strands of the debates on language and mind in Berlin during the 1750s. Among the most intensely discussed topics was the symbolic nature of human thinking, as well as the Epicurean-naturalistic theory of human evolution. This thesis was introduced to the Academy by Maupertuis in works written or publicly read from the late 1740s to the mid-1750s. Rousseau's discussion of the emergence of language in his *Discours sur l'inégalité* (1755) was perceived in Berlin as a serious challenge to the naturalistic thesis, and it attracted several immediate and well-argued replies. This chapter also covers a parallel debate over the 'genius of language', or the reflection of a people's character in its national idiom. The convergence of this discourse with the debates on mind and language led to the dedication of the 1759 contest to the reciprocal influence of language and opinions. But before delving into the vibrant debates at the Berlin Academy, we have to become better acquainted with the institution and its prize contests.

INSTITUTIONAL PRELIMINARIES

Nineteenth- and early twentieth-century accounts of the Berlin Academy tended to emphasize the significance of its foundation by Leibniz, seen in retrospect as the begetter of modern German philosophy.[1] Though Leibniz was indeed the main figure behind the establishment of the Academy, its early history did not owe much to his original design. The first two Hohenzollern kings condemned the new institution to a slow decay, under-funded and ill-reputed.

Long before 1700 Leibniz had conceived several plans for learned societies, which he submitted to his first employer, the Elector of Mainz, in 1669–70. The institution envisaged in these plans, headed by natural philosophers, was to reform almost all scientific activities throughout the Holy Roman Empire. Among its many responsibilities Leibniz mentioned mathematical, physical, and medical research. It would have included archives, a printing press, laboratories, botanical and zoological gardens, and anatomical theatres. The institution should have also promoted commerce by drawing skilled foreigners to the Empire, supported the sea trade in the Hanseatic cities, adjusted interest rates, and reformed education by founding orphanages, schools, seminaries, and universities.[2]

The schemes designed by Leibniz exhibited some of the characteristic features of the seventeenth-century academy movement, envisioning education as a means of moral and religious reform. This post-Reformation view of science as furthering redemption could be perceived in the seventeenth-century works of Wolfgang Ratke, Johann Valentin Andreae, Joachim Jungius, Johann Heinrich Alsted, Jan Amos Comenius, Samuel

---

[1] See, for example, the fullest history of the Academy: Carl Gustav Adolf von Harnack, *Geschichte der Königlich Preußischen Akademie der Wissenschaften zu Berlin*, 4 vols. in 3 (Berlin: Reichsdruckerei, 1900). Despite his professed wish to do justice to the *Aufklärung*, Harnack's account tends to treat the 'French' Academy under Frederick II as an aberration in what is otherwise the confident march of German scholarship. Cf. the older work by Christian Bartholmess, *Histoire philosophique de l'Académie de Prusse depuis Leibniz jusqu'à Schelling*, 2 vols. (Paris: Franck, 1850).

[2] Harnack, *Geschichte*, ii. 8–26; Martha Ornstein, *The Rôle of Scientific Societies in the Seventeenth Century* (Chicago: University of Chicago Press, 1913), 183–6; Wilhelm Totok, 'Leibniz als Wissenschaftsorganisator', in Carl Haase and Wilhelm Totok (eds), *Leibniz: Sein Leben, sein Wirken, seine Welt* (Hanover: Verlag für Literatur und Zeitgeschehen, 1966), 293–320; Ayval Ramati, 'Harmony at a Distance: Leibniz's Scientific Academies', *Isis* 87 (1996), 430–52.

Hartlib, and John Webster. Their plans for learned societies frequently assumed the form of scientific utopias, emphasizing tolerance, a reconciliation of the confessional divide, and the experimental study of nature. This pursuit of encyclopaedic knowledge and socio-political harmony could be traced back to the collapse of Christian humanism, widely perceived as a catastrophe resulting in the fragmentation of several domains: the political (incessant warfare reaching its apogee in the Thirty Years War), the religious (persecution and intolerance), and the scholarly (the disintegration of the Erasmian Republic of Letters). Many of the academic projects of the seventeenth century were endeavours to reinstate late humanist values, frequently expressing intellectual malaise in the face of disharmony and disorder.[3]

By incorporating science and education into their political programme, some German rulers merged this scholarly-religious current with contemporary mercantile or cameralist discourses. Following the widespread devastation of the Thirty Years War, these rulers initiated a process of inner colonization and accelerated economic development through *Polizei*, the regulation of internal order by a series of ordinances.[4] The convergence of economic, religious, and scholarly interests was particularly manifest in Brandenburg in Elector Frederick III's sponsorship of Pietism and its educational programme, resulting in the foundation of the University of Halle (1694) and its accompanying educational compound. In the case of Brandenburg, the post-war economic policy and the Elector's religious irenicism (being a Calvinist ruler of a largely Lutheran territory) also coincided with his active pursuit of a throne. Provoked by the attempts of neighbouring Electors to obtain royal status, especially the Saxons in Poland and the Hanoverians in England, Frederick III embarked on a campaign to demonstrate Brandenburg's cultural preeminence. Apart from the University of Halle, the Elector founded in the 1690s a medical college and an academy of arts.

Leibniz, who had established a close personal relationship with the Elector's wife Sophie Charlotte, seized the day. When the Protestant German states adopted the Gregorian calendar (February 1700), Leibniz saw the opportunity to realize Sophie Charlotte's plan to erect an observatory in Berlin. Both the observatory and a new scientific academy would be funded,

[3] R. J. W. Evans, 'Learned Societies in Germany in the Seventeenth Century', *European Studies Review* 7 (1977), 129–51; Miriam Eliav-Feldon, *Realistic Utopias: The Ideal Imaginary World of the Renaissance, 1516–1630* (Oxford: Clarendon Press, 1981); Howard Hotson, *Johann Heinrich Alsted, 1588–1638: Between Renaissance, Reformation, and Universal Reform* (Oxford: Clarendon Press, 2000).

[4] Marc Raeff, *The Well-Ordered Police State: Social and Institutional Change through Law in the Germanies and Russia, 1600–1800* (New Haven: Yale University Press, 1983), 33–42.

Leibniz proposed, by a new calendar monopoly. The Elector approved an outline to which he made some changes, commissioning the new institution to cultivate German language and history after the model of the Académie Française.[5] His request, alongside Leibniz's own penchant for universal scholarship, accounted for a unique feature of the institution (which was initially called Societät der Wissenschaften): the inclusion of philology, history, metaphysics, and literature under the aegis of a primarily scientific organization. This was one of the few institutional characteristics that were not altered in the major reform of Frederick the Great and Maupertuis.

The royal charter was granted in July 1700, yet the newly founded body faced a grim future when the Elector finally managed to acquire a throne in the following year, becoming King Frederick I in Prussia. The representational rationale behind a royal academy became marginalized; its development was further hindered by the tacit understanding between Leibniz and the Elector that it would not be directly funded from the royal coffers. Eight years passed before the observatory was completed, experiments were conducted in private residences, most members did not measure up to Leibniz's standards, and the first volume of the *Miscellanea Berolinensia* appeared as late as 1710. The official inauguration of the Society took place only a year later. Leibniz was forbidden long sojourns in Berlin by his patron in Hanover, and his prestige in Berlin was declining after Sophie Charlotte's untimely death in 1705. The lethargic state of the institution, mocked as *Academia obscurorum virorum*, prompted members of the council to assume control.[6] Shortly after the publication of the *Miscellanea*, Baron von Printzen was appointed Protector and Director. The inauguration ceremony in 1711 reflected Leibniz's merely honorary status within the Society, as it was celebrated in his absence. In 1713, wishing to acquire a former member's cabinet of curiosities, the Academy stopped transferring to Leibniz his presidential salary. Upon his death in 1716, the Berlin Society of Sciences did not dedicate to its founder as much as a memorial address.[7]

The accession of Frederick William I, the so-called 'soldier king', in 1713 did little to improve the fortunes of the Society of Sciences. The

---

[5] Harnack, *Geschichte*, i/1. 78–9. On issues related to local time measurement, see Michael Sauter, 'Clockwatchers and Stargazers: Time Discipline in Early Modern Berlin', *American Historical Review* 112 (2007), 685–709.

[6] Hans-Stephan Brather, *Leibniz und seine Akademie: Ausgewählte Quellen zur Geschichte der Berliner Sozietät der Wissenschaften 1697–1716* (Berlin: Akademie Verlag, 1993), xxxvii.

[7] The Académie des Sciences in Paris was the only scientific institution whose membership Leibniz held to commemorate him with an official obituary, read by Fontenelle. Harnack saw the treatment of Leibniz as 'the darkest page in the Society's history' (*Geschichte*, i/1. 197).

new ruler perceived anything impractical or non-profitable as a waste of resources, raging in particular at scholars and university professors. He assumed neither direct responsibility for the activities of the Society nor its protectorate. Under its protectors-ministers Printzen, Creuz, and Viereck, the Society published only five thin volumes of the *Miscellanea*, approximately one in six years. The infrequent publications of its proceedings attested to the Academy's grim condition under the leadership of its new directors: the king appointed three of his fools as its presidents. While these were not royal entertainers in the traditional sense but established scholars designated official fools, the act was clearly symbolic. The inscription in state accounts concerning the Society's finances was 'on behalf of the king's fools'.

Jacob Paul Gundling and David Fassmann, successive royal fools and Presidents of the Society, were made the target of hoaxes at the king's *Tabakscollegium*, where they had to endure physical abuse. Due to the intervention of Viereck (1733), the first protector of the Academy under Frederick William I to have genuine concern for the institution, the king found it sufficient to make his next fool, Otto von Graben zum Stein, merely Vice-President of the Society. His inaugural decree obliged the institution to inquire into sorcery and Serbian vampires.[8] Viereck finally managed to convince the king to appoint the Society member Daniel Ernst Jablonski as its President, leaving Frederick William's last learned fool, Salomo Jacob Morgenstern, with the title 'Vice Chancellor of All the Imaginary Realms'.[9] The king forced other office holders upon the Society, mainly relatives of courtiers who required a pension. New decrees obliged the institution to contribute revenues from its meagre calendar monopoly to the maintenance of a military medical school, and new projects were seldom approved. The scorn with which Frederick William I treated the Society channelled intellectual life in Berlin into alternative, unofficial forms of intellectual socialization such as reading clubs and salons. Those who wished to stay closer to centres of active scholarship had to enrol at one of the new universities in Halle or Göttingen.

One of the first endeavours undertaken by Frederick II upon his accession to the Prussian throne (1740) was a complete overhaul of the malfunctioning Society, as part of his attempt to enhance Berlin's cultural appeal. Representational royal culture once again became a major preoccupation of a Hohenzollern ruler; the young Frederick II renovated royal residences after contemporary fashion, built an opera house, and lured to

---

[8] Ibid. i/1. 233–4.
[9] 'Vicekanzler derer sämmtlichen Espaces imaginaires' (ibid. i/1. 225). See also Dorinda Outram, 'The Work of the Fool: Enlightenment Encounters with Folly, Laughter, and Truth', *Eighteenth-Century Thought* 1 (2003), 281–94.

his court musicians, scientists, poets, and philosophers. These measures may all be regarded as elements in Frederick's self-fashioning as an enlightened philosopher-king, an image he cultivated and relished in clear contrast to his predecessor. Berlin lacked, however, the scientific tradition and infrastructure which had been well established in Paris before the incorporation of its own Royal Academy of Sciences. Frederick's first achievement in this respect was his acquisition of the prominent Swiss mathematician Leonhard Euler from the St Petersburg Academy of Sciences. Another prestigious recruit was Pierre Louis Moreau de Maupertuis, who was appointed *Président perpétuel* of the newly rechristened Royal Academy of Sciences and Belles-Lettres. As its new title suggests, this was the first time that a Prussian king assumed explicit patronage of the institution. New statutes for the Academy were approved in 1744, but its final constitution was redrawn on Maupertuis's arrival in 1746. Recent scholarship has suggested that under Maupertuis the Academy was transformed into an organization befitting the ideology of so-called Enlightened Absolutism: new academicians were chosen by the President alone with the king's approval, not elected by the full membership as had previously been the case.[10] Maupertuis introduced several structural innovations such as the annual essay competitions and obligatory plenary sessions, to be attended by members of all four academic classes: mathematics, experimental philosophy, speculative philosophy, and belles-lettres. Major changes in the intellectual and public outlook of the Academy followed the structural reform. Due to the king's cultural preferences and the President's background, a strong French accent could be perceived in most of its enterprises. The number of French and Swiss members grew substantially, and French became the official language of the Academy. The topics examined by the Academy were up to date with the latest developments in Parisian circles.

The transformation of the old Societät der Wissenschaften into an Académie Royale des Sciences et Belles-Lettres, a hub of scholarship under manifest royal patronage, attracted mixed responses in Prussia and other German states. Throughout the 1740s and 1750s most of Prussia's professors positioned themselves in opposition to the Academy, largely

---

[10] Mary Terrall, 'The Culture of Science in Frederick the Great's Berlin', *History of Science* 28 (1990), 333–64, and *The Man Who Flattened the Earth: Maupertuis and the Sciences in the Enlightenment* (Chicago: University of Chicago Press, 2002), 236–43; William Clark, 'The Death of Metaphysics in Enlightened Prussia', in William Clark et al. (eds), *The Sciences in Enlightened Europe* (Chicago: University of Chicago Press, 1999), 423–73. See also Harcourt Brown, 'Maupertuis *Philosophe*: Enlightenment and the Berlin Academy', *Studies on Voltaire and the Eighteenth Century* 24 (1963), 255–69, and Hans Aarsleff, 'The Berlin Academy under Frederick the Great', *History of the Human Sciences* 2 (1989), 193–206.

following Christian Wolff. Having been reinstalled at Halle by Frederick II, following his expulsion from Prussia in 1723, Wolff was offered the presidency of the reformed Academy. The king's offer was declined as soon as Wolff learned he would probably have to share his authority with Maupertuis and rule over a largely Francophile institution.[11] Though Wolff and his followers interpreted the renewal of the Academy as a concerted assault on German philosophy, the situation was not strictly dichotomous. The Wolffian system had several sympathizers within the Academy, including Formey, its Perpetual Secretary from 1748, and his Huguenot collaborators at the institution. For his part, Maupertuis had a few allies at the universities, such as the mathematician Abraham Gotthelf Kästner, a professor at Leipzig and later in Göttingen, whom Maupertuis ineffectively tried to lure to Berlin. Wolffian or otherwise, university professors could not resist the temptation to engage in quarrels and conflicts on the academicians' premises, participating in the prize contests sponsored by the Academy and generating debates over its activities.

The new prize competitions were open to the public, a mediating forum between academicians, university professors, foreign scholars, civil servants, clergymen, and other educated laymen. These contests enhanced the image of the Royal Academy as an intellectual authority while enabling its members to interact more closely with the German press and universities, as well as with the wider Republic of Letters. The second contest sponsored by the Academy (in 1746, on the theory of winds) was won by d'Alembert in Paris; Condillac wrote an unsuccessful entry for the following competition on monads. Contrary to contemporary perception, German thinkers were not discriminated against—at least not in the prize contests. A few telling examples would be the 1751 competition on moral duties, won by Kästner in Leipzig; Mendelssohn's updated Wolffianism that carried the day in the 1763 contest on certitude in metaphysics; and the crowning of Herder with no fewer than three different prizes. Johann David Michaelis's prize essay of 1759 was another demonstration of the openness of the supposedly foreign-orientated institution towards different German voices, in this case a university professor of a Pietist background.[12]

---

[11] Harnack, *Geschichte*, i/1. 255–6.
[12] For a complete list of the prize questions and laureates under Frederick II, see Harnack, *Geschichte*, ii. 305–9. The Berlin contests exerted a particularly strong influence on the University of Göttingen, whose graduates and teachers were awarded the prize or an *accessit* more frequently than scholars elsewhere. (Cornelia Buschmann, 'Die philosophischen Preisfragen und Preisschriften der Berliner Akademie der Wissenschaften im 18. Jahrhundert', in Wolfgang Förster (ed.), *Aufklärung in Berlin* (Berlin: Akademie Verlag, 1989), 165–228.)

As Maupertuis's statutes prevented ordinary members of the Academy from participation in the contests, many of them contributed to the public debate by publishing their views privately. Other scholars preferred discussing the prize questions in the press without submitting their entries to the Academy's judgement. This was particularly the case with authors who doubted the sincerity of the academic proceedings, and therefore criticized the Academy while still stoking the public debates generated by its contests. Lessing and Mendelssohn published independently their mock entry for the 1755 contest on Pope's (and implicitly Leibniz's) optimism, entitled *Pope—ein Metaphysiker!*, and Hamann's early works stemmed mainly from his reflections on the Berlin contests on language.[13] From 1746 until 1800 twenty-two prize topics were proposed by the class of speculative philosophy, including the 1759 question on the reciprocal influence of language and opinions. The ensuing contest in 1771 on the origin of language was likewise sponsored by this class; only in the 1780s did the literary class assume responsibility for competitions concerning language.

The topics of academic contests in Berlin were usually advertised two years prior to the choice of prize essays. The subject for 1759, for example, was announced in mid-1757 with 31 December 1758 as a deadline; the decision was made in May 1759. If the Academy deemed the received essays inadequate, a contest could be delayed by a year or two to allow the submission of additional entries. The average number of entries per contest was twenty, and they gradually grew in length from anything between two and fifty pages up to more than one hundred towards the end of the century. Submissions were sent anonymously, accompanied by a separate envelope containing the author's name and the *symbolum* (prefatory quote) of the essay. After assessing the anonymous essays, members of the jury would open only the envelope bearing the *symbolum* of the winning entry, consigning all other envelopes to the fire. This eighteenth-century practice makes it particularly difficult to identify the authors of the anonymous entries still preserved in the institutional archive. As authors of unsuccessful entries sometimes reclaimed their work, it is impossible to determine the actual number of submissions per contest unless it was specifically noted by the jurors.

Though only two academic contests on language fall within the scope of this project, an intensive debate was conducted before, between, and after the competitions in other forums at the Academy and outside it. A substantial number of lectures given at the weekly academic sessions were

---

[13] In Mendelssohn, *JubA*, ii. 43–80. On Hamann's response to the 1759 contest, see Chapter 5.

dedicated to language and mind. Some of the most significant treatises on the subject began as papers delivered in these weekly meetings, such as Maupertuis's paper on the origin of language and Süßmilch's fierce rebuttal (1756), Formey's review of conjectural histories of language and mind (1762), and Sulzer's contribution (1767). As these meetings were plenary, papers on language were subject to the close scrutiny of members from all four classes of the Academy, not only those pertaining to the speaker's own section. The Berlin contests on language engendered considerable interest among *Aufklärer*, even if not always in a manner favourable to the Academy and its laureates. The public fascination with issues raised by the Academy also resulted in books, pamphlets, public letters, and other media. While the forthcoming chapters refer to all these forms of public debate, the material aspect of publication is particularly emphasized in Chapter 6, in the context of a controversy involving Prémontval, Formey, and Michaelis.

DEBATING LANGUAGE

La Mettrie's barren suggestion

Though the topic of the 1759 contest, the reciprocal influence of language and opinions, had been the subject of a lively discussion in France ever since the Port Royal works of the 1660s, it received a new impulse in 1746 with the publication of Condillac's *Essai*. In the *Essai*, as we have seen in Chapter 1, signs and language were not only prerequisites for the emergence of the arts and the sciences, but for man's self-conscious control of his surroundings. Condillac drew a clear line between such a uniquely human capacity and the mental operations of animals, but this distinction became significantly blurred in a notoriously radical work of the following year. The author of *L'Homme-machine* (*Machine-Man*), Julien Offray de La Mettrie, was invited to Prussia by Frederick II, and his presence in the king's close *Tafelrunde* was a cause of much consternation to more conservative intellectuals such as Albrecht von Haller.[14] La Mettrie's works went virtually unmentioned in the debates of the 1750s, even if his materialist views were very relevant to the anthropological discussions of language and mind.

---

[14] La Mettrie, who had been living in Prussia since 1748, choked to death in 1751 while enjoying a meal at the Potsdam court. Ostensibly offended by La Mettrie's anti-religious proclamations, Albrecht von Haller rejected Frederick II's invitation to join the Berlin Academy. Maupertuis wrote to Haller after La Mettrie's death that the notorious materialist exhibited the most sociable virtues (Maupertuis, 'Réponse à une lettre de M. de Haller', in *Œuvres*, iii. 343–7).

The frequent references to human and animal language in *L'Homme-machine* marked the extreme frontier where nearly all authors feared to tread: La Mettrie explicitly argued that there was no qualitative distinction between human and animal language, and by extension between their mental capacities. This conviction underlay his claim that an ape could be taught to speak if a proper scientific method was applied to the task. In the same vein, human beings unable to use language, such as feral children, were considered by La Mettrie human only in form rather than in mind. A speaking ape would become 'a little man of the town', while a feral child was essentially a beast in human disguise. There was, therefore, no fixed point distinguishing the human from the bestial or nature from artifice. In effect, La Mettrie used language here for exactly the opposite purpose of Descartes's *Discours de la méthode*. For Descartes, the creativity of human language demonstrated the immateriality of the mind and its transcendence of the mechanist domain; for La Mettrie, language proved there was no categorical difference between the human and bestial spheres, because articulate speech was merely the result of conditioning from an early age. In La Mettrie's framework, there was no need to ponder in detail a difficult transition from natural cries to artificial signs, as they had always existed alongside each other, available to both humans and animals properly instructed.[15] If Rousseau came dangerously close to La Mettrie in his views on the link between man and ape, we shall see that he nevertheless sharply distinguished between natural and articulate signs, doubting whether the transition between them could have been naturally achieved.[16]

Maupertuis after Condillac

The President of the Academy, Maupertuis, who knew personally La Mettrie and Condillac, was also well acquainted with their views on language. Yet in his first work on language, probably written in 1748, Maupertuis chose to follow another current of the debate. He elaborated the contemporary critique of Condillac's account, highlighting the Berkeleian implications of a sensualist psychology fully reliant on the data of the senses while having no access to their causes. Maupertuis made this point in *Réflexions philosophiques sur l'origine des langues et la signification des mots* (*Philosophical Reflections on the Origin of Languages and the Meaning of Words*), first published in 1752 in the Dresden edition of his

---

[15] La Mettrie, 'L'Homme-machine', in *Œuvres philosophiques*, ed. Francine Markovits (Paris: Fayard, 1984), i. 75–87.
[16] Robert Wokler, 'Perfectible Apes in Decadent Cultures: Rousseau's Anthropology Revisited', *Daedalus* 107 (1978), 107–34.

collected works.[17] In this work Maupertuis tried to reconstruct the first human notions by imagining his own mind empty of ideas and assaulted by sensations. He attributed a sign to each of his new perceptions in order to distinguish between them: 'I see a tree' was marked by A, and B stood for 'I see a horse'. With the multiplication of perceptions Maupertuis's imagined self could not maintain an independent sign for each phenomenon. 'I see a tree' was therefore divided into CD, 'I see a horse' into CE and so forth: 'I see two lions' eventually became CGH, while 'I see three crows' was CIK. According to Maupertuis, the analysis of perceptions by signs might be performed in various ways, leading human knowledge through diverse trajectories. Different nations had therefore incommensurable 'planes of ideas', determined not by their initial perceptions but by the ways in which these were linguistically analysed.[18] In Maupertuis's eyes, the most important role of language, the internal analysis of sense impressions, significantly influenced national character and opinions.

The central function attributed to signs in processing sense data further led Maupertuis to doubt the common concept of existence. He argued that a proposition such as 'there is a tree' consisted merely of the repeated notions 'I saw a tree', 'I returned to the same place and saw the tree,' and the assumption that 'every time I arrive there I shall see the tree.' Existence thus amounted to a mere agglomeration of perceptions that did not necessarily resemble their causes or external objects. Having demonstrated how the mind's dependence on signs undermined our knowledge of external reality, Maupertuis concluded by questioning the familiar notions of time, memory, and self-consciousness.[19]

Maupertuis's interest in the origins of ideas and language was apparent in some of the academic papers he publicly read at the Academy. Talking in 1750 to the academicians about their duties, Maupertuis suggested that the class of speculative philosophy explore the origin of language. The President noted that linguistic inquiries had been a respectable occupation at the Academy ever since Leibniz's time, and observed that a reconstruction of the original language could be a 'nice endeavour' (*beau*

---

[17] David Beeson claimed that Maupertuis referred to this work already in 1740; Ronald Grimsley, among others, adhered to the traditional publication date of 1748. See Beeson, *Maupertuis: An Intellectual Biography* (Oxford: Voltaire Foundation, 1992), 153–4; Grimsley, 'Introduction', in Maupertuis et al., *Sur l'origine du langage*, ed. Ronald Grimsley (Geneva: Droz, 1971), 1–25. Maupertuis sent the *Réflexions* to Condillac only in summer 1750, which seems to corroborate the traditional dating (Condillac, *Œuvres*, ii. 535).
[18] Maupertuis, *Œuvres*, i. 253–85, here 275–6.
[19] Ibid. 284–5. For Turgot's critique of Maupertuis's *Réflexions*, see Avi Lifschitz, 'Language as the Key to the Epistemological Labyrinth: Turgot's Changing View of Human Perception', *Historiographia Linguistica* 31 (2004), 345–65.

projet) if it were possible.[20] In another programmatic vision of scientific inquiry, *Lettre sur le progrès des sciences* (*Letter on the Progress of Science*), Maupertuis suggested 'useful experiments', physical and metaphysical. In the latter category he included the origin of language, proposing to raise several groups of infants in isolation in order to solve the controversy over linguistic mono- or polygenesis (whether there was a single original language or several ones in different regions).

This was a new version of an experiment supposedly conducted by the Egyptian king Psammetichus I, as reported by Herodotus.[21] According to the ancient account, two children were given to a shepherd to be raised in isolation, having no social or linguistic contact with other human beings. Even the shepherd was not allowed to talk to them; the children were suckled by goats housed in the same hut. After two years of muttering meaningless sounds, the children addressed the shepherd distinctly with the Phrygian word for bread, *bekos*, from which Psammetichus reluctantly concluded that the Phrygians were the most ancient nation on earth.[22] The strong hold of Psammetichus' experiment on the imagination of Enlightenment thinkers may be ascribed to their preoccupation with human origins, as well as to the espousal of the premisses behind the experiment. It seems that the ancient king closely associated ontogeny with phylogeny, assuming that young children of his own day would re-enact the emergence of basic human capacities. Maupertuis was similarly convinced that artificially isolated children would create a language.

> Two or three children raised together from the earliest age, without any exchange with other human beings, would surely form a language, however limited in extension. It would shed great light on the preceding question [of the origin of language], if we could observe whether this new language resembled any of those spoken today, and see to which language it was most closely linked. [...] This experiment would not only teach us about the origin of languages; it could also tell us much about the origin of ideas themselves, and on the fundamental notions of the human mind.[23]

---

[20] Maupertuis, 'Des devoirs de l'académicien', in *Histoire de l'Académie, 1753* (Berlin: Haude & Spener, 1755), 511–24, here 518. The speech was delivered in the public assembly of 18 June 1750; see Eduard Winter (ed.), *Die Registres der Berliner Akademie der Wissenschaften 1746–1766* (Berlin: Akademie Verlag, 1957), 151–2.

[21] Herodotus, *The Histories*, trans. Robin Waterfield, ed. Carolyn Dewald (Oxford: Oxford University Press, 1998), ii/2. 95–6.

[22] Antoni Sułek, 'The Experiment of Psammetichus: Fact, Fiction, and Model to Follow', *Journal of the History of Ideas* 50 (1989), 645–51; Gera, *Ancient Greek Ideas*, 68–111; Margaret Thomas, 'The Evergreen Story of Psammetichus' Inquiry into the Origin of Language', *Historiographia Linguistica* 34 (2007), 37–62.

[23] Maupertuis, 'Lettre sur le progrès des sciences', in *Œuvres*, ii. 343–99, here 396–8.

The assumptions underlying Maupertuis's proposal were clearly linked to the Epicurean theory as recast by Condillac: the origin of language was also that of ideas, and their mutual evolution occurred naturally among human beings.

Maupertuis's final engagement with the question of language and its origin was in a paper he read at the Academy on 13 May 1756, a few weeks before leaving for France. (He would stay away from Berlin until his death in 1759.) The essay, *Dissertation sur les différens moyens dont les hommes se sont servis pour exprimer leurs idées* (*Dissertation on the Different Means Employed by Human Beings to Express Their Ideas*), was considerably different from the *Réflexions*, abandoning the Berkeleian critique of sensualist epistemology. It repeated Condillac's distinction between two phases in the emergence of language: a primary, expressive language of action, followed by an analytic idiom of artificial signs. According to the *Dissertation*, human beings initially expressed their most pressing needs by simple gestures and cries. Conventional interjections became gradually mixed with the natural ones, and articulate language eventually replaced the original natural sounds.[24] Less dramatically than the different 'planes of ideas' of his *Réflexions*, Maupertuis postulated in the *Dissertation* a universal correspondence between a nation's vocabulary and the range of its ideas. Following Condillac in this essay more closely than in his earlier work, Maupertuis fully subscribed here to the joint evolution of language and mind. He went on to describe the emergence of different systems of writing, echoing Warburton's thesis by seeing the shift from pictorial to phonetic representation as the natural equivalent of the transition from gestures and cries to articulate language.[25] The *Dissertation* ended with a discussion of attempts to create a universal language. Considering the Chinese script as approaching such an ideal, Maupertuis nevertheless acknowledged the failure of most projects for a scientific language, ascribing it to the difficult composition of a dictionary of basic concepts. As a substitute, he repeated the suggestion made in *Des devoirs de l'académicien* concerning the grammatical simplification of either Latin or a modern vernacular. The elimination of superfluous conjugations, declensions, and genders would render such a language so simple that its rules could be learned within an hour.[26]

The *Dissertation* of 1756 concluded a prolific decade in Berlin in which Maupertuis published various works on physics, cosmology, biology, and

---

[24] *Histoire de l'Académie, 1754* (Berlin: Haude & Spener, 1756), 349–64. Due to delays in editing and printing, recent papers were sometimes incorporated into the proceedings of previous years; this was the case of Maupertuis's essay, delivered in 1756 but printed that year in the volume for 1754.
[25] Ibid. 353–5.   [26] Ibid. 360–4.

metaphysics. All these undertakings were accompanied throughout his presidency by a profound fascination with language, its origin, and its influence on the human mind, an interest he imparted to the Academy as a whole. Eulogizing the deceased President, the Perpetual Secretary Formey suggested that Maupertuis's essays on language, despite their brevity, elaborated the relevant issues more significantly than hefty volumes. Formey considered the *Réflexions* and the *Dissertation* to be among Maupertuis's greatest works, if not the best of them all.[27]

Responses to Rousseau's conundrums

Though singling out in the *Réflexions* the unintended implications of Condillac's psychology, Maupertuis genuinely endorsed the naturalistic-Epicurean tenets of his thesis, including the problematic transition from natural to arbitrary signs. Jean-Jacques Rousseau was, however, less easily convinced by Condillac's theory. In his *Discours sur l'inégalité* (1755) he suggested Condillac might have endowed the first speechless human beings with either too much reason or excessively extended social skills for the explanation of the emergence of language. Rousseau doubted whether man could ever pull himself independently out of his initial immersion in the senses, arguing that the conscious use of arbitrary signs entailed a logical leap from the preceding stage of communication by natural cries and gestures. This was demonstrated mainly through the reconstruction of a hypothetical state of nature, according to the methodological guidelines introduced in the preface to the *Discours*.

In Rousseau's eyes, his predecessors in the natural law tradition had not ventured far enough in their quest for the natural, still ascribing to humans in the state of nature many of their socially developed characteristics. Rousseau followed seventeenth-century authors such as Hobbes in describing civil society as an arrangement constructed artificially by human beings interacting with one another. Despite his diatribe against the earlier uses of the term 'natural law', Rousseau too tried to derive fundamental principles of conduct from the essential and natural human constitution, famously arriving at the conclusion that only 'two principles prior to reason' speak to human beings 'immediately with the voice of nature': self-preservation and pity, the latter being defined as 'a natural repugnance to see any sentient Being, and especially any being like ourselves, perish or suffer'.[28] To these two principles Rousseau later added perfectibility, a

---

[27] Formey, 'Eloge de Monsieur de Maupertuis', *Histoire de l'Académie, 1759* (Berlin: Haude & Spener, 1766), 464–512, here 495–6. The obituary was delivered on 24 January 1760 (Winter, *Registres*, 254).
[28] Rousseau, *Discourses*, 127.

faculty enabling the improvement of one's condition with the help of circumstances.[29] What perplexed most of Rousseau's eighteenth-century readers was the instinctive or bestial character of his man of nature, mute in the absence of language and devoid of reflection and self-consciousness. This condition was crowned by natural man's self-sufficient isolation and lack of any form of dependence on others, which accounted for his silence and natural freedom. The point was clearly and consistently argued by Rousseau, to the exclusion of familial life in the state of nature.

Examining the naturalistic account offered by Condillac, Rousseau identified three challenges. First, the 'immense distance' between the 'pure state of nature' and a condition in which humans were in need of language, a problem which he set aside in order to consider what he saw as two greater difficulties: consent and abstraction. The substitution of arbitrary sounds for natural interjections could have hardly occurred accidentally or as an unforeseen response to needs, as described by earlier authors from Lucretius to Condillac. The conventional character of human language would have required common consent, an all but impossible act in the absence of speech, especially as 'this unanimous agreement must have been motivated'. In conclusion, 'speech seems to have been very necessary in order to establish the use of speech' within the naturalistic framework.[30]

Finally, Rousseau wondered how human beings with no reflective reason could have invented conventional signs for abstract, non-physical notions. This could only be the result of thinking in general terms—for which, however, artificial signs would have already been required. Rousseau ended his examination of the origin of language by admitting he was 'frightened by the increasing difficulties and convinced of the almost demonstrated impossibility that Languages could have arisen and been established by purely human means'.[31] Yet this acknowledgement seems to undermine Rousseau's entire edifice. If the shift from a linguistic state of nature to a socially based language had been impossible, how could the same transition have occurred in the political sphere? If language had not been established 'by purely human means', the same conclusion might apply to the emergence of conventionally constructed political institutions.

Rousseau's exasperation at the difficulties posed by the human invention of language became a focal point for conservative authors, from Beauzée to de Maistre, who wished to undermine naturalistic theories of human evolution.[32] For such critics of the naturalistic account of human origins,

---

[29] Ibid. 141.   [30] Ibid. 147.   [31] Ibid. 149.
[32] See Joseph de Maistre's agreement with Rousseau on this point in *Les Soirées de Saint-Pétersbourg* (Paris: Librairie Grecque, Latine et Française, 1821), i. 116.

Rousseau not only exposed its Achilles heel—the impossibility of the transition from the natural to the artificial—but also demonstrated its capricious character by randomly ascribing some features rather than others to his man of nature. Condillac and fellow *philosophes* tried to repair the methodological damage wrought by Rousseau in order to demonstrate that no recourse to supernatural intervention was required to explain the emergence of language. Yet at the same time, critics of the naturalistic account did capitalize on its problematization in the *Discours sur l'inégalité* to the fullest extent. Nicolas Beauzée, the prolific author of grammatical entries in the *Encyclopédie*, constructed his refutation of the natural emergence of language around Rousseau's discussion, which he quoted at length. Given the conundrums identified by Rousseau at the core of the naturalistic thesis, Beauzée concluded that language must have been pre-programmed by God into human nature. Beauzée proceeded further, focusing on the shift from nature to artifice. If language and society must have conditioned one another, and if language could not have emerged 'by purely human means', Beauzeé asked Rousseau to admit that human society too must have been created by God.[33]

A similar use of Rousseau's point about language against his own wider narrative can be found in a reply to the *Discours sur l'inégalité* composed in Utrecht by a local professor of mathematics, Jean de Castillon (originally Giovanni Salvemini di Castiglione). Castillon was an associate member of the Berlin Academy who would move to Berlin in 1764 and become an ordinary member, eventually heading the class of mathematics at the Academy (1787–91).[34] His response to Rousseau, published in 1756, was among the first essays to identify the *Discours sur l'inégalité* as a problematic revival of the Epicurean account of human evolution.[35] The main problem with this naturalistic narrative was, for Castillon, the transition from silent bestial existence to the social life of speaking human beings. If human beings had not possessed reason, language, and sociability at the outset, they would have always remained in that condition, Castillon argued. He could not see how such aspects of human nature could have naturally evolved from rudimentary material elements. By contrast to Rousseau's assertion that he was presenting 'a state which no longer exists, which perhaps never did exist, which probably never will

---

[33] Nicolas Beauzée, 'Langue', in *Encyclopédie, ou Dictionnaire raisonné des sciences, des arts et des métiers, par une société de gens de lettres*, 17 vols. (Paris and Neufchâtel: Briasson, 1751–65), ix (1765), 249–66 (252).

[34] Friedrich von Castillon, 'Éloge de M. de Castillon, père', in *Histoire de l'Académie, 1792–93* (Berlin: Decker, 1798), 38–60.

[35] Jean de Castillon, *Discours sur l'origine de l'inégalité parmi les hommes: pour servir de réponse au Discours que M. Rousseau, Citoyen de Géneve, a publié sur le même sujet* (Amsterdam: J. F. Jolly, 1756), pp. vi, xxx, 20.

exist,' Castillon argued that the man of nature exists, always existed, and will forever exist. One only had to examine oneself introspectively in order to see what was essential in human nature.[36]

However, in the midst of his frontal attack on Rousseau's narrative, Castillon bestowed some praise on the 'orator of Geneva' for exposing the difficulties surrounding the emergence of language 'with such force'. Without a model for the articulation of conventional syllables (which children receive from their speaking parents) and due to the initial rigidity of their speech organs, human beings without language would have never felt the urge to invent one.[37] Castillon did not, however, elaborate the implications of this point. His agreement with Rousseau's questioning of the natural emergence of language could have been used to demolish the whole Epicurean account of human origins, as this thesis relied on an allegedly smooth transition from nature to artifice in various other domains. This point would be made in Berlin in the same year by critics who saw Rousseau's *Discours sur l'inégalité* as a refutation of the Epicurean evolutionary account rather than its revival.

The full impact of the *Discours* in Berlin was secured by its first translation into German by Moses Mendelssohn, just months after the appearance of the original French edition. This translation originated in discussions of Rousseau's controversial piece between Mendelssohn and his close friend, Gotthold Ephraim Lessing.[38] It was at Lessing's enthusiastic encouragement that Mendelssohn had published his first works, *Philosophische Gespräche* (*Philosophical Conversations*) in 1754 and *Briefe über die Empfindungen* (*Letters on the Sentiments*) in the following year. The second work contributed to the positive reassessment of symbolic cognition and the sense-based faculties of the mind. Perhaps unsurprisingly, one of the issues both Lessing and Mendelssohn found particularly disconcerting in Rousseau's *Discours* was its problematization of the natural emergence of language.[39]

Mendelssohn published the translation at the beginning of 1756, appending an essay, *Sendschreiben an den Herrn Magister Lessing in Leipzig*

---

[36] Ibid. pp. xv, xxi, 18, 59; Rousseau, *Discourses*, 125.
[37] Castillon, *Discours*, 83–4.
[38] On the intellectual development of the young Mendelssohn, see Alexander Altmann, *Moses Mendelssohn: A Biographical Study* (London: Routledge & Kegan Paul, 1973), 25–83, and Dominique Bourel, *Moses Mendelssohn: la naissance du judaïsme moderne* (Paris: Gallimard, 2004), 96–147.
[39] Moses Mendelssohn, *JubA*, ii. 104. Lessing mentioned in the entry 'Babel' in his *Collectanea* (1769) a planned though never completed treatise on language, which he may have conceived as an essay for the 1771 contest at the Berlin Academy. (Lessing, *Sämtliche Schriften*, eds Karl Lachman and Franz Muncker (Leipzig: G. J. Göschen'sche Verlagshandlung, 1900), xv. 119, 152.)

(*Letter to Magister Lessing in Leipzig*), in which he replied to Rousseau. At the outset, the translator tried to distinguish himself from the Franco-German choir of scornful critics by paying tribute to Rousseau's 'excellent mind'.[40] The available philosophical idiom was, however, heavily influenced by Wolff's German works, and Mendelssohn's *Sendschreiben* reinterpreted various terms in Rousseau's *Discours* along the Wolffian lines apparent in his published works of 1754–5. As to Rousseau's conundrums about the shift from natural cries to arbitrary signs, Mendelssohn grounded it a theory of the association of ideas. Mendelssohn argued that just as he was vividly reminded of Lessing each time he searched for his friend in the garden where they used to chat, human beings had the natural capacity to connect ideas that had been perceived together due to proximity in space, time, or causal relations. This basic association of ideas could have been mastered even by a man of nature ('a savage', as Mendelssohn called him throughout his comments).

In this way, human beings in the state of nature might have encountered a sheep surrounded by flowers in a meadow. The sound of bleating would initially be used to refer only to its source, the sheep, but in some people's minds it might also summon the entire original setting. Gradually, they would leave out the middle link in this associative chain to refer by the sheep's bleating directly to the flowers. As bleating had a merely arbitrary relation to flowers, depending on circumstances rather than inherent in nature, Mendelssohn claimed that this process demonstrated how natural sounds could be transformed into arbitrary ones.[41] Yet he did not consider Rousseau's second conundrum about the social and conventional aspect of linguistic evolution: while one person would associate the bleating with flowers, others could equally link it to the whole meadow, to the rain, or to a pressing feeling of hunger. Mendelssohn also tried to explain the shift from natural to artificial signs by referring to the large span of time during which cumulative change must have occurred. But Rousseau had already rejected the reduction of the transition between two incommensurable categories to a slow transition over time, wondering at

---

[40] Claus Süßenberger, *Rousseau im Urteil der deutschen Publizistik bis zum Ende der französischen Revolution* (Frankfurt am Main: Peter Lang, 1974), 86–8; Ursula Goldenbaum, 'Einführung', in Rousseau, *Abhandlung von dem Ursprunge der Ungleichheit unter den Menschen*, trans. Moses Mendelssohn (Weimar: Hermann Böhlaus Nachfolger, 2000), 18–19. For local responses to Rousseau's *Discourse on the Arts and the Sciences* (1750), see Alexander Schmidt, 'Letters, Morals and Government: Jean-Henri-Samuel Formey's and Johann Gottfried Herder's Responses to Rousseau's *First Discourse*', *Modern Intellectual History* 9 (2012), 249–74.

[41] Mendelssohn, *JubA* ii. 107–9. For a twentieth-century version of the indeterminacy of reference in situations comprising dissimilar components, see the famous 'gavagai' example introduced by W. v. O. Quine in *Word and Object* (Cambridge, Mass.: MIT Press, 1960), 26–79.

which precise point the quantitative enlargement of vocabulary could have been qualitatively transformed into abstract signification.

This was one of the main themes taken up by Johann Peter Süßmilch in two papers delivered at the Berlin Academy on 7 and 15 October 1756. A provost at the Petrikirche in Berlin-Cölln, Süßmilch was elected to the Berlin Academy in 1745 and specialized in demographic and social statistics. His most renowned work, *Die Göttliche Ordnung in den Veränderungen des menschlichen Geschlechts* (*The Divine Order in the Transformations of Mankind*, 1741), exhibited in its title Süßmilch's fondness for proofs of providence. Rummaging through local archives and foreign records, he tried to discover the divinely ordained laws that governed changing patterns of birth and death rates across Europe.[42] He also had a profound interest in languages, which was, however, expressed in traditional etymological exercises.[43] Süßmilch was not at ease with Maupertuis's new regime after 1746, as attested by his protests to Formey that he was ignored and poorly remunerated. He also pleaded with the Perpetual Secretary to talk on his behalf with Maupertuis.[44] However, Süßmilch was apparently not disturbed by the possible repercussions of his direct attack on Maupertuis's *Dissertation*. Like most of his other works, Süßmilch's papers on the origin of language were not printed in the French academic proceedings; they were published together only in 1766 under the title *Versuch eines Beweises, daß die erste Sprache ihren Ursprung nicht vom Menschen, sondern allein vom Schöpfer erhalten habe* (*Attempt at a Demonstration that the First Language Had Its Origin Not in Man but in God Alone*).

Despite the theological connotations of the title, this was a shrewd attempt to present a philosophical proof 'from the realm of nature' against the naturalistic-Epicurean theory of the emergence of language.[45] Süßmilch admitted that the occasion for its composition was Maupertuis's naturalistic account in the *Dissertation* he had read at the Academy in May 1756, but claimed he became aware of Mendelssohn's translation of the *Discours sur l'inégalité* only after delivering his own papers.[46] In any case, Süßmilch incorporated into the printed edition of 1766 numerous references to Rousseau's *Discours* and appended to it a response to Mendelssohn's suggestions, in which he restated Rousseau's conundrums against the naturalistic school. Süßmilch's main thesis may be seen as a

---

[42] Jacqueline Hecht, 'Johann Peter Süssmilch: A German Prophet in Foreign Countries', *Population Studies* 41 (1987), 31–58.
[43] Winter, *Registres*, 141, 178–9, 232, 281; Hecht, 'Süssmilch', 40–1.
[44] Kraków, Biblioteka Jagiellońska, Autographa Collection, Süßmilch to Formey, 4 September 1749.
[45] Süßmilch, *Versuch eines Beweises, daß die erste Sprache ihren Ursprung nicht vom Menschen, sondern allein vom Schöpfer erhalten habe* (Berlin: Buchladen der Realschule, 1766), 97.
[46] See the preface in *Versuch*, 3^r, and the third and fourth appendices, 110–24.

version of Rousseau's vicious circle concerning language and reason. On the one hand, language was the sole means for the exercise of higher mental operations, while on the other, its structure must have required deliberate design by a fully rational mind. Hence language could not have been formed by man, the only alternative being a superior entity whose intellect did not depend on the use of signs.[47]

Süßmilch's originality lay less in his argument than in the ingenious application of the naturalists' own philosophical corpus to the confirmation of the divine origin of language. He noted that modern thinkers drew on ancient accounts of human evolution, as elaborated by Lucretius, Diodorus of Sicily, and Vitruvius. Süßmilch summarized the Epicurean thesis as resting on four tenets: human beings initially led a chaotic, rudimentary life; at this stage they were speechless; they came together out of fear and for mutual defence, beginning to communicate by natural signs; finally they moved on to associate arbitrary signs with things, developing a fully-fledged language. This ancient theory, Süßmilch observed, was revived by Richard Simon, who followed Gregory of Nyssa in assuming that Adam did not receive a ready-made language on his creation but a mere capacity to be further developed. This powerful argument enabled modern philosophers, either of a radical bent (Hobbes) or more orthodox ones (Süßmilch's former teacher, Jacob Carpov) to revive the Epicurean theory. It now became possible to embrace the biblical account while simultaneously espousing the natural emergence of language.[48] Süßmilch's main problem with this Enlightenment synthesis was precisely the one that troubled Rousseau: the transition between two incompatible categories, the shift from natural interjections to arbitrary words. He identified the tendency to stretch this transition over long millennia as an ineffective methodological device.[49]

By the mid-1750s the revived Epicurean theory had been combined with the modern thesis of the close interdependence between signs and thinking. Just like Condillac's *Essai*, Süßmilch's *Versuch* illustrated the indispensability of signs in our cognition by references to Wolff's examples of a Frenchman born deaf and mute and a feral child reared by bears in a Lithuanian forest. Süßmilch agreed wholeheartedly with Wolff's conclusion that one could not have general ideas without signs.[50] Yet mere natural signs would not be of use here; man had to acquire full control of artificial signs, or symbols that have an arbitrary relation to their objects.[51] This was the main difference between animal and human language, according to Süßmilch: in nature sounds were necessary and thus similar,

---

[47] Ibid. preface, 5ʳ⁻ᵛ. [48] Ibid. 5–12. [49] Ibid. 58–9.
[50] Ibid. 47–51. [51] Ibid. 42.

but they varied substantially among human languages. Süßmilch advocated a strong version of the arbitrariness of the sign, contrary to the seminatural origin of signification in Epicurus, Leibniz, or Condillac. For Süßmilch, human language exemplified complete freedom in the imposition of names. Arguing, therefore, that arbitrary signs were the prerequisite for human reasoning, Süßmilch did not neglect the opposite side of the equation: the hypothesis that human language must have been the product of intelligent design. If Lucretius' dumb brutes had produced such an artefact out of need and pure chance, we might as well assume that a well-designed clock could have naturally created itself.[52]

One of Süßmilch's main arguments was levelled at the Epicurean assumption that natural needs and social interaction could have prompted human beings to turn natural signs into arbitrary words. Like Castillon, he wondered what could have spurred such bestial creatures to improve their means of communication if the language of action satisfied all their initial needs. Habitude and comfort, Süßmilch argued, would have impeded any such attempt. Referring to Tacitus' reports on the Germanic tribes and to ascetic Brahmins, Süßmilch emphasized that the fewer needs a nation had, the happier it actually was. If the Lucretian brutes had ever existed, he concluded, they would have been far more content with cries and gestures than the spoiled Europeans were with their articulate language. Further imitation and arbitrary signs would have neither increased nor diminished the happiness of human beings in a state of nature.[53]

Playing in the Epicureans' own arena, Süßmilch mounted an impressive attack on the naturalistic thesis of the emergence of language. More elaborately than Rousseau, Süßmilch demonstrated that the interdependence of signs and human cognition could be reclaimed as a central weapon in the arsenal of the divine party. In line with Wolff's (and implicitly with Condillac's) equation between language and reason, Süßmilch argued that God must have either bestowed them on human beings upon their creation or not at all; in the latter case, they would have forever possessed rudimentary, bestial mental capacities. Those who argued for a natural emergence faced the conundrum of primacy and had to decide what came first, reason or language, an impossible task according to Rousseau and Süßmilch. The only alternative the *Versuch* offered its readers was a supernatural launch of reason and language at the same time, the beginning of time.

In a final appendix, Süßmilch admitted that Mendelssohn's attempt to solve Rousseau's problems was among the best he knew, for Mendelssohn 'trod a different path' from others.[54] Süßmilch conceded that the transition from natural to arbitrary signs could have happened according to

---

[52] Ibid. 31–2.   [53] Ibid. 88–90.   [54] Ibid. 117.

Mendelssohn's example of the sheep and its bleating, but added that this could only explain the emergence of onomatopoeic words, a marginal part of most vocabularies. The counter-argument relied heavily on Süßmilch's notion of the structural similarity and intentional design supposedly observable in all human languages.[55] Mendelssohn probably repaid the tribute by considering the arguments made in Süßmilch's *Versuch* in a few notes and an unpublished essay entitled *Notizen zu Ursprung der Sprache* (*Notes on the Origin of Language*).[56] Here Mendelssohn succinctly examined two main questions: whether speechless human beings could ever invent a language, and if it were possible, whether that language would be as orderly and uniform as any human tongue.[57] The problem would indeed be unsolvable and the divine origin of language vindicated, Mendelssohn admitted, if we considered man's original mental capacities as minimal and bestial. Mendelssohn rejected this hypothesis, for although human beings did not seem to differ much from animals in the state of nature, they had a latent capacity for language and higher mental skills. Drawing on Leibniz and Wolff, Mendelssohn saw this capacity as part of man's unique design.[58] Birds sang a variety of tunes without conveying different ideas, Mendelssohn argued, but human beings must have the intention to denote objects by arbitrary signs if they were ever to use language. Mendelssohn therefore postulated a hard-wired mental capacity for reason and language, *Vernunftanlage*, activated by natural circumstances and developed by human means.[59]

Mendelssohn's stance in the *Notizen* resembled his response to Rousseau in the *Sendschreiben* of 1756 in some respects. The fact that wild men, feral children, and deaf-mutes did not possess a fully fledged language might indeed entail that they could not think in general terms. Mendelssohn emphasized, however, that this could teach us practically

---

[55] Ibid. 121–3.
[56] These remained unpublished until 1981. Their editor, Eva J. Engel, assumes the essay was written in 1756, after the publication of Mendelssohn's translation of the *Discours sur l'inégalité*. See Mendelssohn, *JubA*, vi/2. xv–xix; Engel, '"Die Freyheit der Untersuchung": Die Literaturbriefe 72–5 (13. und 20. Dezember 1759)', in Eva J. Engel and Norbert Hinske (eds), *Moses Mendelssohn und die Kreise seiner Wirksamkeit* (Tübingen: Max Niemeyer, 1994), 249–68.
[57] Mendelssohn, *JubA*, vi/2. 27.
[58] On Mendelssohn's engagement with the debate over human design or destiny, see Anne Pollok, *Facetten des Menschen: Zur Anthroplogie Moses Mendelssohns* (Hamburg: Meiner, 2010), 79–116.
[59] Mendelssohn, *JubA*, vi/2. 7; Ulrich Ricken, 'Mendelssohn und die Sprachtheorien der Aufklärung', in Michael Albrecht and Eva J. Engel (eds), *Moses Mendelssohn im Spannungsfeld der Aufklärung* (Stuttgart-Bad Cannstatt: Frommann-Holzboog, 2000), 195–241; Avi Lifschitz, 'Language as a Means and an Obstacle to Freedom: The Case of Moses Mendelssohn', in Quentin Skinner and Martin van Gelderen (eds), *Freedom and the Construction of Europe* (Cambridge: Cambridge University Press, forthcoming).

nothing about human nature. The potential capacity for higher mental operations would remain repressed without a proper outlet, just as the human drive for reproduction might not bear fruit in the absence of suitable opportunities. For Mendelssohn it was man's social impulse that unleashed the capacity for language and reason. Even Rousseau's basic social unit of mother and child could have provided the motive for the activation of our linguistic capacity, but this instinct atrophied to no effect in children brought up by bears.[60] Mendelssohn's argument may be seen as a theoretical *coup de grâce* to Psammetichus' experiment as a reconstruction of the state of nature. Maupertuis was certain that language would emerge among isolated children, seeing it as a confirmation of the naturalistic thesis, while Süßmilch believed the infants would forever babble natural sounds as a vindication of the divine origin of language. Mendelssohn, by contrast, suggested an innate latent capacity for language, thereby rejecting the heuristic potential of any experiment involving an artificial environment.

Though Mendelssohn's unpublished notes were not part of the public debate, they may be regarded as a prototype of the solution that would emerge in Herder's 1771 prize essay on the origin of language. According to Mendelssohn, we must assume man had some innate platform for reason and language if we were to reject the divine endowment of language. This left a theoretical door open to both intelligent design and natural evolution. Whereas in Condillac the evolutionary scheme had been combined with the Wolffian theory of signs in cognition, Mendelssohn's view implied its further fusion with the Leibnizian concept of self-realization as the unfolding of innate capacities.

The genius and politics of language

While discussions of language in Berlin in 1756 were dominated by the question of its emergence, the special bilingual predicament of the Academy was coming to a head. As indicated by Süßmilch's grievances and his public critique of Maupertuis, what some perceived as the inferior status of German members became the focus of increasing tensions at the Academy. Maupertuis's essay *Des devoirs de l'Académicien*, read in 1750 but published in 1755, testified to the complex situation. The President justified the choice of French as the official language of the Academy by emphasizing the international prestige the institution must acquire and maintain. To reach the broadest audience, the Academy had to publish in the most universal language. But Maupertuis also felt the need for an

[60] Ibid. 7–9.

'argument from perfection'. French had been incomparably enriched since the preceding century by an abundance of excellent literary and scientific works. Maupertuis claimed that by his day, French had superseded Greek and Latin in the quantity and the quality of its texts, now serving as a model for all other tongues.[61] He was aware that some Germans resented the French appropriation of *bel esprit*, taking their revenge by denying the French language seriousness and profundity. Such German critics must be wrong, Maupertuis argued, if by gravity they meant an ostensibly erudite mélange of obscure Greek, Latin, and Hebrew citations with a 'diffuse style'. What endeared French to 'a monarch for whom taste is the most decisive suffrage' was a mutual fertilization between the language and its speakers: the clarity and precision of French authors depended on the genius of the language, as much as the status of the language depended on its speakers' cast of mind.[62] As in his earlier *Réflexions*, Maupertuis clearly endorsed here the reciprocal influence of language and opinions.

Another Francophone member of the Academy was more aware of the fragility of French universality. The young Louis Isaac de Beausobre, son of the renowned émigré scholar Isaac de Beausobre, suggested that the constant changes in living languages, especially French, should be halted. On 18 September 1755 Beausobre read to the Academy a paper on the changes of orthography and pronunciation in living languages, in which he presented any change in a language as its corruption or decline, arguing that the most perfect language must therefore be a dead one.[63] Beausobre's lecture was prompted by the publication in 1754 of a new edition of the Port Royal Grammar, revised by Charles Pinot Duclos. In this edition Duclos proposed the reform of orthography according to actual pronunciation, seeing contemporary French spelling as an ossified testimony to scholarly vanity.[64] Beausobre replied that linguistic matters should indeed be addressed by pedantic grammarians rather than courtiers or philosophers.[65] According to Beausobre, Duclos's reform would have made French even more irregular and unpredictable than it was. Instead of repeating errors committed in other languages, Beausobre argued, French should retain its traditional orthography, guard its vocabulary against any loss or change, and watch out for the dangers of neologism.[66]

[61] *Histoire de l'Académie, 1753* (Berlin: Haude & Spener, 1755), 519.
[62] Ibid. 520.
[63] Louis Isaac de Beausobre, 'Réflexions sur les changemens des langues vivantes par rapport à l'orthographe et à la prononciation', *Histoire de l'Académie, 1755* (Berlin: Haude & Spener, 1757), 514–29, here 515.
[64] Charles Pinot Duclos, 'Remarques à la Grammaire de Port-Royal' (1754), in Arnauld and Lancelot, *Grammaire*, 109–57, here 124.
[65] Beausobre, 'Réflexions', 518–20.   [66] Ibid. 528–9.

In Beausobre's purist endorsement of an orthography codified by Louis XIV's court grammarians, one may perceive the political implications of the interdependence of language and thought. If all speakers could naturally alter words or their meanings, there was no rationale behind the codifying authority of scholars or academies. This point was explicitly made by Duclos in 1754 in his *Remarques* on the Port Royal Grammar.

> To know who should make decisions about usage, one has to see who its author is. It is the people as a body who makes a language through the convergence of infinite needs, ideas, physical and moral causes, varied and combined over successive centuries, with no indication of the period of changes, alterations or progress. [...] The people are therefore the absolute master of the spoken language, and it is an authority [*empire*] it exercises without being aware of it.[67]

The socio-political dimension of Duclos's comments was certainly not lost on Jean-Jacques Rousseau, who confessed they had provoked him to write his own *Essai sur l'origine des langues*. Rousseau's essay, probably written between 1756 and 1761, ended with a brief chapter on the relationship between language and government. Rousseau repeated here his thesis that moral decline was paralleled by a linguistic loss of expressivity. A language like French, for example, in which one could not properly address a public assembly, was a servile idiom whose speakers could never be free. These musings on language and politics were concluded with a tribute to Duclos's remarks on the Port Royal Grammar.

> I shall conclude these reflections which, though superficial, may give rise to more profound ones, with the passage that suggested them to me.
> *To note and to show by means of examples the extent to which a people's character, morals, and interests influence its Language would provide matter for a rather philosophical inquiry.*[68]

The idea that a nation's socio-political character reflected its language, and vice versa, was thus a common topos by the mid-1750s. But contemporary discussions of the genius of language differed from similar debates in the preceding century. While earlier writers dealt mainly with the surface attributes of language, the mid-eighteenth century discussion focused on its cognitive evolution and deep structure.[69] This change may have

---

[67] Duclos, 'Remarques', 124.
[68] Rousseau, *Discourses*, 299; *Œuvres complètes*, v. 429. Cf. Duclos, 'Remarques', 112.
[69] Cordula Neis, '*Génie de la langue*, Apologie der Nationalsprachen und die Berliner Preisfrage von 1771', in Gerda Haßler (ed.), *Texte und Institutionen in der Geschichte der französischen Sprache* (Bonn: Romanistischer Verlag, 2001), 69–88; Christiane Schlaps, 'The "Genius of Language": Transformations of a Concept in the History of Linguistics', *Historiographia Linguistica* 31 (2004), 367–88.

been triggered by the parallel developments that converged in Condillac's *Essai* of 1746: the naturalistic-Epicurean theory of the mutual emergence of language and mind, and the Leibnizian-Wolffian notion of the indispensability of signs for complex mental operations.

The tendency to link linguistic differences to epistemological and psychological outlooks was also demonstrated in Maupertuis's *Réflexions*, where he postulated different national 'planes of ideas'. Maupertuis could have drawn this conclusion from Condillac, who had argued in his *Essai* that it was natural for nations to combine ideas in different ways, on which their subsequent genius depended. This interplay of natural constraints and spontaneous internal activity was also, in Condillac's eyes, the main spring of poetic genius. In a chapter of his *Essai* entitled 'The Genius of Languages', Condillac demonstrated how government, climate, and languages constantly conditioned each other.[70] As a result, national character evolved historically in tandem with the character of the nation's language. This national genius of language also accounted, according to Condillac, for an ultimate incommensurability between different languages, so that one could never translate poetry faithfully from one language to another. Condillac further emphasized the role of great authors in the evolution of language and its genius. Such writers enabled their contemporaries, hitherto incapable of penetrating the expressive depths of language, to follow their example in other domains. Yet just as they contributed to the perfection of language, classic authors could appear only after their mother tongue had made considerable progress. In 1759 Johann David Michaelis would advocate in his prize essay a similar notion of classic poets as creative engines, pulling the other arts and sciences towards perfection.

The conviction that the genius of language depended on psychological processes, and that these operations simultaneously depended on linguistic signs, was forcefully expressed by Diderot in the influential article 'Encyclopédie', published in 1756 in volume five of the eponymous project. The entry followed the tenets of Condillac's theory and clothed its discussion of dictionaries and classification in sensualist-Epicurean terminology. Diderot saw a people's vocabulary as a comprehensive matrix of its knowledge: by examining a nation's linguistic treasury, one could allegedly follow its progress.[71] In the entry 'Langage', written in 1759–60 but published in 1766, the relationship between a language and its speakers' character was mentioned at the outset. Jaucourt began the article by presenting language as the 'manner in which men communicate their thoughts to

---

[70] Condillac, 'Essai', II.i.15, in *Œuvres*, i. 98–104.
[71] Diderot, 'Encyclopédie', in *Encyclopédie*, v (1756), 637.

one another through a succession of words, gestures, and expressions adapted to their genius, customs, and climates'.[72] Quoting Condillac and Warburton, Jaucourt presented the emergence of language as thoroughly natural, prompted by needs and extending over a long period in which human beings substituted artificial signs for gestures and physical actions. Jaucourt also referred to the Epicurean-biblical compromise devised by Richard Simon, arguing that even if God had originally endowed human beings with language, this must have been a rudimentary idiom in need of constant elaboration.[73]

Back in Berlin, the Perpetual Secretary of the Academy addressed this theme in his edition of César Chesneau Du Marsais's grammatical-philosophical bestseller *Des tropes* (*On the Figures of Speech*, 1730), published in Leipzig in 1757. In the preface Formey stressed the influence of words upon all mental operations. This was followed by the Secretary's call for a further propagation of the 'grammatical spirit' in Europe, since it had profound influence on human reasoning in all other domains.[74] Another member of the Academy interested in the influence of language on thinking was Prémontval. One of his most contentious assertions was that the French translation of works composed in Latin or German could reveal their errors. French, in Prémontval's eyes, possessed particular lucidity that made it an indicator of logical fallacies.[75] This opinion, reflecting the controversial view that French mirrored the linear order of thought, was accompanied by Prémontval's attacks on Wolff's geometrical method. Even the anonymous translator of Wolff's psychological works into French rejected the author's method while praising his account of the human mind. The translator's disparaging comments on Wolff's style in the introduction to the French edition (1745) could have contributed to Prémontval's comparative views on philosophizing in Latin, German, and French.[76]

The prize question for 1759

Having sat on the jury of the 1755 prize contest on Pope's optimism, two years later Prémontval believed he had another opportunity to deal a

---

[72] Jaucourt, 'Langage', in *Encyclopédie*, ix (1766), 242.
[73] Ibid. Note the contrast with Beauzée's espousal of the divine endowment of language in his own article 'Langue' in the *Encyclopédie*.
[74] Formey, 'Préface de l'éditeur', in César Chesneau du Marsais, *Traité des tropes*, ed. J. H. S. Formey (Leipzig: La Veuve Gaspard Fritsch, 1757), 4ᵛ.
[75] Prémontval, 'Deux pièces en forme d'essais, concernant, l'une le principe de la raison suffisante, et l'autre la loi de continuité', *Histoire de l'Académie, 1754* (Berlin: Haude & Spener, 1756), 418–39.
[76] Wolff, *Psychologie ou traité sur l'âme* (Amsterdam: Pierre Mortier, 1745), 13.

public blow to his intellectual scapegoat, Wolffian philosophy. In 1757 he seized upon the vigorous discussion of language, mind, and their joint origins, convincing Formey that the topic for the next contest, organized by the class of speculative philosophy, should be the reciprocal influence of language and opinions. The Perpetual Secretary would later admit that the Republic of Letters owed to Prémontval the excellent work produced in the wake of the question he had conceived.[77] Merian, the Deputy Secretary, also wrote to Maupertuis that it was Prémontval who 'conceived the terms of our question', while adding that the querulous Prémontval knew less than anyone else at the Academy about this topic.[78] Prémontval's own motives were indeed, as we have seen, much more circumscribed than the problem of innate potentials versus acquired skills, or the question of the evolution of language among speechless human beings. In a footnote to the French edition of the subsequent prize essay (translated by himself and Merian), Prémontval would trace the origin of the question back to his own concern with Wolff's method. Repeating the thesis set forth in the papers he had read at the Academy, Prémontval argued that false reasoning might only be revealed once translated into French, while it remained 'marvellously shrouded' in German or in Latin. The German language was therefore especially liable to sophistry. This was, as Prémontval claimed hyperbolically, 'one of the most singular traits in the history of the human mind'.[79]

Prémontval's line of reasoning reiterated a rather traditional view of the special clarity of the French language. Yet by 1757 it had already been argued by Condillac, Diderot, and Rousseau that the analytic character of French came at a significant cost. They all regarded ancient languages as closer to the primordial, expressive language of action, and saw the suitability of French for scientific discourse mirrored in its failure to reflect instantaneous feelings. Prémontval, however, was less interested in the genetic aspects of the subject, and the emergence of language was therefore mentioned only in passing at the end of the official prize question.

---

[77] Formey, Letter XL, 2 October 1759, in *Lettres sur l'état présent des sciences et des moeurs*, July–December 1759 (Berlin: Haude & Spener, 1760), ii. 224. Condillac assumed in the 1770s that Maupertuis had set the topic for the 1759 contest (*Œuvres*, ii. 90–4). Yet given Maupertuis's absence from Berlin since 1756, this seems questionable.

[78] Paris, Académie des Sciences, Fonds Maupertuis, 43 J 121.18, Merian to Maupertuis, 25 October 1757. See also Merian's earlier letter of 3 May 1757 (43 J 121.16). I am grateful to Alexander Schmidt for this reference.

[79] Footnote in Johann David Michaelis, *De l'influence des opinions sur le langage et du langage sur les opinions*, trans. Jean Bernard Merian and André Pierre Le Guay de Prémontval (Bremen: George Louis Förster, 1762), 90–1. When translating the prize essay, Merian wrote to Michaelis that the note was Prémontval's own addition. (Göttingen, Niedersächsische Staats- und Universitätsbibliothek, Codex Michaelis 325 (Briefwechsel, VI), undated letter from Merian to Michaelis (May/June 1760), 52.)

The topic for the 1759 prize contest was announced by Formey at the public assembly of 9 June 1757 and published in the press immediately afterwards.[80]

> The Class of Speculative Philosophy proposes for the ordinary Prize of 1759 the following question: *What is the reciprocal influence of the Opinions of a People on the language, and of the Language on the Opinions?* This should be demonstrated by a number of selected examples:
> 1. How many strange turns of phrase and expressions there are in Languages, born manifestly from certain opinions received among the peoples where these Languages were formed: this first point will be the easiest.
> 2. It will be essential to show, in certain turns of phrase typical of each language, in certain expressions, and even in the roots of certain words, the seeds of this or that Error or the obstacles to the reception of this or that Truth.
>
> This double point of view should give rise to very important reflections. After explaining *how a turn of mind forms a Language, which then imparts to the mind an outlook more or less favourable to true ideas*, one could search for the most practical means of remedying the inconveniences of Language.[81]

While the main question uses the term 'opinions', it is important to note that the second, more challenging task and the final comment focus firmly on the epistemological and cognitive aspects of language. The second, 'essential' requirement is to discuss linguistic terms as conducive to the attainment of truth and knowledge; the final paragraph refers to the cognitive issue of how the human mind forms linguistic signs and the subsequent involvement of such signs in human thinking. While the tenor of the prize question resembles the prescriptive tirades of Beausobre and Prémontval, it also reflects some of the main points of the anthropological debate on language, mind, and their evolution. Indeed, as we shall see in Chapter 5, this is how most contestants understood the question, rather than in Prémontval's narrower sense.

This prize question would have sounded completely incoherent in the context of Cartesian dualism and its strict dichotomy between physical signs and immaterial thought. Even Süßmilch, the only Academy member who resolutely rejected the Epicurean thesis in the 1750s, still followed Wolff on the indispensability of signs for higher mental operations—a very un-Cartesian notion. The mere equation of the workings of the human mind (in the final section of the prize question) with 'opinions' (in the title), a term which had traditionally implied uncertain or indistinct

---

[80] Winter, *Registres*, 233.
[81] *Nouvelle Bibliothèque germanique*, July–September 1757 (Amsterdam: Pierre Mortier), 202–3.

knowledge, testifies to the mid-century assimilation of the Leibnizian, anti-Cartesian point about the indispensability of signs in most mental operations.[82] The phrasing of the question assumed that the human mind and linguistic signs did form one another, with all the ensuing difficulties for the purity of human knowledge. Our understanding and intellectual skills were moulded by language while at the same time transforming it; clear and distinct ideas could not be detached from the social and environmental contexts of their users. A century after its initiation, the long journey launched by Arnauld, Lamy, and Pascal in their re-evaluation of Descartes's theory of language had reached a theoretical terminus, where it was about to begin a further transformation.

* * *

The contest announced in June 1757 had a rather prosaic immediate origin in Prémontval's crusade against Wolffian philosophy, but his concerns merged with the wider intellectual currents in contemporary Berlin. A critical discursive mass on the mutual relationship between language and mind, the origin of language, and the genius of language reached its heyday around 1756. The first months of 1756 saw the publication of the German translation of Rousseau's *Discours sur l'inégalité* with its problematization of the Epicurean thesis, and Mendelssohn's riposte upholding the natural origin of language. Maupertuis opted in May for the naturalistic position in the *Dissertation* he read to the Academy; in October came Süßmilch's reply. Meanwhile, volume six of the *Encyclopédie* appeared in Paris, incorporating important discussions of language, mind, and national vocabularies in Diderot's entry 'Encyclopédie' and Turgot's articles on etymology and existence. All these publications in 1756, alongside slightly earlier ones such as Duclos's *Remarques* on the Port Royal Grammar and academic papers by Maupertuis and Prémontval, could be woven together in different manners, as demonstrated by the essays submitted to the Academy's judgement.

The future laureate of the prize contest, Johann David Michaelis, followed these debates from Göttingen, especially through his correspondence with Prémontval. Following a peculiar path of intellectual development, Michaelis came to regard language as the gateway to the investigation of past human experience—a task on which he avidly embarked.

---

[82] Cf. the largely Cartesian entry 'Opinion' in *Encyclopédie*, xi (1765), 506–7.

4

J. D. Michaelis on Language and Vowel Points

From Confessional Controversy to Naturalism

One of the crucial questions raised by an examination of the 1759 contest at the Berlin Academy may be succinctly summarized as 'why Michaelis?' The competition was largely modelled after what Hans Aarsleff termed 'the tradition of Condillac', conjectural essays on the mutual development of language and the human mind. The crowned author was, however, a German orientalist of a Pietist background, who was inspired to a large extent by Albrecht von Haller, Robert Lowth, and the Baumgarten brothers. At first glance it is not clear what could have endeared Michaelis's essay to academicians acquainted with works by Rousseau and Maupertuis—and why Michaelis, whose orientalist ancestors accorded to Hebrew a special status, should resort to a naturalistic or Epicurean account of language. This chapter attempts to answer such questions by tracing a significant shift in Michaelis's view of Hebrew, which triggered a wholesale change in his theory of the evolution of language. Michaelis launched his career in the early 1740s with a defence of the long-held Protestant thesis about the exceptional antiquity and durability of the Hebrew vowel points. But by the late 1750s he presented a very different account of Hebrew as a natural language, evolving and changing like any other. Michaelis's *volte face* concerning the Hebrew vowel points will be considered against the background of his academic pursuits in the late 1750s: annotating Robert Lowth's lectures on biblical poetry, organizing a scientific expedition to the Arabian peninsula, and teaching ancient Jewish law. This exploration of Michaelis's intellectual development is not primarily meant to illuminate his biblical criticism or orientalist scholarship, aspects of his work that have been recently and fruitfully examined.[1]

---

[1] Jonathan Sheehan, *The Enlightenment Bible: Translation, Scholarship, Culture* (Princeton: Princeton University Press, 2005), 182–217; Carhart, *Science of Culture*, 27–68; Suzanne L. Marchand, *German Orientalism in the Age of Empire* (Cambridge: Cambridge University Press, 2009), 36–42, and Michael Legaspi, *The Death of Scripture and the Rise of Biblical Studies* (Oxford: Oxford University Press, 2010). Other recent studies focused on

My engagement with Michaelis's early career should elucidate his anthropological and philosophical musings on the links between language, the human mind, and their joint evolution.

PRELUDE: IN DEFENCE OF THE ANCIENT VOWEL POINTS

Born into a family of academic orientalists, Johann David Michaelis was first educated privately by his father Christian Benedict Michaelis, professor of theology and oriental languages at Halle. Aged 12 he was sent to the prestigious Orphanage School (*Waisenhaus*) at Halle, one of the gems in the crown of the Pietist education enterprise. The instructors were university lecturers who tried to foster scholarly excellence and diligence among small groups of students. It was at the *Waisenhaus* that Michaelis first met Siegmund Jacob Baumgarten, who left an indelible mark on the young pupil in his attempts to reconcile reason and revelation, Wolffianism and theology, Scripture and critical history.[2] As a teenager Michaelis developed what he termed 'a half-Pelagian private theology'. Some of his doubts were countered successfully by the preacher who prepared him for Confirmation but he remained sceptical towards the Lutheran version of the mass, in which one had 'to follow the written words without exercising reason'. Only later, when he understood ancient Greek well enough to read the New Testament in the original, was Michaelis able to see how his qualms could be recast as matters of interpretation.[3]

Michaelis belonged to a group of select pupils to whom Baumgarten taught the principles of Wolffian philosophy, officially proscribed at Halle after Wolff's expulsion from the Prussia at the encouragement of Joachim Lange and the Pietist old guard. In a revealing testimony to the formation of the new Wolffian-Pietist synthesis by progressive theologians at Halle, Michaelis recounted in his autobiography that Baumgarten did not adopt all of Wolff's principles, omitting pre-established harmony. This was one of the concessions Wolffians usually made in their attempt at reconciliation with Pietists who attacked their alleged determinism. Once Michaelis was admit-

---

Michaelis's attitudes towards contemporary Jews: Anna-Ruth Löwenbrück, *Judenfeindschaft im Zeitalter der Aufklärung: Eine Studie zur Vorgeschichte des modernen Antisemitismus am Beispiel des Göttinger Theologen und Orientalisten Johann David Michaelis* (Frankfurt am Main: Peter Lang, 1995), and Jonathan M. Hess, *Germans, Jews and the Claims of Modernity* (New Haven: Yale University Press, 2002), 50–89.

[2] Among Michaelis's fellow students at school were Baumgarten's younger brothers, Alexander and Nathanael. (J. D. Michaelis, *Lebensbeschreibung von ihm selbst abgefaßt* (Leipzig: Johann Ambrosius Barth, 1793), 3–5.)

[3] Ibid. 25.

ted to the University of Halle (1733), he knew—thanks to Baumgarten—more than his peers about the fashionable Wolff. While some students succumbed wholeheartedly to the charms of the forbidden philosophy, Michaelis was well trained not to accept all of its tenets at face value.[4]

Apart from this early encounter with Wolff's philosophy, Michaelis was inculcated with oriental languages by his father at home, at school, and at the university. Christian Benedict Michaelis's view of oriental languages, and Hebrew in particular, was moulded by the theological concerns of the first generation of Pietist reformers. Christian Benedict was one of the teachers at the Collegium Orientale Theologicum of the University of Halle, founded in 1702 and headed by his uncle Johann Heinrich Michaelis. In 1728 an Institutum Judaicum with its own printing press was added to the Collegium. At both institutions students could learn Semitic languages such as biblical and 'rabbinic' (Talmudic) Hebrew, Arabic, Aramaic, Chaldean, Samaritan, and Ethiopian (Amharic), alongside modern oriental languages like Turkish, Persian, and Chinese. The most significant project undertaken by Johann Heinrich Michaelis, a new annotated edition of the Hebrew Bible, was published in Halle in 1720.[5] The foundation of both the Collegium Orientale Theologicum and the Institutum Judaicum was firmly grounded in the missionary ambitions of Halle Pietism, as represented by Johann Heinrich Callenberg, a close collaborator of both Johann Heinrich and Christian Benedict Michaelis. A considerable number of Hebrew teachers at Halle and other German universities were Jewish converts to Christianity.[6]

In early eighteenth-century Halle, the foremost view on Hebrew was a common Protestant thesis seeing it as the oldest language, self-contained and unsullied by other tongues. This stance, deeply rooted in post-Reformation debates over the reliability of the biblical text, was espoused by the young Johann David Michaelis in his doctoral dissertation at Halle on the antiquity of the Hebrew vowel points and accents (1739). Michaelis's dissertation, written under his father's supervision, may be seen as a contribution to a venerable family tradition; his great uncle, Johann Heinrich Michaelis, had already written a popular Hebrew grammar and a treatise on the accents in the Old Testament.[7] Yet by vindicating the

---

[4] Ibid. 4–5.
[5] Karl Heinrich Rengstorf, 'Johann Heinrich Michaelis und seine *Biblia Hebraica* von 1720', in Hinske (ed.), *Zentren der Aufklärung*, i. 15–64.
[6] Dominique Bourel, 'Die deutsche Orientalistik im 18. Jahrhundert: Von der Mission zur Wissenschaft', in Reventlow et al. (eds), *Historische Kritik*, 113–26; Christopher Clark, *The Politics of Conversion: Missionary Protestantism and the Jews in Prussia, 1728–1941* (Oxford: Oxford University Press, 1995), 47–57.
[7] J. H. Michaelis, *Gründlicher Unterricht von den Accentibus prosaicis u. metricis* (Halle: Verlegung des Wäysenhauses, 1700); *Erleichterte hebräische Grammatica* (Halle: Zeitler, 1702).

antiquity of the Hebrew vowel points, the young Michaelis also delved straight into the depths of a confessional controversy engaging European scholars for more than two centuries.

The initial absence of letters signifying vowels in the Hebrew script confronted Protestant theologians with an acute problem. Vowels are indicated in Hebrew by diacritical marks placed below, above, and within the letters, so that the same cluster of consonants can have very different meanings according to the position of its vowel points: בָּגַד stands for 'he betrayed', while בֶּגֶד is a garment or vestment. However, Luther's *sola scriptura* principle and the emphasis on the direct impact of the biblical text upon individual readers required a stable and reliable version of the Bible. In the case of the Hebrew Old Testament, most Protestants accepted as immutable or divinely inspired the sixteenth-century Venetian edition of the Pentateuch (1525), vowel-pointed according to the established Jewish convention, the Masorah.[8] Catholic apologists such as Robert Bellarmine tended, on the other hand, to assert the necessity of the Church as an institutional interpreter of Scripture by undermining the authority of the biblical Hebrew text. One of the Catholic strategies was to argue that vowel points were added to the Hebrew consonantal script at a late stage, not fixed by Ezra the Scribe and his Great Synagogue in the fifth century BC (as accepted by the Jewish tradition). This argument had serious implications, since the addition, change or removal of vowel points could alter the meaning of entire phrases in the Old Testament; the Catholic stance implied that rabbinic scholars could have tampered with the biblical text in response to Jewish-Christian controversies. Mainstream Catholic scholars thus argued for the primacy of the Vulgate Latin translation over the Hebrew original by maintaining that errors, deliberate or inadvertent, had occurred in the process of vocalization, the adding of vowel points to the Old Testament at a later stage. It was therefore crucial for Protestant scholars to defend the reliability and antiquity of the sixteenth-century Hebrew text and its vowel points, used by Luther in his translation of the Old Testament into German (even if in a relatively free manner).

One of the primary defenders of the antiquity of the Hebrew vowel points was the Protestant Hebraist Johannes Buxtorf the elder. By arguing that it was Ezra and his Great Synagogue who fixed the Hebrew text,

---

[8] Richard A. Muller, 'The Debate over the Vowel Points and the Crisis in Orthodox Hermeneutics', *Journal of Medieval and Renaissance Studies* 10 (1980), 53–72; Maurice Olender, *The Languages of Paradise*, trans. Arthur Goldhammer (Cambridge, Mass.: Harvard University Press, 1992), 23–8; Noel Malcolm, 'Hobbes, Ezra and the Bible: The History of a Subversive Idea', in *Aspects of Hobbes* (Oxford: Oxford University Press, 2002), 383–431.

including the vowel points, Buxtorf subjected philology to confessional ends, trying to counter Catholic claims about the late origin of the vowel points that made them prone to misinterpretations.[9] Despite Buxtorf's reputation as the foremost contemporary Hebraic scholar, Louis Cappel, a Huguenot lecturer at the academies of Saumur and Sedan, challenged his thesis. Unlike Buxtorf, Cappel admitted the Septuagint and other Greek versions of the Old Testament as evidence that the Hebrew text was unpointed at the time of its translation. Cappel wished to reclaim the argument about the late origin of the vowel points for the Protestant cause by demonstrating that reliable meaning could be attributed to the consonantal text without recourse to the authority of the Catholic Church.[10]

As a student, Johann David Michaelis was well aware of the long controversy over the Hebrew vowel points. In his dissertation he tried to counter Cappel's thesis, controversial in Protestant circles ever since its publication, with a wide array of sources, ranging from medieval to contemporary scholars.[11] Despite some reservations, his overall defence of Buxtorf's view of the antiquity of the vowel points placed him in the traditional Protestant camp alongside his father and great uncle. It is important, however, to emphasize that the orientalists of the Michaelis clan strayed away from the topical Renaissance discussion of Hebrew as the original, divine language. Such questions, as Christian Benedict Michaelis stated, were not relevant to the philological study of Hebrew.[12] At the same time, both Johann Heinrich and Christian Benedict Michaelis endorsed the Protestant view that the Hebrew vowel points were exceptionally ancient. Johann Heinrich Michaelis's Hebrew grammar started, for example, with the assertion that 'the ancient Hebrews wrote just as they spoke; and especially in the Bible they made an effort to express with

---

[9] Buxtorf's main argument was made in *Tiberias* (Basel: König, 1620), a refutation of the hypothesis expounded by the Jewish scholar Elias Levita (1468–1549) concerning the late vocalization of the Bible. See Stephen G. Burnett, *From Christian Hebraism to Jewish Studies: Johannes Buxtorf (1564–1629) and Hebrew Learning in the Seventeenth Century* (Leiden: Brill, 1996), 203–28.

[10] Louis Cappel, סוד הניקוד נגלה *Hoc est Arcanum punctationis revelatum* (1624). Cappel was not, however, the only Protestant scholar to doubt the antiquity of the vowel points; see Muller, 'The Debate', 65–70, Anthony Grafton, *Joseph Scaliger*, ii: *Historical Chronology* (Oxford: Oxford University Press, 1993), 734–7, and Anthony Grafton and Joanna Weinberg, '*I Have Always Loved the Holy Tongue': Isaac Casaubon, the Jews, and a Forgotten Chapter in Renaissance Scholarship* (Cambridge, Mass.: Harvard University Press, 2011), 307–28.

[11] J. D. Michaelis, *Dissertatio inauguralis de punctorum hebraicorum antiquitate, sub examen vocans* (Halle: J. F. Grunert, 1739).

[12] C. B. Michaelis, 'Vorrede', in J. D. Michaelis, *Anfangs-Gründe der hebräischen Accentuation, nebst einer kurzen Abhandlung von dem Alterthum der Accente und Hebräischen Puncte überhaupt* (Halle: Verlegung des Wäysenhauses, 1741), 8–9.

convenient signs everything related to pronunciation.'[13] In 1741 his great-nephew, Johann David, published in Halle his first book, a treatise on the Hebrew accents based on his doctoral dissertation. Prefaced by his father, *Anfangs-Gründe der hebräischen Accentuation* (*The Basics of Hebrew Accentuation*) was a clearly presented textbook, yet it concluded with a robust argument in defence of the antiquity of the vowel points. Despite his father's qualms about the early publication (Johann David Michaelis was only 24 at the time), this was very much a family venture. Christian Benedict Michaelis used the preface to defend the Hebrew textbook by his uncle against a recent critic, while introducing the treatise in which his son (and former doctoral student) followed in the footsteps of the venerable great uncle.[14]

Towards the end of this treatise, Johann David Michaelis reviewed the traditional battleground between Protestants and Catholics concerning the antiquity of the Hebrew vowel points. He then opted for his great uncle's thesis that the vowel points always existed in Hebrew, long before Ezra the Scribe; in fact, Michaelis claimed, they were in use already at the time of Moses. Michaelis noted that Ezra never mentioned his alleged innovation in the biblical book he composed, a strange omission given its far-reaching hermeneutic ramifications. Furthermore, Michaelis asserted that the traditional Jewish account of Ezra's introduction of the vowel points could not be trusted. Yet his most substantial arguments against the Catholics' (and Cappel's) claims for the novelty of the vowel points were based on a holistic view of language and its functions. For the young Michaelis it was simply inconceivable that a language could be created or invented without a full apparatus, namely signs representing both consonants and vowels. It was impossible, Michaelis argued, that whoever came up with signs for consonants did not see the necessity of expressing vowels by similar notation. If the comparative philologists of eighteenth-century Europe could read unpointed Hebrew texts only with extreme difficulty, the challenge must have been all the greater at the time of the ancient Israelites and the Phoenicians. The latter, using a cognate Semitic language, could not have embarked on their maritime commercial endeavours without vowel points, for these enabled much smoother communication with foreigners.[15]

Following his arguments about the inventors of language and the convenience of its use, Michaelis turned to what may be termed an argument

---

[13] J. H. Michaelis, *Gründlicher Unterricht*, 1.
[14] The critical book was Christoph Sancke's *Vollständige Anweisung zu den Accenten der Hebräer* (Leipzig: Gleditsch, 1740). For Christian Benedict Michaelis's uncertainty about some of his son's points, see his preface to *Anfangs-Gründe*, 25–6.
[15] Ibid. 62–3.

from perfection. The Hebrew vowel points were so well ordered, endowing the consonantal letters with such a natural sense, that one could not possibly ascribe their introduction to 'new and blind Jews'. By the Middle Ages, Michaelis argued, the Jews had lived for a long time with a faded tradition and an unspoken Hebrew, and hence were incapable of producing such a linguistic feat as the vowel points. Had the points been introduced into Hebrew so late, Michaelis asserted, they would have been much more 'confused'. But Michaelis's opponents could have readily agreed with his case for the perfection of the vowel points, arguing that an uncouth people at the dawn of history could not have used such an exquisite device. Michaelis anticipated this objection by noting that not all ancient Israelites were 'unlearned', singling out the prophet Amos's use of a cultivated and delicate style despite his poverty. He also noted that the ancient Israelites at the time of Moses were not as coarse and unrefined as the Greeks. Finally, the young Michaelis promised his readers a much more elaborate defence of the antiquity of the Hebrew vowel points, a pledge he would later be relieved not to have fulfilled.[16]

SACRED POETRY WITHOUT VOWELS: ENGLISH ENCOUNTERS

The modification of Michaelis's professional outlook began as he was travelling to England in spring 1741, having accepted an invitation to assist the German preacher at the royal chapel of St James. En route to London, Michaelis met in Leiden the most famous Arabist of the day, Albert Schultens. Though reliable studies of Arabic grammar had been available for several generations, this language did not attract as much scholarly attention as Hebrew.[17] Schultens was among the first scholars who emphasized the significance of Arabic for an understanding of the Hebrew Old Testament: due to their Semitic proximity, words in Arabic could illuminate the etymology of difficult Hebrew terms. Michaelis would use Schultens's method extensively, without failing to draw some conclusions about the historical evolution of Hebrew. Nevertheless, both Schultens and Michaelis treated Arabic less as an independent field of inquiry than an instrumental support in the study of Hebrew.

Michaelis stayed in London from April 1741 until September 1742, but the pinnacle of the visit was a month spent in Oxford, which he later

---

[16] Ibid. 61, 77–8. For echoes of this debate among Jewish scholars, see Andrea Schatz, *Sprache in der Zerstreuung: Die Säkularisierung des Hebräischen im 18. Jahrhundert* (Göttingen: Vandenhoeck & Ruprecht, 2009), 176–91 and 241–59.
[17] Bourel, 'Deutsche Orientalistik', 122–3.

remembered as 'the most delightful time of my life'.[18] He considered himself fortunate to attend the second of Robert Lowth's lectures on the sacred poetry of the Hebrews. Though he did not approach Lowth at the time, this was the beginning of a close alliance between the two.[19] Lowth, Professor of Poetry at Oxford from 1741 until 1750, later Bishop of London, delivered thirty-four addresses on biblical poetry thoughout his tenure, published as *De sacra poesi Hebraeorum praelectiones* (*Lectures on the Sacred Poetry of the Hebrews*) by the Clarendon Press in 1753. The second lecture, attended by Michaelis, laid out the design of the entire series, legitimizing the application of modern aesthetic criteria to biblical poetry. The main justification rested on the Bible's human audience and the sensual perception of its readers.[20] Lowth argued that poetry should be treated not as a product of reason but rather as a work of nature, organically stimulated in man's mind upon his creation. In further lectures Lowth elaborated his influential view of the poet as a prophet and the prophet as a poet. For Lowth, oriental poetry was written in an enthusiastic, parabolic mode still discernible in modern music and dance. Content and form were closely entwined in this style, which was rich in sensual representations of nature.[21] Lowth's depiction of a primordial language expressing the sublime in an unmediated way, untouched by reason, resembled closely the emphasis placed by Condillac and Diderot in the 1740s on the instantaneous character of sensual perception, as opposed to its later analytic expression. Condillac's language of action and Diderot's hieroglyph were the parallels of Lowth's imaginative oriental poetry. Unlike his French contemporaries, however, Lowth was not interested in tracing the gradual evolution of human language and cognition from this primordial condition.

In the field of biblical criticism Lowth's main contribution was his analysis of parallelism, the expression of the same idea by analogous members of two or more groups of words (as in Genesis 4: 23, according to the King James Version: 'Adah and Zillah, Hear my voice; ye wives of Lamech, hearken unto my speech: for I have slain a man to my wounding, and a young man to my hurt.')[22] Lowth's turn to parallelism and away from verse and metre was justified by his reference to the absence of vowels in written Hebrew. His views on the issue contrasted sharply with the

---

[18] Michaelis, *Lebensbeschreibung*, 29. All further references under this surname are to Johann David Michaelis.

[19] On Lowth's active help to Michaelis in the 1760s, see Lifschitz, 'Translation in Theory and Practice: The Case of Johann David Michaelis's Prize Essay on Language and Opinions (1759)', in Stockhorst (ed.), *Cultural Transfer*, 29–43.

[20] Robert Lowth, *Lectures on the Sacred Poetry of the Hebrews*, trans. G. Gregory (London: Chadwick & Co., 1847), 33–4.

[21] Ibid. 48–60.   [22] Ibid. 45.

tradition the young Michaelis adhered to in his recently published first book: Lowth regarded the Hebrew vowel points as a late, untrustworthy invention, following Cappel rather than Buxtorf.

> It is, indeed, evident, that the true Hebrew pronunciation is totally lost. The rules concerning it, which were devised by the modern Jews many ages after the language of their ancestors had fallen into disuse, have been long since suspected by the learned to be destitute of authority and truth.[23]

This lack of reliable vocalization of the Hebrew Bible led Lowth to search for poetic value in its syntax and figurative vocabulary, and therefore to parallelism as the paradigmatic feature of biblical poetry.[24] Lowth's ideas fascinated Michaelis, who edited and annotated his Oxford lectures in two volumes, published in Göttingen in 1758 and 1761. Though not approving of all of Lowth's observations, Michaelis praised him as a prodigious interpreter of oriental poetry.[25] Michaelis later began his translation of the Old Testament into German with the book of Job, the subject of a detailed analysis in Lowth's *Lectures* and the focal point of a stormy controversy between Lowth and Warburton.[26]

Lowth's appreciation of Hebrew prophecy as a mine of powerful primitive poetry coincided with a similar re-evaluation of Homer's works following the Quarrel of the Ancients and the Moderns, as epitomized in Thomas Blackwell's *An Enquiry into the Life and Writings of Homer* (1735) and Robert Wood's *Essay on the Original Genius and Writings of Homer* (1775). Both Homer and Moses became representatives of an age of lost innocence, sensuality, and creativity, before reason and abstraction launched the march of civilization; their works came to be regarded as documenting the primordial energies of the human mind. Indeed, Michaelis's rich annotation of Lowth's *Lectures* was one of the stimuli leading Wood to compose his travel accounts of Greece and the Near East in the 1750s. Wood stressed the crucial significance of environmental and cultural background for the proper understanding of classical poetry, arguing that the Iliad and the Odyssey could be truly appreciated only in (or in knowing about) the places where Achilles fought and Odysseus

---

[23] Ibid. 44.
[24] James Kugel, *The Idea of Biblical Poetry: Parallelism and Its History* (New Haven: Yale University Press, 1998), 274–86.
[25] 'Praefatio editoris', in Lowth, *De sacra poesi Hebraeorum praelectiones academicae Oxonii habitae*, ed. Johann David Michaelis (Göttingen: Pockwitz & Barmeier, 1758–61), i. p. vi.
[26] Jonathan Lamb, *The Rhetoric of Suffering: Reading the Book of Job in the Eighteenth Century* (Oxford: Oxford University Press, 1995), 110–27; Young, *Religion and Enlightenment*, 190–212; Sheehan, *Enlightenment Bible*, 160–8. See also John Jarick (ed.), *Sacred Conjectures: The Context and Legacy of Robert Lowth and Jean Astruc* (New York: T&T Clark, 2007).

sailed.[27] In 1769 Wood sent to Michaelis one of the seven pre-printed copies of his *Essay on the Original Genius and Writings of Homer*. The *Essay* was enthusiastically received in Göttingen, praised by Christian Gottlob Heyne in the *Göttingische Anzeigen* and translated into German by Michaelis's son, Christian Friedrich, even before its publication in England.[28] The close link Michaelis forged with English orientalists in 1741–2 proved long-lasting and fruitful both in Germany and in Britain.

To cap his encounter with new methods and ideas, Michaelis claimed he underwent in England a theological change as well. Though as an adolescent he could not detect signs of divine grace or undergo the personal conversion required by his Pietist mentors, Michaelis still adhered to the doctrines of grace and supernatural occurrences as a common article of faith. It was in England that he began to apply his long-lasting doubt to biblical scholarship, convinced that Scripture should not be interpreted literally.[29]

FROM GÖTTINGEN TO ARABIA: RESEARCH AND DISCOVERY

Reviewing Michaelis's writings posthumously, Johann Gottlob Eichhorn observed a marked turn in his scholarship around the early 1750s:[30] it seems that the stimuli Michaelis had received in England yielded their scholarly fruit only in a new academic environment. In 1745 Michaelis, then a freelance teacher in Halle, gladly accepted Gerlach Adolf von Münchhausen's invitation to teach at the newly founded University of Göttingen, where he followed a fast track of professional promotion.[31] In 1751 he became Secretary of the Royal Society of Sciences, in 1753 editor of its influential review journal, *Göttingische Anzeigen von gelehrten Sachen*,

---

[27] *The Ruins of Palmyra, otherwise Tedmor in the Desert* (1753) and *The Ruins of Balbec, otherwise Heliopolis in Coelosyria* (1757).

[28] Wood died in 1771 and his *Essay* was published posthumously in 1775. The German edition is *Robert Woods Versuch über das Originalgenie des Homers* (Frankfurt am Main: Andreäische Buchhandlung, 1773). See Hans Hecht, *T. Percy, R. Wood und J. D. Michaelis: Ein Beitrag zur Literaturgeschichte der Genieperiode* (Stuttgart: Kohlhammer, 1933), 19–31.

[29] Michaelis, *Lebensbeschreibung*, 36; Legaspi, *Death of Scripture*, 117–19. On the Pietists' strict demand of a self-denying spiritual conversion, see Anthony La Vopa, *Grace, Talent, and Merit: Poor Students, Clerical Careers, and Professional Ideology in Eighteenth-Century Germany* (Cambridge: Cambridge University Press, 1988), 137–55.

[30] Johann Gottlieb Eichhorn, 'Johann David Michaelis', *Allgemeine Bibliothek der biblischen Literatur*, iii/5 (Leipzig: Weidmannsche Buchhandlung, 1791), 860.

[31] Semler suggested that Michaelis had rivals in Halle in the early 1740s; see his own *Lebensbeschreibung*, i. 96.

and in 1761 Director of the Royal Society. For a considerable time in the 1760s Michaelis also headed the philological seminar at Göttingen, held temporarily the professorship of classical eloquence, and acted as Director of the University Library. Unsurprisingly, some referred to him as 'the regent of Göttingen'.[32]

Michaelis owed his initiation into the Royal Society of Sciences to its founder, the natural philosopher and poet Albrecht von Haller. It is not clear whether their close friendship began as Michaelis claimed, when Haller heard him reciting a German poem, but the young lecturer did become Haller's protégé and was greatly inspired by his concept of science.[33] Haller may have been the model for Michaelis's archetype of the classic author in his 1759 prize essay, an expert in the life sciences who applied his vast knowledge of nature to the composition of poetry in German. As one of the most distinguished scholars at Göttingen, Haller was entrusted by Münchhausen with drawing the outline for the local Royal Society (founded in 1751 with Haller as its Director and Michaelis as Secretary). Haller's own research and the peculiar organization of the Society, comprising mainly university professors, led him to assert a different ideal of scholarship from the contemporary division of labour between universities (dedicated to teaching and training) and royal academies or societies (focused on research and discovery). According to Haller, university professors should aspire to make new discoveries and teaching had to be research based. Metaphysics, theology, and jurisprudence were excluded from the new Society, while history and philology constituted an independent class, reflecting Haller's view of these disciplines as 'sciences which promise the widening of knowledge and discoveries through observations, experiments, deep understanding of nature, and the application of the known unto the unknown'.[34] Michaelis imbibed this notion of

---

[32] Rudolf Smend, 'Johann David Michaelis und Johann Gottfried Eichhorn—zwei Orientalisten am Rande der Theologie', in Bernd Moeller (ed.), *Theologie in Göttingen* (Göttingen: Vandenhoeck & Ruprecht, 1987), 60. Michaelis renounced the editorship of the *Anzeigen* and the directorship of the Royal Society in 1770 due to tensions with his colleague C. G. Heyne. See Ferdinand Frensdorff, 'Eine Krisis in der Königlichen Gesellschaft der Wissenschaften zu Göttingen', *Nachrichten von der Königlichen Gesellschaft der Wissenschaften* (1892), 53–104; Richard Fick, 'Michaelis und die Krisis des Jahres 1763', in *Beiträge zur Göttinger Bibliotheks- und Gelehrtengeschichte* (Göttingen: Vandenhoeck & Ruprecht, 1928), 40–54.

[33] Michaelis, *Lebensbeschreibung*, 41–3.

[34] Richard Toellner, 'Entstehung und Programm der Göttinger Gelehrten Gesellschaft unter besonderer Berücksichtigung des Hallerschen Wissenschaftsbegriffes', in Fritz Hartmann and Rudolf Vierhaus (eds), *Der Akademiegedanke im 17. und 18. Jahrhundert* (Bremen and Wolfenbüttel: Jacobi, 1977), 104; Otto Sonntag, 'Albrecht Von Haller on the Future of Science', *Journal of the History of Ideas* 35 (1974), 313–22; Hubert Steinke, Urs Boschung, and Wolfgang Pross (eds), *Albrecht von Haller: Leben—Werk—Epoche* (Göttingen: Wallstein, 2008).

scholarship from Haller himself as well as from the contemporary professor of classical literature at Göttingen, Johann Matthias Gesner. Gesner and his successor, Chrisian Gottlob Heyne, aimed at a new understanding of antiquity which would edify citizens of the modern state. Instead of philological hypotheses and writing exercises, they emphasized reading and comprehension, trying to convey the aesthetic characteristics of ancient texts. Their colleague Michaelis shared this methodology and the adherence to Haller's scientific ethos, seeing history and philology as disciplines engaged in the advancement of knowledge and its critical assessment rather than mere transmission.[35]

Michaelis propagated Haller's notion of scholarship after his mentor's early departure for Bern (1753) in his own academic activities and as Secretary and Director of the Göttingen Royal Society. Vestiges of this conviction may be perceived in a project Michaelis was pursuing at the time he worked on the prize essay and its extended French version: a scientific expedition to the Arabian peninsula. The idea was first expounded by Michaelis in a letter to the Danish foreign minister 1756, in which he suggested sending a scholar to *Felix Arabia* to examine biblical references to the fauna, flora, customs, rites, and miracles mentioned in the Bible.[36] From the outset Michaelis insisted that the explorer should not be a missionary or a clergyman, emphasizing the academic standards of the envisaged expedition.[37] King Frederick V was persuaded to fund the expedition, which gradually grew to include six participants: the Swedish botanist Peter Forsskål, a student of Linnaeus's who learned oriental languages under Michaelis in Göttingen; the Danish philologist Friedrich von Haven, another student of Michaelis's; the German engineer and mathematician Carsten Niebuhr; the Danish physician Christian Kramer; the German illustrator Georg Baurenfeind; and a Swedish butler named Berggren. The explorers embarked on their voyage in January 1761, but by 1763 all but Niebuhr died in the East. Niebuhr finally returned to Europe only in 1767, publishing his Description of Arabia in 1772.[38]

---

[35] Thomas Howard, *Protestant Theology and the Making of the Modern German University* (Oxford: Oxford University Press, 2006), 118–19; Legaspi, *Death of Scripture*, 53–78.
[36] Michaelis, *Literarischer Briefwechsel*, ed. Johann Gottlieb Buhle (Leipzig: Weidmannsche Buchhandlung, 1794–6), i. 297–333 and 348–66.
[37] Michaelis, *Lebensbeschreibung*, 66.
[38] Carsten Niebuhr, *Beschreibung von Arabien: Aus eigenen Beobachtungen und im Lande selbst gesammleten Nachrichten* (Copenhagen: Nicolaus Möller, 1772); *Reisebeschreibung nach Arabien und andern umliegenden Ländern* (Copenhagen: Nicolaus Möller, 1774–8). See also Michaelis, *Lebensbeschreibung*, 66–76; Thorkild Hansen, *Arabia Felix: The Danish Expedition of 1761–1767*, trans. James and Kathleen McFarlane (London: Collins, 1964); Stig Rasmussen (ed.), *Carsten Niebuhr und die Arabische Reise 1761-67* (Heide: Boyens, 1986); Wolf Feuerhahn, 'A Theologian's List and an Anthropologist's Prose: Michaelis, Niebuhr, and the Expedition to *Felix Arabia*', in Peter Becker and William Clark (eds),

This ill-fated expedition was a unique case among eighteenth-century scientific voyages. While earlier expeditions were supposed to put scientific theories to practical test or gather information on unknown territories as a prelude for colonization, Michaelis's idea was to explore a region not too distant from Europe for the roots of western civilization itself. The Arabian peninsula and its inhabitants, allegedly maintaining some original biblical features, were supposed to yield insights into the obscure origins of ancient language and law. Instead of providing the explorers with general guidelines, as in expeditions aimed at commercial profit or mapping, Michaelis consulted the entire Republic of Letters in order to produce the most detailed set of instructions. In an advertisement in the *Göttingische Anzeigen* he introduced von Haven, Forsskål, and Niebuhr, explaining the all-encompassing aims of the planned expedition.[39] By presenting the expedition as a project of the entire scholarly community Michaelis may have attempted to attract attention to his—and Göttingen's—energetic pursuit of 'discovery and research' in what would later become the humanities. This strategy was indeed successful, resulting in questions from professors, pastors, civil servants, physicians, botanists, and biblical scholars based in Germany, Britain, the Netherlands, and France. The Parisian Académie des Inscriptions even sent in an entire treatise on relevant topics, which Michaelis printed as a supplement to his instructions to the explorers. His volume of instructions included a hundred questions, many of them accompanied by detailed background information. They concerned, among other issues, biblical references to the habitats and behaviour of animals, local diseases, the taste and use of oriental plants, climatic phenomena, the ebb and flow in the Red Sea, stones and gems, and local dialects in their relation to enigmatic Hebrew phrases.

In his programmatic preface Michaelis presented his model of a scientific expedition as distinct from commercial and colonial ones. Scholarly explorers must be intensively prepared for their mission, equipped with profound knowledge of the land and its languages before they set sail. Communication by means of an interpreter was not enough: the travellers had to note down proper names in local characters and memorize their exact pronunciation.[40] Beyond their insufficient knowledge of

---

Little Tools of Knowledge: Historical Essays on Academic and Bureaucratic Practices (Ann Arbor: University of Michigan Press, 2001), 141–68; Sheehan, *Enlightenment Bible*, 186–99; Carhart, *Science of Culture*, 27–44.

[39] *Göttingische Anzeigen von gelehrten Sachen*, 7 February 1760 (Göttingen: Pockwitz & Barmeier), 130–1.
[40] Michaelis, 'Vorrede', in *Fragen an eine Gesellschaft gelehrter Männer, die auf Befehl Ihro Majestät des Königes von Dännemark nach Arabien reisen* (Frankfurt am Main: Johann Gottlieb Garbe, 1762), a3^v–a4^r.

indigenous languages, Michaelis deemed most travellers useless for scholarship because they were 'abandoned to their own curiosity'. As reflected by the number and profundity of his questions, Michaelis's purpose was to maintain total control from Göttingen over the explorers' methods of inquiry. Upon arriving in a foreign country, exposed to a completely different culture, travellers were usually struck by wonder, seeing too many things at once while unable to perceive any of them distinctly. Back in Europe they produced enthusiastic tales of marvel and exoticism, focused on personal experience and lacking a systematic analysis of their findings. According to Michaelis, only the European scholar could properly direct the gaze of the travellers from a critical distance, assisted by a serious library.[41]

The training and control of the explorers' gaze, so significant in Michaelis's conception of a scientific expedition, led him to criticize cabinets of curiosities and collections of natural history, some of the traditional ways of learning about nature. Cabinets might indeed contain some relevant information, but they were intended to overwhelm visitors in the same way that exotic phenomena engulfed the unprepared traveller abroad. There was too much for the eye to perceive and scrutinize in those cabinets, where nature was fashionably domesticated for no practical purpose.[42] Michaelis, who was advocating a systematic approach to learning, had no time for such cabinets nor for the commercial use of curiosities. Science was for Michaelis an unquantifiable and edifying enterprise. Accordingly, he derided mercantile expeditions and encouraged monarchs to fund journeys for the sake of scholarship alone instead of treating science as a financial venture.[43]

For all their meticulous compilation, Michaelis's instructions did not have the intended impact on their addressees. Though the manuscript was sent to the explorers in Egypt, it did not reach them there. Niebuhr first received the instructions in Tranquebar, before his second visit to the Arabian peninsula. Many of the questions were intended for Forsskål and Haven, who had already died. In his autobiography, written more than twenty years after the fact, Michaelis still seemed to resent the explorers for their premature deaths. The tragedy was amplified for him by the disorderly manner in which they kept their notes, contrary to his instructions.[44] Michaelis's handbook to the Arabian explorers nevertheless remains a milestone of Enlightenment scholarship and the perspicuous distillation of an academic creed, mirroring some of the themes he tackled

---

[41] Ibid. a4ᵛ–a5ʳ. See Jürgen Osterhammel, *Die Entzauberung Asiens: Europa und die asiatischen Reiche im 18. Jahrhundert* (Munich: Beck, 1998), chs. 6 and 7.
[42] Michaelis, *Fragen*, b5ʳ–b5ᵛ.
[43] Ibid. c1ᵛ–c2ʳ.   [44] Michaelis, *Lebensbeschreibung*, 75.

in the prize essay. This volume became a comprehensive guide to scientific exploration in general, widely read before and after Niebuhr's return. Robert Wood was not its only admirer: Johann Reihnold Forster kept a copy of Michaelis's *Fragen* aboard James Cook's expedition to the Pacific.[45]

ANCIENT LEGISLATION: THE CASE OF THE HEBREWS

By the late 1750s Michaelis's name as an innovative researcher had been established to the extent that foreign scholars made a special pilgrimage to Göttingen to consult him on all matters oriental. In 1757, a year before Michaelis wrote his entry for the Berlin contest, he gave a series of private tutorials to Olaus Rabenius, professor of law at the University of Uppsala. The work that originated in these tutorials would be published in the early 1770s as a six-volume book entitled *Mosaisches Recht* (*Mosaic Law*), but a short overview of its background may elucidate the new ideas Michaelis was entertaining in the late 1750s.[46]

The ecumenical interest in all aspects of Near Eastern antiquity, so manifest in Michaelis's Arabian project, was reiterated over the pages of *Mosaisches Recht*—which indeed partly drew on the instructions to the explorers and on Niebuhr's account of Arabia. In its six volumes Michaelis discussed Jewish public, private, international, and criminal law; analysed social norms (such as polygamy and revenge in the name of family honour); reviewed environmental and zoological phenomena; and observed agricultural and economic practices, from horse- and sheepbreeding to international commerce. This work was not merely intended for philologists, orientalists, and theologians. Michaelis addressed it specifically to statesmen and civil servants interested in the evolution of legal systems. It is in this respect that Michaelis saw Montesquieu as his main inspiration, though his language also betrayed a debt to Leibniz, Wolff, and the application of their philosophy to historical scholarship by the pioneers of the so-called Göttingen School (particularly Chladenius and Gatterer). Like them Michaelis believed that a historical phenomenon, be it a singular event, a social custom or a legislative act, must be seen within

---

[45] Michaelis, *Briefwechsel*, iii. 55, 373–4; Thomas Biskup, 'The University of Göttingen and the Personal Union, 1737–1837', in Brendan Simms and Torsten Riotte (eds), *The Hanoverian Dimension in British History* (Cambridge: Cambridge University Press, 2007), 146–8.

[46] Michaelis, *Mosaisches Recht* (Frankfurt am Main: Johann Gottlieb Garbe, 1770–5). My references are to the third Frankfurt edition of 1793.

a Wolffian *nexus rerum* or its *Zusammenhang*, the mutual connection and agreement of facts that wove them into a harmonious whole. Only by delving into the intricate relations between environmental, social, and intellectual factors could interpreters attain sufficient knowledge of their subject.[47] By closely analysing a legal system that seemed on its surface absurd or illogical, Michaelis repeated the lesson he wished to convey to the Arabian explorers. Just as the eye must be trained not to fall prey to overwhelming wonders, the mind should strive to consider historical records in their myriad contexts, comparing them to similar documents from other cultures and periods.

Michaelis's aims were not too different from those of Giambattista Vico, who had generalized from accounts of classical antiquity a universal theory of human evolution (even if the two differed on the place of ancient Israel within this scheme). This method of generalization and comparative analysis rendered improbable any direct contact between distant cultures. It was not necessary to postulate immediate influence in order to explain comparable laws and customs: such resemblances could be traced to analogous circumstances in the two cultures. Noting a similarity, for example, between reports on Mongolian marital patterns and a relevant account in the Old Testament, Michaelis rejected the hypothesis that the Mongolians could have descended from the ten lost tribes of Israel.[48] All nations followed universal stages of progress from 'childhood' or a 'state of nature' to civil society. The state of nature posited here was not a hypothetical condition but an actual one, observable in distant civilizations, from which Europeans might learn about the emergence of their own culture. Michaelis wished to show that the familiar Bible could, just like travel accounts, endow its readers with insights that would relativize their social and legal systems.[49] Such a view of cultural development prized empirical observation, as testified by the popular fascination with American and Pacific cultures beyond the more elitist appeal of classical Greece and Rome. Michaelis believed that Near Eastern civilization could make both ends meet: like Homeric Greece it had ancient records attesting to

---

[47] Michaelis, *Mosaisches Recht*, i. 1–2. See also Rudolf Vierhaus, 'Montesquieu in Deutschland: Zur Geschichte seiner Wirkung als politischer Schriftsteller im 18. Jahrhundert', in *Collegium Philosophicum: Studien Joachim Ritter zum 60. Geburtstag* (Basel: Schwabe, 1965), 403–37.

[48] Ibid. ii. 197–200. In *Mosaisches Recht*, ii. 13–18, Michaelis similarly discarded the identification of Plato's Atlantians with biblical Jews, as expounded by Frédéric Charles Baer in *Essai historique et critique sur les Atlantiques, dans lequel on se propose de faire voir la conformité qu'il y a entre l'Histoire de ce peuple, & celle des Hébreux* (Paris: Michel Lambert, 1762).

[49] For the larger framework of such developments, see Sheehan, *Enlightenment Bible*, 93–217.

original genius, while it could also be observed in its unadulterated form. For Michaelis, the tents of Abraham and his folk still existed among nomadic Bedouins in the Arabian peninsula, a region where history stood still.[50]

Contemporaries like Eichhorn did not fail to perceive a conspicuous difference between Michaelis's analysis and the Renaissance scholarship of Olaus Rudbeck and Samuel Bochart, whose works Michaelis reassessed in the light of new data.[51] Whereas comparative etymology between distant languages had been a common scholarly tool in the preceding century, still employed by Michaelis's father, he circumscribed its application. Unlike some of his predecessors, Michaelis also did not interpret biblical chronology in a literal manner. Though Genesis explained geographical and other phenomena in a causal way, it did not constitute a reliable account of global history. The Old Testament could teach us only about the predicament of the ancient Hebrews and their neighbours, from which, however, important lessons could be gleaned.[52]

According to Michaelis, Mosaic law replaced and improved an older, nomadic legal code, a *jus consuetudinarium* (customary or common law).[53] This primitive law, discernible in the Book of Job or among Arabian nomads, was superseded by the legal and social innovations Moses borrowed from Egypt, where he had been raised as a prince. As the Egyptians had built a sophisticated polity over generations, Moses followed their example by basing the Jewish state on systematic agriculture in order to keep his people self-sufficient and independent.[54] Contradictions between biblical laws exposed the tensions between Moses's philosophical system and the rawer customary law, for Moses could not have forced his people to abandon their old habits at once. He had to accommodate his legislation to popular customs and beliefs, maintaining such older nomadic norms as polygamy or the obligatory marriage of a childless widow to her brother-in-law. This observation demonstrates Michaelis's view of legislation in the *longue durée*, which he regarded as one of the main lessons of the Old Testament. Legislators must respect deep-rooted rights and conduct, and reforms could only be gradually implemented. No single set of principles could be universally valid for all states or immutably followed

---

[50] Michaelis, *Mosaisches Recht*, i. 13.   [51] Eichhorn, 'Michaelis', 848–50.
[52] Michaelis admitted that the Old Testament provided no reliable chronology, while arguing that its historical account was still more reliable than others. (Michaelis, *Zerstreute kleine Schriften* (Jena: Akademische Buchhandlung, 1793–4), 267–8.)
[53] Michaelis, *Mosaisches Recht*, i. 10–14.
[54] Michaelis's benign account of Egyptian culture (*Mosaisches Recht*, i. 16) may have served as a template for Herder's similar view in 1774 (Herder, *Schriften zu Philosophie, Literatur, Kunst und Altertum 1774–1787*, ed. Jürgen Brummack and Martin Bollacher (Frankfurt am Main: Deutscher Klassiker Verlag, 1994), 19–30).

even in a single polity. Against religious zealots Michaelis argued that Moses allowed for future modifications of his laws, such as the establishment of a monarchy, while repeatedly declaring that Mosaic laws did not bind modern Europeans. Their value lay in illuminating the elaborate links between natural circumstances, social traditions, and actual legislation. Should eighteenth-century lawgivers wish to follow Moses' lead, they must enact laws suitable to their own circumstances—which differed substantially from those of the ancient Jews in Sinai.

Michaelis's treatment of the Bible as cultural history was accompanied by his refusal to read into the Old Testament typological or symbolic announcements of Christ's coming. In this respect *Mosaisches Recht* could be perceived as echoing new, controversial interpretations of the Old Testament, from Spinoza's *Tractatus Theologico-Politicus* (1670) to Johann Lorenz Schmidt's Wertheim Bible (1735). Michaelis was well aware of this point, raised by conservative critics following the publication of the first instalment of *Mosaisches Recht*. He retorted that symbolic interpretation was simply irrelevant to an analysis of the Old Testament by 'a jurist or someone who philosophises on legislative wisdom'.[55] However, despite this distinction between theological exegesis and historical-critical analysis, Michaelis did not go as far as some of the Neologists. His analysis of Mosaic laws reads as a genuine confirmation of God's providence rather than mere lip service to tradition. Michaelis never denied the divine nature of biblical laws or Moses' authorship of the Pentateuch, but in his eyes providence worked indirectly, by inspiring Moses to borrow certain political structures from the Egyptians.[56] In a commentary on a French essay about the crossing of the Red Sea, Michaelis justified in 1758 the interpretation of miracles as extreme natural phenomena rather than cases of direct divine intervention. He saw the supernatural aspect of the story in Moses' foreknowledge that a peculiar storm would occur. The actual exposure of the seabed was an exceptional yet entirely natural event.[57]

Michaelis's belief in divine providence, accompanied by his sharp historical sense, led him to criticize some of the more radical methods espoused by contemporary interpreters such as Johann Salomo Semler. As mentioned in Chapter 2, Semler tried to separate divine content from historical context, regarding the latter as superfluous to the purely ethical

---

[55] Michaelis, *Mosaisches Recht*, iv. 3–4. See also Michaelis's earlier work, *Entwurf der typischen Gottesgelartheit*, 2nd edn (Göttingen: Universitäts-Buchhandlung, 1753).

[56] Michaelis presented multiple reasons for upholding the Mosaic authorship of the Pentateuch in *Einleitung in die göttlichen Schriften des Alten Bundes* (Hamburg: Bohnsche Buchhandlung, 1787), i. 150–229.

[57] Pierre Hardy, *Essai physique sur l'heure des marées dans la mer rouge, comparée avec l'heure du passage des Hébreux*, ed. J. D. Michaelis (Göttingen: Pockwitz & Barmeier, 1758), 4.

core of the Bible and thus irrelevant to moral edification. Michaelis, by contrast, argued that one could glean from the Old Testament illuminating insights into culture and history even without distilling its moral core. In his review of the first volume of Semler's *Abhandlung von freier Untersuchung des Canon* (*Treatise on the Free Examination of the Canon*, 1771) Michaelis politely but forcefully rejected what he saw as a 'pick and choose' attitude to the Bible. First, as demonstrated in his instructions to the explorers and in *Mosaisches Recht*, Michaelis regarded the Old Testament as a mine of botanical, statistical, and historical facts, even if it could not be read as a reliable chronology. Secondly, treating certain biblical books as devoid of ethical utility was anachronistic in Michaelis's eyes. The laws of Moses were not enacted for the betterment of eighteenth-century readers; they had been carefully grafted on to nomadic customs to forge a settled nation out of a wandering tribe. Finally, Michaelis saw Semler's distinction between inspired and superfluous biblical loci as arbitrary if not dangerous, for it could easily play into the hands of radical deists and atheists.[58]

Michaelis mounted here a serious attack on personal claims to know the so-called 'ethical core' of things, especially in regard to the Bible. Referring to Semler and others as preferring some 'emotional stirrings of the soul' to sound knowledge, Michaelis alluded to radical Pietists and other fervent reformers, usually derided by Enlightenment thinkers as 'enthusiasts' (*Schwärmer*).[59] It is clear, however, from the general tone of Michaelis's review that he regarded Semler as a fellow *Aufklärer* rather than a foe: the slight antagonism may be attributed to Semler's disregard of the cultural insights that could be teased out of the Old Testament. For Michaelis, traces of providence were not to be found only in moral precepts or symbolic prophecies but in the correspondence between the natural circumstances of the ancient Israelites and their laws and literature. As he emphasized in *Mosaisches Recht*, Moses' were not the perfect laws in an absolute sense. The lawgiver's divine inspiration consisted in devising the best system for a concrete, historically given group of human beings in their transition from a state of nature to a higher stage of civilization.[60]

---

[58] Michaelis, *Orientalische und exegetische Bibliothek*, iii (Frankfurt: Johann Gottlieb Garbe, 1772), 26–96, here 69.

[59] On reactions to religious enthusiasm, see A. J. La Vopa, 'The Philosopher and the *Schwärmer*: On the Career of a German Epithet from Luther to Kant', in L. E. Klein and A. J. La Vopa (eds), *Enthusiasm and Enlightenment in Europe, 1650–1850* (San Marino, Calif.: Huntington Library, 1998), 85–115. See also Michael Heyd, '*Be Sober and Reasonable': The Critique of Enthusiasm in the Seventeenth and Early Eighteenth Centuries* (Leiden: Brill, 1995); J. G. A. Pocock, *Barbarism and Religion*, i: *The Enlightenments of Edward Gibbon, 1737–1764* (Cambridge: Cambridge University Press, 1999), 13–27 and 50–71.

[60] Michaelis, *Mosaisches Recht*, i. 20.

NATURAL EVOLUTION: THE CASE OF HEBREW

The change contemporaries perceived in *Mosaisches Recht* from older modes of scholarship to systematic analysis was arguably all the more apparent in Michaelis's theory of language. As Michaelis let his first book be reprinted in 1753, we can assume that his change of heart concerning the antiquity of the Hebrew vowel points was completed only in the mid-1750s.[61] From 1757 onwards, he frequently criticized any exceptional treatment of Hebrew and its vowel points. This was part of his assault on scholars who, inspired by the biblical account of Adam's language, were trying to recover a bygone correspondence between words and world. As noted in Chapter 1, various early modern authors believed that Adam's prelapsarian wisdom endowed him with direct insight into the essence of things. Words in his idiom should have accurately conveyed the structure, function, and meaning of what they stood for, without recourse to the imperfections of human understanding. Michaelis's critique was levelled at scholars who tried to trace the vestiges of such an Adamic idiom either in European vernaculars or in such ancient languages as Hebrew. The target here was a mélange of Christian Hebraism, religious millenarianism, and the seventeenth-century search for 'real characters'.

The Hermetic tradition, tracing the origin of clandestine forms of knowledge back to ancient Egypt, was another significant source on which Michaelis's culprits drew. The discovery of Horapollo's *Hieroglyphica* in 1419 stimulated what Jan Assmann has called a 'semiotic revolution': an increasing attention to the Platonic suggestion of an essential connection between signs and things, at the expense of Aristotle's doctrine of linguistic conventionality. Renaissance Neo-Platonism and the general interest in the hieroglyphic script channelled the debate between Aristotelian conventionalists and Platonic essentialists into the realm of writing systems. Scholars from Marsilio Ficino to Ralph Cudworth and Thomas Browne lamented the transition from a pictorial script to a phonetically based alphabet as one of the main impediments to human communication.[62]

In the eighteenth century William Warburton's influential *Divine Legation of Moses* (1738–41) countered the Hermetic hypothesis that the Egyptian hieroglyphs concealed esoteric wisdom. Warburton argued that

---

[61] In 1769 Michaelis admitted that after 1750 he increasingly deviated from the common Protestant view of the vowel points. ('Vorrede der ersten Ausgabe', in *Deutsche Uebersetzung des Alten Testaments* (Göttingen and Gotha: Johann Christian Dieterich, 1773), xii.)

[62] Jan Assmann, *Moses the Egyptian: The Memory of Egypt in Western Monotheism* (Cambridge, Mass.: Harvard University Press, 1997), 102–4.

the hieroglyphic script was merely a primitive form of writing by images, intended for popular use and arising out of natural necessity. Refuting Athanasius Kircher's thesis that the hieroglyphs concealed recondite wisdom, Warburton presented a naturalistic history of language and mind, arguing that no script had ever been invented for cryptic purposes. On the contrary, ease of communication was always the main impulse for the notation of sounds.[63] The regrettable abuse of the hieroglyphs for cryptic, political purposes was a later development occurring after the introduction of a phonetic alphabet. No admirer of Warburton, Michaelis still shared with the quarrelsome Bishop of Gloucester the refusal to see in the hieroglyphs—or in any human script—vestiges of recondite wisdom and mysterious first meanings.[64] Though Michaelis took care to refute Warburton's central argument about Jewish uniqueness, he might have gleaned from *The Divine Legation* some pertinent ideas about language, just as Condillac and Rousseau did in the 1740s and 1750s.[65]

Michaelis was particularly concerned to refute what he called the 'hieroglyphic thesis', a quasi-Cabbalistic view of language. His critique was elaborated in a treatise on the study of Hebrew, *Beurtheilung der Mittel welche man anwendet die ausgestorbene hebräische Sprache zu verstehen* (*Assessment of the Means Used to Understand the Dead Hebrew Language*, 1757). 'Hieroglyphic' interpreters ascribed first meanings to the Hebrew letters independently of their combination or context. For example, the letter Aleph (א) represented action and movement, while Beth (ב) allegedly denoted three-dimensional bodies. Words were therefore clusters of significations constructed out of letters according to their coalesced meanings.[66] While mentioning Friedrich Christian Koch and Caspar Neumann as advocates of this theory, Michaelis referred to a broader scholarly tradition, namely the view that Hebrew was extraordinarily exempt from constant change. Michaelis noted by contrast that in Hebrew, as in all other tongues, one could discern orthographic alterations, contraction of forms, and various registers employed in different times. The empirical observation of natural linguistic change would, according to Michaelis in 1757, suffice to refute the hieroglyphic theory, with clear consequences. The Hebrew of the Old Testament could not have been Adam's God-given

---

[63] Warburton, *Divine Legation*, ii. 4.4, 150–5. See also Chapter 1 above: cf. David Porter, *Ideographia: The Chinese Cipher in Early Modern Europe* (Stanford, Calif.: Stanford University Press, 2001).

[64] Though in 1753 Michaelis compared the typological interpretation of the Old Testament to signification through hieroglyphs, he did not suggest that the Hebrew script itself had any recondite meanings (*Entwurf der typischen Gottesgelartheit*, 4–11).

[65] For Michaelis's critique of Warburton's argument, see *Mosaisches Recht*, i. 51–2.

[66] Michaelis, *Beurtheilung der Mittel, welche man anwendet, die ausgestorbene hebräische Sprache zu verstehen* (Göttingen: Abram van den Hoeks Witwe, 1757), 94, 114–17.

language due to the myriad modifications it must have undergone since creation—if it had ever been a perfect, essence-revealing language.[67] Though Michaelis did not refer here directly to the antiquity of the vowel points, his stance in 1757 ran contrary to his views around 1740 about the exceptional antiquity of the Hebrew accents and vowel points, their relative lack of change over millennia, and the assumption that these diacritical marks were already in use at the time of Moses.

Michaelis's attempt to refute the Cabbalistic-hieroglyphic view of Hebrew led him to an extensive discussion of the origin of language, which he would soon complement with his prize essay on language and opinions. His pivotal arguments against the hieroglyphic theory were that all languages had been spoken before they were written; that the first and basic units of language were syllables, not letters or single consonants; and that words emerged naturally over time without intentional design.[68] Methodologically, Michaelis recommended an empirical approach to the question of linguistic origins, consisting either in the examination of ancient literature or in the present observation of language acquisition by children and the impaired. In a similar manner to the Epicurean account of the origin of language, Michaelis likened its emergence among sociable human beings to its development in infants. The latter, Michaelis insisted, did not learn language by imitation but through vocal experimentation, a self-motivated process with minimal environmental input.[69] Michaelis argued that the emergence of language followed natural trajectories dictated by material needs, emotions, and social interaction. The space for manoeuvre available to the first speakers was further limited by human physiology, so that no original correspondence between sound and meaning could have been devised. Michaelis's preference for children as his 'master instructors' on this front instead of those who 'philosophize in another world' was targeted at the hieroglyphic thesis, but it may well be considered as a general comment about method. Generalizations were better drawn from experience rather than from abstract reasoning about the perfection of language or the convenience of its speakers—the very arguments Michaelis himself had used in 1741.[70]

This naturalistic theory of the emergence of language would eventually lead Michaelis to acknowledge publicly the errors in his initial view of Hebrew and its vowel points. The full retraction of his youthful defence of the antiquity and immutability of the Hebrew vowel points was made in an essay published in 1769, *Von dem Alter der Hebräischen Vocalen und übrigen Punkte* (*On the Age of the Hebrew Vowels and Other Points*).

---

[67] Ibid. 93. [68] Ibid. 91–3, 99–101, 108–14.
[69] Ibid. 100. [70] Ibid. 103.

Michealis wrote the essay to justify his frequent departure from the Masoretic vowel points in his forthcoming German translation of the Old Testament. It was his 'debt to the public', Michaelis claimed, to disown what he had asserted in his doctoral dissertation and in his first book. Even if the Jews did use vowel points in ancient times, as he had previously argued, the points in modern editions of the Bible were a new 'Masoretic invention'.[71] Reviewing once again the confessional debate, Michaelis categorically rejected any theological presuppositions. In stark contrast to his father, great uncle, and his own early views, Michaelis criticized any case for the antiquity of the vowel points based on the perfection of Hebrew, the needs of its modern readers, or God's foreknowledge. Instead, Michaelis pleaded with his readers to treat the whole question on historical rather than theological ground.

> In a historical question, concerned with what happened or did not happen, one must not resort to theological motives derived from God's wisdom or benevolence. We are too short-sighted to see in advance what God must have done, designed, allowed, or prevented. Our issue is merely historical, for the question of whether the Bible was originally written with vowel points presupposes another: have the oriental languages always had vowel points? How certain would it be to suggest so only because providence owes it to us to have formed with vowel points the alphabet of any language in which Revelation would later be given?[72]

Michaelis also went on to argue that reading without vowels, a difficult challenge to contemporary scholars, must have actually been very natural for ancient Jews who spoke Hebrew fluently.

From the denial that certain features of Hebrew have been immutably maintained throughout history, Michaelis extended his critique to the notion that language could have ever been intentionally designed. Here we find one of the tenets of his mature theory of linguistic evolution: emergence over a large span of time, based on necessary change through trial and error. Michaelis finally ascribed the omission of vowels to frequent use and haste, both natural impulses requiring no premeditation or conscious decision.[73]

* * *

The projects Michaelis undertook at the end of the 1750s shared a noteworthy similarity. A strong emphasis on the empirical examination of historical records and living models (such as children and Bedouin nomads) was discernible in all of them, alongside a resolute critique of

---

[71] Michaelis, 'Von dem Alter der Hebräischen Vocalen, und übrigen Punkte', in *Vermischte Schriften*, ii (Frankfurt am Main: Johann Gottlieb Garbe, 1769), 2.
[72] Ibid. 91.   [73] Ibid. 103.

earlier scholarship. The methods of Kircher, Rudbeck, and Michaelis's own ancestors were rejected; fantastic narratives and fanciful genealogies were replaced by the critical assessment of data. This scholarly outlook—so closely identified with Michaelis's name in the late eighteenth century—should not be underestimated, for his education was not necessarily conducive to such later views.

Michaelis annotated Lowth's *Lectures*, planned the Arabian expedition and taught Mosaic legislation at the time he was completing his change of mind concerning the Hebrew vowel points. He resorted to naturalistic arguments about the regular emergence of Hebrew, as well as all other languages, following his rejection of two interchangeable notions: the belief that Hebrew was the original, divinely inspired tongue, and the search for a perfect language reflecting the nature of things. It was through an original critique of the views he had been inculcated with that Michaelis arrived at similar conclusions to those expounded in conjectural histories in the Epicurean vein. Michaelis's critical engagement with his ancestral legacy demonstrates that innovative syntheses could originate in a philological debate that might have seemed merely antiquarian to Enlightenment observers.[74] The early modern controversy over the Hebrew vowel points served Michaelis as a launchpad for his mature theory of how linguistic signs shape the human mind, how the mind transforms these signs, and how language and the understanding evolved together over time.

The public withdrawal of his initial endorsement of the antiquity of the vowel points could not have been easy for a scholar whose expertise was renowned across Europe. Indeed, Michaelis presented his new views on Hebrew in the late 1750s, whereas the actual retraction of his early claims was printed only in 1769. It seems that the widespread acclaim following the French translation of the prize essay (1762), perhaps also his father's death (1764), enabled Michaelis to be more open about his change of mind and to disclaim publicly his ancestral legacy. In later years he would criticize his great uncle's 'blind enthusiasm' for the Masoretic text of the Bible and his father's penchant for unsound etymologies.[75] However, even without explicit references to his own early work, Michaelis's mature views of language were amply manifest in his prize essay of 1759.

---

[74] On antiquarianism and the Enlightenment, the classic statement remains Arnaldo Momigliano, 'Ancient History and the Antiquarian', *Journal of the Warburg and Courtauld Institutes* 13 (1950), 285–315. See also Peter N. Miller (ed.), *Momigliano and Antiquarianism: Foundations of the Modern Cultural Sciences* (Toronto: University of Toronto Press, 2007).

[75] *Orientalische und Exegetische Bibliothek*, ii (1771), 142–3; Michaelis, *Lebensbeschreibung*, 26.

5

A Point of Convergence and New Departures

The 1759 Contest on Language and Opinions

On the evening of 31 May 1759 André Pierre Le Guay de Prémontval could hardly hold his breath. Having rushed from the Berlin Academy on Unter den Linden back to his home on the nearby Behrenstraße, he immediately wrote to his close correspondent in Göttingen, Johann David Michaelis. Wishing his letter were airborne, Prémontval conveyed personally what the Academy had officially declared.

> I have just come out of our public Assembly; I put my hand to the quill and wish I could give wings to my letter, so that it would precede the one in the name of the Academy which you will probably receive in the same delivery. If CHANCE, for which I have struggled so much, will serve me well in this case, you will open my own letter first, and I shall have the joy of informing you of the success of your excellent Piece, which WE HAVE JUST CROWNED![1]

This chapter is dedicated to the prize essay Prémontval was so enthusiastic about. The examination of Michaelis's treatise is preceded by a tentative reconstruction of the procedure that led to its crowning and a review of some of the submitted entries. These essays can provide significant insights into the ways in which the prize question was interpreted by contemporaries. The analysis of the prize essay itself is then followed by a survey of several responses to it. Some of the reactions might have been expected from thinkers who had been involved in the Berlin debates before 1759, such as Mendelssohn and Formey. But the contest also attracted the keen interest of intellectuals throughout Europe, from d'Alembert in Paris to the self-styled 'magus of the north', Johann Georg Hamann in Königsberg, and even further afield in America. These responses played a significant

---

[1] Michaelis, *Briefwechsel*, i. 151–2. By 'chance' Prémontval referred to his book *Du Hazard sous l'empire de la Providence, pour servir de préservatif contre la doctrine du Fatalisme moderne* (Berlin: J. C. Kluter, 1755).

role in keeping language, mind, and their joint origins the topic of vigorous discussions in Berlin throughout the 1760s.

ACADEMIC ARRANGEMENTS AND EXPECTATIONS

According to the Academy's instructions, entries for its contests were submitted anonymously, accompanied by a separate envelope including the author's name and the *symbolum* (prefatory quote) of the essay. If their work was not successful, authors sometimes reclaimed their essays. It is not clear why no entries from the 1759 contest remain today in the Academy's archive, where one can find only Michaelis's confirmation of his receipt of the actual prize, a golden medal worth 50 ducats.[2] In the absence of such documentation, the scant available information on the institutional aspects of the prize contest must be gleaned from the correspondence between Prémontval and Michaelis.

Along with Prémontval, the jury was composed of the Academy's Perpetual Secretary Formey, his deputy Jean Bernard Merian, and Johann Georg Sulzer. Sulzer, an ordinary member since 1750, was usually allied with the Wolffians at the Academy who rallied around Formey in the bitter debates over Leibniz and Wolff. In the late 1750s Sulzer believed that Merian and Prémontval were defaming Wolffian philosophy at the service of the President Maupertuis, whose scientific merit Sulzer questioned.[3] Prémontval can certainly be viewed as one of the most anti-Wolffian among local academicians, but the controversy over Wolff's philosophy did not entail a clear national or linguistic divide. Leonhard Euler, a German-speaking Swiss like Sulzer, championed the anti-Wolffian cause early on, while the French-speaking Huguenots tended to follow Wolff. The Swiss Merian trod his own careful path between the camps, despite Sulzer's suspicions. Maupertuis does not seem to have played a significant role in the 1759 contest, suffering from a terminal illness which had kept him away from Berlin since 1756. He died at the Bernoulli household in Basel in July 1759.

In the case of the prize essay it seems that Merian, Prémontval, and Sulzer voted together for Michaelis's (as yet anonymous) piece, whereas Formey preferred a French essay. Though Michaelis and Prémontval had

---

[2] Berlin, Archiv der Berlin-Brandenburgischen Akademie der Wissenschaften, Michaelis to the Academy, I-XVI-125 (22), 231.

[3] Winter (ed.), *Registres*, 58. On Sulzer see Hans Erich Bödeker, 'Konzept und Klassifikation der Wissenschaften bei Johann Georg Sulzer (1720–1779)', in Fontius and Holzhey (eds), *Schweizer im Berlin*, 325–39; Johan van de Zande, 'Orpheus in Berlin: A Reappraisal of Johann Georg Sulzer's Theory of the Polite Arts', *Central European History* 28 (1995), 175–208. On Merian see Jens Häseler, 'Johann Bernhard Merian—ein Schweizer Philosoph an der Berliner Akademie', in *Schweizer im Berlin*, 217–30.

been close correspondents since 1753, it is hard to believe Prémontval knew which entry was his friend's—especially as he required his colleagues' assistance in mastering the sense of most German entries.[4] Prémontval believed that Michaelis had composed one of the Latin entries but still voted for the German essay. Writing to Michaelis after the fact, Prémontval proudly claimed that his professional standards prevailed over friendship to the benefit of all involved.[5]

A substantial number of Academy members became acquainted with the prize essay through the summary read by Merian in the public assembly of 31 May 1759, the meeting that Prémontval hurriedly left in order to write to Michaelis. Merian's overview of the prize essay was also printed in the official collection next to the German original.[6] The Deputy Secretary wished, first of all, to explain retrospectively why the class of speculative philosophy had chosen the reciprocal influence of language and opinions as its prize question. His justification might explain the academicians' receptivity to Prémontval's initial proposal and their interpretation of the main points under discussion. Merian cast the entire issue in the mould of French conjectural histories, taking for granted the sensualist, anti-Cartesian edifice erected by Condillac. A master plan of the complex interactions between language and mind would constitute the general map of human understanding, Merian asserted, while admitting that solutions to the problem were 'more obscure than the sources of the Nile'. Merian suggested what seems to have become a philosophical commonplace by the end of the 1750s: that the key to the mutual influence of language and opinions should be found in the question of the origin of language, and more specifically in the first formation of artificial sounds.[7] It is noteworthy that Merian singled out so briefly and nonchalantly the precise problem with which so many intellectuals had grappled in Berlin, as we saw in Chapter 3. For him, the origin of language was practically interchangeable with the reciprocal influence of language and mind.

---

[4] According to Prémontval, Formey favoured a French entry because it would have spared him the translation of the prize essay, usually one of the Perpetual Secretary's duties (Göttingen, Niedersächsische Staats- und Universitätsbibliothek, Codex Michaelis 327, Briefwechsel VIII, Prémontval to Michaelis, 27 June 1759, 208^r–208^v).

[5] Michaelis, *Briefwechsel*, i. 152–3.

[6] Though bearing the date 1760, the volume of selected essays was published in October 1759: Michaelis (and anonymous authors), *Dissertation qui a remporté le prix proposé par l'académie royale des sciences et belles lettres de Prusse, sur l'influence réciproque du langage sur les opinions et des opinions sur le langage. Avec les pièces qui ont concouru* (Berlin: Haude & Spener, 1760).

[7] Jean Bernard Merian, 'Précis du discours qui a remporté le prix', in Michaelis et al., *Dissertation qui a remporté le prix*, p. iv. Merian's extensive summary of the prize essay was also published in Formey's journal *Nouvelle Bibliothèque germanique*, October–December 1759, 237–67.

Reviewing Michaelis's prize essay, Merian interleaved his exposition with his own references to some of the recurring topics in the Berlin debates. Following Diderot and Maupertuis, Merian argued that spontaneous ideas and internal sentiments are transitory modes, disappearing almost at the moment they surface in the mind. The only means to fix such fleeting mental states was to give them 'body and colour', or to analyse them by means of signs. Merian suggested that Michaelis could have dwelled in more detail on examples of speechless human beings such as deaf-mutes and feral children, 'those animals of a human figure found in the forests'. He used these cases to highlight what he saw as common knowledge, namely that 'it is only through language that man truly becomes human'. Merian also projected the nexus of signs and cognition from the individual on to the national level, arguing that the interdependence of language and opinions stemmed from their cognitive link, not from the inherent genius or particular excellence of different tongues.[8]

ORIGINS VERSUS MUTUAL INFLUENCE: REPLIES TO THE PRIZE QUESTION

As we do not have access to the full array of submitted essays, it is difficult to know whether those printed in the Academy's collection are fully representative. However, the fact that the Academy regarded precisely these entries as meriting publication, together with Michaelis's prize essay and Merian's summary, may hint at the ways in which it wished to see the question tackled. Indeed, the anonymous authors of the printed entries tended to view the reciprocal influence of language and opinions not only in the context of the discourse on the genius of language, as Prémontval had interpreted it, but as a different version of the question of the origin of language. This led most competitors to cast their essays as conjectural histories of language and mind, ending with a few offhand observations on the means to improve languages or to eschew their detrimental effects. The pronounced interest in origins may be attested by the striking shift of focus right at the outset of the only German entry in the Academy's collection (beyond the prize essay).

> Question: To what extent do the opinions of a people influence its language, and alternately how does language influence the opinions? We should be permitted to preface this double question with another, which is the following: How would languages emerge, if one placed newly born children under the invigilation of mute people, as Psammetichus had done, and let them

---

[8] Ibid. p. xiii.

grow up within a walled-in wilderness, where they must erect a society in separation from all other human beings?[9]

Obviously fascinated by the implications of Psammetichus' experiment, as Maupertuis himself was, the author of this piece forgot to return to the original question as phrased by the Academy, tracing instead the gradual evolution of language. Focusing on a 'Natur-Sprache', an idiom of gestures and natural sounds roughly equivalent to Condillac's language of action, the author suggested it might also have been the source of all writing systems. A savage could have inscribed in the sand figures resembling his gestures, resulting after further refinement in a pictorial script.[10] Based on travel literature and the examples of feral men, the author concluded that the first words must have been onomatopoeic. Initially names differed according to the ways in which objects had been perceived, and subsequently changed over a long time. This entry claimed that a tenth of the Latin vocabulary derived from variations on fowl names and sounds, while mammals such as dogs, oxen, bears, goats, and horses were the source of a much larger portion of figurative words in all languages. Having examined the human capacity to transform natural sounds into figurative expressions, the author concluded that reason had a crucial impact on the formation of languages. The concluding recommendation, without any practical details, was simply to improve the human intellect.[11]

The first printed French entry is arguably the most interesting of the extant submissions beyond the prize essay. While lacking a strong unifying thesis, some of the author's remarks shed light on contemporary views of the interrelations between language and mind. This entry too began with the desire to reconstruct the origin of language. An isolated person, the author argued, would have no conventional signs, as he or she would not need to communicate ideas; this 'self-evident' observation was allegedly supported by 'the example of the few truly savage people whom one has observed so far'. Language, therefore, originated in the mutual communication of simple human needs and wants.[12] This essay is seemingly untouched by Rousseau and Süßmilch's critiques of the Epicurean account, or their problematization of the transition from natural sounds to

---

[9] (Anon.), 'Abhandlung über die Frage Von dem Einfluß der Meinungen in die Sprache und der Sprache in die Meinungen eines Volckes', in *Dissertation*, 85–124, here 87 (German section). Essays in each language were grouped together and page-numbered separately from other entries, presumably to allow booksellers to bind the collection in different ways.
[10] Ibid. 92.
[11] Ibid. 123–4.
[12] (Anon.), 'Dissertation sur l'influence réciproque des opinions sur le langage et du langage sur les opinions', in *Dissertation*, 1–48 (French section), here 3.

artificial signs. The author assumed the tenets of the naturalistic thesis as the self-evident foundations of the evolution of language, taking human needs to be the mother of linguistic invention.

Reflecting the fashionable discourse on the national genius of language, the author of this French piece believed that a language could reflect the political predicament of its speakers. Servile nations, occupying themselves with frivolities, could easily be led astray by rhetoric, while the language of a free nation was continuously invigorated with words for new ideas and discoveries. In a similar manner to Michaelis's prize essay, the author seemed to link political liberty with the absence of linguistic authority: a free nation's tongue could be fixed only with great difficulty. The author argued that French had been standardized too early, and thereby prevented from attaining a higher level of perfection. Since the language of a free nation smoothly acquired new expressions, the lamentable condition of French could only cast a grim shadow over France's political condition.[13]

Unlike the German entry, this first French essay seems to have engaged seriously with the question of mutual influence alongside the problem of origins. Its emphasis on the inextricable cognitive link between language and mind, as well as on its practical and political implications, was manifest in the author's resort to an organic metaphor in the portrayal of national languages. The stages in one's life and one's different personae at any given time were compared to the various registers of language and its evolutionary phases. All these different linguistic facets bore a unifying countenance, just as an individual personality anchored one's different frames of mind. This solid aspect of language was moulded by stable cognitive patterns, as well as by religion, climate, legislation, and social circumstances.[14]

The second French essay printed in the Academy's collection shared with the others an initial focus on origins and a commitment to the naturalistic hypothesis of the evolution of language. The author's attitude to the biblical account was an instance of the contemporary attempt to bypass divine creation by focusing on a post-diluvian state of bestiality. The exact nature of Adam's language was insignificant, the author argued, for it was not relevant to the question under discussion; one should rather investigate the evolution of language after the Deluge.[15] This entry was cast less as a conjectural account than a universal history of language and its fortunes in ancient Egypt, Asia, Greece, Rome, and thereafter. The evolution

---

[13] Ibid. 40–2.   [14] Ibid. 34.
[15] (Anon.), 'Discours sur la question proposée par l'Académie royale des sciences et belles lettres de Berlin: Quelle est l'Influence réciproque des Opinions du Peuple sur le Langage, & du Langage sur les opinions?', in *Dissertation*, 49–72, here 52.

of language supposedly reflected political history: languages must have progressed and declined simultaneously with their nations. The author also shared the common dissatisfaction with projects for universal languages, arguing that such idioms required an intuitive perception of nature which went beyond human capacities.[16]

The French section ended with a very short, unfinished submission. Its place within the official collection should probably be traced to Formey's patronage of its author; it was introduced as the work of a young man who 'inspires the greatest hopes' within the Republic of Letters.[17] The inclusion of this short piece in the collection was curious not only due to its brevity but because its main thesis ran against the grain of most other entries. The author thought it would be impossible to reconstruct the opinions that had given rise to languages or to find the original roots of words. This would entail going too far back in time to an age whose language contemporary scholars could not hope to comprehend.[18] The entry emphasized the ultimate impenetrability of the origin of language, in a similar manner to Rousseau's problematization of the question in the *Discours sur l'inégalité*. This final French entry implied that investigations of distant cultures might not be helpful even when conducted in a hypothetical manner, as proposed in the prize question.

The first Latin entry could be the one which Prémontval initially believed to have been composed by Michaelis. Steeped in oriental and classical erudition, its tenor was, however, more conservative than Michaelis's essay. Though starting with the Wolffian notion of the indispensability of signs in cognition, the essay continued with a rigid conception of linguistic evolution.[19] The author divided etymologies into rational and vulgar. Rational etymologies traced the manner in which human reason had built up language from its basic bricks, closely corresponding to the structure of things in the world. Terms constructed this way reflected the natural essence of their objects. Vulgar etymologies, by contrast, did not clearly distinguish between objects and their attributes. Often stemming from the ungrounded opinions of the common people, these were mostly homonyms, synonyms, or just 'empty words' that failed to convey reality.[20] After myriad examples from Hebrew, Arabic, Aramaic, and Greek, the author concluded that errors occurred when rational etymology was not exercised.

---

[16] Ibid. 61.
[17] (Anon.), 'Sur l'Influence réciproque des Opinions du Peuple sur le Langage, & du Langage sur les Opinions', in *Dissertation*, 73–6, here 73.
[18] Ibid. 76.
[19] (Anon.), 'De Mutuo influxu opinionum populorum in linguas, et linguarum in opiniones', in *Dissertation*, 1–12 (Latin section), here 3.
[20] Ibid. 4.

In this essay language was viewed as a fixed, closed, and immutable system. The author's rational etymologies implied that morphology and vocabulary had been rationally devised and had to be so maintained. Michaelis's prize essay would make, as we shall see, the opposite assumption.

The author of the second Latin piece adhered to the naturalistic thesis, stating briefly that language emerged through the human imitation of natural sounds. Its author reviewed the various parts of speech and their functions, and traced changes of meanings over time and the impact of customs, religion, and political events upon language. The author observed, for example, that Roman rhetoric must have been infected by the polytheistic prejudices in Latin, and that ancient conceptions of life inspired the terms for animals in Greece and Rome. Though arguing that the first words mirrored a superior judgement of the natural characteristics of things, the author did not address the shift from natural sounds to artificial words.[21]

The final Latin essay traced the vestiges of religious beliefs, social customs, and metaphysical systems in different languages (Arabic, Greek, Latin, Dutch, and German). The author showed how cosmological terms such as the sky and the sun were moulded by prior concepts of the universe, and likewise examined words from the domains of myth, medicine, and natural philosophy. Extensive examples suggested that change always occurred over time. Dividing all languages into primitive or derivative, the entry argued that primitive tongues could contain some divine vestiges, preserved after the Deluge but concealed by subsequent historical change.[22] As to remedies for linguistic inconvenience, the author conceded that usage was the ultimate arbiter, probably following Horace (as Michaelis did in his own essay). This admission was, however, immediately countered by a vindication of the importance of prescriptive grammar and rules of rhetoric. Only their proper study would purify both language and opinions.[23]

To different degrees, all the extant submissions made use of common notions in the debates over language and mind in the 1750s. First among them was the fusion of the synchronic perspective—how language and the human understanding constantly form one another—with a diachronic inquiry into their joint origins and evolution. This confusion, or sometimes conscious combination, of present and historical perspectives on the operation of language testifies to the contemporary significance of

---

[21] (Anon.), 'De lingua vulgarium opinionum teste et interprete', in *Dissertation*, 13–36, here 26.

[22] (Anon.), 'De linguarum in opiniones et opinionum in linguas influxu', in *Dissertation*, 37–64, here 39–40.

[23] Ibid. 64.

the evolutionary viewpoint. The historical growth of language complemented, even if in a conjectural manner, Leibniz and Wolff's rehabilitation of symbolic cognition as a central aspect of the human mind. Most authors also saw the natural element in the first languages in the Epicurean manner, as the psychological response of primordial human beings to environmental stimuli. Another important reference in these entries is to the tight link between speakers' circumstances—physical, social, and political—and the genius of their language. This discourse had, indeed, a long history before the mid-eighteenth century, yet it was reinvigorated following the turn to conjectural histories of human society.

LANGUAGE AS A DEMOCRACY: MICHAELIS'S PRIZE ESSAY

The prize essay was unique among the finalists both in its scholarly apparatus and in its dimensions: 84 quarto pages in the German version, or 176 octavo pages in its extended French edition of 1762. As befitted the offspring of an academic dynasty, familiar with disputations since his childhood, Michaelis was among the very few entrants who directly addressed the question as posed.[24] Though recognizing the inevitable relevance of an evolutionary perspective to the reciprocal influence of language and opinions, Michaelis was the only contestant to make a clear distinction between the two issues. He deliberately confined himself to the actual topic, suggesting the Academy dedicate a different contest to the emergence of a fully fledged language among non-speaking human beings. The Academy would indeed take up his suggestion almost verbatim as its prize question for 1771 on the origin of language.[25] Illustrating his response with numerous references to ancient and modern languages, European and Oriental, Michaelis divided his essay into four parts: the influence of a people's opinions on its language, the advantageous influence of language on opinions and science, the harmful influence of language, and the means to prevent such detrimental effects.

At the outset of his entry, written in late 1758, Michaelis made it clear that he subscribed, as in his 1757 treatise on Hebrew, to the thesis that all

---

[24] On Michaelis's training in disputation at Halle, see his *Lebensbeschreibung*, 6–7.
[25] The prize question for 1771 was: 'Considering men abandoned to their natural faculties, are they in a position to invent language? By what means would they make this invention on their own?' (Harnack, *Geschichte*, ii. 307.) Michaelis's suggestion in 1759 was: 'How could language emerge among men who had hitherto lacked it—and how can it be developed to its present-day perfection and extension?' ('Beantwortung der Frage von dem Einfluß der Meinungen eines Volcks in seine Sprache, und der Sprache in die Meinungen', in *Dissertation*, 1–84 (German section), here 78.)

languages were the natural creations of entire communities rather than conscious inventions of individuals. No language was exempt from the grind of constant use, abuse, change, and exchange. As in the Epicurean-Lucretian narrative, words first expressed the physical aspects of objects that struck their speakers most vividly. What attracted human attention to nature's abundance was, above all, the utility of different objects. It was only subsequent change, superimposed on the original sounds over a very long time, that made words seem completely arbitrary.[26] Michaelis was not at all disturbed by the fact that language, as an indispensable tool of cognition, could lead to epistemological mistakes and errors of judgement. In an anti-Cartesian manner he actually celebrated the contingent and impure nature of historically evolved languages: 'This is how thousands of men contribute their contingency to the immense mass of truths and errors of which national languages are depositors.' As Michaelis added, we all use libraries while being aware that some books are utterly unreliable; language is just such a rich yet uncertain treasury of knowledge.[27]

Michaelis's argument that all languages contained something natural in their origins, based on speakers' initial reactions to their environment, rendered his essay a manifesto for the use of the vernacular. It may have been surprising to find a scholar of ancient Semitic languages, influenced by his colleagues' teaching of the classical legacy, espousing scientific instruction in German and criticizing the use of Latin in the Republic of Letters. These were, however, some of Michaelis's main points in the prize essay, which was also strewn with political metaphors. As Michaelis now saw language as a natural artefact crafted through common use, its master must be the entire speech community. Following Horace's claim that usage is the supreme law of language, Michaelis went further and declared that 'language is, in a word, a democracy, where the will of the majority determines usage'.[28] The right of creating new words or changing their common use belonged, according to Michaelis, to 'the people who is the sovereign legislator', and within it to two groups in particular: women and classic authors. Only poets and other creative writers could be counted as members of the latter group, and here again the people, the 'sovereign legislator', decided who was to become a classic author. This approach to linguistic usage was very different from the definition of *bon usage* by

---

[26] Michaelis, 'Beantwortung', 4; *De l'influence des opinions sur le langage et du langage sur les opinions*, trans. J. B. Merian and A. P. de Prémontval (Bremen: G. L. Förster, 1762), 7–8. I am juxtaposing the original German essay with the French version of 1762, revised and extended by Michaelis.

[27] Michaelis, 'Beantwortung', 6, 16–17; *De l'influence*, 11, 29–30.

[28] Michaelis, 'Beantwortung', 5; *De l'influence*, 8. Cf. Horace, 'Ars poetica', lines 70–2, in *Satires, Epistles and Ars Poetica*, trans. H. Rushton Fairclough (Cambridge, Mass.: Harvard University Press, 1970), 456–7.

Claude Vaugelas, the renowned seventeenth-century prescriptive grammarian. According to Vaugelas, good or exemplary usage was to be found in the 'best part of the court', not in common patterns of speech.[29]

In Michaelis's essay, language was not an anarchic democracy but a well-ordered and well-functioning one. Every person could contribute to it through constant use, but her or his influence remained trivial and diluted in the general stream of everyday conversation. Respect was paid to merit and education, resulting in the emulation of classic authors. 'There is one point where the empire of language seems to distance itself from democracy', Michaelis conceded, referring to the deference of the common people to classic authors. 'Yet isn't it so in all democratic states?' he wondered, concluding that 'nothing obliges us to abandon a comparison that represents so well what it has to represent.'[30] Unlike some of his contemporaries, Michaelis saw linguistic or political democracy neither as a dictatorship of the mediocre masses nor as a realm of essential disorder. Michaelis defended this benign, meritocratic character of linguistic democracy—and, by extension, his vision of political democracy—throughout the essay, and he must have been aware of the overtones of such a forthright espousal of a very problematic term.[31] He was sufficiently familiar with works by ancient authors, as well as with contemporaries such as Montesquieu, Hume, and Rousseau, to know that the image of ancient democracy was a highly contested issue.[32] Similar emphases are discernible in other works by Michaelis. In the 1757 treatise on Hebrew he proclaimed that the European Republic of Letters operated under the 'rights of a democracy', and in *Mosaisches Recht* he conceived of the ancient Jewish polity as a republic turned into a limited, quasi-constitutional monarchy.[33]

---

[29] Vaugelas, *Remarques sur la langue françoise* (Paris: Jean Camusat and Pierre Le Petit, 1647), p. ii. Michaelis's reference to women as setting the norms of linguistic use is also noteworthy against the background of derisive attitudes towards their spelling. (Dena Goodman, '*L'Ortografe des dames*: Gender and Language in the Old Regime', in Sarah Knott and Barbara Taylor (eds), *Women, Gender and Enlightenment* (Basingstoke: Palgrave Macmillan, 2005), 195–223.)

[30] Michaelis, 'Beantwortung', 5; *De l'influence*, 9.

[31] Cf. the more sombre view of language as a democracy in Johann Heinrich Lambert, *Neues Organon* (1764), ed. Günter Schenk (Berlin: Akademie Verlag, 1990), ii. 465; Mario Marino, 'Die Sprache: Demokratie oder Tyrannei?' in Sabine Groß and Gerhard Sauder (eds), *Der frühe und der späte Herder: Kontinuität und/oder Korrektur* (Heidelberg: Synchron, 2007), 343–53.

[32] See Hans Maier's overview of contemporary views of democracy as the degeneration of political entities in 'Demokratie', in Otto Brunner, Werner Conze, and Reinhart Koselleck (eds), *Geschichtliche Grundbegriffe* (Stuttgart: Klett, 1972), i. 842–3.

[33] Michaelis, *Beurtheilung*, 3; *Mosaisches Recht*, i, dedication, *4ᵛ, 8, and 298–325. Michaelis may have been drawing on an earlier view of the Jewish state, recently presented by Eric Nelson in *The Hebrew Republic* (Cambridge, Mass.: Harvard University Press, 2010), 23–56. However, unlike English radicals, Michaelis highlighted the match between Mosaic legislation and its contexts rather than the actual laws and arrangements.

It is important to note who was cast in the prize essay as the arbitrary tyrant, an anti-democratic rogue. This role was reserved for none other than professional scholars, mostly academics, such as Michaelis himself and his ancestors. A scholar, Michaelis argued, could criticize the common way of speaking about the sunrise and the sunset by declaring that Berlin sets in the evening rather than the sun—for after all it is the earth, with Berlin on its surface, that revolves around the sun. Such a scholar would, however, be rightly denounced as a pedant, even if scientific truth was on his side. The generic figure of the scholar appeared several times in the prize essay as the perfect linguistic villain, wishing to impose on his surroundings an unnatural way of speaking and thinking. The use of arbitrariness here is significant, as Michaelis took the scholar's dictates to be as arbitrary as the edicts of a political despot, undermining the genuine democracy that was human language. Scholars, 'perhaps the hundredth part of humanity', were theoretically prejudiced and thus could not see what the common people perceived clearly. By contrast, the exemplary figures capable of clear perception were illiterate people, whom Michaelis regarded as closer to nature; heretics, who could usually think more freely and widely than the orthodox; and young children, who were relatively free of prejudices.[34] Even among 'enlightened nations' we should distinguish, Michaelis proposed, those that merely produced many scholars from others where the majority of the nation was enlightened.[35]

Michaelis's grim view of scholarly language, codifying dictionaries, and prescriptive manuals was manifest in his attack on two particularly great evils, arbitrary scientific classification and projects for the creation of universal languages. Linnaeus' recent designation of all flora and fauna by double Latin names was seen by Michaelis as a barbarous invention, depriving the scholarly world of the riches accumulated in folk wisdom and nomenclature.[36] Already in antiquity Latin was poor in terms for natural history, Michaelis argued on the basis of comparisons with Hebrew and Arabic, and it was no surprise to him that Linnaeus forged 'a new barbaric Latin, not a word of which Cicero would have understood'.[37] Michaelis feared much of the same in other new taxonomies, as well as in older projects for universal languages. Indeed, the largest addition to the French version of the essay concerned universal scientific idioms.[38] Michaelis saw such idioms as systems in which each idea would have an

---

[34] Michaelis, 'Beantwortung', 15–16; *De l'influence*, 27–8.
[35] Michaelis, supplement to *De l'influence*, 73.
[36] Michaelis, 'Beantwortung', 26–32; *De l'influence*, 45–56.
[37] Michaelis, 'Beantwortung', 73–4; *De l'influence*, 138.
[38] This supplement was first read at a meeting of the Academy on 13 March 1760 (Winter, *Registres*, 256).

unequivocal character, based on a rigid classification of nature (as had been suggested in various seventeenth-century projects). He then doubted both the practicality and the feasibility of such an enterprise. Furthermore, Michaelis rejected any parallel between natural languages and mathematical notation. Like his contemporaries in Berlin, discussed in Chapter 2, Michaelis was unimpressed by the perspicuity of mathematics and geometry, arguing that their definitions were man-made and did not depend on external reality. Representations of the outside world were, by contrast, much more challenging. Since there was no agreement about the nature of things, the riches of local taxonomies should be preserved rather than crushed under the weight of a universal language.[39] His main concern was that a universal scientific idiom would lack the consensual character of historically evolved languages. Such an idiom would therefore amount to the despotic imposition of a single person's point of view, or that of a sect, upon the common people. The terminologies invented by Linnaeus or Adanson would, he feared, lead to a new scholarly Babel 'which is prevented by the democratic form of our ordinary languages'. He therefore pleaded with his colleagues to teach botany in the vernacular rather than in Latin.[40]

Michaelis's rejection of universal languages was also related to his view that the malleability of language mirrored the intellectual range of the mind. If a scientific idiom were to be imposed on all human inquiries, the general fund of knowledge would be significantly diminished. On the basis of such claims, Michaelis has been identified as a forerunner of twentieth-century linguistic relativism, the hypothesis that the scope of particular languages moulds the intellectual capacities of their speakers. Michaelis did argue that human beings cannot perceive what they cannot name, and also noted that without signs we cannot acquire ideas of large numbers or abstract terms. However, he clearly endorsed the thesis of a *mutual* influence of language and mind, which meant that human beings could also actively modify their language. They were not merely passive prisoners within the thick web of language.[41]

---

[39] *De l'influence*, 157–8.
[40] Ibid. 171. The work Michaelis referred to was Michel Adanson, *Histoire naturelle du Sénégal: Coquillages* (Paris: Claude-Jeane-Baptiste Bauche, 1757). See also Londa Schiebinger, 'Naming and Knowing: The Global Politics of Eighteenth-Century Botanical Nomenclatures', in Pamela H. Smith and Benjamin Schmidt (eds), *Making Knowledge in Early Modern Europe: Practices, Objects, and Texts, 1400–1800* (Chicago: University of Chicago Press, 2007), 90–105.
[41] Lionel Gossman, 'Berkeley, Hume and Maupertuis', *French Studies* 14 (1960), 304–24; Robert Politzer, 'On the Linguistic Philosophy of Maupertuis and its Relation to the History of Linguistic Relativism', *Symposium* 17 (1963), 5–16; Raoul N. Smith, 'The Sociology of Language in Johann David Michaelis's Dissertation of 1760', *Journal of the History of the Behavioral Sciences* 12 (1976), 338–46; Haßler, *Sprachtheorien*, 43–63.

For all these reasons Michaelis argued that when it came to the improvement of language, scholars should be kept at an arm's length. Any prescriptive rule would infringe on 'the rights of the people'.

> I also believe that the scholar is obliged to behave like every other individual in the realm of language. It is not for him to give the law or proscribe customary expressions. If he does so, he is justly mocked; this is the punishment he deserves for his ambition and his infringement on the rights of the people. Language is a Democratic State: the savant citizen has no authority at all to abolish accepted usage before he has convinced the entire nation that this usage is abusive. And if he substitutes a new term for the one commonly used to refer to a certain object, how can he demand to be heard?[42]

Michaelis's last point, about the refusal of the majority to follow the scholar's rational lead, closely resembled Lucretius's argument against any single inventor at the origins of language.[43] As mentioned in Chapter 1, this was probably a rejection of Plato's suggestion that name-givers could have coined the first words of languages. For Plato, norms of propriety could not be democratically determined, whereas the Epicureans saw no alternative to common use as the arbiter of correctness. According to Lucretius, at no point in human evolution was there a human being equipped with substantially better faculties than his peers, allowing for a superior insight into the nature of things. Even if there had been such a superman, no one would have understood him or seen much sense in adopting his new inventions, however rational they could have been. Like the ancient Epicureans, Michaelis used here the universality of cognitive faculties and their naturalistic evolution to discard the Platonic notion of privileged individuals in the realm of language.

The prize essay is a fascinating statement not only because of Michaelis's naturalistic stance and his depiction of language as an open space where the sheer weight of the whole nation prevents despotic action. His espousal of an account of language that resembled the ancient Epicurean narrative was not necessarily radical. Beyond such controversial figures as Mandeville or Rousseau, more orthodox authors like Leibniz, Vico, and Warburton expounded very similar theories of the evolution of language. Yet Michaelis's examples in the prize essay were illuminating in themselves, including recurrent condemnations of literal interpretations of Scripture and, as mentioned above, a positive reference to free-thinking heretics. Though Michaelis, like most contemporary authors, did not explicitly declare his debt to the ancient Epicureans on the issue of linguistic evolution, he did pay them a public tribute in the prize essay. In a

---

[42] Michaelis 'Beantwortung', 80; *De l'influence*, 148.
[43] Lines 1046–55 in Lucretius, *De rerum natura*, v. 460–1.

discussion of how accessory ideas coloured our attitude to different terms, Michaelis's main example was the Roman vilification of Epicureanism. What had simply meant pleasurable emotion for the Hellenistic philosophers was denoted in Latin by *voluptas* with its connotations of excessive lust and corruption. No wonder, Michaelis claimed, that this idea was ill-received by a nation admiring military virtue. He went on to demonstrate how he would convince a friend to see the sense of Epicurean ethics, making it respectable by substituting the term *angenehme Empfindung* (agreeable feeling) for *voluptas* or the German *Wollust*.[44] Once he did so, there was no need to resort to the 'chicanes and bad arguments with which the Roman orator [Cicero] attacked the Greek philosopher [Epicurus]'. In the same breath Michaelis tried to distance himself rhetorically from a dangerous self-identification with a much maligned school, conceding that some Epicureans might have confused pleasant sentiments with voluptuousness.[45]

Michaelis held a similar grudge against contemporary German translations of the French word *luxe* (luxury). By the late 1750s the effects of luxury had been debated by Fénelon, Mandeville, Rousseau, and Hume, among many others.[46] On this issue, Michaelis did not qualify his clearly pro-luxury stance. He noted that recently suggested German terms for luxury, such as *Üppigkeit* or *Überfluß*, were theologically and morally overloaded with negative associations. His ire was reserved for self-appointed reformers 'who believe they perform a marvel for the public good in recommending to the citizen a sordid thriftiness', whereas luxury (within certain limits) should be 'approved by sound politics, and no state can prosper without it'.[47]

On another front, Michaelis lamented the equivocal character of terms such as 'natural law' and 'the sovereign good'. *Summum bonum* could refer to the ultimate end of all good or to the greatest good, while natural law (*jus naturae* or *das Recht der Natur*) was an unclear term due to the

---

[44] 'Wollust' was the term used in the entry on Epicurus in Zedler's *Universal-Lexicon*, viii (1734), 1388–90.

[45] Michaelis, 'Beantwortung', 24–6; *De l'influence*, 42–5. References to an allegedly unjust interpretation of Epicureanism were common at the time: see Diderot's article 'Epicuréisme ou Epicurisme' in the *Encyclopédie*, v (1756), 779–85, and Johann Jakob Brucker's account of the defamation of Epicureanism in *Historia critica philosophiae* (Leipzig: Breitkopf, 1742–44), i. 1237–48. See also the introduction and Natania Meeker's contribution in Leddy and Lifschitz (eds), *Epicurus in the Enlightenment*, 1–12 and 85–104.

[46] Christopher J. Berry, *The Idea of Luxury: A Conceptual and Historical Investigation* (Cambridge: Cambridge University Press, 1994); Istvan Hont, 'The Early Enlightenment Debate on Commerce and Luxury', in Mark Goldie and Robert Wokler (eds), *The Cambridge History of Eighteenth-Century Political Thought* (Cambridge: Cambridge University Press, 2006), 379–418.

[47] Michaelis, 'Beantwortung', 50; *De l'influence*, 98–9.

different senses of *jus* and *Recht* as both law and right. Michaelis argued that this unclarity prompted a confusion between ethics as ordained by Scripture and what he saw as a new discipline of natural law, starting with Grotius and dealing with social obligations even in the absence of God. Here he defended another notorious figure, the Göttingen law professor Johann Jacob Schmauß, whose voluntarist natural law theory contained strong Epicurean impulses. As in Epicurus' case, Michaelis claimed he did not completely agree with the culprit, while suggesting that the uproar had mostly been caused by mutual misunderstanding. The new discipline of natural law should be called, he suggested, 'natural powers' or 'the authority of nature'.[48]

The prize essay also elaborated Michaelis's mature view of etymology, which he contrasted with earlier fanciful inquiries into the history of words. Building on his own metaphor of language as a library, Michaelis warned against taking etymologies at face value just because they had been published by once-respectable authors. Etymology, Michaelis argued, could never provide perspicuous demonstrations or real definitions. It could only confirm that at a given time, in a certain place, an author thought in a particular manner. Accordingly, etymology should not concern itself with the truth of past assertions, whose validation depended on rigorous scientific procedures.[49] The circumscription of the domain of etymology by quasi-Newtonian hypotheses was one of the main themes of Turgot's article *Étymologie* in volume six of the *Encyclopédie* (1756). Like Michaelis, Turgot rejected earlier etymological methods while recognizing the great potential of inquiries into the history of language. Properly conducted, such investigations would illuminate the evolution of the human mind and constitute 'an interesting branch of experimental metaphysics'. The words that etymologists examined, Turgot explained, could be the 'grains of sand that the human mind has left behind on its path', or our clues in tracing a lost trail of mental evolution.[50] Turgot's sandy path is comparable to Michaelis's library: both were treasuries of the history of human ideas.

Though Michaelis could have read Turgot's recent entry on a topic so close to his own interests, a more probable route of influence may be traced back to Leibniz. Both Michaelis and Turgot followed Leibniz in

---

[48] Michaelis, 'Beantwortung', 48–9. On Schmauß, see Frank Grunert, 'Das Recht der Natur als Recht des Gefühls: Zur Naturrechtslehre von Johann Jacob Schmauß', *Jahrbuch für Recht und Ethik* 12 (2004), 137–53; Thomas Ahnert, 'Epicureanism and the Transformation of Natural Law in the Early German Enlightenment', in Leddy and Lifschitz (eds), *Epicurus in the Enlightenment*, 53–68.

[49] Michaelis, 'Beantwortung', 16–17; *De l'influence*, 29–30.

[50] Turgot, 'Étymologie', in *Œuvres*, i. 473–516, here 506; Daniel Droixhe, *De l'origine du langage aux langues du monde: études sur les XVIIe et XVIIIe siècles* (Tübingen: Gunter Narr, 1987), 40–54; Lifschitz, 'Language as the Key', 353–8.

arguing for a certain natural element in all languages. Leibniz also rejected far-fetched etymologies, maintaining that they must be conducted with no geographical or historical leaps between distant languages, and on the basis of the widest range of materials. Overall, Leibniz saw etymologies as mere conjectures rather than demonstrations, an observation shared by both Turgot and Michaelis.[51] They all agreed that in order to trace the history of ideas one should distance oneself from the casual meanings of words and examine hypotheses against the historical evidence. Once such critical distance was kept, as in the case of the Arabian explorers, the stacks of the cognitive library were open to the discerning investigator. Michaelis ended the extended French edition of his prize essay by envisaging a new science of language and mind. Its further development required detailed inquiries into human nature and linguistic evolution, which Michaelis urged the Berlin Academy to promote.[52]

THE LABYRINTH OF LANGUAGE: RESPONSES TO THE PRIZE ESSAY

Always alert to new works on language and mind, Moses Mendelssohn provided readers of the Berlin-based *Literaturbriefe* with an extensive, four-part review of the collection of entries published by the Berlin Academy following the 1759 contest. Despite a shaky start to their relationship, Michaelis and Mendelssohn maintained a friendly correspondence in the late 1750s, especially after Michaelis reviewed favourably Mendelssohn's *Philosophische Gespräche* and his translation of Rousseau. Following his own discussions of language, Mendelssohn declared himself 'a friend of such speculations' who turned to the 1759 prize essay with 'uncommon eagerness'.[53] Though Michaelis's essay was in his opinion one of the most significant works in the field, this tribute was somewhat attenuated by Mendelssohn's more critical remarks on the contest. He began by asking why it was so difficult to investigate the origin of language. No hypothesis had so far succeeded in penetrating the tangled thicket of language, mind, and their joint origins, Mendelssohn argued, thereby implicitly admitting his own failure to solve the same problem. A potential reason for the persistent opacity of the issue was the fact that language was the very medium of mental operations: human beings could barely extract their thinking from its linguistic instrument.

[51] Aarsleff, *From Locke to Saussure*, 84–100.
[52] Michaelis, supplement to *De l'influence*, 176.
[53] Mendelssohn, *JubA*, v/1. 105.

When they [philosophers] cannot tell us how languages genuinely emerged, why don't they at least explain to us how they *could* have emerged? Does it not stem from the fact that we cannot think without language? The mind can perhaps examine the instrument of its thoughts, language, all the way to its origin just as little as the eyes in their natural condition can clearly perceive rays of light, the tool of sight.[54]

Mendelssohn crystallized here the Leibnizian theory of symbolic cognition, which also stood at the centre of his own aesthetic writings. He conceded, however, that this observation could only serve as an excuse until someone offered a more adequate solution. Having enjoyed Michaelis's examples of the reciprocal influence of language and opinions, Mendelssohn nevertheless argued that the essay failed to engage with one of the points mentioned in the prize question. This was not Michaelis's fault as much as an awkward requirement made by the Academy, according to Mendelssohn. The official announcement had requested competitors, among other tasks, to contemplate how languages prevent us from grasping certain truths. Mendelssohn observed that since the question alternately referred to languages in the plural and to human language in general, its authors must have assumed that the obstruction of truth was natural and common to all languages. He then pointed out that in order to examine this universal barrier to cognition, one had to step outside language altogether and direct a telescope straight into nature and truth. Yet as Michaelis had shown, such an idea was futile if not self-contradictory. Mendelssohn wondered if the authors of the prize question could have earnestly expected contestants to think outside language, and compared it to asking a blind person to guide another.[55] When it came to thinking without language, we were all blind, unable to imagine how our mind would function without the signs, sounds, and gestures that enabled symbolic cognition. This point had significant implications for inquiries into the origin of language which, as we have seen, regularly assumed a transition from a speechless human condition to articulate social communication. If we could not imagine human beings without language, the whole naturalistic shift from silent nature to speech-based society would be undermined. In fact, Mendelssohn elaborated in this review one of the main points made by Rousseau in the *Discours sur l'inégalité*.

Another critique of the prize question and Michaelis's answer was *Versuch über eine akademische Frage* (*Essay on an Academic Question*), a review published by Johann Georg Hamann in June 1760 in a Königsberg

---

[54] Ibid.   [55] Ibid. 107.

journal.⁵⁶ Criticizing the 'dry profundity' of scholars like Michaelis, Hamann complained that neither the Academy nor Michaelis had bothered to clarify the terms mentioned in the prize question. 'Opinions' could mean either the natural cast of a people's mind (the sense understood by most contestants) or prejudices and intellectual fashions, among which Hamann included the mathematical method and trendy translations from French and English. The term 'language' was, according to Hamann, a more ambiguous term, extending from spelling issues to poetry, philosophy, taste, and criticism. Therefore, the Academy should have determined the precise sense in which it wished language to be discussed. Hamann concluded with his own examples of the reciprocal influence of language and opinions. An author writing in a foreign language must familiarize himself with it like a lover, while an author writing in his mother tongue enjoyed the 'household rights of a husband'. Furthermore, a writer thinking at his own expense would always make inroads into language, unlike one commissioned by a learned society. Hamann, the independent scholar, reminded his readers that Michaelis conducted his research under the aegis of one academic institution at Göttingen while winning the prize offered by another, in Berlin.

Hamann countered Michaelis's entire endeavour in a further essay, *Kleeblatt hellenistischer Briefe* (*Cloverleaf of Hellenistic Letters*), published in 1762 in a collection of Hamann's works. Referring to Michaelis's treatise on Hebrew (1757) and his edition of Lowth's *Lectures on the Sacred Poetry of the Hebrews* (1758–61), Hamann ridiculed Michaelis's account of the oriental style as exceptionally rich in figurative expressions.⁵⁷ His attitude towards Michaelis's works was moulded by a principled objection to the historicization of Scripture. Approaching the Old Testament as a product of specific historical and cultural settings meant, for Hamann, its inevitable alienation from present readers. The divide between Michaelis and Hamann was also mirrored in their theories of language. While Michaelis adhered by the late 1750s to a naturalistic account of linguistic evolution, Hamann believed language could have never emerged into being but must have been invented together with the universe as a whole. Language was not only an instrument of cognition or a tool of representation; in Hamann's eyes, it was a creative power independent of the mind. Both Michaelis and Hamann believed that language endowed human

---

⁵⁶ Johann Georg Hamann, 'Versuch über eine akademische Frage', originally in *Wochentliche Königsbergische Frag- und Anzeigungsnachrichten*, in *Sämtliche Werke*, ii, ed. Josef Nadler (Vienna: Herder, 1950), 119–26.

⁵⁷ Hamann also alluded to Michaelis in his *Aesthetica in Nuce* (1762) as 'the archangel on the ruins of Canaan's language' (*Sämtliche Werke*, ii. 197).

beings with all their expressive patterns, but in Michaelis's account human beings could have also moulded language.[58]

A more comprehensive critique of the sense and the effectiveness of inquiries into language and mind was presented at the Berlin Academy by its Perpetual Secretary, Formey, shortly after the publication of the French edition of Michaelis's prize essay (1762). In his *Réunion des principaux moyens employés pour découvrir l'origine du langage, des idées et des connoissances des hommes* (*Collection of the Principal Means to Discover the Origin of Language, Ideas, and Human Knowledge*), Formey levelled a shrewd attack at Michaelis's essay and the tradition it represented.[59] Formey rejected resolutely most conjectural inquiries into the origins of human institutions, suggesting instead a detailed new version of Psammetichus' experiment. Ten children of each sex were to be isolated from society, served by mute observers, and subjected to different tests. Like Süßmilch before him, Formey was certain that the children would never develop a proper human language, thus empirically confirming the biblical account. Referring to the milestones of the language debate, including works by Locke and Wolff, Formey argued they were either irrelevant or unreliable as guides to the question of origins. Formey likewise discarded most of the empirical observations hitherto conducted, those he termed 'physical' (brain operations) as well as 'historical' (language acquisition in children and feral men). Such observations could only teach us what we already knew: that we are what the circumstances of our birth and life made us.[60]

The paper was occasioned by a rereading of Michaelis's argument that the emergence of language was natural, and his proposal to dedicate a contest to the origin of language among speechless human beings. Formey pointed out that such a question presupposed the naturalistic thesis which he rejected.

> I deny both the principle and the consequence: I believe that if men had been born without language [...] they would have invented neither language nor the simplest things that are most necessary for satisfying their

---

[58] Helmut Weiss, *Johann Georg Hamanns Ansichten zur Sprache* (Münster: Nodus, 1990); Ian Hacking, 'How, Why, When, and Where Did Language Go Public?', in Robert S. Leventhal (ed.), *Reading after Foucault: Institutions, Disciplines, and Technologies of the Self in Germany, 1750–1830* (Detroit: Wayne State University Press, 1994), 31–50. More generally, see John R. Betz, *After Enlightenment: The Post-Secular Vision of J. G. Hamann* (Oxford: Wiley-Blackwell, 2008).

[59] Formey, 'Réunion des principaux moyens [...]', in *Histoire de l'Académie, année 1759* (Berlin: Haude & Spener, 1766), 367–77. Formey did not wait for the publication of this essay in the delayed academic proceedings, attaching it as a supplement to his *Anti-Émile* (1763).

[60] Ibid. 369–70.

needs. It follows that the Question about the way in which language would emerge and perfect itself is not susceptible to any discussion.⁶¹ Consequently Formey regarded as nonsensical all accounts of a pre-social human condition and of the gradual emergence of language and mind. The more he reflected on this issue, the firmer he grew in his conviction that 'the supreme Being, author of our existence, is also the author of our first ideas and of our habitual capacity to express them'. It would therefore be a 'total waste to examine the Problem of Mr Michaelis'. Formey was willing to allow only empirical demonstrations of man's helplessness and speechlessness if left to his own devices.⁶²

This was a striking intervention by a senior figure at the Berlin Academy on behalf of the divine party, as well as a rather unkind attack on an author whom the same institution had crowned with its highest honour. Yet at the same time that Formey was criticizing Michaelis in Berlin, the latter published in Bremen the extended French translation of his prize essay which made it widely accessible across Europe. In his autobiography, Michaelis noted that the prize essay would not have been such a landmark in his career had it not been for the excellent French version by Merian and Prémontval.⁶³ As Göttingen was occupied by French troops for most of the years 1758–63, Michaelis became particularly aware of the importance of translation into French. He befriended French officers (who procured for him rare manuscripts from Parisian libraries) and tried to improve his skills in their mother tongue. It is no coincidence that what he regarded as the best translations of his works, the prize essay and the instructions to the explorers in Arabia, were executed by Merian at that time. (Prémontval was responsible mainly for the stylistic revision of the prize essay.)

The French edition of the prize essay, whose main supplement included Michaelis's arguments against a universal language, was indeed a success. It was selectively distributed in Paris by the regent of the local faculty of medicine, who expressed his admiration for the new views introduced by Michaelis to the language debate and requested more copies for local scholars.⁶⁴ One of the copies reached d'Alembert, who was consulting Frederick II on academic matters after Maupertuis's death in 1759. As part of the king's attempts to reinvigorate the Academy following the Seven Years War, d'Alembert also spent summer

---

⁶¹ Ibid. 372.   ⁶² Ibid. 376.
⁶³ Michaelis, *Lebensbeschreibung*, 57–8. Merian and Prémontval discussed with Michaelis the different stages of the translation over three years, and Michaelis reviewed all proofs.
⁶⁴ Göttingen, Niedersächsische Staats- und Universitätsbibliothek, Codex Michaelis 329, Thierry to Michaelis, 12 May 1762, 273ʳ–273ᵛ.

1763 in Berlin, where he attended several meetings of the Academy.[65] Having read the new edition of the prize essay, d'Alembert complimented Michaelis on his perfect French, which would have been the envy of any *bel esprit* in Paris. This tribute was followed by the offer of a position in Berlin, which Michaelis declined politely while correcting d'Alembert's mistake and paying his translators their due.[66] This comedy of errors can shed some light on the mechanisms of academic appointments in Berlin: the Prussian king was apparently willing to acquire a major German scholar only at the recommendation of a Parisian *philosophe*, partly made on the basis of his elegant French. Yet beyond academic politics, this episode attests to contemporary fascination with the prize essay far beyond the circles of German orientalists and theologians. It was further translated into English (1769) and Dutch (1771), and widely read well into the nineteenth century. The prize essay also largely influenced Noah Webster's cultural projects in the young United States—perhaps paradoxically, given Michaelis's attitude towards prescriptive scholars.[67]

* * *

The 1759 contest was a watershed in the mid-century debates on language and mind. Despite Merian's enthusiastic introduction of Michaelis's essay within the conjectural framework, almost all its immediate reviewers not only criticized the question but commented on serious problems with all contemporary inquiries. In 1757–8, when the contest was announced and the entries written, the evolution of language seemed inextricably linked to symbolic thinking, or the indispensability of signs in human cognition. The joint emergence of language and mind, progressive or detrimental, became the basis of the notion that language could provide insights into the history of human civilization. Within this historically orientated framework of an ongoing evolution, a universal language became obsolete: it might only forestall the natural growth of knowledge, even if arguably advancing a particular scientific discipline.

---

[65] Harnack, *Geschichte*, i/1. 354–63; Winter, *Registres*, 70–4 and 288.

[66] Michaelis, *Lebensbeschreibung*, 59. The offer was declined in July 1763 by Michaelis, who was grateful to the Hanoverian authorities. In the 1770s he felt that his loyalty had not been rewarded and tried to regain the favour of Frederick II through d'Alembert. (Ferdinand Frensdorff, 'J. D. Michaelis und die Berliner Akademie', *Internationale Monatsschrift für Wissenschaft, Kunst und Technik* 15 (1921), 261–90.)

[67] Webster used Michaelis's ideas and examples in his own 'Dissertation Concerning the Influence of Language on Opinions and of Opinions on Language', in *A Collection of Essays and Fugitiv Writings* (Boston: I. Thomas and E. T. Andrews, 1790), 222–8. See V. P. Bynack, 'Noah Webster's Linguistic Thought and the Idea of an American National Culture', *Journal of the History of Ideas* 45 (1984), 99–114. On the English translation of the prize essay see Lifschitz, 'Translation in Theory and Practice', 39–42.

Most of the submitted entries testified to the common equation between these topics, sometimes investigating origins in more detail than language and opinions.

Michaelis's reformulation of the problematic relations between language, mind, and society had considerable impact on subsequent inquiries, including those written by his critics. One of his main contributions was the endowment of such traditional issues as etymology and universal languages with a bold political dimension. The links between politics and the evolution of language had been explored by Duclos and Rousseau, but Michaelis's allusions to the democracy of language and to scholarly tyranny were more firmly grounded in a critique of earlier theories of language. If language could have never been intentionally designed, all speakers enjoyed the same rights in its 'democratic state'—scholars and fishwives alike. The perceptive critique of new scientific taxonomies merged seamlessly with a vindication of the vernacular, linked to a vision of language as the malleable product of a living community of speakers.

Michaelis's mature theory of language, as presented in the prize essay, may also indicate that naturalism, Epicureanism, and other widely applied labels often conceal more than they reveal about the diverse features of eighteenth-century thought. The incorporation of some Epicurean elements did not necessarily undermine religious belief, as manifest in Michaelis's career.[68] Despite his flirtation in the prize essay with democracy and Epicurean ethics, the main bulk of Michaelis's scholarship displayed moderate conservatism and a Montesquieu-inspired appreciation of slow change over time. Like many of his colleagues across Europe, Michaelis did not see any contradiction between religious belief and his newly found, thoroughly naturalistic account of the evolution of language and human civilization. Others, however, refused to subscribe to this synthesis between the biblical and the Epicurean narratives. Formey concluded, after Rousseau and Süßmilch, that there was no attainable or tenable solution to the questions of how language functioned in the mind and where it originated. Formey's discontent resulted in a reformulation of Psammetichus' experiment, while Mendelssohn and Hamann followed another path. Each believed in his own manner that language and cognition were indistinguishable sides of the same coin, so that their reciprocal influence could never be concretely spelled out.

---

[68] A similar point has been recently made by Ann Thomson in relation to early eighteenth-century debates on the materiality of the human mind; see her *Bodies of Thought: Science, Religion and the Soul in the Early Enlightenment* (Oxford: Oxford University Press, 2008).

The new directions identified in the prize essay and its reviews would powerfully recast the debate on language and mind in the 1760s. Even Formey, so convinced of the futility of such discussions, could not stem the rising tide that culminated in two further contests on language at the Academy before Frederick II's death. This new urgency was not merely speculative; it had much to do with social tensions and group identities in contemporary Berlin.

6
Language and Cultural Identity

The Controversy over Prémontval's *Préservatif*

A few weeks after the Academy crowned Michaelis with its prize, the Prussian minister Karl Ludolf von Danckelmann, President of the Privy Council of Justice and Supreme Curator of local universities, found a periodical publication in Berlin significant enough to merit his active involvement. On 12 July 1759 Danckelmann issued an official edict reprimanding the publishers Grynäus and Decker for neglecting their duty to submit the periodical to state censorship. The Privy Council was asked to summon the publishers for investigation, and the courts of the French colony in Berlin were informed of the alarming publication as the author belonged to their constituency. Given the constant threat of occupation in the middle of the Seven Years War, a struggle that was straining Prussia's resources to their limit, it seems rather remarkable that the publication at stake was a guide to French style. The troubling periodical was entitled *Préservatif contre la corruption de la langue françoise* (*Preservative against the Corruption of the French Language*), written and edited by Michaelis's close correspondent, André Pierre Le Guay de Prémontval.[1]

In the *Préservatif* Prémontval wished to draw attention to common mistakes in the use of French, eradicate the influence of inappropriate models, and provide his readers with the principles of eloquence. This seemingly innocent enterprise attracted the attention of Prussian officials only five days after the publication of its first instalment. The ensuing threat to ban it became the subject of a lengthy affair, involving some of the main protagonists of the 1759 contest. The personal animosity between Prémontval, an Academy member since 1752, and Formey, the powerful Perpetual Secretary, was amply demonstrated over the pages of the *Préservatif*, offering a rare insight into the complex web of tensions in

---

[1] Prémontval, *Préservatif contre la corruption de la langue françoise en France, & dans les pays où elle est le plus en usage, tels que l'Allemagne, la Suisse, & la Hollande* (Berlin: Georg Ludwig Winter and Grynäus & Decker, 1759–61). On Danckelmann, see Formey's 'Eloge de M. le Baron de Danckelmann', in *Histoire de l'Académie, année 1765* (Berlin: Haude & Spener, 1767), 541–54.

mid-eighteenth-century Berlin.[2] Though the ostensible topic of the periodical concerned the reciprocal influence of language and opinions, the *Préservatif* affair was not confined to linguistic and theoretical matters. It touched upon the social status and philosophical outlook of local Huguenots in contrast to that of French authors granted asylum in Prussia by Frederick II. The debate also concerned academic freedom under an absolutist regime, the material production and distribution of texts, conduct and etiquette in the Republic of Letters, determinism and free will, and the formation of group identities in eighteenth-century Berlin.

The *Préservatif* affair demonstrated that philosophical and anthropological debates over language were not conducted in a void. The passionate argumentation and surprising alliances of its participants underscored the socio-cultural stakes implicit in these discussions, which only rarely surfaced with such vehemence. The link between philosophy and cultural identity becomes even clearer if we note that the quarrel took its course around the announcement of Michaelis's triumph in the 1759 contest, the publication of selected entries, and the translation of the prize essay on which Michaelis worked intensively with Merian and Prémontval.[3]

HOW TO GERMANIZE ONESELF: PRÉMONTVAL'S *PRÉSERVATIF*

Born in 1716 in Charenton, Prémontval was educated in Paris, where he experienced an intellectual crisis upon his initial introduction to philosophy. As recounted in Prémontval's *Mémoires*, at a very young age he became a Pyrrhonist and an atheist. In the following years, however, he modified his views into moderate deism. Denying most central dogmas of Christianity, he still believed in a God creator who was essentially good and just.[4] It was when Prémontval decided to challenge traditional forms

---

[2] On Formey's position in the Republic of Letters, see Jens Häseler, 'Samuel Formey, pasteur huguenot entre Lumières françaises et *Aufklärung*', *Dix-huitième siècle* 34 (2002), 239–47, and 'Jean Henri Samuel Formey—L'homme à Berlin', in Christiane Berkvens-Stevelinck, Hans Bots, and Jens Häseler (eds), *Les grands intermédiaires culturels de la République des Lettres* (Paris: Champion, 2005), 413–34; Werner Krauss, 'Ein Akademiesekretär vor 200 Jahren: Samuel Formey', in *Studien zur deutschen und französischen Aufklärung* (Berlin: Rütten & Loening, 1963), 53–62.

[3] The Marquis d'Argens, head of the class of belles-lettres at the Academy, regarded the affair as one of the most famous quarrels of the time; see his *Histoire de l'esprit humain, ou Mémoires secrets et universels de la république des lettres* (Berlin: Haude & Spener, 1765–8), viii. 559–66.

[4] *Mémoires d'André Pierre Le Guay de Prémontval, Prof. en mathématiques et belles-lettres* (The Hague: n.p., 1749). See also Prémontval's 'Profession de foi' in his *Le Diogène de D'Alembert, ou Diogène décent* (Berlin: Aux dépens de la Compagnie, 1754), 114–15.

of education by giving free public lessons in mathematics that he met Denis Diderot. Diderot, possibly one of Prémontval's students, shared his passion for mathematics. Perhaps the most famous reference to the now-forgotten Prémontval was made by Diderot in *Jacques le fataliste*, whose main theme resembles Prémontval's discussions of free will in the mid-1750s.[5]

> Did you ever hear of a man named Prémontval who used to give public mathematics lessons in Paris? [...] Mademoiselle Pigeon went [there] every day with her portfolio under her arm and her case of mathematical instruments in her muff. One of the teachers, Prémontval, fell in love with his pupil and in the midst of propositions concerning solid bodies inscribed within a sphere, a child was conceived.

There is no evidence, however, that Diderot ever read the works Prémontval published in Berlin; he may have relied on early memories when writing *Jacques le fataliste* at the end of the 1770s.[6]

Following disputes with the Jesuits and professors of mathematics, Prémontval and his future wife fled France in 1744 to spend several years in the Netherlands and Switzerland, where they married and became Protestant (1746). Prémontval's arrival in Berlin (1752) prompted a detailed study of Leibniz and Wolff, which forced him to reassess his views on providence and determinism in a series of publications.[7] In these works Prémontval unleashed a fierce attack on Leibniz and Wolff, whom he saw as enemies of free will and advocates of fatalism (a word he was probably the first to coin in its modern sense).[8] As a prolific member of the class of speculative philosophy at the Berlin Academy, Prémontval sat on the jury of the 1755 prize contest on philosophical optimism and the 1763 contest on certainty in metaphysics. As we have seen, he also proposed the subject for the 1759 competition, the reciprocal influence of language and opinions. When Prémontval announced the publication of his *Préservatif* in January 1759, it was interpreted by contemporaries as a

---

[5] Denis Diderot, *Jacques the Fatalist*, trans. David Coward (Oxford: Oxford University Press, 1999), 55; *Œuvres*, ed. Laurent Versini (Paris: Robert Laffont, 1994), ii. 759. On Prémontval in Paris see Georges Dulac, 'Louis-Jacques Goussier, encyclopédiste et... "original sans principes"', in Jacques Proust (ed.), *Recherches nouvelles sur quelques écrivains des Lumières* (Geneva: Droz, 1972), 63–110, and Elisabeth Badinter, *Les Passions intellectuelles*, i: *désirs de gloire* (Paris: Fayard, 1999), 220–1.

[6] Franco Venturi, *Jeunesse de Diderot (1713–1753)*, trans. Juliette Bertrand (Paris: Albert Skira, 1939), 33–6.

[7] *Pensées sur la liberté* and *Le Diogène de D'Alembert* (both 1754), *Du Hazard sous l'empire de la providence* (1755), and *Vues philosophiques* (1757).

[8] Georges May, 'Le fatalisme et *Jacques le fataliste*', in Raymond Trousson (ed.), *Thèmes et figures du siècle des Lumières: mélanges offerts à Roland Mortier* (Geneva: Droz, 1980), 162–74; Christophe Paillard, 'Le Problème du fatalisme au siècle des Lumières', PhD dissertation, Jean Moulin University, Lyon III, 2000.

change of course. He appeared to have moved from the controversial critique of a popular system to a more prosaic, practically orientated project. But these expectations were proven to be misplaced when the first issue appeared in July 1759. Prémontval examined the use of French in Germany in a provocative manner, directing his critique at both Huguenot scholars and German adherents of Leibniz.

Despite the purist associations the title evokes, in the *Préservatif* Prémontval presented an innovative perspective on linguistic genius and change. In the prospectus for subscribers, published in February 1759, Prémontval claimed that if French were to change significantly outside France, it would lose its status as the common language of merchants, aristocrats, and the Republic of Letters. French would thus become a common language only nominally, due to the widening gap between its local dialects across Europe and a literary 'high French' taught and learned in the same manner as Latin. This ominous vision was the main motive behind Prémontval's linguistic preservative. The entire work was grounded in a desire to maintain a practical cross-European idiom rather than in an endorsement of any inherent qualities in the French language. Indeed, Prémontval argued that this language was quite poor compared to others. Less sweet then Italian, less majestic than Spanish, less concise than English, and certainly less energetic than German, French owed its primacy to an arbitrary combination of all these properties—or to what Prémontval called 'a certain temperament of mediocre qualities'.[9]

The same opinion concerning the relative merits of French was reiterated in 1760 in the fourth issue of the *Préservatif* in an essay against the so-called Gallicomania of Germans who preferred French to their own language. Prémontval claimed he had met Germans acquainted with a single German dialect in its crudest form, entirely ignorant of contemporary German literature, and proud to read only French. They were surprised to hear that Prémontval, a Frenchman in Berlin, held their mother tongue in high esteem, as well as several German authors—particularly Albrecht von Haller, Michaelis's mentor at Göttingen. Such a state of affairs, according to Prémontval, was extremely detrimental to both languages. French was being distorted and abused in Germany, its speakers emulating the most superficial Parisian fashion. Locals used Germanized French words for numerous terms, even when there were three or four better German names for the same objects. They thus discouraged potential authors of German works and delayed the desired emergence of classic authors in German—the same writers whose importance was vindicated in Michaelis's prize essay of 1759. Prémontval contrasted this situation

[9] Prémontval, *Préservatif*, pp. iii–iv.

with the relationship between French and English, a healthy and enriching literary rivalry, since the English—unlike the Germans—did not suffer from an excessive passion for French and did not subjugate themselves to a foreign culture while abandoning their own. Eventually, Prémontval wrote, most Germans were 'making themselves doubly barbaric in their own country,' mastering neither German nor French.[10]

> A German will exude the same delicacy as the Frenchman, the same extent of profundity and elevation as the Englishman, when he is on the right course: but he is not yet there. I attribute it to the excessive passion he has for our Language, and perhaps for all Languages except his own [...] His language is prepared for all tasks; why should he not cultivate it as he ought to?[11]

This critique of the flawed use of French in Germany was not meant to denigrate the German nation. In a footnote to the first issue of the *Préservatif*, Prémontval admitted that 'our Frenchmen would do well to *Germanize* themselves, and even I am working on *Germanizing* myself as much as I can.'[12]

Prémontval's view that each language possessed its own merit, immeasurable by foreign standards, was accompanied by his account of the inner workings of language. It was usage more than any intrinsic attributes that bestowed on certain expressions what we call beauty or propriety.[13] This authorization by usage, so central also in Michaelis's prize essay, was linked in the *Préservatif* to the artificial nature of human language. Prémontval followed Michaelis in treating language as a communal work in progress, even if he did not concern himself with its political dimension, origins, or the complex links between cognition and signs. His example of the pivotal role of usage was the French numerical system. It might have been deemed 'absolutely better' to say *septante*, *huitante*, and *nonante* instead of *soixante-dix*, *quatre-vingts*, and *quatre-vingt-dix*, but once common use had sanctioned this manner of counting, it was conventionally crowned *bon usage*.

Unlike Michaelis, however, Prémontval thought that common usage had to be codified and approved by certain authorities. Language required a single cultural centre to function as its arbiter—and this was, Prémontval suggested, Germany's misfortune. Though superior to French in various respects, the German language had not been codified in widely accepted dictionaries nor moulded into exemplary forms by classic authors, a

---

[10] Ibid. 293–4; Prémontval, *Diogène de D'Alembert*, 42–3, and *Du Hazard*, pp. iii–iv. See also Jürgen Storost, *300 Jahre romanische Sprachen und Literaturen an der Berliner Akademie der Wissenschaften* (Frankfurt am Main: Peter Lang, 2001), 57–77.
[11] Prémontval, *Préservatif*, 295–6.   [12] Ibid. 92.   [13] Ibid. 254.

process French had undergone in the seventeenth century. Moreover, the fragmentation of the Holy Roman Empire had prevented the emergence of a single capital, encouraging the reign of French in the different courts of the Empire. Prémontval noted, for example, that when an aristocrat returned to London or to Madrid from a sojourn in France, his recently acquired enthusiasm for all things French was usually attenuated by the need to conform to local cultural codes. In Germany, by contrast, there was no centre attracting the nation's best authors, administrators, and courtiers, with the effect that the reign of French went uncontested.[14]

Prémontval provided his readers with little practical advice while dedicating most of the *Préservatif* to severe attacks on the propagators of bad style in Germany, the 'half-Frenchmen' or 'self-appointed Frenchmen'. Behind the façade of an introduction into the secrets of purer French, Prémontval drew the dividing line between native speakers in the literal sense—French speakers born and bred in France—and foreigners, or native speakers of French who were raised abroad and exposed only to corrupt local dialects. In several of his remarks, Prémontval explicitly addressed the 'Colonists', members of the large Huguenot community in Berlin.

Driven out of France in 1685 by Louis XIV's revocation of the Edict of Nantes, the Huguenots were lured to Brandenburg by the Great Elector Frederick William, who offered them various privileges. The Huguenot community in Berlin was the largest in Brandenburg-Prussia, amounting in 1700 to a fifth of the town's population.[15] Asserting his authority as the only French-speaking member of the Berlin Academy who was actually French, Prémontval further distinguished himself from the Huguenots, the most noticeably bilingual community in Berlin.[16] Unlike some of the French figures at the king's entourage, the Huguenots respected the German language and used it as a vehicle of integration into Prussian society. Prémontval's sharp critique of the Franco-German mélange was therefore aimed not only at young Germans wishing to fashion themselves as *gens du monde*, but at the literary style and cultural identity of the Huguenots. Bad style was allegedly epitomized by Formey, whom Prémontval saw as the chief promoter of the corruption of the French language in Germany.

---

[14] Ibid. 238–53.
[15] Gottfried Bregulla (ed.), *Hugenotten in Berlin* (Berlin: Union, 1988), 476–7; Jürgen Wilke, 'Die französische Kolonie in Berlin', in Helga Schulz (ed.), *Berlin 1650–1800: Sozialgeschichte einer Residenz*, 2nd edn (Berlin: Akademie Verlag, 1992), 352–430.
[16] Prémontval's account is inaccurate. Several other Frenchmen, apart from the President Maupertuis, were members of the Academy or spent extended periods in Berlin (for example, La Mettrie and Voltaire); the Marquis d'Argens headed the class of belles-lettres from 1750 until his death in 1771.

The first issue of the *Préservatif* was interspersed with barely concealed references to Formey, though the Perpetual Secretary was never explicitly mentioned. Prémontval talked, for example, of 'a certain author who, since the deaths of Beausobre and Lenfant, enjoys the reputation of these great men'.[17] It may have been expected that Prémontval, a vigilant opponent of Leibniz and Wolff, would attack the philosophical content of works by Formey, who devoted considerable efforts to the dissemination of Wolffian philosophy. Yet the critique dealt almost exclusively with Formey's style, likened by Prémontval to the frivolity and superficiality of the leading *philosophes*. Prémontval criticized Fontenelle, the former Perpetual Secretary of the Parisian Académie des Sciences, for applying the shallow style of worldly chatter and flirtation to scientific theories, while portraying Formey as Fontenelle's lame imitator.[18] Prémontval also denounced the local taste for *pagnoteries*, which he defined by binding together all the impertinent quips, jibes, and other verbal mischief he encountered in France, capping them with obscenity. This fashion was allegedly encouraged by men of letters who, while ostensibly transmitting philosophical truths, 'prostitute themselves in lowly works and an obscene style', turning scholarly journals into a 'detestable genre of *bel esprit*'.[19] Prémontval's examples were all taken from works by Formey, in which the Perpetual Secretary tried to infuse theological and philosophical treatises with lively references to the relationship between the sexes. Formey modelled, for example, his serial introduction to Wolffian philosophy, *La belle Wolfienne* (*The Beautiful Wolffian Lady*, 1741–53), on Fontenelle's *Entretiens sur la pluralité des mondes* (*Conversations on the Multiplicity of Worlds*): the conversations in Formey's work centred on Espérance, a lady strolling along the Spree and the gardens of Charlottenburg. In another work Formey, also a Calvinist pastor, proposed the formation of a public institution to release the clergy from the burden of marriage while 'satisfying their natural needs'. He further explained the Wolffian concepts of attraction and force by reference to the self-restraint required to resist the charms of a beautiful woman.[20] Rather than seeing these instances as harmless attempts to popularize complex philosophical theories, Prémontval regarded them as a coarse debasement of the fine and delicate style codified in Louis XIV's *grand siècle*.

---

[17] Prémontval, *Préservatif*, 3. Isaac de Beausobre and Jacques Lenfant were prominent scholars in the first generation of the Berlin Refuge; Formey assisted Beausobre in the 1730s in editing his periodical *Bibliothèque germanique*. On Huguenot scholarship in Berlin, see Sandra Pott, Martin Mulsow, and Lutz Danneberg (eds), *The Berlin Refuge, 1680–1780: Learning and Science in European Context* (Leiden: Brill, 2003).
[18] Prémontval, *Préservatif*, 52.
[19] Ibid. 58, 61.
[20] More references can be found in part III of the *Préservatif* (131–3 and 151–4).

Contemplating the question of linguistic corruption in France itself, Prémontval distinguished between the grammatical and stylistic aspects. Vaugelas and other prescriptive scholars had brought about a grammatical revolution, aided by the great works of Corneille, Molière, and La Fontaine. Style, however, was an entirely different matter. France's problem was not that its writers lacked *esprit*, but that they had far too much of it. According to Prémontval, contemporary French authors usually expressed themselves in a light style, full of witticisms and specious brilliance.[21]

FREEDOM OF THE PRESS AND ACADEMIC MANNERS

This unusual attack by a member of the Berlin Academy on its Perpetual Secretary did not go unnoticed, as attested by Danckelmann's prompt warning to the publishers and the threat of legal procedures against Prémontval. The edict declared that Prémontval, like other academicians, did not enjoy in his private publications the privileges accorded to the Academy as a corporate body.

> Concerning the most indecent and punishable proceedings by Prémontval against the Professor Formey, we present you [the Privy Council of Justice] with this merciful resolution. Since only books published by the Academy of Sciences itself and under its name are exempt from ordinary censorship, whereas its members do not enjoy the same freedom, you should summon the printers of Prémontval's work, Grynäus and Decker, to examine what they intend to call upon for their justification, and afterwards report about it in writing.[22]

Censorship under Frederick II was decentralized and exercised by a number of officials and institutions who were responsible for different sorts of publications. Contrary to the king's self-propagated image of an enlightened defender of truth and reason, freedom of the press was not unlimited in Prussia. This was demonstrated in an epistolary exchange between Gotthold Ephraim Lessing and Friedrich Nicolai in 1769. While Lessing argued that freedom of expression in Prussia amounted to the unfettered abomination of religion, a liberty which a decent man should

---

[21] Ibid. 109.
[22] A handwritten copy of the edict is attached to an undated letter from Formey to Michaelis in Göttingen, Niedersächsische Staats- und Universitätsbibliothek, Codex Michaelis 324 (Briefwechsel, V), 243ʳ. Danckelmann issued the edict on 12 July 1759 as a reply to an inquiry from the Privy Council, dated 6 July; the first issue of the *Préservatif* bears the publication date of 1 July. The court of the French Colony eventually found Prémontval guilty of libel and personal affront (Wilke, 'Die französische Kolonie', 429).

be ashamed to use, Nicolai claimed that the Prussian policy was much more tolerant than its Austrian counterpart, particularly concerning scholarly publications.[23] Though the king issued a relatively strict order concerning censorship in 1749, it was never completely implemented and depended on various censors, most of whom were officials fulfilling their part-time duties as censors quite leniently. The authorities regarded political newspapers as potentially more dangerous than books; learned journals were usually not meticulously censored, if at all.[24] Nicolai, for example, recounted that in 1759 the censor for philosophical affairs was surprised to receive the manuscripts of his journal *Literaturbriefe*, for it had apparently been a very long time since anyone bothered to submit a learned journal for censorship.[25]

Control of works authored by members of the Academy was a different issue, since the Academy as a whole was exempt from state censorship and supposed to censor its own publications. However, as noted in Danckelmann's edict, Academy members did not enjoy this privilege when writing in a private capacity. Prémontval was well aware of this rule, as attested by the disclaimers to the critiques of Wolffian philosophy he published in 1754–5, where he noted that the Academy could not be held responsible for his private views.[26] Academy members recruited as censors were usually either Huguenots or Wolffian associates of Formey, like Louis de Beausobre, Johann Georg Sulzer, and Johann Peter Süßmilch. It is thus not surprising that, although Prémontval volunteered in December 1758 to become censor of historical works, the appointment was eventually turned down.[27]

As Maupertuis had been absent from Berlin since the beginning of the Seven Years War, Leonhard Euler (head of the class of mathematics) and Formey became the most senior figures at the Academy for all practical purposes—bar its curators, who were not scholars. Prussian administrators may have seen any personal assault on Formey, particularly under

---

[23] Bodo Plachta, *Damnatur Toleratur Admittitur: Studien und Dokumente zur literarischen Zensur im 18. Jahrhundert* (Tübingen: Niemeyer, 1994), 102–3.

[24] Ulrike Schömig, 'Politik und Öffentlichkeit in Preußen: Entwicklung der Zensur- und Pressepolitik zwischen 1740 und 1819', PhD dissertation, Julius-Maximilians-Universität, Würzburg, 1988, 102–45; Edoardo Tortarolo, 'Censorship and the Conception of the Public in Late Eighteenth-Century Germany', in Dario Castiglione and Lesley Sharpe (eds), *Shifting the Boundaries: Transformations of the Languages of Public and Private in the Eighteenth Century* (Exeter: Exeter University Press, 1995), 131–50.

[25] Schömig, 'Politik und Öffentlichkeit', 124.

[26] Prémontval, *Diogène décent*, 80; *Du Hazard*, pp. x–xi.

[27] Berlin, Geheimes Staatsarchiv, Euler to Frederick II, 21 December 1758, Rep 9 AV, F 2a. Fasz. 12, fo. 134^r; Euler to Maupertuis, 16 December 1758, in *Correspondance de Leonhard Euler avec P.-L. M. de Maupertuis et Frédéric II*, eds Pierre Costabel, Eduard Winter, Ašot T. Grigorijan, and Adolf P. Juškevič (Basel: Birkhäuser, 1986), 249.

these circumstances, as an insult to the entire Academy and to the king, its protector. More generally, Prémontval's vehement attack on Formey was regarded by local scholars, native Frenchmen as well as Huguenots, as an intolerable violation of academic sociability, exposing publicly the inner tensions within the Academy.

Recognizing how well connected and powerful his enemy was, Prémontval opted for a strategy of defiance and an appeal to public opinion, representing himself as a victim of crude censorship and champion of the freedom of speech, so cherished (at least theoretically) by the Prussian king. Following the imminent ban on the printing of the *Préservatif*, Prémontval published in October 1759 its second issue as a two-page copper engraving, which technically did not qualify as a printed work. A shrewd way to evade the publishers' prosecution, this mode of publication might have also been designed to amplify Prémontval's image as a maltreated defender of the freedom of the press. Unsurprisingly, the engraved leaflet included a bold personal attack on Formey, who was now explicitly named. Having requoted the Perpetual Secretary's foulest stylistic errors, Prémontval noted that Formey had been 'authorized to pursue him' and promised a firm retaliation.

> It is an obstruction of the freedom of the Press, which my Academician brothers have hitherto enjoyed *even in much more serious Matters*; because it is here merely a question *of Style*, nothing more. It is unfortunate that Baseness and indecency characterize the Works against which I rebel, and which find such zealous Defenders. This literary Inquisition can certainly not last much longer; and isn't that due to its perfect uselessness, *as long as there are Printers in places where the prefatory Dedications [Epîtres dédicatoires] of M. FORMEY enjoy less credit*.[28]

Asserting his victimization by a literary inquisition, Prémontval also tried to present his periodical as nothing but an advice sheet for authors. As shown above, however, there was more to the *Préservatif* than matters of style. The personal aspect of the quarrel was highlighted by the Marquis d'Argens who saw the *Préservatif* as Prémontval's personal vendetta against Formey. D'Argens claimed in 1767 that Prémontval told him he simply needed an illustrious victim to enhance the appeal of his own writings, and he also recalled the official rage greeting Prémontval's copper-engraved pamphlet. The magistrates saw themselves mocked; as d'Argens argued, engraving a banned journal instead of printing it was a 'measure that would have landed him [Prémontval] in Bicêtre,' the Parisian mental asylum.[29]

---

[28] Prémontval, *Préservatif*, 117.
[29] D'Argens, *Histoire de l'esprit humain*, viii. 562–4; Dieudonné Thiébault, *Mes souvenirs de vingt ans de séjour à Berlin*, v (Paris: F. Buisson, 1804), 67.

bien de m'en empêcher. Au lieu d'une Procédure si irrégulière, on a pris le parti de gêner la liberté de la Presse, dont mes Confreres les Académiciens ont joui jusqu'à présent, même en Matieres plus graves; car il n'est ici question que de Style, rien de plus. Le malheur est que la Bassesse et l'Indécence, sont le caractere des Ecrits contre lesquels je m'éleve, et qui trouvent de si zélés Défenseurs. Cette Inquisition littéraire sans doute ne durera pas; ne fut-ce qu'à cause de l'inutilité parfaite dont elle seroit, tant qu'il y aura des Presses, en lieu où les Epitres dédicatoires de M. FORMEY ayent moins de crédit. Je prie mes Souscrivans de prendre patience, de relire en attendant ma 1e. Partie avec toute l'attention possible, et d'être persuadés que de façon ou d'autre le Public n'y perdra rien.

A Berlin, le 1. Octobre, 1759.

De Prémontval

P.S. Les Personnes qui demeurent à Berlin, et qui seroient curieuses de connoître l'importance et la légitimité de ma Critique dans cette 2e. Partie, sont priées de se trouver chez moi tous les jeudis après midi, depuis trois heures jusqu'à quatre. Elles pourront d'ailleurs se convaincre, qu'il n'est pas vrai que mon Ouvrage, ainsi qu'on le veut faire croire, ne roule absolument que sur M. Formey.
L'Adresse, dans la Bährenstrass au coin de la Charlottenstrass.

Illustration 1. The end of the second instalment of Prémontval's *Préservatif* (October 1759), copper-engraved in order to evade the official threat to ban its printing. Courtesy of the Staatsbibliothek zu Berlin—Preußischer Kulturbesitz.

The following issue of the *Préservatif* (early 1760) was printed outside Prussia, as Prémontval disclosed in the *avertissement*, lamenting his inability to check the final proofs personally.[30] Though Prémontval denied the *Préservatif* was a libel and called it 'a serious critique', he maintained a sarcastic tone throughout. In this issue the implicit references to Formey's works were replaced by direct assaults on the Perpetual Secretary himself, while Formey's influence in the local intellectual scene was depicted as despotic rule, similar to the scholarly tyranny Michaelis mentioned in his prize essay. Moreover, Prémontval suggested that the legal procedures against him were contrary to Frederick II's own preferences, a serious allegation in contemporary Prussia. 'Louis XIV was far less enlightened than Frederick II,' Prémontval argued, adding that 'the freedom of the press had never been as great' as in contemporary Berlin. He then rhetorically wondered whether Frederick approved of printing outside Prussia a work as innocent as the *Préservatif*, which would have encountered no opposition elsewhere.[31] Accusations of censorship and oppression were reiterated even in the errata to the volume encompassing the first four issues of the *Préservatif*. Prémontval claimed that the printing of his *Préservatif* was conditional upon the suppression of certain references to Formey as well as to Voltaire and d'Alembert, favourites of the Prussian king.

Having repeated his assertion that Formey's reputation owed more to connections and politics than to intellectual merit, Prémontval directly challenged the Perpetual Secretary. He asked Formey to find a single established French author, such as Condillac or d'Alembert, who would declare Prémontval's accusations wrongheaded after reading a dozen of Formey's best books.[32] Formey, however, was too astute to fall into Prémontval's trap, displaying consistent indifference to an attack by a scholar of an inferior rank at his own institution and in the wider Republic of Letters. Having edited two well-known journals, *Nouvelle Bibliothèque germanique* (1746–59) and *Bibliothèque impartiale* (1751–8), Formey maintained a wide web of correspondents across Europe, enabling him to update readers with the latest literary news. He could have probably capitalized on these contacts, as well as on his superior experience in editing and publishing. But he chose to remain publicly silent, as if to declare that his rival did not deserve a serious counter-attack or indeed any reference at all. By implying that wrestling with Prémontval in the public sphere was beneath his dignity, Formey may have also sought to emphasize the stylistic differences between them or to turn Prémontval's allegations upside down. While Prémontval attacked him in an acrimonious manner, Formey retained his equanimity. The Perpetual Secretary's refusal to enter his rival's arena and

[30] Prémontval, *Préservatif*, 117–18.   [31] Ibid. 181–2.   [32] Ibid. 164–5.

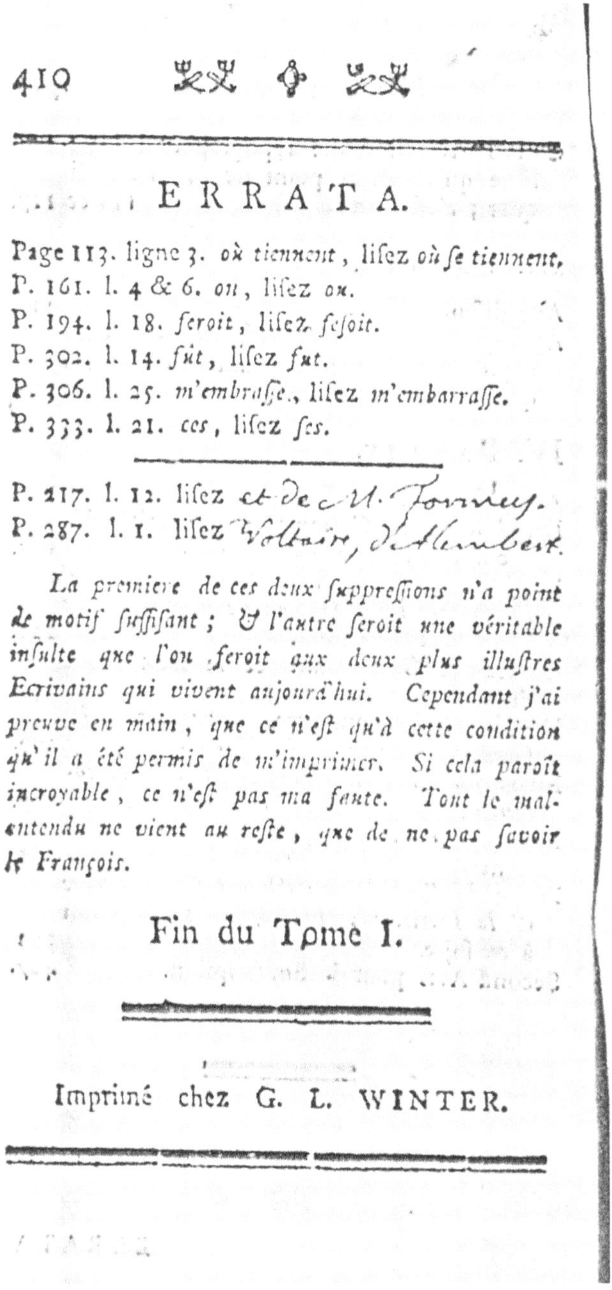

410

ERRATA.

Page 113. ligne 3. où tiennent, lisez où se tiennent.
P. 161. l. 4 & 6. on, lisez ou.
P. 194. l. 18. feroit, lisez sesoit.
P. 302. l. 14. fût, lisez fut.
P. 306. l. 25. m'embrasse., lisez m'embarrasse.
P. 333. l. 21. ces, lisez ses.

P. 217. l. 12. lisez *et de M. Formey*.
P. 287. l. 1. lisez *Voltaire, D'Alembert*.

La première de ces deux suppressions n'a point de motif suffisant; & l'autre seroit une véritable insulte que l'on feroit aux deux plus illustres Ecrivains qui vivent aujourd'hui. Cependant j'ai preuve en main, que ce n'est qu'à cette condition qu'il a été permis de m'imprimer. Si cela paroît incroyable, ce n'est pas ma faute. Tout le malentendu ne vient au reste, que de ne pas savoir le François.

Fin du Tome I.

Imprimé chez G. L. WINTER.

Illustration 2. The errata of the first volume of the *Préservatif* (1761). Left as blank spaces but later filled in with a pen are the names Prémontval claimed he was forced to suppress: Formey, Voltaire, and D'Alembert. Courtesy of the Staatsbibliothek zu Berlin—Preußischer Kulturbesitz.

play by his rules can thus be seen as the combination of a forced stance, prompted by Prémontval's self-presentation as a victim of academic tyranny, with a conscious choice to protect his reputation through silence.

Formey's attitude became clearer in his reaction to a short review of the engraved pamphlet in the *Göttingische Anzeigen*. In its issue of 3 November 1759 Michaelis reported about Prémontval's short engraving, assuming it concluded the publication of the *Préservatif*. Michaelis urged Formey to provide a good reason for the official ban, a different one from mere personal insult. If Prémontval was forced to continue its publication in the foreign press, Michaelis argued, the Prussian sanction would only draw the attention of many more readers.[33] Though Michaelis tried to maintain a neutral stance, Formey saw his review of the polemical engraving as a violation of the unwritten rules governing scholarly journals, if not a wholesale mobilization to Prémontval's cause. In an emotional letter to Michaelis, Formey wrote he was surprised to see a scholar of Michaelis's reputation challenge him to answer Prémontval's libellous engraving. Formey was all the more hurt as he had rendered Michaelis 'the justice that was his due'.[34] This was probably a reference to the prize the Academy had recently bestowed on Michaelis, though as we have seen, Formey did not find Michaelis's piece to his particular liking.

Formey further explained to Michaelis that ever since Prémontval's arrival in Berlin, he had assisted his colleague in any possible way. The works Prémontval published in 1754 (*Diogène décent* and *Pensées sur la liberté*) embarrassed him for containing 'manifestly dangerous' opinions, but he refrained from refuting them in his journals. As editor, Formey claimed he had declined a review critical of Prémontval and refused to recommend its author to local publishers. In short, Formey concluded, 'had M. de Prémontval been my oldest and most loyal friend, even my own brother, I could not have acted differently'.[35] Inadvertently, however, Formey revealed in this letter how influential he was in Berlin. The control of local and foreign journals, connections across Europe, and a senior academic position turned him into a literary arbiter, being able to determine the fate of future publications by recommending them to local *libraires*. As to Prémontval's allegations of academic oppression, Formey assumed an innocent stance, claiming he had nothing to do with the official procedures against Prémontval, which were complete and legitimate. If his adversary gave up writing, it was his own decision, though at the same time Formey

---

[33] *Göttingische Anzeigen*, 3 November 1759, 1150.
[34] Göttingen, Niedersächsische Staats- und Universitätsbibliothek, Codex Michaelis 324, Formey to Michaelis (undated, probably November–December 1759), 241ʳ.
[35] Ibid. 242ʳ. Formey announced the forthcoming publication of the *Préservatif* in *Nouvelle Bibliothèque germanique* 24 (January–March 1759), 234.

admitted that Prémontval had been forbidden to write 'in such a tone'.[36] This letter, which Formey pleaded with Michaelis to keep private, reveals much about the code of conduct in contemporary academia. Institutions such as the Berlin Academy and the Royal Society in Göttingen tended to become personalized and identified with their presidents or secretaries. By the same token, newspapers and journals were employed by their editors-authors for the promotion of their favourite theories, scholars, and causes in public debates. Even when editors of review journals assumed the cloak of neutral spectators, as Michaelis did in the *Göttingische Anzeigen*, they were nevertheless suspected by the quarrelling parties of taking sides.[37]

The publication of the *Préservatif* ceased in 1761. Apart from the lack of interest among readers who might have expected linguistic instruction but found themselves in the maelstrom of an academic quarrel, Prémontval could not resist the pressure of his own allies and even his wife. Prémontval's spouse, Anne-Marie Victoire (née Pigeon d'Osangis), a reader to prince Henry's consort, expressed her reservations before and after her husband's death. In 1757 she wrote to Formey that 'had everyone thought of you the way I do, you surely would have had nothing to complain about'.[38] After her husband's death she would tell Formey that her way of thinking 'has always been so opposed to that of my dear deceased Husband. He liked to sparkle and make noise; I wanted to be completely ignored; but I was not the master, *you know that.*'[39] The Academy's Deputy Secretary, Merian, confessed his own discontent with Prémontval's campaign in a letter to Formey. He was considerably embarrassed by the lavish praise Prémontval bestowed on him in the *Préservatif*, where it was suggested that Merian was worthier of the Secretary's position than Formey.[40] Under such pressure, Prémontval tried to modify the tone of his *Préservatif*. The first four issues were titled 'Preservative against the corruption of French in Germany,' whereas in further issues the corruption of French was relocated to 'France and the countries where it is mostly used'. The final reconciliation occurred in 1763, when Prémontval beseeched Formey for forgiveness, promising a thorough review and even self-censorship of the second edition of the *Préservatif*.

> I wish, Monsieur, to do away with the unfortunate Work, monument of our disagreements. [...] I shall finish the Work, because it has to be done, but

---

[36] Formey to Michaelis, undated (as above), 241ʳ.
[37] Cf. Anne Goldgar, *Impolite Learning: Conduct and Community in the Republic of Letters* (New Haven: Yale University Press, 1995).
[38] Kraków, Biblioteka Jagiellońska, Varnhagen von Ense collection, Mme de Prémontval to Formey, 2 November 1757.
[39] Kraków, Mme de Prémontval to Formey, 9 January 1765, emphasis in the original.
[40] Kraków, Merian to Formey, 27 August 1760.

in a manner that would not compromise you, Monsieur; and I give you my Word of honour that each time the previous material passes under my hands will be such a serious Blow for me, that it ought to make you quite satisfied. If these Inclinations are not disagreeable to you, I throw myself into your arms with the resolution not to separate myself from them for the rest of my Life.[41]

The rest of Prémontval's life was not to last long. He died in Berlin in September 1764, leaving the last word in the affair to Formey. Since eulogizing deceased academicians was one of the Perpetual Secretary's tasks, Formey delivered Prémontval's obituary to the Academy in 1765. This was the first occasion in which Formey referred publicly to the *Préservatif* affair, vindicating his self-restraint in the face of adversity. In a curious reversal of roles, Formey presented himself in the obituary as the suffering victim of an unjust attack.

> I have now said more on this topic than I had done during the entire publication of the *Préservatif*, when I subjected myself to the rule of a most perfect silence, and when my heart itself kept silent even while it seemed to be ulcerated, because I have never ceased not only to hold in high esteem M. *de Prémontval* the Writer, but also to love the man. At the end I had the satisfaction of seeing him convinced of it, and to hold him in my arms as cordially as he threw himself into them.[42]

Concerning the *Préservatif*'s main claim, Formey referred his readers to France. If one took seriously the incessant critiques of the French language by French authors, the source of its corruption must be sought in Paris itself. But the obituary was not a detailed scholarly reply to the *Préservatif*, as Formey infused it with references to Prémontval's tempestuous character. Prémontval believed people were constantly conspiring against him, Formey told his academic audience, whereas 'we have always been disposed only to love and cherish him'.[43]

FATALISM AND PROVIDENCE, CONTENT AND FORM

In the same obituary Formey mentioned several times Prémontval's 'emotional aversion' to Leibniz and Wolff, thus demonstrating that the *Préservatif* affair was also part of the wider philosophical controversies of

---

[41] Kraków, Prémontval to Formey, 25 November 1763.
[42] Formey, 'Eloge de M. de Prémontval', in *Histoire de l'Académie, année 1765* (Berlin: Haude & Spener, 1767), 539.
[43] Ibid. 540.

the day. Prémontval's publications before the *Préservatif* had addressed the question of free will, and criticized both Leibniz and Wolff as fatalists. In *Pensées sur la liberté* (*Reflections on Freedom*, 1754) Prémontval argued that Leibniz subjugated freedom to pre-established harmony and to the principle of sufficient reason. According to Prémontval, human freedom was inextricably linked to arbitrariness, the absolute liberty to act as one chooses even without a cause—just as his theory of language emphasized arbitrariness in contrast to Leibniz's views.

In *Du Hazard sous l'empire de la providence* (*On Chance under the Rule of Providence*, 1755), Prémontval defined chance as a cause whose effect was contingent and not determined by design.[44] He divided all philosophers into two classes: those who strictly denied chance ('rigorous fatalists', as he labelled Spinoza and Leibniz) and authors who recognized some arbitrariness either in divine or in human actions, but rejected the name or label of chance (various adherents of predestination, ascribing arbitrary action to God but not to his creatures). Prémontval tried to present the latter as resembling his own views, once they admitted the possibility of real contingency. Their main difference, according to Prémontval, was the extent to which human action was directed by God and whether God could be regarded as the source of evil.

Replying to accusations by German theologians who identified any rejection of both predestination and pre-established harmony with materialism, Prémontval undertook the difficult task of reconciling arbitrariness with providence. Like the Epicureans, he admitted an open and unpredictable future, subject to the interaction of chance and necessity. But he simultaneously recognized the existence of an omnipotent, wise, and benevolent creator, who maintained providence and distributed grace. God, according to Prémontval, did not determine a priori the course of things to come, but intervened a posteriori to minimize evil without recourse to miracles. Prémontval's conclusion was that God's existence supported the case for chance and arbitrariness: 'If there is a God, there is chance; if there is no chance, there is no God.'[45] This curious espousal of complete arbitrariness together with full divine providence proved difficult to digest. As Prémontval noted in the introductions to the works he published in 1754–5, he was misinterpreted by both 'impious philosophers' and 'zealous theologians'.[46] The hostile reception only deepened his sense of isolation and persecution in Berlin a few years before the official edict against the *Préservatif*.

---

[44] Prémontval, *Du Hazard*, 5.   [45] Ibid. 122.
[46] Ibid. 147. In a letter of 21 February 1754 to Baculard d'Arnauld in Paris, Prémontval reported he found it difficult to find a publisher in Berlin (Berlin, Staatsbibliothek, Darmstädter collection, H 1754, 2).

The common misunderstanding of Prémontval's writings concerned not only their philosophical content. While Prémontval disagreed with Formey and his Wolffian peers on various theoretical issues, he seems to have shared their critique of the *philosophes*. This is a perplexing stance for a mid-eighteenth-century author: most contemporary thinkers aligned themselves either with the *philosophes* or with their critics, conservative or otherwise. The key to this difficulty may be found in a distinction between philosophical content and stylistic form. Formey and other Wolffians were alarmed by Prémontval's disparaging remarks on the Leibnizian concepts of freedom and pre-established harmony, considering him a dangerous author. In matters of form, however, Formey successfully adapted himself to the latest fashions in the publishing market both formally (journals, abridged versions, translations, and reviews) and stylistically (a playful prose peppered with references to sexual attraction). Prémontval, by contrast, seems to have been stuck in the seventeenth century, clinging to a rigid ideal of classicism. Prémontval's critique of the *philosophes* concerned their allegedly superficial style much more than the content of their works, while Formey's concern with materialists and sceptics was content-orientated rather than stylistically minded. It seems, therefore, that neither Formey nor Prémontval suits the common images of eighteenth-century men of letters. Formey moulded his enlightened conservatism and Wolffian philosophy into the most up-to-date literary devices; Prémontval rejected Leibniz and Wolff along with the *philosophes*, but despite their theoretical affinity he stood firmly against the *littérateurs mondains* and closer to the *érudits* of the seventeenth century. This stance mirrored Prémontval's espousal of the official codification of French, whose further alteration should only be regarded as its corruption.

GROUP IDENTITIES BETWEEN FRENCH AND GERMAN

Prémontval's critique of bilingualism and linguistic mixture struck at the heart of an increasingly crucial dilemma in the local French Colony. Throughout the eighteenth century the percentage of German-speaking Huguenots soared as the result of social and commercial integration. At the same time, the Huguenot privileges concerning church services, education, and self-administration in French were closely guarded by community leaders. The pace of linguistic assimilation corresponded to the social stratification within the Colony. Because the Prussian court enthusiastically adopted French culture, the higher ranks of the *réfugiés*, as well as scholars in the first generations of the *Refuge*, found it convenient to use their mother tongue in Prussia. The middle and lower classes were, however, forced to integrate much more quickly into Berlin's commercial and social life, acquiring German relatively early. German was taught, for example, in Huguenot charity schools, while students at the Colony's prestigious *Collège français* were instructed only in French and the classical languages.[47]

A few years before the *Préservatif* affair, in the early 1750s, Voltaire perceived in Berlin a certain *style réfugié*, an outdated French interspersed with provincial expressions and infused with an exaggerated, quasi-biblical rhetoric. Most of the first *réfugiés* in Berlin were indeed pastors trained in provincial Protestant academies in France before 1685.[48] Some of the ensuing Franco-German neologisms persisted in the Berlin dialect well into the nineteenth and twentieth centuries. They included terms such as 'Bouletten' (meat balls *à la berlinoise*), 'Muckefock' (*mocca faux*), and 'Schislaweng' (*ainsi cela vint*).[49] In the 1780s prominent Huguenots defended their *style réfugié* as a creative idiom in constant evolution. Responding to an attack along the lines of Prémontval's *Préservatif*, Jean Pierre Erman and Frédéric Reclam saw the French dialect of Berlin as a resourceful linguistic device powered by bilingualism, arguing that it was actually French in the mainland that had been ossified. In a restatement of Michaelis's principle of linguistic democracy, Erman and Reclam argued that every expression was adequate as long as it was intelligible: anyone could borrow from a foreign language and create a neologism. By arguing that the sole arbiter was common usage—not dictionaries, the Académie Française, or overweening scholars—Erman and Reclam discredited the linguistic pretensions of French newcomers who deemed the Colonists' idiom inadequate.[50]

---

[47] Wilke, 'Die französische Kolonie', 426–7.

[48] Voltaire's observation is in the entry on Jacques Saurin in the supplement to *Du siècle de Louis XIV* (*Œuvres complètes de Voltaire*, ed. Louis Moland (Paris: Garnier, 1877–83), xiv. 133). See also Germaine de Staël, *De l'Allemagne*, ed. Simone Balayé (Paris: Garnier-Flammarion, 1968), i. 135; Jürgen Eschmann, 'Die Sprache der Hugenotten', in Jürgen Eschmann (ed.), *Hugenottenkultur in Deutschland* (Tübingen: Stauffenberg, 1988), 9–35; Miryam Yardeni, 'Le Refuge allemande et la France: histoire d'une alienation', in *Le Refuge huguenot: assimilation et culture* (Paris: Champion, 2002), 187–203.

[49] Wilke, 'Die französische Kolonie', 429; Agathe Lasche, '*Berlinisch*': *Eine berlinische Sprachgeschichte* (Berlin: R. Hobbing, 1928), 64–139.

[50] Viviane Rosen-Prest, *L'Historiographie des Huguenots en Prusse au temps des Lumières* (Paris: Champion, 2002), 420–7, 642–3; Manuela Böhm, 'Berliner Sprach-Querelen: Ein Ausschnitt aus der Debatte über den *style réfugié* im 18. Jahrhundert', in Elisabeth Berner, Manuela Böhm, and Anja Voeste (eds), *Ein grofs vnnd narhafft haffen: Festschrift für Joachim Gessinger* (Potsdam: Universität Potsdam, 2005), 103–15; Gerda Haßler, 'Bon usage et langue parfaite: la présence des remarqueurs dans le débat sur l'universalité de la langue française au XVIIIe siècle', in Philippe Caron (ed.), *Les Remarqueurs sur la langue française du XVIe siècle à nos jours* (Rennes: Presses Universitaires de Rennes, 2004), 167–83.

The tensions between the quick pace of integration and the efforts to maintain a unique identity came to the fore in the 1770s and 1780s, when Prémontval's concern with the corruption of French away from its homeland was shared by Huguenots and foreign observers alike. In 1774 the pastor Abraham Robert Bocquet suggested that school instruction and certain church services be conducted in German, but it was only in 1815 that services in German were officially condoned in the French Colony.[51] Its authorities faced a double dilemma from the mid-eighteenth century onwards: whether to admit into the community Germans who spoke French fluently, and how to deal with Huguenots whose knowledge of their ancestral language had all but diminished over the generations. On the one hand, it was the use of French that legitimized the communal privileges, originally grounded in an ethno-linguistic special status. Yet on the other hand, the Huguenot identity had also been construed around a confessional core. The danger was a growing alienation of community members from religious dogmas preached and discussed in what for many had become a foreign language.

Outside the Huguenot community, authors were tackling similar questions concerning French and German. Prémontval's call for an autonomous development of national literatures offered contemporaries an alternative to the bilingualism of the Huguenots and the royal courts. This approach was applauded by Michaelis, who blamed French-speaking German monarchs for the exaggerated foreign influence in Germany. In his review of parts 4 and 5 of Prémontval's *Préservatif*, Michaelis criticized Frederick II implicitly though sharply.

> [...] It is not yet sufficiently customary to teach German as part of our education, to read our classic authors and poets with the young, and to practise with them the writing of German. This flaw of education, which is gradually being improved among the middle classes, dominates the palaces. When the prince knows only the language of the crowd, when he cannot read anything well-written in German, no sublime poet, no Haller; then he will despise his mother tongue, in which he recognizes only the deficient, and at the most only the *** Muse of the Counter-Parnassus, and his example will be contagious in court and in the army.[52]

Similar tones were perceptible in the review of the *Préservatif* in the *Literaturbriefe*. The reviewer, either Moses Mendelssohn or Friedrich Gabriel Resewitz, noted that Prémontval preached against the neglect of the ver-

---

[51] Frédéric Hartweg, 'Influence culturelle et intégration linguistique du Refuge Huguenot à Berlin au XVIIIe siècle', in *Le Refuge Huguenot en Allemagne* (Paris: CNRS, 1981), 47–55.
[52] *Göttingishe Anzeigen*, 22 May 1762, 510.

nacular 'with real German diligence'. However, the critic seemed offended by Prémontval's assertion that no regional dialect had been acknowledged by Germans as their literary language, suggesting that High German was the preserve of Saxony and Brandenburg-Prussia. The review also noted that excellent literature in the vernacular was much more important than a national capital.[53]

These reviews of the *Préservatif* reveal that Prémontval's quarrelsome periodical exerted, in a somewhat serendipitous manner, significant influence upon authors concerned with the establishment of German as a literary language. Johann Gottfried Herder was certainly one of these, and he was indeed well acquainted with Prémontval's works. Already in the first collection of his *Fragments on German Literature* (1767) Herder quoted Prémontval's 'not unjust' verdict on the questionable merits of French.[54] Contemplating in 1769 his contribution to the prize contest on the origin of language at the Berlin Academy, Herder fiercely attacked Frederick II and his academicians. Though generally not impressed by the Berlin intellectual scene, he demonstrated his profound acquaintance with it. The only works to prove somewhat useful, according to Herder, were the essays on language by Prémontval and Michaelis.

> What sort of philosophers are his [Frederick II's] Maupertuis, Prémontvals, Formeys, d'Argens? What have they crowned as [prize] essays? They did not understand Leibniz and Wolff and fostered the style of the Hazard by a Prémontval, the Monadology by a Justi,[55] the Free Will by a Reinhard,[56] the ethics and cosmology of a Maupertuis, and the style of a Formey. What is he [Formey] against Fontenelle? What are the *philosophes* themselves with their agreeable style against the Lockes and Leibnizs? On language they turned out to be more useful. Michaelis, Prémontval, and the current task [on the origin of language]; but still nothing of great measure and to serve as an eternal model.[57]

Categorically condemned by Herder, the Berlin Academy eventually bestowed its prestigious prize on the essay he wrote in the following year. Even if they were 'not to serve as an eternal model', it is noteworthy that the theories of language propounded by Prémontval and Michaelis had a long-lasting impact on Herder. In 1784 he translated a large section of

---

[53] The review is included in Mendelssohn, *JubA* v/1. 262–3, but Jürgen Storost has argued for Resewitz's authorship in *300 Jahre romanische Sprachen*, 74.
[54] 'Über die neuere deutsche Literatur', in Johann Gottfried Herder, *Frühe Schriften 1764–1772*, ed. Ulrich Gaier (Frankfurt am Main: Deutscher Klassiker Verlag, 1985), 256.
[55] The prize essay of the 1747 contest on monadology.
[56] The prize essay of the 1755 contest on Pope's optimism.
[57] Herder, *Journal meiner Reise im Jahr 1769; Pädagogische Schriften*, ed. Rainer Wisbert (Frankfurt am Main: Deutscher Klassiker Verlag, 1997), 71.

Prémontval's essay against Gallicomania, the German over-enthusiasm for the French language, which had been published as part 4 of the *Préservatif*. Having introduced Prémontval as a witness to the detrimental domination of French in Europe, Herder concluded his extract from the *Préservatif* with a tribute. The addiction to French in Germany, Herder argued, 'has wounded us much more deeply than the good Prémontval indicates. In his position he could say no more, and he had surely already said too much.'[58]

* * *

By emphasizing the relevance of language to the maintenance of cultural identities in Berlin, the *Préservatif* affair complemented the theoretical discussion of the genius of language, its origins, and its role in the mind. Prémontval's condemnation of the Huguenots' idiom may have stemmed from his part-time occupation as a language tutor, but the resonance of the *Préservatif* among German authors testified to a genuine receptivity to this sort of discourse.[59] Michaelis endorsed Prémontval's critique of the allegedly shallow use of French in Prussia, while Herder invoked the *Préservatif* when writing on cultural distinctiveness. What could have been deemed a forgotten literary quarrel may thus not only shed new light on issues of censorship and academic conduct but also reveal an unexpected contribution to the emergence of a new discourse on German literature. Yet this evolving discussion was also linked to the theoretical conundrums with which local authors, German and French alike, were left after the 1759 prize contest.

---

[58] Herder, *Briefe zu Beförderung der Humanität*, ed. Hans Dietrich Irmscher (Frankfurt am Main: Deutscher Klassiker Verlag, 1991), 597. For differences between Prémontval and Herder, see Krämer, '"Welcher Gestalt..."', and Clémence Couturier-Heinrich, 'Herders Übersetzung aus Prémontvals *Contre la gallicomanie* in den *Briefen zu Beförderung der Humanität*', *Herder Jahrbuch/Herder Yearbook* 10 (2010), 37–56.

[59] Prémontval, *Projet de conférences publiques sur l'éducation et sur l'éducation françoise en particulier* (Berlin: C. M. Vogel, 1763). On the saturated market of French tutors in Germany, see Henri Duranton, '"Un métier de chien": précepteurs, demoiselles de compagnie et bohême littéraire dans le refuge allemand', *Dix-huitième siècle* 17 (1985), 297–315.

7

Tackling the Naturalistic Conundrum

Instincts and Conjectural History to 1771

Despite the deadlock following the 1759 contest, the pertinent issues continued to occupy the Berlin Academy, as well as German authors from Riga to Göttingen. This chapter attempts, first, to trace various theoretical threads in the 1760s that increasingly led contemporaries to view language as an innate instinct. It then examines renewed attempts to cope with the problem of the joint origins of language and civilization over the 1760s, and the accompanying difficulties addressed by Abbt, Herder, Sulzer, and Garve. The persistence of the theoretical crisis in the 1760s finally led the Academy to dedicate another contest to language and mind. By contrast to the 1759 question, which was presented as a synchronic discussion of the constant interrelations between signs and the mind, the question for the 1771 contest dealt with the same topic from a diachronic, historical perspective: the Academy asked authors to trace the natural emergence of language among initially speechless human beings. Two of the entries submitted for this competition, Herder's prize essay and Michaelis's submission, bore the impact of the new epistemological and anthropological currents of the 1760s. Yet these entries should still be regarded as points on the theoretical continuum established by Leibniz's symbolic cognition and Condillac's genetic perspective on language in the mind.

Herder's major attempt to break the stalemate will be reviewed towards the end of this chapter, which emphasizes the continuity between 1759 and 1771, or between the question of the reciprocal influence of language and mind and that of the origin of language. Despite the theoretical developments of the 1760s, the main themes of the discussion remained fairly stable. These included the blurred boundary between animal language (or the natural expression of the passions) and human speech. By extension, such questions touched upon the natural or artificial character of human sociability and the human use of active reflection. A related topic troubling authors between the two contests on language was the degree of certainty attainable in philosophical inquiries, in comparison to both the mathematical method and the biblical account of human origins. Combined with new works in physiology and anthropology, the effect of these discussions was to highlight the problematic status of contemporary naturalism, or of the attempts to trace the transition from nature to human artifice.

LANGUAGE, METHOD, AND THE ANIMAL–HUMAN BOUNDARY

In spite of Formey's public avowal of his frustration with conjectural inquiries into language and mind, the Berlin Academy continued to explore various aspects of this disconcerting issue. The discussion, as before 1759, was conducted through extramural publications, essays read in academic meetings, and academic prize contests. The latter maintained their role as a mediating forum between the Academy, universities, and educated lay persons (*Gebildeten*). The common fascination in Berlin with language and its role in the mind was expressed also in prize contests whose ostensible topics were different from those of 1759 and 1771. A case in point is the announcement in 1761 of a competition (scheduled for 1763) on evidence and certainty in metaphysics, compared to the certitude available in geometry and mathematics. Prospective authors were asked whether 'metaphysical truths in general', and especially the first principles of ethics and natural theology, could be demonstrated with the same kind of evidence as mathematical truths. In case they could not, the Academy asked what degree of certainty metaphysics could attain, and whether it would suffice for philosophical persuasion.[1] This was the culmination of the intense debate over Christian Wolff's deductive method, which was to a large extent a controversy over the language of philosophy. The main question at stake was whether the objects of mathematics and metaphysics required treatment in completely different idioms. As noted in Chapter 2, criticism of the application of the mathematical method to philosophy was almost unanimous in the Germany of the 1750s. It was not only heralded by Maupertuis or anti-Wolffian sensualists like Crusius, but shared by professed Wolffians such as Gottsched and Formey. Most of them traced the distinctive certainty of the geometrical method back to its objects of inquiry. Mathematics owed its infallibility to its man-made imaginary objects; philosophy, on the other hand, was concerned with real things outside the human mind, and thus required different principles of verification.

[1] Harnack, *Geschichte*, ii. 306–7.

The prize went to Moses Mendelssohn's essay, an updated Wolffian approach to the question. Only one author gained the *accessit*: a young *Privatdozent* from Königsberg, Immanuel Kant. In his prize essay Mendelssohn argued that while mathematics dealt either with quantities or with the qualities of extended objects, natural philosophy was concerned with intensive or non-extended qualities such as speed and light. In the absence of an exact science of such qualities, philosophy did not have 'real signs' corresponding directly to the nature of its objects and their images in the mind. A further complication was that metaphysics required verification of the actual existence of its objects, in contrast to the mathematical focus on logical possibility.[2] A similar assertion was made in Kant's essay, where he claimed that mathematics dealt with mind-dependent, predetermined definitions, while philosophy must proceed by analysis of confused or inaccessible concepts. However, instead of following in the footsteps of Leibniz and Wolff, who strove for the full analysis of basic concepts (whenever possible), Kant took for granted that some of the main notions in philosophy were simply unanalysable: they were immediately given to our minds. The task of metaphysics was therefore to find out those aspects of things that seemed wholly intuitive, defying demonstrative analysis.[3]

Kant might have been influenced here by Crusius, whose Pietist attack on Wolffianism stressed the limits of human understanding. Refusing to deduce all knowledge from general principles such as the laws of non-contradiction and sufficient reason, Crusius based his criteria of truth on experience and self-evidence, arguing that what cannot be thought of as false must therefore be true.[4] Though Kant did not accept Crusius' subjective criteria of truth, he did use the resort to epistemological immediacy as the marker of our most fundamental concepts. This notion was strengthened in Kant's 1763 *Essay on Negative Magnitudes*, where he distinguished between logical negativity, amounting to contradiction or impossibility, and 'real' or actual negativity expressed as opposition or interaction between opposites, as in the case of natural forces.[5] Kant's distinction between the logical and the real in the *Essay on Negative Magnitudes* (together with

---

[2] Mendelssohn, 'Abhandlung über die Evidenz in metaphysischen Wissenschaften', *JubA*, ii. 281; Cornelia Buschmann, 'Wie bleibt Metaphysik als Wissenschaft möglich? Moses Mendelssohn und seine Konkurrenten um den Preis der Preußischen Akademie für 1763', in Albrecht and Engel (eds), *Mendelssohn im Spannungsfeld*, 37–49.
[3] *Kants gesammelte Schriften* (Berlin: Georg Reimer, 1900–), ii. 284 (henceforth *Akademieausgabe*).
[4] See the discussion in Chapter 2 above, as well as Giorgio Tonelli, 'Der Streit über die mathematische Methode', 55–8, and Carlos Spoerhase, 'A Case against Skepticism: On Christian August Crusius' Logic of Hermeneutical Probability', *History of European Ideas* 36 (2010), 251–9.
[5] Kant, 'Versuch den Begriff der negativen Grössen in die Weltweisheit einzuführen', in *Akademieausgabe*, ii. 165–204.

his treatise *The Only Possible Ground for a Demonstration of God's Existence*, 1763) advocated the primacy of the actual and the immediate over the logical and merely possible.[6] Herder, who attended Kant's lectures at Königsberg in 1762–4, internalized this lesson.[7] This was one of several developments in the 1760s pointing increasingly in the direction Mendelssohn had identified as a possible solution to Rousseau's conundrums: viewing language as an innate capacity in need of environmental activation.

The renewed emphasis on the actual and the real in both the natural and the human sciences, as opposed to the logical and the imaginary in mathematics, prized a view of language as always existing in a certain form. This stance was clear in Formey's attack in 1762 on naturalistic conjectural histories: language could not have appeared *ex nihilo* in initially speechless creatures. If this had ever been the case, the original creatures could not be considered human at all. Yet as we do not know of any other species equipped with a fully fledged language, so went the anti-Epicurean objection, there had never been a natural transition from natural sounds to arbitrary human words: mankind must have always been a linguistic species, the only speaking animal.[8]

Another significant contribution to this emerging perspective was the first publication in 1765 of Leibniz's *New Essays on Human Understanding* (written in 1703–5) by Rudolf Erich Raspe.[9] In this reply to Locke's *Essay*, Leibniz tried to reconcile his innatism with a double source of knowledge in human psychology. He thus resorted in the *New Essays* to the notion of inherent knowledge as a latent potential in need of activation by conscious reflection and attention. These, in turn, could be provoked by confused sense perceptions. The innate capacities and structures of human knowledge were alternately called by Leibniz 'dispositions', 'tendencies', 'habits', and sometimes 'instincts', though this latter term was different from physical drives. According to Leibniz, the universal functions of the mind presupposed matching innate instincts.[10] Even if, as Giorgio Tonelli pointed out, the psychological aspects of the *New Essays* were not clearly perceived in the immediate reviews, its publication coincided with a

---

[6] Kant, 'Der einzig mögliche Beweisgrund zu einer Demonstration des Daseins Gottes', *Akademieausgabe*, ii. 63–163.

[7] Zammito, *Kant, Herder, and the Birth of Anthropology*, 71–5.

[8] Formey, 'Réunion des principaux moyens' (see Chapter 5).

[9] Raspe (1736–94) worked at the Royal Library in Hanover, where he had access to Leibniz's manuscripts. He wrote an adaptation of Robert Hooke's geological works and an essay introducing Macpherson's Ossian to German readers. However, today he is renowned mostly for publishing Baron Munchhausen's adventures (1785). See Rudolf Hallo, *Rudolf Erich Raspe: Ein Wegbereiter von deutscher Art und Kunst* (Stuttgart: Kohlhammer, 1934).

[10] Leibniz, 'Nouveaux essais sur l'entendement humain', in *Sämtliche Schriften*, vi/6, I. ii.§3, 90.

widespread dissatisfaction with Wolff's method and an increasing tendency of younger intellectuals to bypass Wolff by independently re-examining Leibniz's original works.[11]

Debates on human cognition and language in the 1760s were further stimulated by a treatise by Hermann Samuel Reimarus, *Allgemeine Betrachtungen über die Triebe der Thiere, hauptsächlich über ihre Kunsttriebe* (*General Observations on Animal Instincts and Primarily Their Artful Instincts*). This work, first published in 1760, appeared in revised editions in 1762, 1773, and 1798, and was translated into Dutch and French in the 1760s. Reimarus, retrospectively known mainly as the author of heterodox fragments which Lessing published after his death, collected in this book observations by academic experimenters, professional hunters, and animal breeders. He concluded, in the contemporary anti-Cartesian manner, that the mind and instincts of animals were not strictly mechanical. Their natural drives included, according to Reimarus, capacities of representation and arbitrary action, instincts of self-preservation and self-love, and skilful drives for the intricate production of artefacts (the eponymous *Kunsttriebe*). Reimarus criticized Buffon for clinging in his *Histoire naturelle* to a largely Cartesian view of animals while simultaneously ascribing to them life, soul, and feelings.[12] Yet even Reimarus' vindication of the robust cognitive faculties of animals was capped by a commitment to modified dualism. The target-orientated actions of animals were not acquired through experience and reasoning, Reimarus argued. They consisted in divinely predetermined natural powers of both body and mind, different from the similar albeit undetermined and progressively perfectible human capacities.[13]

Language played a significant role in this argument. While some observers suggested that animals could link the past with the present and intelligibly communicate with one another, Reimarus emphasized that a proper human language always consisted of consciously introduced artificial signs. By contrast to the tacit transition in conjectural histories from natural signs to conventional words, Reimarus pointed out that onomatopoeic sounds could not have enabled human communication: they were exces-

---

[11] Tonelli, 'Leibniz on Innate Ideas and the Early Reactions to the Publication of the *Nouveaux Essais* (1765)', *Journal of the History of Philosophy* 12 (1974), 437–54. Hamann drew Herder's attention to Raspe's edition as early as January 1765 (Hamann, *Briefwechsel*, ii. 296–303).

[12] Reimarus, *Allgemeine Betrachtungen über die Triebe der Thiere, hauptsächlich über ihre Kunsttriebe*, 4th edn, ed. Johann Albert Heinrich Reimarus (Hamburg: Carl Ernst Bohn, 1798), 282.

[13] Ibid. pp. vi–viii; 302–11. See also Hans Werner Ingensiep, 'Der Mensch im Spiegel der Tier- und Pflanzenseele: Zur Anthropomorphologie der Naturwahrnehmung im 18. Jahrhundert', in Hans-Jürgen Schings (ed.), *Der ganze Mensch: Anthropologie und Literatur im 18. Jahrhundert* (Stuttgart: Metzler, 1994), 54–79.

sively subjective and reflected far too different circumstances. Only artificial signification could express the general similarities and differences between phenomena on an intersubjective level.[14] Artificiality as a proof of human intelligence was demonstrated, according to Reimarus, by the diversity of languages, whereas animal sounds were everywhere uniform, not invented but innately 'pre-planted'.[15]

Reimarus referred in his treatise to Condillac's similar critique of Buffon in his *Treatise on the Animals* of 1755, taking up one of its main arguments. Condillac claimed that animals could feel, compare, judge, and store ideas, but drew a clear line between mankind and the rest of nature. Unsurprisingly for an author who based human thinking on the manipulation of signs, Condillac postulated language as the essential trait of human beings alone.[16] This boundary between human and animal cognition was manifest in the famous case of the statue Condillac endowed with the different senses in his *Treatise on the Sensations* (1754). Though this thought experiment would later be considered as the hallmark of extreme materialism, Condillac's statue fell short of becoming truly human due to its lack of language. It did not possess the uniquely human ability to process general ideas through artificial signs.[17]

The Berlin Academy, as usual a significant indicator of contemporary trends, dedicated two different contests in 1768 to a reassessment of Leibniz's work (*Éloge de Leibniz*) and to natural instincts. In the latter case, the Academy asked authors to examine specifically whether innate instincts could be overcome or completely inhibited. If these instincts turned out to be 'invincible', the Academy required authors to suggest how such drives could be channelled towards useful targets.[18] As the topics of the contests were announced two years in advance, it seems that the second half of the 1760s witnessed a reinvigorated interest in innatism as expressed in internal drives and dispositions, both intellectual and physical. The Leibniz renaissance merged here with Kant's critical assessment of

---

[14] Reimarus, *Allgemeine Betrachtungen*, 319. Reimarus had made similar arguments about human and animal communication in his popular work of 1754, *Die vornehmsten Wahrheiten der natürlichen Religion*, 3rd edn (Hamburg: Johann Carl Bohn, 1766), 344–6 and 544–5.

[15] Gerda Haßler, 'Diversity of Human Languages and Universals of Thought: An Eighteenth-Century Debate in the Berlin Academy', in David Cram, Andrew Linn, and Elke Nowak (eds), *History of Linguistics 1996* (Amsterdam: John Benjamins, 1999), 163–74.

[16] Condillac, *Traité des sensations; Traité des animaux* (Paris: Fayard, 1984), 369.

[17] Aarsleff, 'Condillac's Speechless Statue', in *From Locke to Saussure*, 210–24. Cf. Ernst Platner, *Anthropologie für Aerzte und Weltweise* (Leipzig: Dyckische Buchhandlung, 1772), 208–15. While wishing to overcome simplistic dichotomies between body and mind, Platner too saw the creation of general ideas and artificial words as an attribute of the immaterial aspects of the human mind.

[18] Harnack, *Geschichte*, ii. 307.

Wolff by way of Crusius, as well as with the anthropological interest in the physiological aspects of man and the artful drives of animals. These new theoretical impulses further complicated the Epicurean account of the emergence of a full human language from cries and gestures. The gauntlet had been thrown down in the 1750s by one of the chief contributors to the revival of naturalistic thesis, Condillac himself. By employing language as the gatekeeper of the uniquely human part of the mind, Condillac might have undermined his own narrative of a slow transition from nature to artifice. His sharp distinction between human and animal language implied that artificial signs were qualitatively different from natural or onomatopoeic sounds.[19]

Reimarus' introduction of the debate on animal cognition between Condillac and Buffon to a German audience amplified Rousseau's similar conundrums. When Johann Peter Süßmilch revised his lectures on the divine origin of language (given in 1756) for publication in 1766, he found it necessary to include an appendix on animal language. Any attempt to find similarities between animal language and human speech, Süßmilch argued, was deliberately meant to 'diminish the eternity of man and the boundary between him and the animals'.[20] Like Condillac and Reimarus, Süßmilch referred to the absence of general or abstract ideas in animal communication, as well as to the inability of apes and domestic animals to learn a grammatical language despite their manifest imitative skills.[21] The new discourse of anthropology, while examining man's entire constitution and attempting to bridge the gap between the mental and the physical, seems to have stumbled on the obstacle of language. Virtually none of the authors who upgraded the animal mind was willing to accept a continuum between bestial communication and human language, or between natural sounds and artificial words. Language was left hovering between the two realms as a mysterious leap from the natural to the civilized: Rousseau's vicious circles retained in the 1760s their full beguiling appeal.

HISTORICAL EVOLUTION FROM UNKNOWN ORIGINS: ABBT, HERDER, AND SULZER

The problems inherent in the natural evolution of language and mind were well perceived, as we have seen, in reviews of the 1759 contest by thinkers interested in these topics. Another such author was Thomas

---

[19] Condillac became well aware of this problem, as recounted in Chapter 1. See also Lifschitz, 'The Arbitrariness of the Linguistic Sign'.
[20] Süßmilch, *Versuch*, 99.   [21] Ibid. 102–3.

Abbt, a close friend of Friedrich Nicolai and Moses Mendelssohn who replaced Lessing as reviewer for their Berlin-based journal *Literaturbriefe*. Better known for his essays on merit and patriotic self-sacrifice, Abbt was deeply interested in language as a philosophical subject and as a means to promote cultural regeneration in Germany.[22] Indeed, Abbt wrote his thesis at Halle in 1758 on the confusion of languages at Babel. According to Abbt, this miraculous event did not consist merely in the erasure of a particular vocabulary and its replacement by several different lexicons: at Babel God transformed the human mind. A mind without words could not simply make up new signs, for it lost its capacity of representing the surrounding world. This miracle was, however, double-edged, equipping human beings with a new capacity to coin words in manifold manners, according to the circumstances in which they first encountered external objects. Abbt's interpretation, therefore, posited a quasi-Epicurean emergence of language after Babel, the consequence of a profound mental upheaval.[23]

A few years later, language was the central example in a methodological essay included in Abbt's posthumously published universal history, entitled *Allerhand Muthmassungen über den ältesten Zustand des Menschen* (*Various Conjectures about the Earliest Condition of Mankind*).[24] A perceptive overview of the questions involved in the contemporary quest for origins, Abbt's essay was strategically placed within what he defined as the second period of universal history, starting after the Deluge. Abbt's meditation on human origins interrupted his narrative at the precise point where various Enlightenment authors inserted an Epicurean account of the evolution of human society into the Judeo-Christian framework: after the divine crushing of human pride and cultural aspirations. Like Süßmilch and Formey, Abbt vindicated the significance of the biblical account of origins not due to its traditional authority but rather as the only alternative to the inadequacy of the naturalistic thesis. He too had wished to play the naturalistic game in the arena of conjectural historians

---

[22] Abbt's most renowned works are 'Vom Tode fürs Vaterland' (1761) and 'Vom Verdienste' (1765), in *Vermischte Werke*, ed. Friedrich Nicolai (Frankfurt and Leipzig: Nicolai, 1783), i, and ii. 1–132. On these works, see Hans Erich Bödeker, 'Thomas Abbt: Patriot, Bürger und bürgerliches Bewußtsein', in Rudolf Vierhaus (ed.), *Bürger und Bürgerlichkeit im Zeitalter der Aufklärung* (Heidelberg: Schneider, 1981), 221–53; Benjamin W. Redekop, *Lessing, Abbt, Herder, and the Quest for a German Public* (Montreal and Kingston: McGill-Queen's University Press, 2000), 123–67; Eva Piirimäe, 'Dying for the Fatherland: Thomas Abbt's Theory of Aesthetic Patriotism', *History of European Ideas* 35 (2009), 194–208.

[23] Abbt, *Vermischte Werke*, vi. 110–16.

[24] Abbt, *Fragment der aeltesten Begebenheiten des menschlichen Geschlechts*, ed. Johann Peter Miller (Halle: Johann Justinus Gebauer, 1767), 36–48; reprinted in *Vermischte Werke*, vi. 146–65.

attempting to reconstruct the evolution of society and the human mind; unfortunately, Abbt informed his readers, this was a precarious pastime.

Much in contemporary inquires into origins was muddled, Abbt argued, by the tendency to combine Genesis with other, 'philosophical' accounts of human origins. There was, as we saw in Chapters 1 and 3, a widely accepted synthesis to be found in works of authors from Vico and Warburton to Condillac and Rousseau. Abbt wished, however, to separate the two images of the first human beings—the biblical and the 'philosophical'—as distinctly from one another as possible. In the so-called Mosaic image of man, the first human beings were already 'grown up', or in full command of the entire range of their cognitive capacities. They had language, and hence did not need to develop it from natural sounds. They also had sociable inclinations, lived in sizeable communities, and were capable of conducting commerce and constructing cities. In short, Abbt noted, most of the intractable difficulties facing investigators into human origins would disappear if one adopted this image of original man. Instead of quarrelling over the essential qualities of abstract, non-existent human beings at the dawn of history, authors could pursue a ready-made thread.

In the alternative 'philosophical' accounts of human origins, Abbt argued, everything was complete conjecture with no added value for the philosopher.[25] In implicit reference to Rousseau's methodology in the *Discours sur l'inégalité*, Abbt noted that such philosophers had to decide arbitrarily whether to consider the first human beings equipped with rudimentary capacities or with developed ones, to choose a couple or a larger human community as their point of origin, and to postulate all kinds of geological and climatic upheavals. As an example of a shrewd attempt to explain the transition from nature to artifice, Abbt related almost verbatim Mendelssohn's reply to Rousseau's conundrums, complete with the shift in the reference of bleating from a sheep (its natural denotation) to the surrounding meadow (of which it was an artificial sign).[26] However, even if Mendelssohn arguably managed to step out of one of Rousseau's vicious circles, Abbt did not see what could be the larger point of his conjecture about the natural emergence of language. Mendelssohn's solution, as many others, assumed the mutual emergence and enhancement of language, society, and the human mind over long ages of barbarism, but its speculative starting point was precisely that, in Abbt's eyes: a conjecture unsupported by any sort of evidence. For Abbt, the biblical narrative was a better heuristic tool for speculations about the evolution of language and society. Its malleability, together with its cul-

[25] Ibid. 151.   [26] Ibid. 155–62.

tural prominence, made it an indispensable and common point of departure. As Johann David Michaelis argued, even if Genesis was not a trustworthy guide to universal history, it was still a fuller and more reliable account than most alternatives.[27] From Abbt's perspective, the wider acceptance of the biblical narrative could spare philosophers much inconsequential quarrelling over unknowable details.[28]

Some of these points were taken up seriously by a new arrival in this troubled field of inquiry, Johann Gottfried Herder, who composed an admiring obituary to Abbt after the latter's death at the age of 28.[29] Herder's first popular publication was the *Fragments on Recent German Literature*, a self-styled supplement and response to the influential *Literaturbriefe*. Herder published a few collections of his *Fragments* in 1767–8, adhering to the programme of contemporary *Popularphilosophie*. He sought to distinguish himself from the aporetic investigations of language conducted by professional academics, addressing his musings to the 'world'—the new *Gebildeten*, as opposed to specialized *Gelehrten*. He took for granted the main tenets of the Berlin debates, namely that language was not just a vehicle for the expression of thought but an indispensable tool for its production. Yet Herder's main concern was, at this stage, practical: how to employ these insights in the service of a German literary renaissance. He wished to 'wake up geniuses and teach readers, not satisfy arbiters of taste!'[30] This preoccupation might explain his receptivity to Prémontval's views on the harmful imitation of French models. Not unlike Michaelis, Herder too envisaged the advent of geniuses who would recast the German language, and in the meantime he examined cultural revivals in foreign literatures.[31]

In the second edition of his first collection of *Fragments* (1768), Herder stressed his impatience with academics, whom he deemed isolated in their ivory tower. Johann David Michaelis became his specific scapegoat. Herder's retrospective assessment of the 1759 prize essay started with the observation that it said 'much that is good but nothing

---

[27] Michaelis, *Zerstreute kleine Schriften*, 267–8.
[28] See also Immanuel Kant's short essay 'Conjectures on the Beginning of Human History', where he suggested that 'the route which philosophy follows with the help of concepts accords with that which the Bible story describes' (Kant, *Political Writings*, ed. Hans Reiss, trans. H. B. Nisbet (Cambridge: Cambridge University Press, 1991), 222; *Akademieausgabe*, viii. 110). For Herder's engagement with the same theme, see Christoph Bultmann, *Die biblische Urgeschichte in der Aufklärung* (Tübingen: Mohr Siebeck, 1999), and Daniel Weidner, 'Secularization, Scripture, and the Theory of Reading: J. G. Herder and the Old Testament', *New German Critique* 94 (2005), 169–93.
[29] Herder, 'Über Thomas Abbts Schriften: Der Torso von einem Denkmal, an seinem Grabe errichtet' (1768), in *Schriften zur Ästhetik und Literatur 1767–1781*, ed. Gunter E. Grimm (Frankfurt am Main: Deutscher Klassiker Verlag, 1993), 565–608.
[30] Ibid. 594.   [31] Herder, *Frühe Schriften*, 273–4.

complete', and continued by levelling at Michaelis two conflicting accusations. The Göttingen professor allegedly failed to specify and elaborate his generalizations, for Herder wished to 'grab him by the arm' and ask for examples, but on the other hand Michaelis flooded readers with numerous etymologies and special cases, thus obscuring his general points. Ridiculing Michaelis as an impractical dreamer, Herder claimed that the prize essay itself demonstrated the detrimental influence of language on opinions.[32] At the same time Herder was particularly interested in applying the mutual links between language and mind to the German predicament. He asked, for example, in what shape or within which limits language moulded human thinking, how one could philosophize about the origin and structure of language if one's own thought was moulded by it (a question posed earlier by Mendelssohn), what a nation should do in order to make its language the vehicle of indigenous literature, and whether foreign impact on the vernacular was a negative phenomenon.

These were all issues Michaelis had examined extensively if not exhaustively. His concern with the democratic nature of language, with the revival of the vernacular, and with the negative effects of scientific idioms may attest to the inadequacy of Herder's critique. It seems that Michaelis was picked as a foil against which Herder could thrust his new insights. At the same time the young author used many of the ideas in Michaelis's prize essay and his works on oriental poetry. In the following year, after all, Herder would single out Michaelis and Prémontval as the most 'useful' authors writing for the Berlin Academy.[33] Herder admitted he had no straightforward solution to the problems involving language and mind, suggesting in his fragment *Von den Lebensaltern einer Sprache* (*On the Life-Stages of a Language*) what had become a rather conventional theory of linguistic evolution. Like Michaelis, Condillac, and Diderot, Herder traced the transition from a childhood of fiery poetry to an old age of abstract but scientifically useful language.[34]

---

[32] Ibid. 563–4.

[33] Herder, *Journal meiner Reise*, 71, as quoted in Chapter 6. For Michaelis's influence on Herder's evolving views of Hebrew, see Weidner, '"Menschliche, heilige Sprache": Das Hebräische bei Michaelis und Herder', *Monatshefte für deutschsprachige Literatur und Kultur* 95 (2003), 171–206, and Jan Loop, '"Von dem Geschmack der morgenländischen Dichtkunst": Orientalistik und Bibelexegese bei Huet, Michaelis und Herder', in Daniel Weidner (ed.), *Urpoesie und Morgenland: Johann Gottfried Herders 'Vom Geist der Ebräischen Poesie'* (Berlin: Kadmos, 2008), 155–83.

[34] *Frühe Schriften*, 181–7. See Ulrich Gaier, *Herders Sprachphilosophie und Erkenntniskritik* (Stuttgart-Bad Cannstatt: Frommann-Holzboog, 1988), 35–74; Anthony La Vopa, 'Herder's *Publikum*: Language, Print, and Sociability in Eighteenth-Century Germany', *Eighteenth-Century Studies* 29 (1996), 5–24.

These comments on language made Herder himself the target of sharp criticism. In a review of Herder's *Fragments*, Christian Garve remarked that the analogy between human life and the evolution of language was far too simplistic. Garve believed that Herder, despite his precocious scholarship, had not sufficiently understood the theoretical impasse of inquiries into the interrelations between language and mind after 1759.

> We doubt whether such a childhood of language [...] has ever existed. To tell the truth, this seems to us, just as much as the so-called *status naturalis*, to belong to philosophical novels: because if there had ever been a time when man just made sounds instead of speaking, he would have forever *made sounds* and never *spoken*.[35]

Unlike Abbt, who tolerated naturalistic speculations about the evolution of language against the receding background of Genesis, Garve seems to have opted here for a more radical stance, similar to some of Süßmilch's arguments in his *Versuch* (published in the previous year, 1766). Süßmilch had argued that if the Lucretian brutes had ever existed, they would have always remained bestial; a community of 4-year olds with no access to grammatical language would likewise forever remain childish.[36] Garve thereby joined the choir of critics emphasizing the most unstable element of the naturalistic account, the transformation of imitative sounds into artificial words. By seeing conjectural histories of language and mind as fictitious 'philosophical novels', Garve also echoed Formey's exasperation at the difficulties inherent in unveiling the distant origins of all human phenomena.

One member of the 1759 jury did not despair. Johann Georg Sulzer read to the Academy in 1767 a paper on the reciprocal influence of reason and language, a conscious confrontation with one of Rousseau's conundrums and the 1759 question. Sulzer opened his essay by presenting the problem: reason presupposed the matching of signs with general ideas, whereas language—the use of signs for these general ideas—seemed to require an already cultivated reason. Pointing out that this 'insurmountable difficulty' had made some authors resort to 'miracles',

---

[35] Christian Garve's review of the first and second collections of Herder's *Fragments* in *Neue Bibliothek der schönen Wissenschaften und der freyen Künste*, iv/1 (Leipzig: Dyckische Buchhandlung, 1767), 40–79, here 74. See also Garve's review of the third collection in the *Neue Bibliothek*, v/2 (1767), 241–91.

[36] Süßmilch, *Versuch*, 69, 88–90. Michaelis, by contrast, regarded children as creative agents who acquired language with no need for direct, explicit instruction (*Beurtheilung*, 100–11).

Sulzer begged to differ: an appeal to supernatural causes, he declared, should be made only after the inadequacy of all natural causes was fully demonstrated.[37] Like Abbt, Sulzer lamented the absence of any fixed point of departure for such inquiries, but he argued that a full reconstruction of the genesis of reason and language was not mandatory. Sulzer suggested taking 'civilized man' (*l'homme instruit*), if considered without language, as a model for 'wild man' (*l'homme brute*).[38] As an active member of the Academy and future head of its class of speculative philosophy, Sulzer must have been well acquainted with Rousseau's challenges—yet he did not heed Rousseau's advice. More than a decade after Rousseau's allegations that natural law theorists had wrongly ascribed to natural man some of his civilized attributes, Sulzer was effectively suggesting that human characteristics could be freely transferred between these two conditions.

On the whole, Sulzer's essay did not seem to have satisfied the expectations it might have evoked in its readers, recapitulating as it did some of the earlier arguments for the natural origin of artificial words in the Epicurean tradition. According to Sulzer's account, all words ultimately derived from onomatopoeia. Brutish people could have never denoted a thing without 'a reason in nature'.[39] He was apparently unimpressed by the argument that only a very small number of words could be explained on this basis, as Süßmilch and some of the reviewers of the 1759 contest pointed out. The Epicurean-naturalistic thesis allowed, indeed, for the subsequent transformation of most onomatopoeic words into completely artificial signs through metaphor and analogy. However, the implied shift of vocabulary was so comprehensive that contemporaries could question the effectiveness of onomatopoeic origins as an explanation of the workings of present-day, artificial language. By the end of the 1760s, linguistic arbitrariness had been largely appropriated by the supernatural party. Naturalists were therefore compelled to adhere to a rudimentary account of the onomatopoeic origin of most words—or confess they could not account for the transformation of natural sounds into the artificial words that characterize an appropriately human language.

---

[37] Johann Georg Sulzer, 'Observations sur l'influence réciproque de la raison sur le langage et du langage sur la raison', *Histoire de l'Académie, année 1767* (Berlin: Haude & Spener, 1769), 413–38; here 413. See also Ralph Häfner, *Johann Gottfried Herders Kulturentstehungslehre: Studien zu den Quellen und zur Methode seines Geschichtsdenkens* (Hamburg: Meiner, 1995), 3–4.
[38] Sulzer, 'Observations', 414.
[39] Ibid. 419–20.

NATURALISM AND INSTINCTS IN THE 1771 CONTEST

In an attempt to break the stalemate, the Academy announced in 1769 another contest on language and mind, this time focused on the evolutionary aspect of their interrelations. The question for 1771 was very similar to the one proposed by Michaelis in his 1759 prize essay, with a trace of the contemporary fascination with Psammetichus' experiment. It could also be seen as an official invitation to challenge the recently deceased Süßmilch by vindicating a naturalistic account of the mutual emergence of language and mind.

> Abandoned to their natural capacities, would human beings be in a condition to invent language? And by what means could they achieve this invention on their own? We require a hypothesis explaining the matter clearly and satisfying all the difficulties.[40]

The final point attests to the troubled status of the question by the late 1760s. If the main difficulties in the naturalistic account of a transition from gestures and cries to artificial words had been exposed by Rousseau, the prize question seemed to return to his own point of departure. Like fellow naturalists, Rousseau had wished in his *Discours sur l'inégalité* to speculate only on the basis of 'the nature of man and of the Beings that surround him, about what Mankind might have become if it had remained abandoned to itself'.[41] The notion of human beings left to their own devices was one of the keys to Rousseau's conjectural account of human evolution, as well as to similar Enlightenment narratives. Though providence may have had a hand in the contingent, actual history of the world, 'mankind abandoned to itself' signalled the potential course of things without the optional intervention of God and the odd natural disaster. Rousseau's account was indeed conjectural, but it traced the unfolding of essence and nature as opposed to history (seen as the record of contingency). By referring to human beings 'abandoned to their natural capacities', the Berlin Academy confronted authors head-on with Rousseau's challenge to himself and to other conjectural historians of humanity.

Unlike the case of the 1759 contest, twenty-four out of the thirty-one entries submitted for the 1771 competition are still preserved in the archive of the Berlin Academy. These have recently formed the basis of a

---

[40] Harnack, *Geschichte*, ii. 307.
[41] Rousseau, *Discourses*, 132; *Œuvres complètes*, iii. 133.

meticulous textual comparison by Cordula Neis, which yielded significant insights into the common *topoi* and points of references in discussions of language and mind in the 1760s.[42] Though much could have been said about entries by Dietrich Tiedemann, Johannes Nikolaus Tetens, and Francesco Soave, among others, my examination here is limited to the arguments made in two essays by authors involved in the discussions reviewed above: Herder's prize essay and Michaelis's renewed attempt to tackle the question.

As a scholar deeply involved with linguistic issues since his youth, it was not surprising that Michaelis participated in the 1771 contest. He might have felt particularly gratified that the Academy took up the topic he had suggested in 1759, despite Formey's condemnation of the entire conjectural genre.[43] As the question this time concerned the origin of language, Michaelis directly engaged with both Rousseau and Süßmilch, the most serious challengers of the naturalistic theory he advocated from the 1750s onwards. Like Herder, Michaelis strictly ruled out any recourse to the divine endowment of language. He therefore had to deny Süßmilch's assumption that all languages shared the same perfect structure across time and over the entire earth, and that this design was replicated in no other system of communication. Michaelis pointed out that the first languages must have been rather rudimentary, lacking most parts of speech, so that qualitative change (rather than mere improvement) must have occurred over time. Faithful to his own critique of earlier theories involving a deliberate design of language, Michaelis argued that languages evolved by strictly human means.

> On the basis of natural features it is not necessary to assume that the first speaker invented language following a pre-made plan. Language will impose itself on him and be invented before he knows it, then extending and enriching itself.[44]

Michaelis argued that language could always emerge within a small, basic human community: a man, a woman, and their young child, united by ties of mutual affection. This claim arose from Michaelis's principled objection to Rousseau's portrayal of the state of nature. The entry elaborated two points Michaelis had already singled out in his 1757 review of Mendelssohn's translation of Rousseau's *Discours*: the importance of mutual

---

[42] Cordula Neis, *Anthropologie im Sprachdenken des 18. Jahrhunderts: Die Berliner Preisfrage nach dem Ursprung der Sprache* (Berlin: De Gruyter, 2003).
[43] I am indebted here to Neis's discovery of Michaelis's manuscript in Göttingen; the entry is not preserved in the Academy's archive in Berlin (*Anthropologie im Sprachdenken*, 507–50).
[44] Göttingen, Codex Michaelis 72, 42.

affection and domestic life for the emergence of language, and the crucial contribution of children's creativity, spurred by emotional bonds with their mothers.[45] He therefore rejected Rousseau's seminal distinction between the physical and moral aspects of mutual affection, or the putative transition from the gratification of physical impulses in the state of nature (physical love) to socially sanctioned conjugal relationship (moral love). According to Michaelis, mutual human affection, the fear of changing a domicile, and inherent jealousy would all have naturally brought men and women together. Anticipating the Rousseau-inspired objection that he transferred to natural man some attributes of his civilized counterpart, Michaelis buttressed his argument by pointing out how affection among animals intensifies the use of gestures and sounds.[46] Like Abbt, Michaelis reprimanded Rousseau for having allegedly assumed a polygenetic origin of mankind, or a sufficient number of males and females to enable different mating possibilities, without considering the biblical alternative of a single original couple.

In 1771 Michaelis attributed the human development of language to the convergence of general dispositions (such as natural affection) and instincts, for example imitation and the combination of sounds with meanings. Some of the natural instincts, like imitation, were shared by animals, while the rest were exclusively human (the gradual perfection of articulate speech). These latent capacities were activated, according to Michaelis, through chance and accident, but only within the framework of mutual affection and familial life. Michaelis used here the anthropological discussion of skilful drives (*Kunsttriebe*) and the Leibnizian notion of innate tendencies in a revision of the Epicurean account. Emphasizing that need and pain could necessitate only rudimentary, inarticulate speech, he rooted the uneasy transition from natural signs to conventional words in the added value of dispositions such as love, mutual care, and the resourcefulness of human infants. Without these tendencies, Rousseau's natural man would have indeed remained as speechless as Süßmilch's Lucretian brutes, forever emitting natural sounds. Michaelis argued, therefore, that 'Language is not the daughter of need but of human love, overflowing joy, play, and a secret pleasure felt at the exchange of thoughts.'[47] As Mendelssohn tried to suggest in the 1750s, the innate channelling of physical drives within a social

---

[45] *Göttingische Anzeigen*, 5 February 1757, 142–3. This review was the first to reveal publicly Mendelssohn's authorship of the anonymous translation and the attached *Sendschreiben*. These stemmed, as Michaelis put it, from 'the pen of a philosophizing Jew' who had previously written the *Briefe über die Empfindungen*.

[46] Göttingen, Codex Michaelis 72, 23–4.

[47] Ibid. 23. Here Michaelis called pleasure 'Wollust', a term he had criticized in the 1759 prize essay.

framework was required to complement the naturalistic narrative and 'humanize' its animalistic overtones.

Herder's prize essay began by tackling exactly this difficulty, memorably exclaiming that 'Already as an animal, the human being has language.'[48] This surprising proposition expressed at the outset of Herder's treatise one of its most pivotal theses. According to Herder, man should be seen in his entirety, as an integrated physical and intellectual being. Human beings did not evolve from a pre-linguistic condition to one of speech and civilization. Language, according to Herder, has always been present in the human mind.[49]

Like Michaelis, Herder wished to uphold the naturalistic account of human evolution while recognizing that it could be saved only by a major reconfiguration. When reviewing previous accounts of the shift from natural signs to artificial words, Herder somewhat caricaturized his predecessors to make his point. Condillac allegedly made animal into man in his *Traité des animaux*, while also ascribing to the first human beings too extensive a use of signs in the *Essai*. Rousseau, however, had reduced man to an animal, and Maupertuis too had apparently disappointed Herder, who admitted he had not read the relevant treatise.[50] Yet Herder's primary intention was not to belittle earlier contributions. He wished to single out for criticism the notion that a passionate language of action could have formed the basis of a properly human idiom of artificial signs. The natural expression of emotions could not have been transformed into an articulate human language through metaphors, analogies, imitation, or any other transference of meaning. What Herder called a language of nature, the language man had 'already as an animal', was basically an instinct for the expression of pain and violent passions.[51] Herder stressed, however, that this natural language, or the natural law making animals and human beings into expressive creatures, was categorically different from proper human language. It lacked the peculiar combination of expression with self-awareness and intention.[52] Herder had apparently learned Rousseau's lesson,

---

[48] Herder, *Philosophical Writings*, 65; *Frühe Schriften*, 697.
[49] On the background of this conviction, see Zammito, *Kant, Herder, and the Birth of Anthropology*; Wolfgang Pross's epilogue to Herder, *Werke*, ii: *Herder und die Anthropologie der Aufklärung* (Munich: Hanser, 1987), esp. 1170–204; articles by Pross, Jean Mondot, and Ulrich Gaier in Pierre Pénisson and Norbert Waszek (eds), *Herder et les Lumières* (*Revue Germanique Internationale* 20 (2003)), 17–71.
[50] Herder, *Philosophical Writings*, 74–7; *Frühe Schriften*, 708–11. See also Bruce Kieffer, 'Herder's Treatment of Süssmilch's Theory of the Origin of Language in the *Abhandlung über den Ursprung der Sprache*: A Re-evaluation', *The Germanic Review* 53 (1978), 96–105.
[51] On the relationship between pain and expression in this idiom, see Ilit Ferber, 'Herder: On Pain and the Origin of Language', *The Germanic Review* 85 (2010), 205–23.
[52] Herder, *Philosophical Writings*, 74; *Frühe Schriften*, 708.

coming to view the language of nature and any human tongue as so different in kind that no transition over time could turn the one into the other.

This was Herder's main point in reference to ancient naturalists such as Diodorus of Sicily and Vitruvius, 'who make men first of all roam for ages as animals with cries in the forests, and then afterwards—God knows whence and God knows for what purpose!—invent language for themselves'.[53] Here was a striking testimony to the extent to which Herder heeded contemporary warnings about the inadequacy of long ages of barbarism as a heuristic device explaining the transition from natural sounds to artificial words. A few years after Formey's essay of 1762 on conjectural histories and the publication in 1766 of Süßmilch's lectures, Herder seemed to be in agreement with them about one of the tenets of the naturalistic narrative. No matter how long the so-called Lucretian brutes roamed the woods, they would have never been able to develop a full human language if they had originally lacked its main features. Most proponents of the natural emergence of language, therefore, 'fought their case from such insecure territory, which others, for example Süßmilch, attacked with such good reason'.[54] But rather than merely ridiculing the Enlightenment champions of naturalism, Herder rushed to their assistance with newly whetted intellectual weapons. He understood very well the damage wrought by Rousseau's questioning of the human origin of language in the *Discours sur l'inégalité*, noting that the failure of one line of naturalistic argumentation did not completely rule it out. Herder's ambition to reintegrate mankind into the natural world led to a passionate rejection of any appeal to divine intervention, which he regarded in his prize essay as a hindrance to the proper understanding of both nature and human beings.

> The higher [divine] origin [of language] is useless and extremely harmful. It destroys all efficacy of the human mind, explains nothing, and makes everything, all psychology and all sciences, inexplicable. For have human beings, then, with language received all the seeds of forms of knowledge from God? So *nothing* comes from the human mind? So the *beginning of every art, science, and form of knowledge* is always *unintelligible*? The human origin lets no step be taken without prospects, and the most fruitful explanations in all parts of philosophy, and in all types and genres of language.[55]

In fact, Herder argued, the divine origin of language was 'entirely irreligious' in making God actively work for the benefit of his creation. It was

---

[53] Herder, *Philosophical Writings*, 77; *Frühe Schriften*, 711.   [54] Ibid.
[55] Herder, *Philosophical Writings*, 163–4 (translation slightly modified); *Frühe Schriften*, 809–10.

much worthier of God to let his creation, the human mind, develop language on its own: 'the origin of language hence only becomes divine in a worthy manner insofar as it is human.'[56]

Part of Herder's solution consisted in an appropriation of the contemporary discussion of instincts and the physiological constitution of organisms. While taking on board Leibnizian notions of force (*Kraft*) and instincts, Herder placed a premium on the empirical study of 'experiences concerning the difference between animals and human beings'.[57] Herder distilled Reimarus' observations into his own 'animal sphere' argument: the smaller a creature's natural environment, the greater its skills and artful drives were, as attested by the intricate structure of beehives and spiders' webs. With the extension of habitat, animals had to relate to more factors over a larger territory, inevitably becoming less focused and skilful. Man was at the opposite end to insects on this natural scale: living all over the earth and engaged in myriad activities, he lacked any naturally concentrated artful drives (*Kunsttriebe*).

Yet Herder differed from Reimarus in an important aspect. While Reimarus claimed that some forms of the artful drives of animals could be discerned in human beings—for example, in our immediate visual perception or in the supposedly innate instinct of infants to represent their desires and pains to others—Herder argued for a categorical difference between animal instincts and the drives of human beings. Referring to the review of Reimarus' book on animal instincts in the *Literaturbriefe*, Herder followed closely Mendelssohn's main argument in that piece: one had to distinguish more clearly between innate inclinations and acquired ones. As Mendelssohn argued, the capacity to cry at the feeling of pain is innate to us, but our ability to prompt sympathy in others or to feel sympathy at the sight of a crying person had to be learned through experience. Not every capacity, or what seems to us as an instinctive action, should be traced back to an innate disposition. The development of such abilities might have actually cost us much mental effort in the first, unconscious stages of our infancy.[58]

Mendelssohn ended his review of Reimarus by prompting his readers to admit they could not properly account for the artful drives of animals.

---

[56] Ibid. Cf. Herder's different approach to language in Books IV.3 and IX.2 of his *Ideen*, 136–42 and 345–55; Wolfgang Pross, 'Das "göttliche Geschenk der Rede"—Hat Herder die Sprachursprungstheorie der *Abhandlung* in den *Ideen* revoziert?', in Jürg Niederhauser and Stanislaw Szlęk (eds), *Sprachsplitter und Sprachspiele* (Bern: Peter Lang, 2000), 223–33.

[57] Herder, *Philosophical Writings*, 77; *Frühe Schriften*, 711.

[58] This fascinating discussion of instincts and innatism was published in four instalments between 30 October and 20 November 1760 (Mendelssohn, *JubA* v/1. 283–302, here 293–4). Reimarus replied in a lengthy supplement to the second edition of his work, which Mendelssohn reviewed in July 1762 (*JubA* v/1. 538–49).

But for Herder, one of Mendelssohn's attentive readers, this was not sufficient. While agreeing with Mendelssohn on the dissimilarity of human and animal instincts, Herder postulated a uniquely human power substituting for artful drives. This power was *Besonnenheit*, active reflection or awareness of the world. Herder emphasized that *Besonnenheit* was not an ethereal reason distinct from matter, but man's organizing principle, directing body and mind alike and orientated towards the surrounding environment.[59] Against Rousseau's postulation of reason as a dormant capacity in man (*réflexion en puissance*), Herder advanced his lesson from Kant's papers of the early 1760s: the primacy of the real and the given over the logical and the possible. Latent but unrealized tendencies were thus a phantom, amounting to nothing in reality. Habit and use could never have transformed such mere potentiality into actual force. *Besonnenheit* was always active and present in man, and human language was both coextensive and coexistent with *Besonnenheit*.[60]

According to Herder, language was the active appropriation of the outer world within the human mind by means of distinguishing marks (*Merkmale*). Resorting to the common image of a man or a child engulfed by confused sensations, Herder argued that the simplest recognition of an object consisted in mentally marking it apart from the whole. Here we find another guest appearance of the useful sheep that had grazed the pages of Mendelssohn and Abbt's works. According to Herder, the sheep and its bleating, or the object and its distinguishing mark, were one and the same thing in the perceiving mind. For the first human beings the sheep *was* the bleating sound. Unlike the description of the same process by Maupertuis and Sulzer, in Herder's prize essay there was no prelinguistic cognition. Human beings did not consciously denote already existing ideas, for ideas were their own signs and vice versa.

> The sheep comes again. White, soft, woolly—the soul sees, feels, takes awareness, seeks a characteristic mark—it bleats, and now the soul recognizes it again! 'Aha! You are the bleating one!' the soul feels inwardly. This soul has recognized it in a human way, that is, with a characteristic mark.[61]

Though Herder repeatedly discussed the case of the bleating sheep, the identity of sign and idea was not restricted to onomatopoeic markers, operating equally with artificial signs. In fact, the identity of words and mental signs tended to undermine the entire distinction between nature and artifice. If active reflection (*Besonnenheit*) and human language were

---

[59] Herder, *Philosophical Writings*, 82–7; *Frühe Schriften*, 716–22.
[60] Herder, *Philosophical Writings*, 86; *Frühe Schriften*, 720.
[61] Herder, *Philosophical Writings*, 88; *Frühe Schriften*, 723.

natural to all human beings, self-motivated signification must have been present all along human history. Herder's equation of word and idea, of language and cognition, prompted a further attack on any attribution of the first words to the imitation of natural sounds, to the physiology of the vocal organs, or to social convention. This solution partly resembled the views of Hobbes, Leibniz, and Condillac, who saw language as an indispensable tool of human thought. Yet Herder went a few steps forward by arguing not only for the linguistic character of our cognition but also for the cognitive nature of human language. One could not think without language, as various Enlightenment authors argued, but at the same time one could not properly speak without perceiving the world in a uniquely human way. This was the crux of the difference between Herder's suggestion and earlier naturalistic narratives. For Herder, human language involved from the outset a peculiar way of self-orientation in the world. Consequently, it could have never emerged from the expressive idiom of nature, from a language of action, or from rudimentary communication among beasts and brutes.[62]

This point, in turn, may be viewed as a return to Leibniz and Wolff's synchronic treatment of the interrelations between signs and the mind. By resorting to this perspective, Herder seems to have admitted that narratives of the gradual evolution of language and mind were unsustainable in the face of the challenges mounted by Rousseau, Formey, and Süßmilch. To understand language properly one had to view it as another facet of the whole entity that was the human being, together with physical organization and mental operations. One could not assume that a single feature of this entity existed without the others—and hence the futility of imagining human beings without language. This was, for Herder, a contradiction in terms: man would not be himself without language and active reflection, while language deserved its name only as a cognitive aspect of the entire human being.

In the first part of the prize essay, Herder depicted the genesis of language as an innate process triggered by sense impressions, not so much an invention as a fundamental characteristic of human beings. Unlike Michaelis's entry for the same contest, in Herder's prize essay human society did not play a role in the generation of language, probably in order to emphasize his break with theories that traced the origin of language back to rudimentary interpersonal communication.[63] The second part of the prize

---

[62] See Jürgen Trabant, 'Herder's Discovery of the Ear', in Kurt Mueller-Vollmer (ed.), *Herder Today* (Berlin: De Gruyter, 1990), 345–66, and Trabant, *Europäisches Sprachdenken*, 219–26. On Herder's subsequent impact see, most recently, Michael N. Forster, *After Herder: Philosophy of Language in the German Tradition* (Oxford: Oxford University Press, 2010).

[63] Herder singled out Rousseau as the most effective speaker against a conventional origin of language: see *Philosophical Writings*, 89; *Frühe Schriften*, 724.

essay balanced the scales by describing the conjectural evolution of human languages in their diversity according to four natural laws, accounting for different sorts, levels, and paces of cultural progress. Finally, at the close of his prize essay, Herder admitted that the identification of language and active reflection (*Besonnenheit*) as necessary conditions of humanity did not constitute an adequate reply to the set question. The question had two explicit references to the invention of language, thereby implying a bygone condition in which human beings did not yet have language. Apologizing for his impertinence, Herder argued it was pointless to mount another hypothesis about the evolution of language from this point of departure. Such diachronic narratives, he thought, had clearly exhausted themselves.

> For just this reason he [the author] has transgressed the command of the Academy and *supplied no hypothesis*. For what would be the use of having one hypothesis outweigh or counterbalance the other? And how do people usually regard whatever has the form of a hypothesis but as a philosophical novel—Rousseau's, Condillac's, and others'? He preferred to work 'at *collecting firm data from the human soul, human organization, the structure of all ancient and savage languages, and the whole household-economy of the human species,*' and at *proving* his thesis in the way that the firmest *philosophical truth* can be proved. He therefore believed that with his disobedience he has achieved the will of the Academy more than it could otherwise have been achieved.[64]

In a possible reply to Garve's critique, Herder separated strictly the cognitive part of his essay (*langage* as a self-realizing human feature) from its historical aspect (individual *langues* in their diachronic evolution). His own account of language, Herder argued, was no longer a fictive 'philosophical novel' like the conjectural narratives of his predecessors. To bypass the question of the primacy of reason or language, Herder recast the problem of the origin of language as a synchronic issue rather than a diachronic one.

* * *

This synchronic analysis of the link between language and mind was precisely the subject of the 1759 contest, when most participants chose to address historical evolution instead of the set topic of constant reciprocal influence. Michaelis was one of the only contestants to focus on the actual question, while emphasizing the ensuing problems such as the emergence of language. The 1771 question was essentially Michaelis's suggestion from 1759, explicitly asking for a diachronic account of the language-mind rapport, and taking as its starting point speechless human beings 'abandoned to their natural faculties'. Yet in a peculiar twist of philo-

---

[64] Herder, *Philosophical Writings*, 164; *Frühe Schriften*, 810.

sophical fate, Herder's solution—as he himself admitted—was not an answer to the Academy's new question but a return to 1759: the expression of a constant reciprocal link between language and the human mind. Michaelis too pointed in the same direction by proposing that mutual affection, combined with children's creativity, would always generate human language. The 1771 contest may thus be regarded as closing a circuit opened in 1759, demonstrating yet again that the question of origins was inseparable from that of language and cognition—or language *as* cognition.

8
Conclusion and a Glimpse into the Future

The 1771 prize essay on the origin of language may have returned full circle to the synchronic, reciprocal influence of language and mind, but it did not lay to rest the underlying problems. Trying to overcome the difficulties confronted in the 1760s by Abbt, Garve, Sulzer, and others, both Michaelis and Herder regarded language in 1771 as an innate human capacity. In their different essays, Michaelis and Herder associated the human capacity for language with other intuitive tendencies such as sociability, familial life, mutual affection, and a basic inclination for poetic expression. This theoretical perspective was similar to contemporary Scottish works on the emergence of cultural phenomena (such as Adam Ferguson's or Adam Smith's) but different from Rousseau's view of the historically evolved, or the artificial in man, as unnatural and even counter-natural.

Yet despite the extensive evidence of cultural exchange, the contours of intellectual debates in Germany and Scotland were not necessarily identical.[1] The issue of natural emergence, for example, was much more of a stumbling stone in the Berlin debates on language. As we have seen, most local authors—Germans, Swiss, Huguenots, and French newcomers alike—pondered very seriously Rousseau's conundrums about the primacy of language or reason and the indispensability of society and language for each other's formation. They focused their attention on the incommensurability of natural gestures and cries on the one hand, and artificial signs on the other—the most vulnerable spot in the revived Epicurean narrative of the evolution of language and civilization. Differently from other thinkers across Europe, most authors writing at and for the Berlin Academy were not satisfied with the projection of this shift onto a large temporal axis. Instead of unintended consequences over long ages of human self-improvement, contributors to the Berlin debates eventually

---

[1] Manfred Kuehn, *Scottish Common Sense in Germany* (Kingston and Montreal: McGill-Queen's University Press, 1987); Fania Oz-Salzberger, *Translating the Enlightenment: Scottish Civic Discourse in Eighteenth-Century Germany* (Oxford: Oxford University Press, 1995); Annette Meyer, *Von der Wahrheit zur Wahrscheinlichkeit: Die Wissenschaft vom Menschen in der schottischen und deutschen Aufklärung* (Tübingen: Niemeyer, 2008).

highlighted innate instincts. This solution was manifest in Mendelssohn and Herder's attitude to feral children: the fact that their innate capacity for language had not been activated did not mean that they had no such disposition.

Herder's combination of innatism with naturalism, part of his larger programme to overcome dualism in natural philosophy and the cultural sciences, was not uncontroversial. Hamann, a keen follower of the Berlin debates on language, chastised Herder for abandoning his own view of language as more than a natural human capacity.[2] In the ensuing debate Herder remained committed to naturalism as the only explanatory method in philosophy and anthropology. Yet as Herder himself would demonstrate in his later works, the notion of language as an innate capacity in need of environmental activation could be regarded as a proof of the divine endowment of all innate human instincts. This synthesis between innatism and naturalism may have contributed to the rise in the 1780s of a new sort of 'religious naturalism' and divine immanence in nature, especially in the context of the bitter quarrel over Lessing's alleged Spinozism. The so-called 'pantheism controversy' gave rise to a new view of Spinoza as a 'man intoxicated with the divine' (*Gotttrunkener Mensch*) which could be attributed, to a large extent, to Herder's own vitalist reconfiguration of seventeenth-century naturalism.[3]

Other aspects of the language debates continued to have long-lasting impact in Berlin, especially the combination of symbolic cognition, or the active role of language in the mind, with the discourse on the national genius of languages. This synthesis was apparent in the stormy discussion of a rare verdict by a monarch on the literary culture of his realm. Frederick II's essay *On German Literature* (1780) is usually seen as demonstrating that his views on German culture changed very little after he acceded the throne.[4] According to the Prussian king, German culture in 1780 was

---

[2] Hamann, 'Des Ritters von Rosencreuz letzte Willensmeynung über den göttlichen und menschlichen Ursrpung der Sprache' and 'Philologische Einfälle und Zweifel über eine akademische Preisschrift', in *Sämtliche Werke*, iii. 25–33 and 35–53.

[3] In Herder's 'Gott, Einige Gespräche' of 1787. Spinoza was characterized as Goddrunk by Novalis (Friedrich von Hardenberg), in *Schriften*, eds Richard Samuel, Hans-Joachim Mähl, and Gerhard Schulz (Stuttgart: Kohlhammer, 1960–88), iii. 651. On the *Spinozismusstreit* or *Pantheismusstreit*, see, among others, Beiser, *Fate of Reason*, 44–126; Wilhelm Schmidt-Biggemann, *Theodizee und Tatsachen: Das philosophische Profil der deutschen Aufklärung* (Frankfurt am Main: Suhrkamp, 1988), 117–61; Ursula Goldenbaum, 'Kants Stellungnahme zum Spinozismusstreit 1786', in Dina Emundts (ed.), *Immanuel Kant und die Berliner Aufklärung* (Wiesbaden: Reichert, 2000), 98–115.

[4] Frederick II of Prussia, 'De la littérature allemande', in *Œuvres philosophiques*, eds Jean-Robert Armogathe and Dominique Bourel (Paris: Fayard, 1985), 423–55. On the extent of Frederick's knowledge of German, see Corina Petersilka, *Die Zweisprachigkeit Friedrichs des Großen: Ein linguistisches Porträt* (Tübingen: Niemeyer, 2005).

'half barbarous', a situation that might be overcome through a massive project of translation from foreign languages.[5] Some of the examples and images used by Frederick were very similar to the idiom used by Michaelis and Prémontval in 1759. According to the king, poets drawing on imaginative metaphors were the main improvers of language, and the common people's ordinary speech was the highest linguistic arbiter. Though Frederick understandably refrained from comparing language to political democracy, he did make a telling reference to the ineffectiveness of political attempts at linguistic reform. According to Frederick, even if the Holy Roman Emperor, supported by all his Prince-Electors, had issued a solemn decree about a new pronunciation of German infinitives, the common people would have ignored it and continued to speak according to custom.[6] Some of these points were quite common, and it seems unlikely that the king borrowed his arguments directly from the 1759 prize essay (which he could have read in its 1762 French edition). Yet Michaelis's salient points had apparently become, through the subsequent language debates, widely held convictions—even at a time when some of them were no longer valid, following the substantial developments in German literature and philosophy between 1759 and 1780.

This link between language and its speakers' frame of mind was further highlighted by the Academy in 1782, when it announced that the 1784 prize contest would concern the universality of the French language. The question required authors to concentrate on the causes of this universal status, assess whether French deserved its 'prerogative', and suggest whether it could retain it in the future.[7] The academicians decided to bestow the prize on an essay by Johann Christoph Schwab, who acknowledged the political and cultural superiority of French in Europe but praised recent breakthroughs in German literature. While mentioning some shortcomings of German language and style, Schwab praised various works by Klopstock, Lessing, Goethe, and Wieland. The Academy was, however, made to divide the prize between Schwab's balanced evaluation and a French piece at the request of the king's brother, prince Henry, who claimed the Academy would 'dishonour itself' if it did not crown a French reply to this particular question.[8] The joint laureate was Antoine

---

[5] Frederick II, *Œuvres philosophiques*, 424.
[6] Ibid. 437.
[7] Harnack, *Geschichte*, ii. 308.
[8] Pierre Pénisson, 'Evolution de la question des langues à l'Académie de Berlin', *Das Achtzehnte Jahrhundert* 25 (2001), 43–54. On the 1784 contest see René Piedmont, *Beiträge zum französischen Sprachbewußtsein im 18. Jahrhundert: Der Wettbewerb der Berliner Akademie zur Universalität der französischen Sprache von 1782/84* (Tübingen: Narr, 1984); Jürgen Storost, *Langue française—Langue universelle? Die Diskussion über die Universalität des Französischen an der Berliner Akademie der Wissenschaften* (Bonn:

de Rivarol, whose essay replicated seventeenth-century arguments for the superior qualities inherent in the French language.[9] Rivarol's arguments for the particular congruity between the word order in French and the natural order of thought had been widely contested since the 1740s by Condillac, Diderot, and Rousseau (as discussed in Chapter 1). In his *Fragments* of the 1760s Herder embraced the revisionist French observations that the so-called natural order—subject, verb, object—was actually a late invention, whereas the first languages must have been full of inversions, closer than modern idioms to the origins of language.[10] Except for mounting a challenge to common prejudices, authors like Diderot meant to highlight the general problem of analytic discourse in all human languages: the incommensurability of instantaneous perception in the mind (a picture) and its representation in words (a linear chain). But Herder could use this epistemological point as a critique levelled at the French language per se. Because German retained its cases and possessed more syntactic inversions than French, it must be much closer to the origin of language, a language of *Vernunft* compared to mere *Verstand* in French.[11] The welding together of the cognitive and socio-cultural aspects of the language debates, already manifest in the 1759 prize question and in the *Préservatif* affair, would become a powerful argumentative tool over the next few decades—and especially at the time of the Napoleonic Wars. It could serve not only to enhance the prominence of German as a literary language against authors of Frederick II's persuasion, but also to elevate German above other languages. Within this framework, French could be seen as an idiom sullied by Latinate structures that eroded its link to the emotive origin of speech.

Frederick II's death in 1786 exacerbated the tensions within the Academy. These frictions were visibly exposed when Count Ewald Friedrich von Hertzberg tried to reform the institution almost single-handedly. Influenced by Joseph II's vision of a German revival, Hertzberg convinced the new Prussian monarch, Frederick William II, to add to the Academy's eighteen regular members (of whom only five were German) no less than fifteen new members—all German except for three members of the bilingual French Colony.[12] The Prussian minister encouraged them to act as a *deutsche Deputation* for the promotion of German culture, triggering a

---

Romanistischer Verlag, 1994); Pierre Pénisson (ed.), *De l'universalité de la langue française, 1784* (Paris: Fayard, 1995).

[9] Antoine de Rivarol, 'Discours sur l'universalité de la langue française', in *Pensées diverses*, ed. Sylvain Menant (Paris: Desjonquères, 1998), 101–57.

[10] *Œuvres complètes de Diderot*, ed. Jules Assézat (Paris: Garnier, 1875), i. 371.

[11] Herder, *Frühe Schriften*, 255–6.

[12] Harnack, *Geschichte*, i/2. 495–522.

cultural war of attrition inside the Academy. These developments were expressed in two prize contests in the early 1790s, one on the purification of German and another on the comparative merits of the main European languages. But the hopes of Hertzberg and his 'German faction' faded with the minister's fall from royal grace, along with the failure of the counter-Austrian *Fürstenbund* to realize and finance the expectations for a new cultural renaissance.[13]

The debate in the 1790s over the language and goals of the Berlin Academy was settled in favour of the status quo: in the new statutes of 1795, phrased by Merian and approved by Frederick William II, French retained its role as the official language of the institution. This was also due to the contemporary perception that after 1789, and especially after Louis XVI's execution in 1793, the Berlin Academy had to preserve the cultural legacy of the defunct French monarchy (among its other activities).[14] The patriotic-bourgeois camp within the Academy had its partial victory in 1804, when the academic proceedings were finally published in German, albeit with no corresponding change in the Academy's organization. The institution would complete its transformation from the Académie Royale conceived by Frederick II and Maupertuis into a different Königliche Akademie only in 1807–12 with the active involvement of the Humboldt brothers, who were simultaneously collaborating with Schleiermacher and Niebuhr on the foundation of the University of Berlin.

This was not merely a change of language and structure at the Berlin Academy. The relationship between universities and academies, the social profile of scholars, and the complex nature of their endeavours were all in constant flux at the turn of the century.[15] Such developments were perhaps the inevitable result of changing political contexts and the ongoing specialization of scholarship, a process initiated at Göttingen and carried on at the new University of Berlin. Furthermore, the retreat of philosophy from the 'world' back into the university following Kant's critical turn did not augur well for the Berlin Academy. Over the final decades of the

---

[13] Jürgen Schiewe, *Sprachpurismus und Emanzipation: Joachim Heinrich Campes Verdeutschungsprogramm als Voraussetzung für Gesellschaftsveränderungen* (Hildesheim: Olms, 1988); Brigitte Schlieben-Lange and Harald Weydt, 'Die Antwort Daniel Jenischs auf die Preisfrage der Berliner Akademie zur "Vergleichung der Hauptsprachen Europas" von 1794', in Ute Tintemann and Jürgen Trabant (eds), *Sprache und Sprachen in Berlin um 1800* (Hanover: Wehrhahn, 2004), 215–43; Edwin H. Zeydel, 'The German Language in the Prussian Academy of Sciences', *PMLA* 41 (1926), 126–50; Claudia Sedlarz, 'Ruhm oder Reform? Der "Sprachenstreit" um 1790 an der Königlichen Akademie der Wissenschaften in Berlin', in Ursula Goldenbaum and Alexander Košenina (eds), *Berliner Aufklärung* (Hanover: Wehrhahn, 2003), ii. 245–76.

[14] Storost, *300 Jahre romanische Sprachen*, i. 132–7.

[15] Bödeker, 'Von der "Magd der Theologie" zur "Leitwissenschaft"'; Howard, *Protestant Theology*, 130–211.

eighteenth century the number of essays submitted to its annual contests declined steadily. In Berlin, as in other European centres, such competitions ceased to function as venues for intellectual exchange between educated laymen and academic experts.

The discussion of the German language or Germanization (*Verdeutschung*) in relation to cultural identity and self-formation (*Bildung*) continued to engage major thinkers in Berlin well into the nineteenth century, though on different terrains from the ones examined in this book. Interest in the cognitive aspects of the discussion lingered for a while, notably in Wilhelm von Humboldt's work, but the rise of comparative philology made the joint origins of language and mind look unfashionably speculative. The eighteenth-century debate became so outdated in retrospect that the statutes of the Linguistic Society of Paris, founded in 1866, explicitly prohibited any conjectures on the origin of language.[16]

To return to the period at the centre of this study, we can now better appreciate the observation made in 1776 by Michael Hißmann, a young lecturer at Göttingen, that 'the question of the origin of language has occupied the thinkers of the last half-century more than those of any earlier period'.[17] In the following year, Hißmann informed his readers that 'investigations of language, its formation [...] and its more or less advantageous influence on the human mind' have become the 'fashionable occupation of philosophical Germany'.[18] The Berlin Academy fully participated in, or actively orchestrated, the emergence of this philosophical pastime. By fostering the debate on language and mind it also engendered a distinctive blend of cross-European philosophical currents. From the mid-1740s onwards, various controversies—over monads and theodicy, about instincts and physiology, on language and mind—all emphasized the intercultural dialogue promoted by the Academy. By openly challenging Wolffian philosophy while frequently recognizing the originality of its adherents and crowning them with its prizes, the Berlin Academy proved a unique centre of intellectual regeneration.

---

[16] Sylvain Auroux, 'La Question de l'origine des langues: ordres et raisons du rejet institutionnel', in Gessinger and von Rahden (eds), *Theorien vom Ursprung*, ii. 122–50. On the new avenues of scholarship see, most recently, Benes, *In Babel's Shadow*; Pascale Rabault-Feuerhahn, *L'Archive des origines: Sanskrit, Philologie, anthropologie dans l'Allemagne du XIXe siècle* (Paris: Cerf, 2008); Markus Messling, *Pariser Orientlektüren: Zu Wilhelm von Humboldts Theorie der Schrift* (Paderborn: Schöningh, 2008); Marchand, *German Orientalism*; Chen Tzoref-Ashkenazi, *Der romantische Mythos vom Ursprung der Deutschen: Friedrich Schlegels Suche nach der indogermanischen Verbindung* (Göttingen: Wallstein, 2009).

[17] Michael Hißmann, 'Ueber den Ursprung der Sprache', *Hannoverisches Magazin*, 30 August 1776, 1145.

[18] Hißmann's preface (unnumbered pages) to *Ueber Sprache und Schrift* (Leipzig: Weygandsche Buchhandlung, 1777), his translation of Charles de Brosses's *Traité de la formation mécanique des langues* (1765).

As argued in the introduction to this work, a close examination of the debates over language and mind undermines Isaiah Berlin's notion of two distinct intellectual camps: the Paris-based champions of 'universality, objectivity, rationality' and their Counter-Enlightenment detractors, based mostly in the German states, who emphasized the frailty of reason and its dependence on the artifice of language.[19] As we have seen, the Enlightenment theory of signs as indispensable cognitive tools implied that all cultural phenomena are constructed and maintained by language. This idea, in turn, entailed the artificiality and historicity of human civilization, in both its intellectual and material manifestations, and its dependence on a combination of internal dispositions, cultural traditions, and socio-political structures. The notion that artificial signs stood at the basis of both self-consciousness and human civilization was equally endorsed by authors writing in Paris, Berlin, or Göttingen. This does not mean, of course, that the Enlightenment had no enemies. It did not lack its intransigent foes, who sometimes regarded reason and tradition as incompatible and irreconcilable. But this contrast should be examined in relation to particular debates, local circumstances, and institutional structures rather than painted with a broad brush along national lines.

Yet it is not only the philosophical content of the debates we have examined that makes Isaiah Berlin's strict distinction between the Enlightenment and its 'other' untenable. Such a dichotomy also mistakes the role of German intellectuals in the intricate web of intellectual exchange that was the eighteenth-century Republic of Letters. Enlightenment discussions of language and mind demonstrate that German cultural and linguistic theories did not stem from an indiscriminate rejection of French ideas.[20] Johann David Michaelis and Johann Gottfried Herder, winners of the prize contests of 1759 and 1771, developed their views of human nature and culture through a serious engagement with foreign ideas and their intellectual backgrounds. This was a case neither of passive reception nor of straightforward resistance, since authors writing in different political and religious contexts did take part in a common conversation. From Glasgow to Riga via Oxford, Paris, Göttingen, and

---

[19] Berlin, *Against the Current*, 20. For a different corrective, see Darrin M. McMahon, *Enemies of the Enlightenment: The French Counter-Enlightenment and the Making of Modernity* (Oxford: Oxford University Press, 2001).

[20] On Franco-German intellectual exchange, see Michel Espagne and Michael Werner (eds), *Transferts: relations interculturelles dans l'espace franco-allemand, XVIIIe–XIXe siècle* (Paris: Recherche sur les Civilisations, 1988); Michel Espagne, *Les Transferts culturels franco-allemands* (Paris: PUF, 1999); Anne Saada, *Inventer Diderot: les constructions d'un auteur en Allemagne au XVIIIe siècle* (Paris: CNRS, 2003); Anne Baillot and Charlotte Coulombeau (eds), *Die Formen der Philosophie in Deutschland und Frankreich—Les formes de la philosophie en Allemagne et en France 1750–1830* (Hanover: Wehrhahn, 2007).

Berlin, Enlightenment authors tackled the emergence of language in order to understand how human beings could have constructed their world naturally and independently. The debates on language in Berlin constituted an active, organic transformation of this wider European conversation. The examination of the Berlin debates can therefore throw a fresh ray of light on a major, but hitherto unclear and indistinct aspect of the eighteenth-century discourse on the emergence of human civilization.

Bibliography

MANUSCRIPTS

Berlin
Archiv der Berlin-Brandenburgischen Akademie der Wissenschaften
  Accounts and receipts concerning Johann David Michaelis's prize, June 1759, I-XVI-125 (22), 231 (224)
Geheimes Staatsarchiv, Preußischer Kulturbesitz
  Leonhard Euler to Frederick II of Prussia, 21 December 1758, in Rep 9 AV, F 2a. Fasz. 12, 134
Staatsbibliothek, Preußischer Kulturbesitz, Darmstädter Collection
  André Pierre Le Guay de Prémontval to François Thomas Marie de Baculard d'Arnauld, 21 February 1754, H 1754 (2)

Göttingen
Niedersächsische Staats- und Universitätsbibliothek
  Karl Ludolf von Danckelmann, official edict of 12 July 1759, attached to an undated letter from Jean Henri Samuel Formey to Johann David Michaelis, Codex Michaelis 324, 243[r]
  Formey to Michaelis, undated (November/December 1759), Codex Michaelis 324, 241–2
  Jean Bernard Merian to Michaelis, 1755–1760, Codex Michaelis 324, 39–62
  Prémontval to Michaelis, 27 June 1759, Codex Michaelis 327, 208[r]–208[v]
  Thierry to Michaelis, 12 May 1762, Codex Michaelis 329, 273[r]–273[v]
  Johann David Michaelis, 'Preisschrift vom Ursprung der Sprache', Codex Michaelis 72–3

Kraków
Biblioteka Jagiellońska, Autographa Collection
  Johann Peter Süßmlich to Jean Henri Samuel Formey, 4 September 1749
Biblioteka Jagiellońska, Varnhagen von Ense Collection
  Merian to Formey: 27 August 1760
  Prémontval to Formey: 4 April 1755, 12 May 1755, 12 May 1757, 21 May 1757, 12 August 1757, 26 November 1757, 20 November 1758, 9 December 1758, 25 November 1763, 29 April 1764
  Anne Marie Victoire de Prémontval to Formey: 2 November 1757, 9 January 1765

Paris
Académie des Sciences, Fonds Maupertuis
  Merian to Maupertuis, 3 May 1757, 43 J 121.16
  Merian to Maupertuis, 25 October 1757, 43 J 121.18

PRIMARY SOURCES

(Anon.), 'Opinion', in Diderot and d'Alembert (eds), *Encyclopédie*, xi (1765), 506–7

Abbt, Thomas, *Fragment der aeltesten Begebenheiten des menschlichen Geschlechts*, ed. Johann Peter Miller (Halle: Johann Justinus Gebauer, 1767)

—— 'Allerhand Muthmassungen über den ältesten Zustand des Menschen', in *Vermischte Schriften*, eds Friedrich Nicolai and Johann Erich Biester, vol. vi (Stettin: Nicolai, 1781), 141–59

Adanson, Michel, *Histoire naturelle du Sénégal: Coquillages. Avec la Relation abrégée d'un Voyage fait en ce pays, pendant les années 1749, 50, 51, 52 & 53* (Paris: Claude-Jeane-Baptiste Bauche, 1757)

D'Argens, Jean-Baptiste de Boyer, Marquis, *Histoire de l'esprit humain, ou Mémoires secrets et universels de la république des lettres* (Berlin: Haude & Spener, 1765–8)

Aristotle, *The Organon* i: *The Categories, On Interpretation, Prior Analytics*, trans. Harold Cooke and Hugh Tredennick (Cambridge, Mass.: Harvard University Press, 1938)

Arnauld, Antoine, *Réflexions sur l'éloquence des prédicateurs*, ed. Thomas M. Carr (Geneva: Droz, 1992)

—— and Claude Lancelot, *Grammaire générale et raisonnée*, ed. Michel Foucault (Paris: Paulet, 1969)

—— and Pierre Nicole, *La Logique ou l'art de penser* (Paris: Charles Savreux, 1662)

Bacon, Francis, *The Major Works*, ed. Brian Vickers (Oxford: Oxford University Press, 2002)

Baer, Frédéric Charles, *Essai historique et critique sur les Atlantiques, dans lequel on se propose de faire voir la conformité qu'il y a entre l'Histoire de ce peuple, & celle des Hébreux* (Paris: Michel Lambert, 1762)

Baumgarten, Alexander Gottlieb, *Aesthetica* (Frankfurt an der Oder: Johann Christian Kleyb, 1750)

—— *Reflections on Poetry—Meditationes philosophicae de nonnullis ad poema pertinentibus*, eds Karl Aschenbrenner and William B. Holther (Berkeley, Calif.: University of California Press, 1954)

Baumgarten, Siegmund Jacob, 'Vorrede', in *Übersetzung der Algemeinen Welthistorie die in Engeland durch eine Gesellschaft von Gelehrten ausgefertiget worden. Nebst die Anmerkungen der holländischen Übersetzung*, ed. Siegmund Jacob Baumgarten, i (Halle: Johann Justinus Gebauer, 1744)

Beausobre, Louis Isaac de, 'Réflexions sur les changemens des langues vivantes par rapport à l'orthographe et à la prononciation', *Histoire de l'Académie royale des sciences et belles lettres, année 1755* (Berlin: Haude & Spener, 1757), 514–29

Beauzée, Nicolas, 'Langue', in Diderot and d'Alembert (eds), *Encyclopédie*, ix (1765), 249–66

Berkeley, George, *The Works of George Berkeley*, ed. G. N. Wright (London: Thomas Tegg, 1843)

Berkeley, George, *Philosophical Works*, ed. Michael Ayers (London: Everyman, 2000)

Brosses, Charles de, *Ueber Sprache und Schrift*, trans. Michael Hißmann (Leipzig: Weygandsche Buchhandlung, 1777)

Brucker, Johann Jakob, *Historia critica philosophiae* (Leipzig: Breitkopf, 1742–44)

Campe, Joachim Heinrich, *Über die Reinigung und Bereicherung der Deutschen Sprache* (Braunschweig: Schulbuchhandlung, 1794)

Castillon, Friedrich von, 'Éloge de M. de Castillon, père', in *Histoire de l'Académie royale des sciences et belles lettres, année 1792–93* (Berlin: Decker, 1798), 38–60

Castillon, Jean de, *Discours sur l'origine de l'inégalité parmi les hommes. Pour servir de réponse au Discours que M. Rousseau, Citoyen de Géneve, a publié sur le même sujet* (Amsterdam: J. F. Jolly, 1756)

Chladenius, Johann Martin, 'Allgemeine Geschichtswissenschaft', in Blanke and Fleischer (eds), *Theoretiker der deutschen Aufklärungshistorie*, i. 226–74

Condillac, Étienne Bonnot de, *Œuvres philosophiques de Condillac*, ed. Georges Le Roy (Paris: PUF, 1947–51)

—— *Lettres inédites à Gabriel Cramer*, ed. Georges Le Roy (Paris: PUF, 1953)

—— *Les Monades*, ed. Laurence Bongie (Oxford: Voltaire Foundation, 1980)

—— *Traité des sensations; Traité des animaux* (Paris: Fayard, 1984)

—— *Essay on the Origin of Human Knowledge*, ed. Hans Aarsleff (Cambridge: Cambridge University Press, 2001)

Crusius, Christian August, *Entwurf der nothwendigen Vernunft-Wahrheiten* (Leipzig: Gleditsch, 1745)

—— *Weg zur Gewißheit und Zuverläßigkeit der menschlichen Erkenntniß* (Leipzig: Gleditsch, 1747)

Descartes, René, *Œuvres et lettres*, ed. André Bridoux (Paris: Gallimard, 1953)

Diderot, Denis 'Encyclopédie' and 'Epicuréisme ou Epicurisme', in Diderot and d'Alembert (eds), *Encyclopédie* v (1756), 635–48 and 779–85

—— *Diderot's Early Philosophical Works*, trans. Margaret Jourdain (Chicago: Open Court, 1916)

—— *Œuvres complètes*, eds Yvon Belaval et al. (Paris: Hermann, 1975–2004)

—— *Œuvres*, ed. Laurent Versini (Paris: Hachette, 1994–6)

—— *Jacques the Fatalist*, trans. David Coward (Oxford: Oxford University Press, 1999)

—— and Jean le Rond d'Alembert (eds), *Encyclopédie, ou Dictionnaire raisonné des sciences, des arts et des métiers, par une Société de Gens de lettres*, 17 vols (Paris and Neufchâtel: Briasson, 1751–65)

Dubos, Jean Baptiste, *Réflexions critiques sur la poesie et sur la peinture* (Paris: Pierre-Jean Mariette, 1733)

Duclos, Charles Pinot, 'Remarques à la Grammaire de Port-Royal', in Arnauld and Lancelot, *Grammaire*, 109–57

Eichhorn, Johann Gottfried, 'Johann David Michaelis', *Allgemeine Bibliothek der biblischen Literatur*, iii (Leipzig: Weidmannsche Buchhandlung, 1791), 827–906

Epicurus, 'Letter to Herodotus', in *The Hellenistic Philosophers*, eds A. A. Long and D. N. Sedley (Cambridge: Cambridge University Press, 1987), i. 97

Bibliography 199

Euler, Leonhard, *Correspondance de Leonhard Euler avec P.-L. M. de Maupertuis et Frédéric II*, eds Pierre Costabel, Eduard Winter, Ašot T. Grigorijan, and Adolf P. Juškevič (Basel: Birkhäuser, 1986)

Formey, Jean Henri Samuel, *Mélanges philosophiques* (Leiden: Elie Luzac, 1754)

—— 'Préface de l'éditeur', in César Chesneau du Marsais, *Traité des tropes* (Leipzig: La Veuve Gaspard Fritsch, 1757)

—— 'Éloge de Monsieur de Maupertuis', *Histoire de l'Académie royale des sciences et belles lettres, année 1759* (Berlin: Haude & Spener, 1766), 464–512

—— 'Réunion des principaux moyens employés pour découvrir l'origine du langage, des idées & des connoissances des hommes', *Histoire de l'Académie royale des sciences et belles lettres, année 1759* (Berlin: Haude & Spener, 1766), 367–77

—— 'Éloge de M. de Prémontval' and 'Éloge de M. le Baron de Danckelmann', *Histoire de l'Académie royale des sciences et belles lettres, année 1765* (Berlin: Haude & Spener, 1767), 526–40 and 541–54

Frederick II of Prussia, *Œuvres philosophiques*, eds Jean-Robert Armogathe and Dominique Bourel (Paris: Fayard, 1985)

Gatterer, Johann Christoph, 'Von der Evidenz in der Geschichtskunde', in Blanke and Fleischer (eds), *Theoretiker der deutschen Aufklärungshistorie*, ii. 466–78

Göttingische Anzeigen von gelehrten Sachen, unter dem Aufsicht der Königl. Gesellschaft der Wissenschaften, 13 June 1754; 5 February 1757; 1 September, 3 November 1759; 7 February, 20 March 1760; 22 May 1762

Hamann, Johann Georg, *Sämtliche Werke*, ed. Josef Nadler (Vienna: Herder, 1949–57)

—— *Briefwechsel*, eds Walther Ziesemer and Arthur Henkel (Wiesbaden: Insel, 1955–1957)

Hardy, Pierre, *Essai physique sur l'heure des marées dans la mer rouge, comparée avec l'heure du passage des hébreux*, ed. Johann David Michaelis (Göttingen: Pockwitz & Barmeier, 1758)

Herder, Johann Gottfried, *Outlines of a Philosophy of the History of Man*, trans. T. Churchill (London: Luke Hansard for J. Johnson, 1803)

—— *Werke in zehn Bänden*, eds Günter Arnold et al., 10 vols in 11 (Frankfurt am Main: Deutscher Klassiker Verlag, 1985–2000)

—— *Philosophical Writings*, ed. Michael N. Forster (Cambridge: Cambridge University Press, 2002)

Herodotus, *The Histories*, trans. Robin Waterfield, ed. Carolyn Dewald (Oxford: Oxford University Press, 1998)

Hobbes, Thomas, Third set of objections to Descartes's *Meditations*, in Descartes, *Œuvres et lettres*, 399–420

—— *Man and Citizen*, trans. C. T. Wood, T. S. K. Scott-Craig, and B. Gert (Indianapolis: Hackett, 1991)

—— *Leviathan*, ed. Richard Tuck (Cambridge: Cambridge University Press, 1996)

Hoffmann, Adolf Friedrich, *Vernunft-Lehre* (Leipzig: n.p., 1737)

Horace, *Satires, Epistles and Ars Poetica*, trans. H. Rushton Fairclough (Cambridge, Mass.: Harvard University Press, 1970)

Jaucourt, Louis Chevalier de, 'Langage', in Diderot and d'Alembert (eds), *Encyclopédie*, ix (1766), 242–3

Kant, Immanuel, *Kants gesammelte Schriften* ('Akademieausgabe') (Berlin: Reimer, 1900–)

——*Political Writings*, ed. Hans Reiss, trans. H. B. Nisbet (Cambridge: Cambridge University Press, 1991)

Lambert, Johann Heinrich, *Neues Organon*, ed. Günter Schenk (Berlin: Akademie Verlag, 1990)

La Mettrie, Julien Offray de, *Œuvres philosophiques*, ed. Francine Markovits (Paris: Fayard, 1984)

Lamy, Bernard, *La Rhétorique ou l'art de parler*, 3rd edn (Paris: André Pralard, 1688)

Leibniz, Gottfried Wilhelm, *Opuscules et fragments inédits de Leibniz: extraits des manuscrits de la Bibliothèque Royale de Hanovre*, ed. Louis Couturat (Paris: Alcan, 1903)

——*Sämtliche Schriften und Briefe*, eds Paul Ritter et al. (Berlin: Akademie Verlag, 1923–)

——*Political Writings*, trans. Patrick Riley (Cambridge: Cambridge University Press, 1988)

——*Philosophical Essays*, eds Roger Ariew and Daniel Garber (Indianapolis: Hackett, 1989)

——*New Essays on Human Understanding*, trans. Peter Remnant and Jonathan Bennett (Cambridge: Cambridge University Press, 1996)

——*The Art of Controversies*, trans. Marcelo Dascal with Quintín Racionero and Adelino Cardoso (Dordrecht: Springer, 2006)

Lessing, Gotthold Ephraim, *Sämtliche Schriften*, eds Karl Lachmann and Franz Muncker (Leipzig and Stuttgart: G. J. Göschensche Verlagshandlung, 1886–1924)

Lettres sur l'état présent des sciences et des moeurs, July–December 1759

Locke, John, *An Essay concerning Human Understanding*, ed. Peter H. Nidditch (Oxford: Oxford University Press, 1979)

Lowth, Robert, *De sacra poesi Hebraeorum praelectiones academicae Oxonii habitae*, ed. Johann David Michaelis (Göttingen: Pockwiz & Barmeier, 1758–61)

——*Lectures on the Sacred Poetry of the Hebrews*, trans. G. Gregory (London: Chadwick & Co., 1847)

Lucretius, *De rerum natura*, trans. W. H. D. Rouse, ed. Martin Ferguson Smith (Cambridge, Mass.: Harvard University Press, 1982)

Maistre, Joseph de, *Les Soirées de Saint-Pétersbourg* (Paris: Librairie Grecque, Latine et Française, 1821)

Mandeville, Bernard, *The Fable of the Bees: or, Private Vices, Publick Benefits*, ed. F. B. Kaye (Oxford: Clarendon Press, 1924)

Maupertuis, Pierre Louis Moreau de, 'Des devoirs de l'académicien', in *Histoire de l'Académie royale des sciences et belles lettres, année 1753* (Berlin: Haude & Spener, 1755), 511–24

——'Dissertation sur les différents moyens dont les hommes se sont servis pour exprimer leurs idées', *Histoire de l'Académie royale des sciences et belles lettres, année 1754* (Berlin: Haude & Spener, 1756), 349–64

—— *Œuvres de M. de Maupertuis* (Lyon: Jean-Marie Bruyset, 1756)
—— 'Examen philosophique de la preuve de l'existence de Dieu employée dans l'Essai de cosmologie', *Histoire de l'Academie royale des sciences et belles lettres, année 1756* (Berlin: Haude & Spener, 1758), 389–424
Mendelssohn, Moses, *Gesammelte Schriften—Jubiläumsausgabe*, eds F. Bamberger et al. (Berlin: Akademie Verlag; Stuttgart-Bad Cannstatt: Frommann-Holzboog, 1929–)
Merian, Jean Bernard, 'Précis du discours qui a remporté le prix', in Michaelis, *Dissertation qui a remporté le prix*, iii–xxiv
Michaelis, Johann David, *Dissertatio inauguralis de punctorum hebraicorum antiquitate, sub examen vocans* (Halle: Johann Friedrich Grunert, 1739)
—— *Anfangs-Gründe der hebräischen Accentuation, nebst einer kurzen Abhandlung von dem Alterthum der Accente und Hebräischen Puncte überhaupt* (Halle: Verlegung des Wäysenhauses, 1741)
—— *Entwurf der typischen Gottesgelartheit*, 2nd edn (Göttingen: Universitäts-Buchhandlung, 1753)
—— *Beurtheilung der Mittel, welche man anwendet, die ausgestorbene hebräische Sprache zu verstehen* (Göttingen: Vandenhoek, 1757)
—— *De l'influence des opinions sur le langage et du langage sur les opinions*, trans. Jean Bernard Merian and André Pierre Le Guay de Prémontval (Bremen: Förster, 1762)
—— *Fragen an eine Gesellschaft gelehrter Männer, die auf Befehl Ihro Majestät des Königes von Dännemark nach Arabien reisen* (Frankfurt am Main: Johann Gottlieb Garbe, 1762)
—— 'Von dem Alter der Hebräischen Vocalen, und übrigen Punkte', in *Vermischte Schriften* (Frankfurt am Main: Johann Gottlieb Garbe, 1769), ii. 1–143
—— *Deutsche Uebersetzung des Alten Testaments, mit Anmerkungen* (Göttingen and Gotha: Vandenhoeck and Dieterich, 1769–85)
—— *Hebräische Grammatik nebst einem Anhange von gründlicher Erkenntniß derselben*, 3rd edn (Halle: Carl Hermann Hemmerde, 1778)
—— *Arabische Grammatik, nebst einer Arabischen Chrestomathie und Abhandlung vom Arabischen Geschmack* (Göttingen: Victorinus Boßiegel, 1781)
—— *Einleitung in die göttlichen Schriften des Alten Bundes*, i (Hamburg: Bohnsche Buchhandlung, 1787)
—— *Lebensbeschreibung von ihm selbst abgefaßt, mit Anmerkungen von Hassencamp, nebst Bemerkungen über dessen literarischen Character von Eichhorn, Schulz, und dem Elogium von Heyne* (Leipzig: Johann Ambrosius Barth, 1793)
—— *Mosaisches Recht*, 3rd edn (Frankfurt am Main: Johann Gottlieb Garbe, 1793)
—— *Zerstreute kleine Schriften* (Jena: Akademische Buchhandlung, 1793–4)
—— *Literarischer Briefwechsel*, ed. Johann Gottlieb Buhle (Leipzig: Weidmannsche Buchhandlung, 1794–6)
Michaelis, Johann David, et al., *Dissertation qui a remporté le prix proposé par l'académie royale des sciences et belles lettres de Prusse, sur l'influence réciproque du langage sur les opinions et des opinions sur le langage. Avec les pièces qui ont concouru* (Berlin: Haude & Spener, 1760)

Michaelis, Johann Heinrich, *Gründlicher Unterricht von den Accentibus prosaicis u. metricis* (Halle: Verlegung des Wäysenhauses, 1700)
—— *Erleichterte hebräische Grammatica* (Halle: Zeitler, 1702)
Neue Bibliothek der schönen Wissenschaften und der freyen Künste, iv/1 and v/2 (1767)
Niebuhr, Carsten, *Beschreibung von Arabien: Aus eigenen Beobachtungen und im Lande selbst gesammleten Nachrichten* (Copenhagen: Nicolaus Möller, 1772)
—— *Reisebeschreibung nach Arabien und andern umliegenden Ländern* (Copenhagen: Nicolaus Möller, 1774–8)
Nouvelle Bibliothèque germanique, ou Histoire littéraire de l'Allemagne, de la Suisse, & des pays du Nord, July–September 1757, January–March 1759, October–December 1759 (Amsterdam: Pierre Mortier)
Orientalische und Exegetische Bibliothek, ii and iii (Frankfurt am Main: Johann Gottlieb Garbe, 1771–2)
Pascal, Blaise, *Œuvres complètes*, ed. Jacques Chevalier (Paris: Gallimard, 1954)
Platner, Ernst, *Anthropologie für Aerzte und Weltweise* (Leipzig: Dyckische Buchhandlung, 1772)
Plato, *Cratylus*, trans. C. D. C. Reeve (Indianapolis: Hackett, 1999)
Prémontval, André Pierre Le Guay de, *Mémoires*, 3 vols (The Hague: n.p., 1749)
—— *Le Diogène de d'Alembert ou Diogène décent* (Berlin: Aux dépens de la Compagnie, 1754)
—— *Pensées sur la Liberté* (Berlin: Voss, 1754)
—— *Du Hazard sous l'empire de la Providence, pour servir de préservatif contre la doctrine du Fatalisme moderne* (Berlin: J. C. Kluter, 1755)
—— 'Deux pièces en forme d'essais, concernant, l'une le principe de la raison suffisante, et l'autre la loi de continuité', 'Remarque sur cette définition de M. Wolf du mot *aliquid*', *Histoire de l'Académie royale des sciences et belles lettres, année 1754* (Berlin: Haude & Spener, 1756), 418–39 and 440–2
—— *Préservatif contre la Corruption de la Langue Françoise, en France, & dans les Pays où elle est le plus en usage, tels que l'Allemagne, la Suisse, & la Hollande* (Berlin: Georg Ludwig Winter, Grynäus & Decker, 1759–61)
—— *Projet de conférences publiques sur l'éducation et sur l'éducation françoise en particulier* (Berlin: C. M. Vogel, 1763)
Pufendorf, Samuel, *Of the Law of Nature and Nations*, trans. Basil Kennett (Oxford: A. and J. Churchill, 1710)
—— *Les Devoirs de l'homme et du citoyen*, trans. Jean Barbeyrac (Trévoux: L'imprimerie de S. Altesse Serenissime, 1741)
—— *Gesammelte Werke*, ed. Wilhelm Schmidt-Biggemann (Berlin: Akademie Verlag, 1996–2004)
Reimarus, Hermann Samuel, *Die vornehmsten Wahrheiten der natürlichen Religion*, 3rd edn. (Hamburg: Johann Carl Bohn, 1766)
—— *Allgemeine Betrachtungen über die Triebe der Thiere, hauptsächlich über ihre Kunsttriebe*, 4th edn. (Hamburg: Carl Ernst Bohn, 1798)
Rivarol, Antoine de, *Pensées diverses*, ed. Sylvain Menant (Paris: Desjonquères, 1998)

Rousseau, Jean Jacques, *Œuvres complètes*, eds Bernard Gagnebin et al. (Paris: Gallimard, 1959–95)
—— *The Discourses and Other Early Political Writings*, ed. Victor Gourevitch (Cambridge: Cambridge University Press, 1997)
Sancke, Christoph, *Vollständige Anweisung zu den Accenten der Hebräer* (Leipzig: Gleditsch, 1740)
Schmidt, Johann Lorenz, *Die göttlichen Schriften vor den Zeiten des Messie Jesus: Der erste Theil worinnen Die Gesetze der Israelen enthalten sind nach einer freyen Übersetzung welche durch und durch mit Anmerkungen erläutert und bestätigt wird* (Wertheim: Johann Georg Nehr, 1735)
Schwab, Johann Christoph, *Le Grand Concours: 'Dissertation sur les causes de l'universalité de la langue française et la durée vraisemblable de son empire'*, trans. Denis Robelot, ed. Freeman G. Henry (Amsterdam: Rodopi, 2005)
Semler, Johann Salomo, *Abhandlung von freier Untersuchung des Canon* (Halle: Carl Hermann Hemmerde, 1771–5)
—— *Lebensbeschreibung von ihm selbst abgefasst*, 2 vols. (Halle, n.p., 1781–2)
Simon, Richard, *Histoire critique du Vieux Testament: suivant la copie imprimée à Paris* (Amsterdam: Elzevir, 1680)
Spinoza, Baruch, *Complete Works*, trans. Samuel Shirley, ed. Michael L. Morgan (Indianapolis: Hackett, 2002)
Staël, Germaine de, *De l'Allemagne*, ed. Simone Balayé, 2 vols (Paris: Garnier-Flammarion, 1968)
Stewart, Dugald, 'Account of the Life and Writings of Adam Smith, LL.D.', in Adam Smith, *Essays on Philosophical Subjects*, eds W. P. D. Wightman and J. C. Bryce (Oxford: Oxford University Press, 1980), 269–351
Sulzer, Johann Georg, 'Observations sur l'influence réciproque de la raison sur le langage et du langage sur la raison', *Histoire de l'Académie royale des sciences et belles lettres, année 1767* (Berlin: Haude &Spener, 1769), 413–38
Süßmilch, Johann Peter, *Versuch eines Beweises, daß die erste Sprache ihren Ursprung nicht vom Menschen, sondern allein vom Schöpfer erhalten habe* (Berlin: Buchladen der Realschule, 1766)
Thiébault, Dieudonné, *Mes souvenirs de vingt ans de séjour à Berlin, ou Frédéric le Grand, sa Famille, sa Cour, son Gouvernement, son Académie, ses Écoles, et ses Amis littérateurs et philosophes* (Paris: F. Buisson, 1804)
Thomasius, Christian, *Von Nachahmung der Franzosen*, ed. August Sauer (Stuttgart: Göschen, 1894)
Turgot, Anne Robert Jacques, *Œuvres de Turgot et documents le concernant*, ed. Gustave Schelle (Paris: Alcan, 1913–23)
Vaugelas, Claude, *Remarques sur la langue françoise* (Paris: Jean Camusat and Pierre Le Petit, 1647)
Vico, Giambattista, *The New Science* (3rd edn), trans. Thomas Goddard Bergin and Max Harold Fisch (Ithaca, NY: Cornell University Press, 1984)
Voltaire (François-Marie Arouet), *Œuvres complètes de Voltaire*, ed. Louis Moland (Paris: Garnier, 1877–83)
Warburthon [sic], William, *Essai sur les hiéroglyphes des Égyptiens*, trans. Marc Antoine Léonard des Malpeines (Paris: Hippolyte-Louis Guerin, 1744)

Warburton, William, *The Divine Legation of Moses Demonstrated, on the Principles of a Religious Deist, from the Omission of the Doctrine of a Future State of Reward and Punishment in the Jewish Dispensation* (London: Fletcher Gyles, 1738–41)

Webster, Noah, 'Dissertation Concerning the Influence of Language on Opinions and of Opinions on Language', in *A Collection of Essays and Fugitiv Writings* (Boston: I. Thomas and E. T. Andrews, 1790), 222–8

Wolff, Christian, *Psychologia rationalis* (Frankfurt and Leipzig: Rengerische Buchhandlung, 1734)

—— *Psychologie ou traité sur l'âme*, anon. trans. (Amsterdam: Pierre Mortier, 1745)

—— *Vernünfftige Gedancken von Gott, der Welt und der Seele des Menschen, auch allen Dingen überhaupt* (Halle: Rengerische Buchhandlung, 1751)

—— *Venünfftige Gedancken von den Kräften des menschlichen Verstandes und ihrem richtigen Gebrauche in Erkänntniß der Wahrheit* (Halle: Rengerische Buchhandlung, 1754)

—— *Gesammelte Werke*, ed. Jean École (Hildesheim: Olms, 1962–)

—— *Discursus praeliminaris de philosophia in genere*, trans. Günter Gawlick and Lothar Kreimdahl (Stuttgart-Bad Cannstatt: Frommann-Holzboog, 1996)

Zedler, Johann Heinrich, and Carl Günther Ludovici (eds), *Großes vollständiges Universal-Lexikon aller Wissenschaften und Künste* (Halle and Leipzig, n.p., 1732–54)

RESEARCH LITERATURE (POST-1850)

Aarsleff, Hans, 'The Tradition of Condillac: The Problem of the Origin of Language in the Eighteenth Century and the Debate in the Berlin Academy before Herder', in *Studies in the History of Linguistics: Traditions and Paradigms*, ed. Dell Hymes (Bloomington, Ind.: Indiana University Press, 1974), 93–156; reprinted in *From Locke to Saussure*, 146–209

—— *From Locke to Saussure: Essays on the Study of Language and Intellectual History* (London: Athlone, 1982)

—— 'The Berlin Academy under Frederick the Great', *History of the Human Sciences* 2 (1989), 193–206

—— 'The Rise and Decline of Adam and his Ursprache', in Allison Coudert (ed.), *The Language of Adam—Die Sprache Adams* (Wiesbaden: Harrassowitz, 1999), 277–95

—— Introduction to Condillac, *Essay on the Origin of Human Knowledge*, trans. Hans Aarsleff (Cambridge: Cambridge University Press, 2001), pp. xi–xxxviii

Abbattista, Guido, 'The English *Universal History*: Publishing, Authorship, and Historiography in a European Project (1736–1790)', *Storia della Storiografia* 39 (2001), 103–8

Adler, Hans, *Die Prägnanz des Dunklen: Gnoseologie—Ästhetik—Geschichtsphilosophie bei Johann Gottfried Herder* (Hamburg: Meiner, 1990)

Ahnert, Thomas, *Religion and the Origins of the German Enlightenment: Faith and the Reform of Learning in the Thought of Christian Thomasius* (Rochester, NY: University of Rochester Press, 2006)

—— 'Epicureanism and the Transformation of Natural Law in the Early German Enlightenment', in Leddy and Lifschitz (eds), *Epicurus in the Enlightenment*, 53–68

Aiton, E. J., *Leibniz: A Biography* (Bristol: Hilger, 1985)

Albrecht, Michael, *Eklektik: Eine Begriffsgeschichte mit Hinweisen auf die Philosophie- und Wissenschaftsgeschichte* (Stuttgart-Bad Cannstatt: Frommann Holzboog, 1994)

—— and Eva J. Engel (eds), *Moses Mendelssohn im Spannungsfeld der Aufklärung* (Stuttgart-Bad Cannstatt: Frommann-Holzboog, 2000)

Allen, Don Cameron, *The Legend of Noah* (Urbana, Ill.: University of Illinois Press, 1949)

Altmann, Alexander, *Die trostvolle Aufklärung: Studien zur Metaphysik und politischen Theorie Moses Mendelssohns* (Stuttgart-Bad Cannstatt: Frommann-Holzboog, 1982)

—— *Moses Mendelssohn: A Biographical Study* (London: Routledge & Kegan Paul, 1973)

Aner, Karl, *Theologie der Lessingzeit* (Halle: Niemeyer, 1929)

Antognazza, Maria Rosa, 'The Defence of the Mysteries of the Trinity and the Incarnation: An Example of Leibniz's "Other" Reason', *British Journal for the History of Philosophy* 9 (2001), 283–309

—— *Leibniz on the Trinity and the Incarnation: Reason and Revelation in the Seventeenth Century*, trans. Gerald Parks (New Haven, Conn.: Yale University Press, 2007)

—— *Leibniz: An Intellectual Biography* (Cambridge: Cambridge University Press, 2009)

Arndt, Hans Werner, 'Rationalismus und Empirismus in der Erkenntnislehre Christian Wolffs', in Schneiders (ed.), *Christian Wolff*, 31–47

Assmann, Jan, *Moses the Egyptian: The Memory of Egypt in Western Monotheism* (Cambridge, Mass.: Harvard University Press, 1997)

Auroux, Sylvain, *La Sémiotique des encyclopédistes* (Paris: Payot, 1979)

—— 'La Question de l'origine des langues: ordres et raisons du rejet institutionnel', in Gessinger and von Rahden (eds), *Theorien vom Ursprung*, ii. 122–50

—— et al. (eds), *History of the Language Sciences*, 3 vols (Berlin: De Gruyter, 2000–6)

Austin, J. L., *How to Do Things with Words* (Cambridge, Mass.: Harvard University Press, 1962)

Baár, Monika, 'From General History to National History: The Transformation of William Guthrie's and John Gray's *General History of the World* in Continental Europe', in Stockhorst (ed.), *Cultural Transfer*, 63–82

Badinter, Elisabeth, *Les Passions intellectuelles*, i: *Désirs de gloire (1735–1751)* (Paris: Fayard, 1999)

Baillot, Anne, and Charlotte Coulombeau (eds), *Die Formen der Philosophie in Deutschland und Frankreich: Les formes de la philosophie en Allemagne et en France 1750–1830* (Hanover: Wehrhahn, 2007)

Barber, W. H., *Leibniz in France from Arnauld to Voltaire* (Oxford: Clarendon Press, 1955)
Barnes, Jonathan, 'Epicurus: Meaning and Thinking', in Gabriele Giannantoni and Marcello Gigante (eds), *Epicureismo greco e romano* (Naples: Bibliopolis, 1996), i. 197–220
Barth, Ulrich, 'Hallesche Hermeneutik im 18. Jahrhundert', in Manfred Beetz and Giuseppe Cacciatore (eds), *Hermeneutik im Zeitalter der Aufklärung* (Cologne: Böhlau, 2000), 69–98
Bartholmess, Christian, *Histoire philosophique de l'Académie de Prusse depuis Leibniz jusqu'à Schelling*, 2 vols (Paris: Franck, 1850)
Beeson, David, *Maupertuis: An Intellectual Biography* (Oxford: Voltaire Foundation, 1992)
Beiser, Frederick, *The Fate of Reason: German Philosophy from Kant to Fichte* (Cambridge, Mass.: Harvard University Press, 1987)
—— *Diotima's Children: German Aesthetic Rationalism from Leibniz to Lessing* (Oxford: Oxford University Press, 2009)
Benes, Tuska, *In Babel's Shadow: Language, Philology, and the Nation in Nineteenth-Century Germany* (Detroit: Wayne State University Press, 2008)
Berlin, Isaiah, *Three Critics of the Enlightenment: Vico, Hamann, Herder* (Princeton: Princeton University Press, 2000)
—— *Against the Current: Essays in the History of Ideas*, ed. Henry Hardy (Princeton: Princeton University Press, 2001)
Berry, Christopher J., *The Idea of Luxury: A Conceptual and Historical Investigation* (Cambridge: Cambridge University Press, 1994)
Betz, John R., *After Enlightenment: The Post-Secular Vision of J. G. Hamann* (Oxford: Wiley-Blackwell, 2008)
Biletzki, Anat, *Talking Wolves: Thomas Hobbes on the Language of Politics and the Politics of Language* (Dordrecht: Kluwer, 1997)
Biskup, Thomas, 'The University of Göttingen and the Personal Union, 1737–1837', in Brendan Simms and Torsten Riotte (eds), *The Hanoverian Dimension in British History* (Cambridge: Cambridge University Press, 2007), 128–60
Blackall, Eric A., *The Emergence of German as a Literary Language 1700–1775*, 2nd edn (Ithaca, NY: Cornell University Press, 1978)
Blanke, Horst Walter, and Dirk Fleischer (eds), *Theoretiker der deutschen Aufklärungshistorie* (Stuttgart-Bad Cannstatt: Frommann-Holzboog, 1990)
Bödeker, Hans Erich, 'Thomas Abbt: Patriot, Bürger und bürgerliches Bewußtsein', in Rudolf Vierhaus (ed.), *Bürger und Bürgerlichkeit im Zeitalter der Aufklärung* (Heidelberg: Schneider, 1981), 221–54
—— 'Aufklärung als Kommunikationsprozeß', in Rudolf Vierhaus (ed.), *Aufklärung als Prozeß* (Hamburg: Meiner, 1987), 89–111
—— 'Von der 'Magd der Theologie' zur 'Leitwissenschaft'. Vorüberlegungen zu einer Geschichte der Philosophie des 18. Jahrhunderts', *Das Achtzehnte Jahrhundert* 7 (1990), 19–57
—— 'Konzept und Klassifikation der Wissenschaften bei Johann Georg Sulzer (1720–1779)', in Fontius and Holzhey (eds), *Schweizer im Berlin*, 325–39

—— (ed.), *Begriffsgeschichte, Diskursgeschichte, Metapherngeschichte* (Göttingen: Wallstein, 2002)

Bödeker, Hans Erich, Philippe Büttgen, and Michel Espagne (eds), *Die Wissenschaft vom Menschen in Göttingen um 1800* (Göttingen: Vandenhoeck & Ruprecht, 2008)

Böhm, Manuela, 'Berliner Sprach-Querelen: Ein Ausschnitt aus der Debatte über den *style réfugié* im 18. Jahrhundert', in Elisabeth Berner, Manuela Böhm, and Anja Voeste (eds), *Ein groß vnnd narhafft haffen: Festschrift für Joachim Gessinger* (Potsdam: Universität Potsdam, 2005), 103–15

Borst, Arno, *Der Turmbau von Babel: Geschichte der Meinungen über Ursprung und Vielfalt der Sprachen und Völker*, 4 vols in 6 (Stuttgart: Hiersemann, 1957–63)

Bourel, Dominique, 'Die deutsche Orientalistik im 18. Jahrhundert: Von der Mission zur Wissenschaft', in Reventlow et al. (eds), *Historische Kritik*, 113–26

—— *Moses Mendelssohn: la naissance du judaïsme moderne* (Paris: Gallimard, 2004)

Brather, Hans-Stephan (ed.), *Leibniz und seine Akademie: Ausgewählte Quellen zur Geschichte der Berliner Sozietät der Wissenschaften 1697–1716* (Berlin: Akademie Verlag, 1993)

Bregulla, Gottfried (ed.), *Hugenotten in Berlin* (Berlin: Union Verlag, 1988)

Brown, Harcourt, 'Maupertuis *Philosophe*: Enlightenment and the Berlin Academy', *Studies on Voltaire and the Eighteenth Century* 24 (1963), 255–69

Brunner, Otto, Werner Conze, and Reinhart Koselleck (eds), *Geschichtliche Grundbegriffe: Historisches Lexikon zur politisch-sozialen Sprache in Deutschland* (Stuttgart: Klett-Cotta, 1972–97)

Bultmann, Christoph, *Die biblische Urgeschichte in der Aufklärung: Johann Gottfried Herders Interpretation der Genesis als Antwort auf die Religionskritik David Humes* (Tübingen: Mohr Siebeck, 1999)

Burnett, Stephen G., *From Christian Hebraism to Jewish Studies: Johannes Buxtorf (1564–1629) and Hebrew Learning in the Seventeenth Century* (Leiden: Brill, 1996)

Bursill-Hall, G. L., *Speculative Grammars of the Middle Ages: The Doctrine of Partes orationis of the Modistae* (The Hague: Mouton, 1971).

Buschmann, Cornelia, 'Die philosophischen Preisfragen und Preisschriften der Berliner Akademie der Wissenschaften im 18. Jahrhundert', in Wolfgang Förster (ed.), *Aufklärung in Berlin* (Berlin: Akademie Verlag, 1989), 165–228

—— 'Wie bleibt Metaphysik als Wissenschaft möglich? Moses Mendelssohn und seine Konkurrenten um den Preis der Preußischen Akademie für 1763', in Albrecht and Engel (eds), *Mendelssohn im Spannungsfeld*, 37–49

Bynack, V. P., 'Noah Webster's Linguistic Thought and the Idea of an American National Culture', *Journal of the History of Ideas* 45 (1984), 99–114

Campbell, Gordon, *Lucretius on Creation and Evolution* (Oxford: Oxford University Press, 2003)

Carhart, Michael, *The Science of Culture in Enlightenment Germany* (Cambridge, Mass.: Harvard University Press, 2007)

Carr, Thomas M., *Descartes and the Resilience of Rhetoric: Varieties of Cartesian Rhetorical Theory* (Carbondale, Ill.: Southern Illinois University Press, 1990)
Cassirer, Ernst, *The Philosophy of Symbolic Forms*, i: *Language*, trans. Ralph Manheim (New Haven: Yale University Press, 1953)
Cherpack, Clifton, 'Warburton and the Encyclopédie', *Comparative Literature* 7 (1955), 226–39
Chilton, C. W., 'The Epicurean Theory of the Origin of Language', *American Journal of Philology* 83 (1962), 159–67
Chomsky, Noam, *Cartesian Linguistics* (Lanham, Md.: University Press of America, 1966)
Clark, Christopher, *The Politics of Conversion: Missionary Protestantism and the Jews in Prussia 1728–1941* (Oxford: Oxford University Press, 1995)
Clark, William, 'The Death of Metaphysics in Enlightened Prussia', in *The Sciences in Enlightened Europe*, eds William Clark, Jan Golinski, and Simon Schaffer (Chicago: University of Chicago Press, 1999), 423–73
Cole, Thomas, *Democritus and the Sources of Greek Anthropology* (Cleveland: Western Reserve University Press, 1967)
Corr, Charles A., 'Christian Wolff and Leibniz', *Journal of the History of Ideas* 36 (1975), 241–62
Couturier-Heinrich, Clémence, 'Herders Übersetzung aus Prémontvals *Contre la gallicomanie* in den *Briefen zu Beförderung der Humanität*', *Herder Jahrbuch/Herder Yearbook* 10 (2010), 37–56
Cram, David, and Jaap Maat, *George Dalgarno on Universal Language* (Oxford: Oxford University Press, 2001)
Dagen, Jean, *L'Histoire de l'esprit humain dans la pensée française de Fontenelle à Condorcet* (Paris: Klincksieck, 1977)
Damis, Christine, 'Metaphern als Elemente der Sprachbeschreibung im 18. Jahrhundert', in Gerda Haßler and Peter Schmitter (eds), *Sprachdiskussion und Beschreibung von Sprachen im 17. und 18. Jahrhundert* (Münster: Nodus, 1999), 163–73
Darmon, Jean-Charles, *Philosophie épicurienne et littérature au XVIIᵉ siècle* (Paris: PUF, 1998)
Dascal, Marcelo, *La Sémiologie de Leibniz* (Paris: Aubier Montaigne, 1978)
—— *Leibniz: Language, Signs and Thought* (Amsterdam: John Benjamins, 1987)
Dawson, Hannah, *Locke, Language and Early Modern Philosophy* (Cambridge: Cambridge University Press, 2007)
Deneys-Tunney, Anne, and Pierre-François Moreau (eds), *L'Epicurisme des Lumières—Dix-huitième siècle* 35 (2003)
Douthwaite, Julia, *The Wild Girl, Natural Man and the Monster: Dangerous Experiments in the Age of Enlightenment* (Chicago: University of Chicago Press, 2002)
Droixhe, Daniel, *La Linguistique et l'appel de l'histoire 1600–1800: rationalisme et révolutions positivistes* (Geneva: Droz, 1976)
—— *De l'origine du langage aux langues du monde: études sur les XVIIe et XVIIIe siècles* (Tübingen: Narr, 1987)

Duchet, Michèle, *Anthropologie et histoire au siècle des lumières* (Paris: François Maspéro, 1971)

Dulac, Georges, 'Louis-Jacques Goussier, encyclopédiste et..."original sans principes"', in Jacques Proust (ed.), *Recherches nouvelles sur quelques écrivains des Lumières* (Geneva: Droz, 1972), 63–110

Dummett, Michael, 'Language and Communication', in *The Seas of Language* (Oxford: Oxford University Press, 1996), 166–87

Duranton, Henri, '"Un métier de chien": précepteurs, demoiselles de compagnie et bohême littéraire dans le refuge allemand', *Dix-huitième siècle* 17 (1985), 297–315

Dutz, Klaus D., '"Lingua Adamica nobis certe ignota est": Die Sprachursprungsdebatte und Gottfried Wilhelm Leibniz', in Gessinger and von Rahden (eds), *Theorien vom Ursprung*, i. 204–40

Eco, Umberto, *The Search for the Perfect Language*, trans. James Fentress (Oxford: Blackwell, 1995)

École, Jean, 'En quel sens peut-on dire que Wolff est rationaliste?', *Studia Leibnitiana* 11 (1979), 45–61

Elias, Norbert, *The Civilizing Process*, trans. Edmund Jephcott (Oxford: Blackwell, 1994)

Eliav-Feldon, Miriam, *Realistic Utopias: The Ideal Imaginary World of the Renaissance, 1516–1630* (Oxford: Clarendon Press, 1982)

Engel, Eva J., '"Die Freyheit der Untersuchung": Die Literaturbriefe 72–75 (13. und 20. Dezember 1759)', in Eva J. Engel and Norbert Hinske (eds), *Moses Mendelssohn und die Kreise seiner Wirksamkeit* (Tübingen: Niemeyer, 1994), 249–68

Engfer, Hans-Jürgen, *Philosophie als Analysis: Studien zur Entwicklung philosophischer Analysiskonzeptionen unter dem Einfluß mathematischer Methodenmodelle im 17. und frühen 18. Jahrhundert* (Stuttgart-Bad Cannstatt: Frommann-Holzboog, 1982)

Ermarth, Michael, 'Hermeneutics and History: The Fork in Hermes' Path through the 18th Century', in Hans Erich Bödeker, Georg G. Iggers, Jonathan B. Knudsen, and Peter H. Reill (eds), *Aufklärung und Geschichte* (Göttingen: Vandenhoeck & Ruprecht, 1986), 191–221

Eschmann, Jürgen, 'Die Sprache der Hugenotten', in Jürgen Eschmann (ed.), *Hugenottenkultur in Deutschland* (Tübingen: Stauffenberg, 1988), 9–35

Escudier, Alexandre, 'Theory and Methodology of History from Chladenius to Droysen: A Historiographical Essay', in Christopher Ligota and Jean-Louis Quantin (eds), *History of Scholarship* (Oxford: Oxford University Press, 2006), 437–86

Espagne, Michel, *Les Transferts culturels franco-allemands* (Paris: PUF, 1999)

—— and Michael Werner (eds), *Transferts: relations interculturelles dans l'espace franco-allemand, XVIIIe–XIXe siècle* (Paris: Recherche sur les Civilisations, 1988)

Evans, Arthur William, *Warburton and the Warburtonians* (Oxford: Oxford University Press, 1932)

Evans, R. J. W., 'Learned Societies in Germany in the Seventeenth Century', *European Studies Review* 7 (1977), 129–51

Everson, Stephen, 'Epicurus on Mind and Language', in Stephen Everson (ed.), *Companions to Ancient Thought*, iii: *Language* (Cambridge: Cambridge University Press, 1994), 74–108
Ferber, Ilit, 'Herder: On Pain and the Origin of Language', *The Germanic Review* 85 (2010), 205–23
Feuerhahn, Wolf, 'A Theologian's List and an Anthropologist's Prose: Michaelis, Niebuhr, and the Expedition to *Felix Arabia*', in Peter Becker and William Clark (eds), *Little Tools of Knowledge: Historical Essays on Academic and Bureaucratic Practices* (Ann Arbor, Mich.: University of Michigan Press, 2001), 141–68
Fick, Richard, 'Michaelis und die Krisis des Jahres 1763', *Beiträge zur Göttinger Bibliotheks- und Gelehrtengeschichte* (Göttingen: Vandenhoeck & Ruprecht, 1928), 40–54
Fontius, Martin, and Helmut Holzhey (eds), *Schweizer im Berlin des 18. Jahrhunderts* (Berlin: Akademie Verlag, 1996)
—— Hartmut Rudolph, and Gary Smith (eds), *Labora diligenter* (Studia Leibnitiana Sonderheft 29) (Stuttgart: Steiner, 1999)
Formigari, Lia, *Signs, Science and Politics: Philosophies of Language in Europe, 1700–1830*, trans. William Dodd (Amsterdam: John Benjamins, 1993)
Forster, Michael N., *After Herder: Philosophy of Language in the German Tradition* (Oxford: Oxford University Press, 2010)
Foucault, Michel, *The Order of Things* (London: Routledge, 2002)
Frensdorff, Ferdinand, 'Eine Krisis in der Königlichen Gesellschaft der Wissenschaften zu Göttingen', *Nachrichten von der Königlichen Gesellschaft der Wissenschaften* (1892), 53–104
—— 'J. D. Michaelis und die Berliner Akademie', *Internationale Monatsschrift für Wissenschaft, Kunst und Technik* 15 (1921), 261–90
Gaier, Ulrich, *Herders Sprachphilosophie und Erkenntniskritik* (Stuttgart-Bad Canstatt: Frommann-Holzboog, 1988)
Gardt, Andreas, *Sprachreflexion in Barock und Frühaufklärung* (Berlin: De Gruyter, 1994)
Gensini, Stefano, 'Epicureanism and Naturalism in the Philosophy of Language from Humanism to the Enlightenment', in Peter Schmitter (ed.), *Sprachtheorien der Neuzeit* i (*Geschichte der Sprachtheorie* IV) (Tübingen: Gunter Narr, 1999), 44–92
—— '*De linguis in universum*': On Leibniz's Ideas on Languages (Münster: Nodus, 2000)
Gessinger, Joachim, and Wolfert von Rahden (eds), *Theorien vom Ursprung der Sprache*, 2 vols (Berlin: De Gruyter, 1989)
Gera, Deborah Levine, *Ancient Greek Ideas on Speech, Language, and Civilization* (Oxford: Oxford University Press, 2003)
Gierl, Martin, *Pietismus und Aufklärung: Theologische Polemik und die Kommunikationsreform der Wissenschaft am Ende des 17. Jahrhunderts* (Göttingen: Vandenhoeck & Ruprecht, 1997)
Goldenbaum, Ursula, 'Leibniz as a Lutheran', in Allison Coudert, Richard H. Popkin, and Gordon M. Weiner (eds), *Leibniz, Mysticism, and Religion* (Dordrecht: Kluwer, 1998), 169–92

—— 'Die *Commentatiuncula de judice* als Leibnizens erste philosophische Auseinandersetzung mit Spinoza nebst der Mitteilung über ein neuaufgefundenes Leibnizstück', in Fontius et al. (eds), *Labora diligenter*, 61–127

—— 'Kants Stellungnahme zum Spinozismusstreit 1786', in Dina Emundts (ed.), *Immanuel Kant und die Berliner Aufklärung* (Wiesbaden: Reichert, 2000), 98–115

—— 'Spinoza's Parrot, Socinian Syllogisms, and Leibniz's Metaphysics: Leibniz's Three Strategies for Defending Christian Mysteries', *American Catholic Philosophical Quarterly* 76 (2002), 551–75

—— 'Einleitung: Die öffentliche Debatte in der deutschen Aufklärung', 'Der Skandal der *Wertheimer Bibel*: Die philosophisch-theologische Entscheidungsschlacht zwischen Pietisten und Wolffianern', in Ursula Goldenbaum (ed.), *Appell an das Publikum: Die öffentliche Debatte in der deutschen Aufklärung 1687–1796* (Berlin: Akademie Verlag, 2004), i. 1–118, 175–508

Goldgar, Anne, *Impolite Learning: Conduct and Community in the Republic of Letters* (New Haven: Yale University Press, 1995)

Goldie, Mark, and Robert Wokler (eds), *The Cambridge History of Eighteenth-Century Political Thought* (Cambridge: Cambridge University Press, 2006)

Goodman, Dena, '*L'Ortografe des dames*: Gender and Language in the Old Regime', in Sarah Knott and Barbara Taylor (eds), *Women, Gender and Enlightenment* (Basingstoke: Palgrave Macmillan, 2005), 195–223

Gossman, Lionel, 'Berkeley, Hume and Maupertuis', *French Studies* 14 (1960), 304–24

Grafton, Anthony, '*Polyhistor* into *Philolog*: Notes on the Transformation of German Classical Scholarship, 1780–1850', *History of Universities* 3 (1983), 159–92

—— 'The World of the Polyhistors: Humanism and Encyclopedism', *Central European History* 18 (1985), 31–47

—— *Joseph Scaliger*, ii: *Historical Chronology* (Oxford: Oxford University Press, 1993)

—— and Joanna Weinberg, '*I Have Always Loved the Holy Tongue*': *Isaac Casaubon, the Jews, and a Forgotten Chapter in Renaissance Scholarship* (Cambridge, Mass.: Harvard University Press, 2011)

Grimsley, Ronald, 'Introduction', in Maupertuis, Turgot, and Maine de Biran, *Sur l'origine du langage*, ed. Ronald Grimsley (Geneva: Droz, 1971), 1–25

Grunert, Frank, 'Das Recht der Natur als Recht des Gefühls: Zur Naturrechtslehre von Johann Jacob Schmauß', *Jahrbuch für Recht und Ethik* 12 (2004), 137–53

Haakonssen, Knud, 'Protestant Natural Law Theory: A General Interpretation', in Natalie Brender and Larry Krasnoff (eds), *New Essays on the History of Autonomy: A Collection Honoring J. B. Schneewind* (Cambridge: Cambridge University Press, 2004), 92–109

Hacking, Ian, 'How, Why, When, and Where Did Language Go Public?', in Robert S. Leventhal (ed.), *Reading after Foucault: Institutions, Disciplines, and Technologies of the Self in Germany, 1750–1830* (Detroit: Wayne State University Press, 1994), 31–50

Häfner, Ralph, *Johann Gottfried Herders Kulturentstehungslehre: Studien zu den Quellen und zur Methode seines Geschichtsdenkens* (Hamburg: Meiner, 1995)

Hallo, Rudolf, *Rudolf Erich Raspe: Ein Wegbereiter von deutscher Art und Kunst* (Stuttgart: Kohlhammer, 1934)

Hansen, Thorkild, *Arabia Felix: The Danish Expedition of 1761–1767*, trans. James and Kathleen McFarlane (London: Collins, 1964)

Harnack, Carl Gustav Adolf von, *Geschichte der Königlich Preußischen Akademie der Wissenschaften zu Berlin* (Berlin: Reichsdruckerei, 1900)

Harris, Roy et al. (eds), *Landmarks in Linguistic Thought*, 3 vols (London: Routledge, 1989–2001)

Hartweg, Frédéric, 'Influence culturelle et intégration linguistique du Refuge Huguenot à Berlin au XVIIIe siècle', in *Le Refuge Huguenot en Allemagne* (Paris: CNRS, 1981), 47–55

—— 'Les Huguenots en Allemagne: une minorité entre deux cultures', in Michelle Magdelaine and Rudolf von Thadden (eds), *Le Refuge Huguenot* (Paris: Armand Colin, 1985), 191–211

Häseler, Jens, 'Johann Bernhard Merian—ein Schweizer Philosoph an der Berliner Akademie', in Fontius and Holzhey (eds), *Schweizer im Berlin*, 217–30

—— 'Samuel Formey, Pasteur huguenot entre Lumières françaises et *Aufklärung*', *Dix-Huitième Siècle* 34 (2002), 239–47

—— 'Jean Henri Samuel Formey—L'homme à Berlin', in Christiane Berkvens-Stevelinck, Hans Bots, and Jens Häseler (eds), *Les grands intermédiaires culturels de la République des Lettres* (Paris: Champion, 2005), 413–34

Haßler, Gerda, *Sprachtheorien der Aufklärung zur Rolle der Sprache im Erkenntnisprozess* (Berlin: Akademie Verlag, 1984)

—— 'Leibniz' Stellung in der Diskussion des Zeichencharakters', in Fontius et al. (eds), *Labora diligenter*, 167–85

—— 'Diversity of Human Languages and Universals of Thought: An Eighteenth-Century Debate in the Berlin Academy', in David Cram, Andrew Linn, and Elke Nowack (eds), *History of Linguistics 1996* (Amsterdam: John Benjamins, 1999), 163–74

—— 'Bon usage et langue parfaite: la présence des remarqueurs dans le débat sur l'universalité de la langue française au XVIIIe siècle', in Philippe Caron (ed.), *Les Remarqueurs sur la langue française du XVIe siècle à nos jours* (Rennes: Presses Universitaires de Rennes, 2004), 167–83

—— and Cordula Neis (eds), *Lexikon sprachtheoretischer Grundbegriffe des 17. und 18. Jahrhunderts*, 2 vols (Berlin: De Gruyter, 2009)

Hecht, Hans, *T. Percy, R. Wood, und J. D. Michaelis: Ein Beitrag zur Literaturgeschichte der Genieperiode* (Stuttgart: Kohlhammer, 1933)

Hecht, Jacqueline, 'Johann Peter Süssmilch: A German Prophet in Foreign Countries', *Population Studies* 41 (1987), 31–58

Hess, Jonathan M., *Germans, Jews and the Claims of Modernity* (New Haven: Yale University Press, 2002)

Heyd, Michael, *'Be Sober and Reasonable': The Critique of Enthusiasm in the Seventeenth and Early Eighteenth Centuries* (Leiden: Brill, 1995)

Hinske, Norbert (ed.), *Zentren der Aufklärung*, i: *Halle. Aufklärung und Pietismus* (Heidelberg: Schneider, 1989)

Hobson, Marian, ' "Nexus effectivus" and "nexus finalis": Causality in Rousseau's *Discours sur l'inégalité* and in the *Essai sur l'origine des langues*', in Marian Hobson, J. T. A. Leigh, and Robert Wokler (eds), *Rousseau and the Eighteenth Century: Essays in Memory of R. A. Leigh* (Oxford: Voltaire Foundation, 1992), 225–50

Hochstrasser, T. J., *Natural Law Theories in the Early Enlightenment* (Cambridge: Cambridge University Press, 2000)

Holmes, Brooke, '*Daedala lingua*: Crafted Speech in *De rerum natura*', *American Journal of Philology* 126 (2005), 527–85

Hont, Istvan, *Jealousy of Trade: International Competition and the Nation State in Historical Perspective* (Cambridge, Mass.: Harvard University Press, 2005)

—— 'The Early Enlightenment Debate on Commerce and Luxury', in Goldie and Wokler (eds), *Cambridge History of Eighteenth-Century Political Thought*, 379–418

Hotson, Howard, *Johann Heinrich Alsted, 1588–1638: Between Renaissance, Reformation, and Universal Reform* (Oxford: Clarendon Press, 2000)

Howard, Thomas A., *Protestant Theology and the Making of the Modern German University* (Oxford: Oxford University Press, 2006)

Hudson, Nicholas, *Writing and European Thought, 1600–1830* (Cambridge: Cambridge University Press, 1994)

Hundert, E. J., 'The Thread of Language and the Web of Dominion: Mandeville to Rousseau and Back', *Eighteenth-Century Studies* 21 (1987–8), 169–91

Hunter, Ian, *Rival Enlightenments: Civil and Metaphysical Philosophy in Early Modern Germany* (Cambridge: Cambridge University Press, 2001)

—— *The Secularization of the Confessional State: The Political Thought of Christian Thomasius* (Cambridge: Cambridge University Press, 2007)

Ingensiep, Hans Werner, 'Der Mensch im Spiegel der Tier- und Pflanzenseele: Zur Anthropomorphologie der Naturwahrnehmung im 18. Jahrhundert', in Hans-Jürgen Schings (ed.), *Der ganze Mensch: Anthropologie und Literatur im 18. Jahrhundert* (Stuttgat: Metzler, 1994), 54–79

Isermann, Michael, *Die Sprachtheorie im Werk von Thomas Hobbes* (Münster: Nodus, 1991)

Israel, Jonathan, *Radical Enlightenment: Philosophy and the Making of Modernity 1650–1750* (Oxford: Oxford University Press, 2001)

—— *Enlightenment Contested: Philosophy, Modernity, and the Emancipation of Man, 1670–1752* (Oxford: Oxford University Press, 2006)

Jarick, John (ed.), *Sacred Conjectures: The Context and Legacy of Robert Lowth and Jean Astruc* (New York: T&T Clark, 2007)

Jolley, Nicholas, *The Light of the Soul: Theories of Ideas in Leibniz, Malebranche, and Descartes* (Oxford: Clarendon Press, 1998)

—— *Leibniz* (London and New York: Routledge, 2005)

Joseph, John E., 'The Natural: Its Meanings and Functions in the History of Linguistic Thought', in Douglas A. Kibbee (ed.), *History of Linguistics 2005* (Amsterdam: John Benjamins, 2007), 1–23

Kästner, Erich, *Friedrich der Grosse und die deutsche Literatur: Die Erwiderungen auf seine Schrift 'De la littérature allemande'* (Stuttgart: Kohlhammer, 1972)
Katz, David, 'The Language of Adam in Seventeenth-Century England', in Hugh Lloyd-Jones, Valerie Pearl, and Blair Worden (eds), *History and Imagination: Essays in Honour of H. R. Trevor-Roper* (London: Duckworth, 1981), 132–45
Kieffer, Bruce, 'Herder's Treatment of Süssmilch's Theory of the Origin of Language in the *Abhandlung über den Ursprung der Sprache*: A Re-evaluation', *Germanic Review* 53 (1978), 96–105
Knowlson, James, *Universal Language Schemes in England and France, 1600–1800* (Toronto: University of Toronto Press, 1975)
Kontler, László, 'William Robertson and his German Audience on European and non-European Civilisations', *Scottish Historical Review* 80 (2001), 63–89
Koselleck, Reinhart, *Futures Past: On the Semantics of Historical Time*, trans. Keith Tribe (New York: Columbia University Press, 2004), 26–42
Krämer, Olav, '"Welcher Gestalt man denen Frantzosen nachahmen solle": Stationen einer Jahrhundertdebatte', in Jens Häseler, Albert Meier, and Olaf Koch (eds), *Gallophobie im 18. Jahrhundert* (Berlin: Berliner Wissenschaftsverlag, 2005), 61–88
Krauss, Werner, 'Ein Akademiesekretär vor 200 Jahren: Samuel Formey', in *Studien zur deutschen und französischen Aufklärung* (Berlin: Rütten & Loening, 1963), 53–62
Kuehn, Manfred, *Scottish Common Sense in Germany* (Kingston and Montreal: McGill-Queen's University Press, 1987)
Kugel, James, *The Idea of Biblical Poetry: Parallelism and Its History* (New Haven: Yale University Press, 1998)
Lamb, Jonathan, *The Rhetoric of Suffering: Reading the Book of Job in the Eighteenth Century* (Oxford: Oxford University Press, 1995)
Lämmert, Eberhard, 'Friedrich der Große und die deutsche Literatur', in Brunhilde Wehinger (ed.), *Geist und Macht: Friedrich der Große im Kontext der europäischen Kulturgeschichte* (Berlin: Akademie Verlag, 2005), 13–21
Lasche, Agathe, *'Berlinisch': eine berlinische Sprachgeschichte* (Berlin: R. Hobbing, 1928)
Laursen, John Christian, 'Swiss Anti-Skeptics in Berlin', in Fontius and Holzhey (eds), *Schweizer im Berlin*, 261–82
—— and Richard H. Popkin, 'Hume in the Prussian Academy: Jean Bernard Merian's "On the Phenomenalism of David Hume"', *Hume Studies* 23 (1997), 153–91
Lauzon, Matthew, *Signs of Light: French and British Theories of Linguistic Communication, 1648–1789* (Ithaca, NY: Cornell University Press, 2010)
La Vopa, Anthony J., *Grace, Talent, and Merit: Poor Students, Clerical Careers, and Professional Ideology in Eighteenth-Century Germany* (Cambridge: Cambridge University Press, 1988)
—— 'Herder's *Publikum*: Language, Print, and Sociability in Eighteenth-Century Germany', *Eighteenth-Century Studies* 29 (1996), 5–24
—— 'The Philosopher and the *Schwärmer*: On the Career of a German Epithet from Luther to Kant', in Lawrence E. Klein and Anthony J. La Vopa (eds),

Enthusiasm and Enlightenment in Europe, 1650–1850 (San Marino, Calif.: Huntington Library, 1998), 85–115

Law, Vivien, *The History of Linguistics in Europe from Plato to 1600* (Cambridge: Cambridge University Press, 2003)

Leddy, Neven, and Avi Lifschitz (eds), *Epicurus in the Enlightenment* (Oxford: Voltaire Foundation, 2009)

Legaspi, Michael, *The Death of Scripture and the Rise of Biblical Studies* (Oxford: Oxford University Press, 2010)

Lestition, Steven, 'Countering, Transposing, or Negating the Enlightenment? A Response to Robert Norton', *Journal of the History of Ideas* 68 (2007), 659–81

Lewis, Rhodri, *Language, Mind and Nature: Artificial Languages in England from Bacon to Locke* (Cambridge: Cambridge University Press, 2007)

Lifschitz, Avi, 'Language as the Key to the Epistemological Labyrinth: Turgot's Changing View of Human Perception', *Historiographia Linguistica* 31 (2004), 345–65

—— 'From the Corruption of French to the Cultural Distinctiveness of German: The Controversy over Prémontval's *Préservatif* (1759)', *Studies on Voltaire and the Eighteenth Century* 2007:06, 265–90

—— 'The Enlightenment Revival of the Epicurean History of Language and Civilisation', in Leddy and Lifschitz (eds), *Epicurus in the Enlightenment*, 207–26

—— 'Translation in Theory and Practice: The Case of Johann David Michaelis' Prize Essay on Language and Opinions (1759)', in Stockhorst (ed.), *Cultural Transfer*, 29–43

—— 'The Arbitrariness of the Linguistic Sign: Variations on an Enlightenment Theme', *Journal of the History of Ideas* 73(4) (2012)

—— 'Language', in Aaron Garrett (ed.), *The Routledge Companion to Eighteenth Century Philosophy* (London: Routledge, forthcoming)

—— 'Language as a Means and an Obstacle to Freedom: The Case of Moses Mendelssohn', in Quentin Skinner and Martin van Gelderen (eds), *Freedom and the Construction of Europe* (Cambridge: Cambridge University Press, forthcoming)

Long, A. A., *Hellenistic Philosophy* (Berkeley, Calif.: University of California Press, 1974)

—— and D. N. Sedley (eds), *The Hellenistic Philosophers* (Cambridge: Cambridge University Press, 1987), 2 vols.

Loop, Jan, '"Von dem Geschmack der morgenländischen Dichtkunst": Orientalistik und Bibelexegese bei Huet, Michaelis und Herder', in Daniel Weidner (ed.), *Urpoesie und Morgenland: Johann Gottfried Herders 'Vom Geist der Ebräischen Poesie'* (Berlin: Kadmos, 2008), 155–83

Losonsky, Michael, *Linguistic Turns in Modern Philosophy* (Cambridge: Cambridge University Press, 2006)

Lough, John, 'Locke's Reading during his Stay in France (1675–9)', *Transactions of the Bibliographical Society* 8 (1953), 229–58

Löwenbrück, Anna-Ruth, *Judenfeindschaft im Zeitalter der Aufklärung: Eine Studie zur Vorgeschichte des modernen Antisemitismus am Beispiel des Göttinger*

Theologen und Orientalisten Johann David Michaelis (Frankfurt am Main: Peter Lang, 1995)

Maat, Jaap, *Philosophical Languages in the Seventeenth Century* (Dordrecht: Kluwer, 2004)

McMahon, Darrin M., *Enemies of the Enlightenment: The French Counter-Enlightenment and the Making of Modernity* (Oxford: Oxford University Press, 2001)

Malcolm, Noel, 'Hobbes, Ezra and the Bible: The History of a Subversive Idea', in *Aspects of Hobbes* (Oxford: Oxford University Press, 2002), 383–431

Mali, Joseph, and Robert Wokler (eds), *Isaiah Berlin's Counter-Enlightenment* (Philadelphia: American Philosophical Society, 2003)

Marchand, Suzanne L., *German Orientalism in the Age of Empire* (Cambridge: Cambridge University Press, 2009)

Marino, Mario, 'Die Sprache: Demokratie oder Tyrannei?' in Sabine Groß and Gerhard Sauder (eds), *Der frühe und der späte Herder: Kontinuität und/oder Korrektur* (Heidelberg: Synchron, 2007), 343–53

May, Georges, 'Le Fatalisme et *Jacques le Fataliste*', in Raymond Trousson (ed.), *Thèmes et figures du siècle des Lumières: mélanges offerts à Roland Mortier* (Geneva: Droz, 1980), 162–74

Medick, Hans, *Naturzustand und Naturgeschichte der bürgerlichen Gesellschaft* (Göttingen: Vandenhoeck & Ruprecht, 1973)

Meeker, Natania, 'Sexing Epicurean Materialism in Diderot', in Leddy and Lifschitz (eds), *Epicurus in the Enlightenment*, 85–104

Megill, Alan, 'The Enlightenment Debate on the Origins of Language and Its Historical Background', PhD dissertation, Columbia University, 1975

Messling, Markus, *Pariser Orientlektüren: Zu Wilhelm von Humboldts Theorie der Schrift* (Paderborn: Schöningh, 2008)

Meyer, Annette, *Von der Wahrheit zur Wahrscheinlichkeit: Die Wissenschaft vom Menschen in der schottischen und deutschen Aufklärung* (Tübingen: Niemeyer, 2008)

Miel, Jean, 'Pascal, Port-Royal, and Cartesian Linguistics', *Journal of the History of Ideas* 30 (1969), 261–71

Miller, Peter N. (ed.), *Momigliano and Antiquarianism: Foundations of the Modern Cultural Sciences* (Toronto: University of Toronto Press, 2007)

Moeller, Bernd (ed.), *Theologie in Göttingen* (Göttingen: Vandenhoeck & Ruprecht, 1987)

Momigliano, Arnaldo, 'Ancient History and the Antiquarian', *Journal of the Warburg and Courtauld Institutes* 13 (1950), 285–315

Monfasani, John, 'The Ciceronian Controversy', in Norton (ed.), *The Cambridge History of Literary Criticism*, iii. 395–401

Mortimer, Sarah, *Reason and Religion in the English Revolution: The Challenge of Socinianism* (Cambridge: Cambridge University Press, 2010)

Muller, Richard A., 'The Debate over the Vowel Points and the Crisis in Orthodox Hermenutics', *Journal of Medieval and Renaissance Studies* 10 (1980), 53–72

Mulsow, Martin, *Moderne aus dem Untergrund: Radikale Frühaufklärung in Deutschland 1680–1720* (Hamburg: Meiner, 2002)

—— and Jan Assmann (eds), *Sintflut und Gedächtnis: Erinnern und Vergessen des Ursprungs* (Munich: Fink, 2006)

Neis, Cordula, '*Génie de la langue,* Apologie der Nationalsprachen und die Berliner Preisfrage von 1771', in Gerda Haßler (ed.), *Texte und Institutionen in der Geschichte der französischen Sprache* (Bonn: Romanistischer Verlag, 2001), 69–88

—— *Anthropologie im Sprachdenken des 18. Jahrhunderts: Die Berliner Preisfrage nach dem Ursprung der Sprache* (Berlin: De Gruyter, 2003)

Nelson, Eric, *The Hebrew Republic: Jewish Sources and the Transformation of European Political Thought* (Cambridge, Mass.: Harvard University Press, 2010)

Niedermann, Josef, *Kultur: Werden und Wandlungen des Begriffs und seiner Ersatzbegriffe von Cicero bis Herder* (Florence: Bibliopolis, 1941)

Norton, Glyn P. (ed.), *The Cambridge History of Literary Criticism*, iii: *The Renaissance* (Cambridge: Cambridge University Press, 1999)

Norton, Robert E., *The Beautiful Soul: Aesthetic Morality in the Eighteenth Century* (Ithaca, NY: Cornell University Press, 1995)

—— 'The Myth of the Counter-Enlightenment', *Journal of the History of Ideas* 68 (2007), 635–58

—— 'Isaiah Berlin's "Expressionism," or: "Ha! Du bist das Blökende!"', *Journal of the History of Ideas* 69 (2008), 339–47

Nye, Edward, *Literary and Linguistic Theories in Eighteenth-Century France: From Nuances to Impertinence* (Oxford: Oxford University Press, 2000)

Olender, Maurice, *The Languages of Paradise*, trans. Arthur Goldhammer (Cambridge, Mass.: Harvard University Press, 1992)

Ornstein, Martha, *The Rôle of Scientific Societies in the Seventeenth Century* (Chicago: Chicago University Press, 1913)

Osterhammel, Jürgen, *Die Entzauberung Asiens: Europa und die asiatischen Reiche im 18. Jahrhundert* (Munich: Beck, 1998)

Othmer, Sieglinde, *Berlin und die Verbreitung des Naturrechts in Europa* (Berlin: De Gruyter, 1970)

Outram, Dorinda, 'The Work of the Fool: Enlightenment Encounters with Folly, Laughter and Truth', *Eighteenth Century Thought* 1 (2003), 281–94

Oz-Salzberger, Fania, *Translating the Enlightenment: Scottish Civic Discourse in Eighteenth-Century Germany* (Oxford: Oxford University Press, 1995)

Paganini, Gianni, 'Signes, imagination et mémoire: de la psychologie de Wolff à l'*Essai* de Condillac', *Revue des sciences philosophiques et théologiques* 72 (1988), 287–300

—— and Edoardo Tortarolo (eds), *Der Garten und die Moderne: Epikureische Moral und Politik vom Humanismus zur Aufklärung* (Stuttgart: Frommann-Holzboog, 2004)

Paillard, Christophe, 'Le Problème du fatalisme au siècle des Lumières', PhD dissertation, Université Jean Moulin, Lyon III (2000)

Paxman, David B., *Voyage into Language: Space and the Linguistic Encounter, 1500–1800* (Aldershot: Ashgate, 2003)

Pénisson, Pierre (ed.), *De l'universalité de la langue française, 1784* (Paris: Fayard, 1995)

—— 'Evolution de la question des langues à l'Académie de Berlin', *Das Achtzehnte Jahrhundert* 25/1 (2001), 43–54

Pénisson, Pierre and Norbert Waszek (eds), *Herder et les Lumières—Revue Germanique Internationale* 20 (2003)

Petersilka, Corina, *Die Zweisprachigkeit Friedrichs des Großen: Ein linguistisches Porträt* (Tübingen: Niemeyer, 2005)

Pettit, Philip, *Made of Words: Hobbes on Language, Mind, and Politics* (Princeton: Princeton University Press, 2008)

Piedmont, René, *Beiträge zum französischen Sprachbesußtsein im 18. Jahrhundert: Der Wettbewerb der Berliner Akademie zur Universalität der französischen Sprache von 1782/84* (Tübingen: Narr, 1984)

Piirimäe, Eva, 'Dying for the Fatherland: Thomas Abbt's Theory of Aesthetic Patriotism', *History of European Ideas* 35 (2009), 194–208

Plachta, Bodo, *Damnatur Toleratur Admittitur: Studien und Dokumente zur literarischen Zensur im 18. Jahrhundert* (Tübingen: Niemeyer, 1994)

Pocock, J. G. A., *Barbarism and Religion*, i: *The Enlightenments of Edward Gibbon, 1737–1764* (Cambridge: Cambridge University Press, 1999)

—— *Political Thought and History: Essays on Theory and Method* (Cambridge: Cambridge University Press, 2008)

Politzer, Robert L., 'On the Linguistic Philosophy of Maupertuis and its Relation to the History of Linguistic Relativism', *Symposium* 17 (1963), 5–16

Pollok, Anne, *Facetten des Menschen: Zur Anthropologie Moses Mendelssohns* (Hamburg: Meiner, 2010)

Porter, David, *Ideographia: The Chinese Cipher in Early Modern Europe* (Stanford, Calif.: Stanford University Press, 2001)

Pott, Sandra, Martin Mulsow and Lutz Danneberg (eds), *The Berlin Refuge, 1680–1780: Learning and Science in European Context* (Leiden: Brill, 2003)

Poulouin, Claudine, *Le Temps des origines: l'Éden, le Déluge et 'les temps reculés'. De Pascal à l'Encyclopédie* (Paris: Champion, 1998)

Pross, Wolfgang, Epilogue to Herder, *Werke*, ii: *Herder und die Anthropologie der Aufklärung*, ed. Wolfgang Pross (Munich: Hanser, 1987)

—— 'Das "göttliche Geschenk der Rede": Hat Herder die Sprachursprungstheorie der *Abhandlung* in den *Ideen* revoziert?', in Jürg Niederhauser and Stanislaw Szlęk (eds), *Sprachsplitter und Sprachspiele* (Bern: Peter Lang, 2000), 223–33

—— 'Naturalism, Anthropology, Culture', in Goldie and Wokler (eds), *The Cambridge History of Eighteenth-Century Political Thought*, 218–47

Quine, Willard van Orman, *Word and Object* (Cambridge, Mass.: MIT Press, 1960)

Rabault-Feuerhahn, Pascale, *L'Archive des origines: Sanskrit, philologie, anthropologie dans l'Allemagne du XIXe siècle* (Paris: Cerf, 2008)

Raeff, Marc, *The Well-Ordered Police State: Social and Institutional Change through Law in the Germanies and Russia, 1600–1800* (New Haven: Yale University Press, 1983)

Ramati, Ayval (1996), 'Harmony at a Distance: Leibniz's Scientific Academies', *Isis* 87 (1996), 430–52

Rasmussen, Stig (ed.), *Carsten Niebuhr und die Arabische Reise 1761–67* (Heide: Boyens, 1986)

Redekop, Benjamin W., *Lessing, Abbt, Herder and the Quest for a German Public* (Montreal and Kingston: McGill-Queen's University Press, 2000)
Reill, Peter Hanns, 'History and Hermeneutics in the *Aufklärung*: The Thought of Johann Christoph Gatterer', *Journal of Modern History* 45 (1973), 24–51
—— *The German Enlightenment and the Rise of Historicism* (Berkeley, Calif.: University of California Press, 1975)
—— 'Die Geschichtswissenschaft um die Mitte des 18. Jahrhunderts', in Vierhaus (ed.), *Wissenschaften im Zeitalter der Aufklärung*, 163–93
Reinhardt, Tobias, 'Epicurus and Lucretius on the Origins of Language', *The Classical Quarterly* 58 (2008), 127–40
Rengstorf, Karl Heinrich, 'Johann Heinrich Michaelis und seine Biblia Hebraica von 1720', in Hinske (ed.), *Zentren der Aufklärung*, i. 15–64
Reventlow, Henning Graf, Walter Sparn, and John Woodbridge (eds), *Historische Kritik und biblischer Kanon in der deutschen Aufklärung* (Wiesbaden: Harrassowitz, 1988)
Ricken, Ulrich, *Leibniz, Wolff, und einige sprachtheoretische Entwicklungen in der deutschen Aufklärung* (Berlin: Akademie Verlag, 1989)
—— *Linguistics, Anthropology and Philosophy in the French Enlightenment*, trans. Robert Norton (London: Routledge, 1994)
—— 'Mendelssohn und die Sprachtheorien der Aufklärung', in Albrecht and Engel (eds), *Mendelssohn im Spannungsfeld*, 195–241
Ringleben, Joachim, 'Göttinger Aufklärungstheologie—von Königsberg her gesehen', in Moeller (ed.), *Theologie in Göttingen*, 82–110
Robertson, John, *The Case for the Enlightenment: Scotland and Naples 1680–1760* (Cambridge: Cambridge University Press, 2005)
Rosenberg, Daniel, 'Making Time: Origin, History, and Language in Enlightenment France and Britain', PhD dissertation, UC Berkeley, 1996
Rosenfeld, Sophia, *A Revolution in Language: The Problem of Signs in Late Eighteenth-Century France* (Stanford, Calif.: Stanford University Press, 2001)
Rosen-Prest, Viviane, *L'Historiographie des Huguenots en Prusse au temps des Lumières* (Paris: Champion, 2002)
Rossi, Paolo, *The Dark Abyss of Time: The History of the Earth and the History of Nations from Hooke to Vico*, trans. Lydia G. Cochrane (Chicago: University of Chicago Press, 1984)
—— *Logic and the Art of Memory: The Quest for a Universal Language*, trans. Stephen Clucas (Chicago: University of Chicago Press, 2000)
Saada, Anne, *Inventer Diderot: les constructions d'un auteur en Allemagne au XVIIIe siècle* (Paris: CNRS, 2003)
Sauter, Michael, 'Clockwatchers and Stargazers: Time Discipline in Early Modern Berlin', *American Historical Review* 112 (2007), 685–709
Scaglione, Aldo, 'Direct vs. Inverted Order: Wolff and Condillac on the Necessity of the Sign and the Interrelationship of Language and Thinking', *Romance Philology* 33 (1980), 496–501
Schatz, Andrea, *Sprache in der Zerstreuung: Die Säkularisierung des Hebräischen im 18. Jahrhundert* (Göttingen: Vandenhoeck & Ruprecht, 2009)

Schiebinger, Londa, 'Naming and Knowing: The Global Politics of Eighteenth-Century Botanical Nomenclatures', in Pamela H. Smith and Benjamin Schmidt (eds), *Making Knowledge in Early Modern Europe: Practices, Objects, and Texts, 1400–1800* (Chicago: University of Chicago Press, 2007), 90–105

Schiewe, Jürgen, *Sprachpurismus und Emanzipation: Joachim Heinrich Campes Verdeutschungsprogramm als Voraussetzung für Gesellschaftsveränderungen* (Hildesheim: Olms, 1988)

Schlaps, Christiane, 'The "Genius of Language": Transformations of a Concept in the History of Linguistics', *Historiographia Linguistica* 31 (2004), 367–88

Schlieben-Lange, Brigitte, and Harald Weydt, 'Die Antwort Daniel Jenischs auf die Preisfrage der Berliner Akademie zur "Vergleichung der Hauptsprachen Europas" von 1794', in Ute Tintemann and Jürgen Trabant (eds), *Sprache und Sprachen in Berlin um 1800* (Hanover: Wehrhahn, 2004), 215–43

Schloemann, Martin, *Siegmund Jacob Baumgarten: System und Geschichte in der Theologie des Übergangs zum Neuprotestantismus* (Göttingen: Vandenhoeck & Ruprecht, 1974)

—— 'Wegbereiter wider Willen: Siegmund Jacob Baumgarten und die historisch-kritische Bibelforschung', in Reventlow et al. (eds), *Historische Kritik*, 149–55

Schmidt, Alexander, 'Letters, Morals and Government: Jean-Henri-Samuel Formey's and Johann Gottfried Herder's Responses to Rousseau's *First Discourse*', *Modern Intellectual History* 9 (2012), 249–74

Schmidt, Johannes, *Leibnitz und Baumgarten: Ein Beitrag zur Geschichte der deutschen Aesthetik* (Halle: Niemeyer, 1875)

Schmidt-Biggemann, Wilhelm, *Theodizee und Tatsachen: Das philosophische Profil der deutschen Aufklärung* (Frankfurt am Main: Suhrkamp, 1988)

Schneiders, Werner (ed.), *Christian Wolff 1679–1754: Interpretationen zu seiner Philosophie und deren Wirkung* (Hamburg: Meiner, 1983)

Schömig, Ulrike, 'Politik und Öffentlichkeit in Preußen: Entwicklung der Zensur- und Pressepolitik zwischen 1740 und 1819', PhD dissertation, Julius-Maximilians-Universität Würzburg, 1988

Schulenburg, Sigrid von der, *Leibniz als Sprachforscher*, ed. Kurt Müller (Frankfurt am Main: Klostermann, 1973)

Schweizer, Hans Rudolf, *Ästhetik als Philosophie der sinnlichen Erkenntnis: Eine Interpretation der 'Aesthetica' A.G. Baumgartens* (Basel: Schwabe, 1973)

Searle, John R., *Speech Acts: An Essay in the Philosophy of Language* (Cambridge: Cambridge University Press, 1969)

—— *Making the Social World: The Structure of Human Civilization* (Oxford: Oxford University Press, 2010)

Sedlarz, Claudia, 'Ruhm oder Reform? Der "Sprachenstreit" um 1790 an der Königlichen Akademie der Wissenschaften in Berlin', in Ursula Goldenbaum and Alexander Košenina (eds), *Berliner Aufklärung: Kulturwissenschaftliche Studien* (Hanover: Wehrhahn, 2003), ii. 245–76

Sedley, David, *Plato's Cratylus* (Cambridge: Cambridge University Press, 2003)

Seguin, Maria Susana, *Science et religion dans la pensée française du XVIIIe siècle: le mythe du Déluge universel* (Paris: Champion, 2001)

Serjeantson, Richard, 'The Passions and Animal Language, 1540–1700', *Journal of the History of Ideas* 62 (2001), 425–44
Sheehan, Jonathan, *The Enlightenment Bible: Translation, Scholarship, Culture* (Princeton: Princeton University Press, 2005)
Skinner, Quentin, *The Foundations of Modern Political Thought* (Cambridge: Cambridge University Press, 1978), 2 vols.
—— *Reason and Rhetoric in the Philosophy of Hobbes* (Cambridge: Cambridge University Press, 1996)
—— *Visions of Politics*, i: *Regarding Method* (Cambridge: Cambridge University Press, 2002)
Slaughter, Mary M., *Universal Languages and Scientific Taxonomy in the Seventeenth Century* (Cambridge: Cambridge University Press, 1982)
Smend, Rudolf, 'Johann David Michaelis und Johann Gottfried Eichhorn—zwei Orientalisten am Rande der Theologie', in Moeller (ed.), *Theologie in Göttingen*, 58–81
Smith, Raoul N., 'The Sociology of Language in Johann David Michaelis's Dissertation of 1760', *Journal of the History of the Behavioral Sciences* 12 (1976), 338–46
Sonntag, Otto, 'Albrecht Von Haller on the Future of Science', *Journal of the History of Ideas* 35 (1974), 313–22
Sorkin, David, *The Religious Enlightenment: Protestants, Jews and Catholics from London to Vienna* (Princeton: Princeton University Press, 2008)
Spalding, Paul S., *Seize the Book, Jail the Author: Johann Lorenz Schmidt and Censorship in Eighteenth-Century Germany* (West Lafayette, Ind.: Purdue University Press, 1998)
Sparn, Walter, 'Vernünftiges Christentum: Über die geschichtliche Aufgabe der theologischen Aufklärung im 18. Jahrhundert in Deutschland', in Vierhaus (ed.), *Wissenschaften im Zeitalter der Aufklärung*, 18–57
—— 'Auf dem Wege zur theologischen Aufklärung in Halle: Von Johann Franz Budde zu Siegmund Jakob Baumgarten', in Hinske (ed.), *Zentren der Aufklärung*, i. 71–89
Spoerhase, Carlos, 'Die "Mittelstrasse" zwischen Skeptizismus und Dogmatismus: Konzeptionen hermeneutischer Wahrscheinlichkeit um 1750', in Carlos Spoerhase, Dirk Werle, and Markus Wild (eds), *Unsicheres Wissen: Skeptizismus und Wahrscheinlichkeit 1550–1850* (Berlin: De Gruyter, 2009), 269–300
—— 'A Case against Skepticism: On Christian August Crusius' Logic of Hermeneutical Probability', *History of European Ideas* 36 (2010), 251–9
Stam, James, *Inquiries into the Origins of Language: The Fate of a Question* (New York: Harper and Row, 1976)
Starobinski, Jean, *Jean-Jacques Rousseau: Transparency and Obstruction*, trans. Arthur Goldhammer (Chicago: University of Chicago Press, 1988)
—— *Blessings in Disguise, or, the Morality of Evil*, trans. Arthur Goldhammer (Cambridge, Mass.: Harvard University Press, 1993)
Steinke, Hubert, Urs Boschung, and Wolfgang Pross (eds), *Albrecht von Haller: Leben—Werk—Epoche* (Göttingen: Wallstein, 2008)
Stockhorst, Stefanie (ed.), *Cultural Transfer through Translation in Eighteenth-Century Europe* (Amsterdam: Rodopi, 2010)

Storost, Jürgen, *Langue française—Langue universelle? Die Diskussion über die Universalität des Französischen an der Berliner Akademie der Wissenschaften* (Bonn: Romanistischer Verlag, 1994)

—— *300 Jahre romanische Sprachen und Literaturen an der Berliner Akademie der Wissenschaften* (Frankfurt am Main: Peter Lang, 2001)

Sułek, Antoni, 'The Experiment of Psammetichus: Fact, Fiction, and Model to Follow', *Journal of the History of Ideas* 50 (1989), 645–51

Süßenberger, Claus, *Rousseau im Urteil der deutschen Publizistik bis zum Ende der französischen Revolution: Ein Beitrag zur Rezeptionsgeschichte* (Frankfurt am Main: Peter Lang, 1974)

Sutcliffe, Adam, *Judaism and Enlightenment* (Cambridge: Cambridge University Press, 2003)

Taylor, Charles, *Human Agency and Language* (*Philosophical Papers*, i) (Cambridge: Cambridge University Press, 1985)

Terrall, Mary, 'The Culture of Science in Frederick the Great's Berlin', *History of Science* 28 (1990), 333–64

—— *The Man Who Flattened the Earth: Maupertuis and the Sciences in the Enlightenment* (Chicago: University of Chicago Press, 2002)

Thomas, Downing A., *Music and the Origins of Language* (Cambridge: Cambridge University Press, 1995)

Thomas, Margaret, 'The Evergreen Story of Psammetichus' Inquiry into the Origin of Language', *Historiographia Linguistica* 34 (2007), 37–62

Thomson, Ann, *Bodies of Thought: Science, Religion and the Soul in the Early Enlightenment* (Oxford: Oxford University Press, 2008)

Toellner, Richard, 'Entstehung und Programm der Göttinger Gelehrten Gesellschaft unter besonderer Berücksichtigung des Hallerschen Wissenschaftsbegriffes', in Fritz Hartmann and Rudolf Vierhaus (eds), *Der Akademiegedanke im 17. und 18. Jahrhundert* (Bremen and Wolfenbüttel: Jacobi, 1977), 97–115

Tonelli, Giorgio, 'Der Streit über die mathematische Methode in der Philosophie in der ersten Hälfte des 18. Jahrhunderts und die Entstehung von Kants Schrift über die "Deutlichkeit"', *Archiv für Philosophie* 9 (1959), 37–66

—— 'Leibniz on Innate Ideas and the Early Reactions to the Publication of the *Nouveaux Essais* (1765)', *Journal of the History of Philosophy* 12 (1974), 437–54

Tortarolo, Edoardo, *La ragione sulla Sprea: coscienza storica e cultura politica nell'illuminismo berlinese* (Bologna: Mulino, 1989)

—— 'Censorship and the Conception of the Public in Late Eighteenth-Century Germany', in Dario Castiglione and Lesley Sharpe (eds), *Shifting the Boundaries: Transformations of the Languages of Public and Private in the Eighteenth Century* (Exeter: University of Exeter press, 1995), 131–50

Totok, Wilhelm, 'Leibniz als Wissenschaftsorganisator', in Carl Haase and Wilhelm Totok (eds), *Leibniz: Sein Leben, sein Wirken, seine Welt* (Hanover: Verlag für Literatur und Zeitgeschehen, 1966), 293–320

Trabant, Jürgen, 'Herder's Discovery of the Ear', in Kurt Mueller-Vollmer (ed.), *Herder Today* (Berlin: De Gruyter, 1990), 345–66

—— *Vico's New Science of Ancient Signs: A Study of Sematology*, trans. Sean Ward (London: Routledge, 2004)

—— *Europäisches Sprachdenken: Von Platon bis Wittgenstein* (Munich: Beck, 2006)

Tunstall, Kate E., 'The Judgement of Experience: Seeing and Reading in Diderot's *Lettre sur les aveugles*', *French Studies* 42 (2008), 404–16

—— 'Pré-histoire d'un emblème des Lumières: l'aveugle-né de Montaigne à Diderot', in Isabelle Moreau (ed.), *Les Lumières en mouvement* (Lyon: ENS, 2009), 173–97

Tzoref-Ashkenazi, Chen, *Der romantische Mythos vom Ursprung der Deutschen: Friedrich Schlegels Suche nach der indogermanischen Verbindung* (Göttingen: Wallstein, 2009)

Ungeheuer, Gerold, 'Sprache und symbolische Erkenntnis bei Wolff', in Schneiders (ed.), *Christian Wolff*, 89–112

Venturi, Franco, *Jeunesse de Diderot (1713–1753)*, trans. Juliette Bertrand (Paris: Albert Skira, 1939)

Verlinsky, Alexander, 'Epicurus and his Predecessors on the Origin of Language', in Dorothea Frede and Brian Inwood (eds), *Language and Learning: Philosophy of Language in the Hellenistic Age* (Cambridge: Cambridge University Press, 2005), 56–100

Vierhaus, Rudolf, 'Montesquieu in Deutschland: Zur Geschichte seiner Wirkung als politischer Schriftsteller im 18. Jahrhundert', in *Collegium Philosophicum: Studien Joachim Ritter zum 60. Geburtstag* (Basel: Schwabe, 1965), 403–37

—— (ed.), *Wissenschaften im Zeitalter der Aufklärung* (Göttingen: Vandenhoeck & Ruprecht, 1985)

Voigt, Christoph, *Der englische Deismus in Deutschland* (Tübingen: Mohr Siebeck, 2003)

Waswo, Richard, 'Theories of Language', in Norton (ed.), *The Cambridge History of Literary Criticism*, iii. 25–35

Weidner, Daniel, '"Menschliche, heilige Sprache": Das Hebräische bei Michaelis und Herder', *Monatshefte für deutschsprachige Literatur und Kultur* 95 (2003), 171–206

—— 'Secularization, Scripture, and the Theory of Reading: J. G. Herder and the Old Testament', *New German Critique* 94 (2005), 169–93

Weiss, Helmut, *Johann Georg Hamanns Ansichten zur Sprache: Versuch einer Rekonstruktion aus dem Frühwerk* (Münster: Nodus, 1990)

Wells, G. A., *The Origin of Language: Aspects of the Discussion from Condillac to Wundt* (La Salle, Ill.: Open Court, 1987)

Wilke, Jürgen, 'Die französische Kolonie in Berlin', in Helga Schulz (ed.), *Berlin 1650–1800: Sozialgeschichte einer Residenz*, 2nd edn (Berlin: Akademie Verlag, 1992), 352–430

Williams, Bernard, 'Cratylus' Theory of Names and its Refutation', in Malcolm Schofield and Martha Nussbaum (eds), *Language and Logos* (Cambridge: Cambridge University Press, 1982), 83–93

Wilson, Catherine, *Epicureanism at the Origins of Modernity* (Oxford: Oxford University Press, 2008)

Winter, Eduard (ed.), *Die Registres der Berliner Akademie der Wissenschaften 1746–1766: Dokumente für das Wirken Leonhard Eulers in Berlin* (Berlin: Akademie Verlag, 1957)

Wokler, Robert, 'Perfectible Apes in Decadent Cultures: Rousseau's Anthropology Revisited', *Daedalus* 107 (1978), 107–34

—— *Rousseau on Society, Politics, Music and Language* (New York: Garland Publishing, 1987)

—— 'Anthropology and Conjectural History in the Enlightenment', in Christopher Fox, Roy Porter, and Robert Wokler (eds), *Inventing Human Science: Eighteenth-Century Domains* (Berekeley, Calif.: University of California Press, 1995), 31–52

Yardeni, Miryam, *Le Refuge huguenot: assimilation et culture* (Paris: Champion, 2002)

Young, B. W., *Religion and Enlightenment in Eighteenth-Century England* (Oxford: Clarendon Press, 1998)

Zammito, John H., *Kant, Herder, and the Birth of Anthropology* (Chicago: University of Chicago Press, 2002)

—— 'Herder and Historical Metanarrative: What's Philosophical about History?', in Hans Adler and Wulf Koepke (eds), *Companion to the Works of Johann Gottfried Herder* (Rochester, NY: Camden House, 2009), 65–91

—— Karl Menges, and Ernest A. Menze, 'Johann Gottfried Herder Revisited: The Revolution in Scholarship in the Last Quarter Century', *Journal of the History of Ideas* 71 (2010), 661–84

Zande, Johan van der, 'In the Image of Cicero: German Philosophy between Wolff and Kant', *Journal of the History of Ideas* 56 (1995), 419–42

—— 'Orpheus in Berlin: A Reappraisal of Johann Georg Sulzer's Theory of the Polite Arts', *Central European History* 28 (1995), 175–208

Zedelmaier, Helmut, *Der Anfang der Geschichte: Studien zur Ursprungsdebatte im 18. Jahrhundert* (Hamburg: Meiner, 2003)

Zeydel, Edwin H., 'The German Language in the Prussian Academy of Sciences', *PMLA* 41 (1926), 126–50

Index

Aarsleff, Hans 10–11, 95
Abbt, Thomas 165, 171–4, 176, 177, 180, 184, 188
abstraction 2, 13, 19–20, 44, 46, 53, 55, 63, 79, 103, 116, 171, 176
Académie des Inscriptions 107
Académie Française 68, 161
accommodation, principle of (exegesis) 55, 57
Adam, language of 4, 12, 17, 21–7, 28, 37, 44 n. 11, 84, 114, 115–16, 124
Adanson, Michel 131
aesthetics 13, 43, 52–3, 56, 58, 60, 63–4, 81, 102, 105–6, 136
Alsted, Johann Heinrich 66
Amos (prophet) 101
analogy 19, 24, 25, 102, 177, 181
analysis 34–5, 39, 42–3, 51–3, 56, 64, 75, 92, 122, 166–7, 191
Andreae, Johann Valentin 66
animal communication 2, 19, 21, 29–30, 42, 73–4, 83–7, 165, 169–71, 180–2, 185
  apes 74, 171
  birds 30, 86
  parrots 41–3
  sheep 19, 82, 86, 173, 184
animal instincts 15, 169–71, 180–1, 183–4
anthropology 7, 14, 73, 93, 96, 165, 166–71, 180, 189
Arabia Felix, Danish expedition to 95, 106–9, 110–11, 118
Arabic 97, 101, 125, 126, 130
arbitrariness 2, 18–21, 23, 28, 36, 44, 78–9, 82, 84, 86, 128, 130, 159, 169, 177
Aristotle 1, 19, 20, 114
Arnauld, Antoine 31, 43, 94
Arnold, Gottfried 59
artifice 2, 3–5, 7, 16, 27–9, 36–7, 47–8, 63–4, 74, 77, 78–87, 121, 123, 126, 128, 136, 147, 165–6, 169–71, 177, 184–5, 188–9, 194–5
artificial, *see* artifice
Aufklärung (German Enlightenment) 10, 11, 39, 59, 61–3, 65, 73, 113, 194–5

Babel, confusion of languages at 22 n. 13, 24, 81 n. 39, 172
Baer, Frédéric Charles 110 n. 48

Baumgarten, Alexander Gottlieb 13, 52–4, 56, 60, 96 n. 2
Baumgarten, Siegmund Jacob 54–8, 96–7
Baurenfeind, Georg 106–9
bestial language, *see* animal communication
Beausobre, Isaac de 149
Beausobre, Louis Isaac de 88–9, 93, 151
Beauzée, Nicolas 79–80
Bellarmine, Robert 98
Berggren, Lars 106–9
Berkeley, George 33, 35
Berlin Academy 9–10, 13, 39, 54, 62, 64, 65–6, 80, 83, 87–8, 163, 175, 191–5
  1755 prize contest 72, 92, 145, 163 n. 56
  1759 prize contest 10–12, 14, 65–6, 71, 91–4, 95, 119–42, 144, 145, 164, 171, 176–8, 186–7, 191
  1763 prize contest 15, 62, 71, 72, 145, 166–8
  1771 prize contest 10–12, 15, 72, 127, 163, 165, 178–87, 188
  1784 prize contest 190–1
  and the *Préservatif* affair 143–4, 150–8
  history of 66–71
  rules of contests at 71–3, 120
Berlin, Isaiah, *see* Counter-Enlightenment
Berlin, University of 192
Blackwell, Thomas 103
blind cognition, *see* symbolic cognition
Bochart, Samuel 111
Bocquet, Abraham Robert 162
Boineburg, Johann Christian von 40
Browne, Thomas 114
Buffon, Georges-Louis Leclerc, Comte de 59, 62, 169, 171
Büsching, Anton Friedrich 56
Buxtorf, Johannes (the elder) 98–9, 103

Cabbala 20, 115
Callenberg, Johann Heinrich 97
Cappel, Louis 99, 100, 103
Carpov, Jacob 84
Cassirer, Ernst 16
Castillon, Jean de 80–1, 85
certainty *or* certitude 15, 43, 55, 60, 61–3, 71, 128, 165, 166–8

226 Index

Chinese characters 25, 77
Chladenius, Johann Martin 60, 109
Cicero 130, 133
Clarke, Samuel 40, 56
classic authors 90, 105, 128–9
clear but indistinct (confused) ideas 13, 39–48, 58, 60, 63
cognition 1–2, 6–7, 13, 14, 29–50, 78–87, 93–4, 122, 125, 135–6, 141, 184–7; *see also* symbolic cognition
Collins, Anthony 56
Comenius, Jan Amos 66
Condillac, Étienne Bonnot de 1, 2, 7, 12, 17, 25, 33, 35–7, 59, 71, 74, 77–9, 80, 85, 92, 102, 121, 154, 165, 175, 186, 191
   Essai sur l'origine des connoissances humaines 10–11, 26–9, 47–8, 73, 84, 90–1, 181
   Grammaire 28
   Traité des animaux 170–1, 181
conjectural histories 3–5, 39, 49, 78–87, 94–5, 118, 121–2, 127, 166, 169, 171–87, 194–5
convention, *see* artifice
Cook, James 109
Corneille, Pierre 150
Counter-Enlightenment 6–7, 15, 194–5
Crusius, Christian August 61–2, 166, 167, 171
Cudworth, Ralph 114
curiosity cabinets 107

D'Alembert, Jean Le Rond 71, 119, 139–40, 154, 155
Danckelmann, Karl Ludolf von 143, 150
D'Argens, Jean-Baptiste de Boyer, Marquis 144 n. 3, 148 n. 16, 152, 163
deaf-mutes 34, 47, 84, 86, 122
Deluge (biblical) 12, 24–7, 124, 126, 172
Descartes, René 1, 7, 17, 29–30, 31, 41, 43–4, 48, 61
   Cartesian dualism 7, 29–33, 46, 93–4, 169, 189
   Discours de la méthode 29, 74
   Meditations 29–30
determinism 96, 144, 145, 158–60
Diderot, Denis 3, 7, 33, 36–7, 59, 92, 102, 122, 175, 191
   'Encyclopédie' 90, 94
   Jacques le fataliste 145
   Lettre sur les aveugles 35
   Lettre sur les sourds et muets 34–5
Diodorus of Sicily 23, 26, 84, 182
Dubos, Jean Baptiste 32

Duclos, Charles Pinot 88–9, 94, 141
Du Marsais, César Chesneau 91

Egypt (ancient) 25–6, 111–12, 114–15, 124; *see also* Psammetichus' experiment
Eichhorn, Johann Gottlob 104, 111
Encyclopédie 25, 33, 90–1, 94, 134
English 137, 146–7
Epicureanism 14, 132–4, 141, 159
and the emergence of language 5, 12, 13, 16–29, 36–7, 65, 89–90, 91, 93, 95–6, 121, 123–4, 127–8, 132, 172, 188–9
criticism of 78–87, 136–9, 168, 170–1, 176, 182
Epicurus 12, 16–18, 19–21, 23, 85, 133, 134
Erman, Jean Pierre 161
Ernesti, Johann August 58
etymology 37 n. 54, 44, 48, 83, 94, 101, 111, 118, 125–6, 134–5, 141, 175
Euler, Leonhard 70, 120, 151
Ezra the Scribe 98, 100

Fassmann, David 69
fatalism, *see* determinism
Fénelon, François de Salignac de La Mothe- 133
feral children 37, 47, 74, 84, 86, 122, 189
Ferguson, Adam 3, 188
Ficino, Marsilio 114
Fontenelle, Bernard Le Bovier de 62, 149, 163
Formey, Jean Henri Samuel 14, 62, 71, 73, 78, 83, 91–3, 120, 125, 142, 160, 163, 172, 176, 179, 185
and the *Préservatif* affair 143, 148–9, 150–8, 166
Réunion des principaux moyens (…) 138–9, 141, 168, 182
Forsskål, Peter 106–9
Forster, Johann Reihnold 109
Francke, August Hermann 54
Francke, Gotthilf August 54
Frederick II of Brandenburg-Prussia ('the Great') 65, 68, 73, 139–40, 142, 144, 150–1, 152, 154, 162, 163, 191, 192
De la littérature allemande 189–90
reforming the Berlin Academy 69–71
Frederick III/I of Brandenburg-Prussia 67
Frederick V of Denmark 106
Frederick William of Brandenburg-Prussia ('the Great Elector') 148
Frederick William I of Brandenburg-Prussia 68–9
Frederick William II of Brandenburg-Prussia 191–2

free will 30, 62, 144–5, 159, 163; *see also* determinism
French Colony, *see* Huguenots (in Berlin)
French 15, 32, 34, 44–6, 70, 87–9, 91–2, 143–64, 174, 190–2
 orthography of 88–9
 and political freedom 89, 124
 see also Huguenots (in Berlin)
French Revolution 37, 192

Garve, Christian 165, 176, 186, 188
Gatterer, Johann Christoph 60–1, 109
general ideas *or* generalization, *see* abstraction
Genesis 17, 21–7, 28, 37, 102, 111, 172–4, 176; *see also* Adam, Babel, *and* Deluge
genius of language 13, 65, 87–94, 122, 124, 127, 189–91
geometric method, *see* mathematical method
German 44–6, 51, 68, 87–8, 91–2, 104, 105, 126, 128, 133–4, 143–64, 189–93
Gesner, Johann Matthias 105
Gibbon, Edward 5
Goethe, Johann Wolfgang von 190
Goeze, Johann Melchior 56
Göttingen, University of 13, 39, 59–61, 71 n. 12, 104–6, 107, 109, 137, 192
Göttingen, Royal Society of 104–6, 157
Göttingische Anzeigen 104, 107, 156–7
Gottsched, Johann Christoph 166
Graben zum Stein, Otto von 69
Greek 32, 34, 88, 96, 98, 125–6
Gregory of Nyssa 23, 84
Grotius, Hugo 134
Gundling, Jacob Paul 69

Halle, University of 14, 39, 45, 46, 50, 51, 54–8, 67, 96–8, 104
Haller, Albrecht von 73, 95, 105–6, 146, 162
Hamann, Johann Georg 14, 16, 72, 119, 189
 and the 1759 contest 136–8, 141
Hardy, Pierre 112 n. 57
Hatrtlib, Samuel 66–7
Haven, Friedrich von 106–9
Hebrew 24–5, 51, 88, 107, 125, 127, 129, 130, 137, 175 n. 33
 'hieroglyphic theory' of 115–16
 natural evolution of 114–18
 teaching of 97
 vowel points in 14, 95, 97–101, 102–3, 114, 116–18

Hebrews, *see* Israelites
Herder, Johann Gottfried 2, 3, 4, 7, 12, 15, 16, 26, 71, 111 n. 54, 165, 168, 194
 prize essay on the origin of language 10–12, 15, 87, 179, 181–7, 188–9
 Fragmente über die neuere deutsche Literatur 163, 174–6, 191
 Ideen zur Philosophie der Geschichte der Menschheit 1, 183 n. 56
 and Prémontval's *Préservatif* 163–4
Hermeticism 20, 114–15
Herodotus 76
Hertzberg, Ewald Friedrich von 191–2
Heyne, Christian Gottlob 103, 105
hieroglyphs, *see* Egypt (ancient)
Hißmann, Michael 193
historical inquiry 13, 17–18, 55–61, 63–4, 96, 105, 109–13
Hobbes, Thomas 1, 22, 23, 24, 26, 29, 30, 44, 48, 49, 78, 84
Hoffmann, Adolf Friedrich 61–2
Homer 103–4
Horace 126, 128
Horapollo 114
Huguenots (in Berlin) 10, 15, 65, 71, 144, 146, 148–9, 152, 160–2, 191
Humboldt, Wilhelm von 192, 193
Hume, David 5, 7, 129, 133

imagination 29–33, 34, 39, 48
immaterialism 33, 35, 41
innatism 31–2, 34, 81–7, 92, 165, 168–71, 178–89
intuitive perception 13, 39, 43, 47, 52, 60, 63, 125, 167
Israelites *or* ancient Israel 14, 24–6, 51, 53, 58, 99–101, 109–13, 117, 129

Jablonski, Daniel Ernst 69
Jaucourt, Louis de 33, 90–1
Joseph II of Austria 191
Jungius, Joachim 66
Justi, Johann Heinrich Gottlob von 163

Kant, Immanuel 167–8, 170, 174 n. 28, 184, 192
Kästner, Abraham Gotthelf 71
Kircher, Athanasius 115, 118
Klopstock, Friedrich Gottlieb 190
Koch, Friedrich Christian 115
Kramer, Christian 106–9

La Fontaine, Jean de 150
Lambert, Johann Heinrich 129 n. 31

La Mettrie, Julien Offray de 30, 33, 73–4, 148 n. 16
Lamy, Bernard 32, 46, 94
Lancelot, Claude 31
Lange, Joachim 51, 54, 96
language
    acquisition by children 24 n. 20, 26, 81, 87, 116, 117–18, 138, 176, 180, 183, 187; *see also* Psammetichus' experiment
    and cultural identity in Berlin 15, 148–50, 160–4, 191–3
    and tyranny 130–2, 141; *see also* French as a democracy 14, 89, 128–32, 141, 190
    constituting thought and reality 2, 8–9, 29, 43–4, 49–50, 53, 64, 75, 83–7, 89–90, 93–4, 118, 121–2, 135–6, 140–1, 184–7, 194–5
    diversity of 2, 6, 20
    divine endowment of 3–5, 7, 13, 16–17, 21–27, 78–87, 91, 117, 137–9, 182–3, 189
    encoding or mirroring thought 1–2, 53
    evolution of 16–29, 36–7, 48–50, 75–87, 88–9, 114–18, 126–8, 134–5, 137–8, 140–1, 165, 168, 171–89
    genius of, *see* genius of language
    vernacular 14, 43–6, 48, 77, 90, 128–9, 131
    women's use of 128, 129 n. 29, 141
    see also signs *and* symbolic cognition
language of action 25, 28, 34, 77, 102, 123, 181–2, 185
Latin 32, 34, 44, 77, 88, 91–2, 98, 123, 125–6, 128, 130–1, 133–4, 146
Leibniz, Gottfried Wilhelm 1, 7, 10, 11, 23–4, 48, 49, 50, 52, 55, 60, 61, 63, 65, 75, 85–6, 109, 126, 132, 134–5, 145, 146, 149, 158–60, 163, 165, 167, 170, 185
    Commentatiuncula de judice controversiarum 42
    Ermahnung an die Teutsche (…) 44
    Meditationes de cognitione, veritate et ideis 43
    Nouveaux essais sur l'entendement humain 15, 46, 168–9
    Unvorgreiffliche Gedancken (…) 44–5
    and the Christian mysteries 13, 39–43
    and the foundation of the Berlin Academy 66–8
    see also symbolic cognition
Leipzig, University of 45
Lenfant, Jacques 149
Lessing, Gotthold Ephraim 56, 72, 81–2, 150–1, 189, 190

linguistic relativism 74–5, 131
Linnaeus, Carl 106, 130–1
Literaturbriefe 135, 151, 162–3, 172, 174, 183
Locke, John 23, 32–3, 46, 48, 138, 163
Louis XIV of France 148, 149, 154
Louis XVI of France 192
Lowth, Robert 95, 102–3, 118, 136
Lucretius 12, 16, 20–1, 23, 24, 25, 30, 79, 84, 85, 132, 176
Lüdke, Friedrich Germanus 56–7
Luther, Martin (translation of the Bible by) 44, 98

Maistre, Joseph de 79
Malebranche, Nicolas 31, 43, 48
Malpeines, Marc Antoine Léonard des 25
Mandeville, Bernard 24, 25, 36, 132, 133
Masorah 98, 117, 118
materialism 14, 30, 33, 73–4, 159, 160, 170
mathematical method 13, 30–1, 52, 61–2, 131, 166–8
Maupertuis, Pierre Louis Moreau de 62, 65, 68, 73, 74–8, 92, 120, 122, 148 n. 16, 151, 163, 166, 181, 184, 192
    Des devoirs de l'Académicien 75–6, 87–8
    Dissertation sur les différens moyens (…) 77, 83, 94
    Lettre sur le progrès des sciences 76–7
    Réflexions philosophiques sur l'origine des langues 74–5
    reforming the Academy 70–2
Mendelssohn, Moses 5, 11, 12, 13, 14, 39, 60, 71, 72, 85, 162, 168, 172, 183–4, 192
    Briefe über die Empfindungen 53
    Notizen zu Ursprung der Sprache 86–7
    Sendschreiben an Lessing (reply to Rousseau) 81–3, 94, 173–4, 179–80
    and the 1763 contest on certainty 167
    on the 1759 contest on language 135–6, 141
Merian, Jean Bernard 92, 119–22, 139–40, 144, 157, 192
metaphor 21, 25–6, 32, 44, 51, 53, 57, 177, 181, 190
Michaelis, Christian Benedict 96–7, 99–100, 111, 118
Michaelis, Christian Friedrich 104
Michaelis, Johann David 5, 7, 15, 39, 57, 58, 71, 73, 94, 95–118, 174, 181, 194
    prize essay on language and opinions 14, 38, 90, 105, 116, 118, 119–22, 126, 127–42, 146, 175–6, 178, 190

Beurtheilung der Mittel (...) 115–16, 127, 129, 137
  Mosaisches Recht 109–13, 114
  Von dem Alter der Hebräischen Vocalen 116–17
  and the 1771 contest 127, 165, 179–81, 185, 188
  and the Danish expedition, *see* Arabia Felix
  and the *Préservatif* affair 143–4, 156–7, 162, 163–4
  education of 96–8
  in England 102–4
  on Hebrew vowel points 97–101, 116–8
Michaelis, Johann Heinrich 97, 99–100, 118
mind, *see* cognition
miracles 3–5, 42, 50, 53, 106, 112, 159, 172, 176, 182–3; *see also* Babel, Deluge, Red Sea, *and* language, divine endowment of
Miscellanea Berolinensia 68–9
Molière, Jean-Baptiste Poquelin 150
Montesquieu, Charles-Louis de Secondat, Baron de 7, 109, 129
Morgenstern, Salomo Jacob 69
Moses 14, 100, 101, 103, 111–13
Münchhausen, Gerlach Adolf von 104

naturalism 3–6, 14, 16, 21–7, 114–18, 119–28, 136, 141, 165–6, 168, 171–89, 194–5
natural law 48–50, 78, 133–4
natural order of thought (theory of) 34, 191
natural religion 42, 50, 63
Neology (exegesis) 57–9, 60, 112
Neo-Platonism 114–15
Neumann, Caspar 115
New Testament 96
Newton, Isaac 40
Newtonian method 3, 6, 134
Nicolai, Friedrich 150–1, 172
Nicole, Pierre 31
Niebuhr, Barthold Georg 192
Niebuhr, Carsten 106–9
Noah 27
Nösselt, Johann August 57
Novalis (Friedrich von Hardenberg) 189 n. 3

Old Testament 23, 26, 50–2, 53, 54–5, 57, 61, 97–9, 101, 115, 117, 118, 137
  Book of Job 103, 111
  legislation and social customs in 109–13
  poetry in 102–3
  see also Amos, Genesis, Pentateuch *and* Scripture
onomatopoeia 86, 123, 169, 171, 177, 184,
  see also signs, natural
opinions 11, 14, 66, 72, 73, 75, 88, 91–4, 116, 119–42, 144, 145, 175; *see also* genius of language; Berlin Academy, 1759 prize contest; Michaelis, Johann David

parallelism, *see* Lowth, Robert
Paris Academy of Sciences 10, 68 n. 7, 70, 149
Paris Linguistic Society 193
Pascal, Blaise 30–1, 94
passions 29–33, 165, 181
Pentateuch 5, 50, 51, 58, 98, 112
philosophes 65, 80, 149, 160, 163
Pietism (*or* Pietists) 13, 14, 39, 51, 52, 54–7, 58, 67, 71, 95–7, 104, 113, 167
Platner, Ernst 170 n. 17
Plato 18–19, 20, 22–3, 27, 114, 132
Popular Philosophy (*Popularphilosophie*) 13, 61–3, 174
Port Royal (*Grammaire* and *Logique*) 31–2, 34, 73, 88–9, 94
Prémontval, André Pierre Le Guay de 13, 62, 73, 174, 175
  Du Hazard sous l'empire de la providence 159
  Préservatif contre la corruption de la langue françoise 144–50, 190
  and the 1759 contest 91–4, 119–22
  and the *Préservatif* affair 15, 143–4, 150–8, 162–4
  early life 144–6
Prémontval, Marie Anne Victoire Pigeon d'Osangis, Mme de 145, 157
Printzen, Marquard Ludwig von 68
probability 5–6, 56, 167–8
providence 4, 26, 83, 112–13, 117, 145, 159, 178
Psammetichus' experiment 76–7, 87, 122–3, 138, 141, 178
Pufendorf, Samuel 22–3, 48–50, 59

Rabenius, Olaus 109
Raspe, Rudolf Erich 168
rationality, *see* reason
Ratke, Wolfgang 66
reason 6–7, 13, 23, 29–38, 39, 40, 50–3, 55–6, 60, 62, 63, 78–9, 80, 84–7, 96, 102–3, 123, 125, 176–7, 184, 186, 188, 194
Reclam, Frédéric 161

Red Sea 107, 112
Reimarus, Hermann Samuel 169–71, 183–4
Reinbeck, Johann Gustav 54
Reinhard, Adolf Friedrich von 163
representation 7–8, 29, 30, 32 n. 44, 33–8, 60–61 63, 77, 131, 137, 169, 172, 191
Republic of Letters 65, 67, 71, 92, 107, 125, 128, 129, 144, 146, 150–8, 194
Resewitz, Friedrich Gabriel 162
Rivarol, Antoine de 190–1
Royal Society 10
Rousseau, Jean-Jacques 3, 12, 25, 26, 35–7, 48, 74, 92, 123, 129, 132, 133, 141, 171, 177, 181, 184, 191
 Discours sur l'inégalité 4–6, 11, 13, 65, 78–9, 94, 125, 136, 178
  Responses to 80–7, 172–4, 179–80, 182–6
 Essai sur l'origine des langues 27, 89
Rudbeck, Olaus 111, 118

Schleiermacher, Friedrich 192
Schmauß, Johann Jacob 48, 134
Schmidt, Johann Lorenz 50–2, 54–5, 112
Schultens, Albert 101
Schwab, Johann Christoph 190
scientific idioms, *see* universal languages
Scripture 22, 24, 42, 50–2, 55–7, 96, 98, 104, 132, 134, 137
Searle, John 8–9
Semler, Johann Salomo 57–9, 112–13
sensualism 13, 16, 17, 30, 32–8, 63, 74, 77, 90, 121, 166
Septuagint 99
Seven Years War 139, 143, 151
signs (generally in language)
 accidental 28
 instituted, *see* artifice
 natural 2, 3, 18–21, 27–9, 44, 46, 74, 77, 78–87, 123, 126, 169–71, 181–7
 artificial, *see* artifice
Simon, Richard 23, 26, 84, 91
Skinner, Quentin 8
Smith, Adam 3, 188
sociability 23, 39, 80, 116, 165, 173, 180, 188
social contract 8–9, 22, 36, 49–50
Socinianism 40
Socrates 18
sola scriptura 51, 98
Sophie Charlotte of Brandenburg-Prussia 67–8

speech, human 1–2, 12, 22, 24, 30–2, 46, 49, 73–4, 78–9, 126, 136, 138–40, 165, 171, 176, 180–1; by gestures, *see* language of action
speech acts 8
Spinoza, Baruch 7, 25, 61, 159, 189
 Tractatus theologico-politicus 41–3, 112
state of nature 4, 8, 78–82, 85–7, 110, 113, 172–4, 176–7, 179–80
Stewart, Dugald 3
St Petersburg Academy of Sciences 70
Sulzer, Johann Georg 73, 120, 151, 165, 184, 188
 Observations sur l'influence réciproque (…) 176–7
supernatural intervention, *see* language, divine endowment of; miracles
Süßmlich, Johann Peter 13, 73, 87, 93, 94, 123, 138, 141, 151, 172, 178
 Versuch eines Beweises (…) 83–6, 171, 176, 177, 179, 182, 185
symbolic cognition 1, 7, 11, 13, 38–43, 46–8, 50, 53, 58, 60, 64, 126, 165, 189

Tacitus 45, 85
Taylor, Charles 8
Thirty Years War 67
Thomasius, Christian 45–6, 48, 59
Tindal, Matthew 56
Toland, John 25, 56
translation 11, 24, 25, 44, 50–2, 54, 81, 83, 94, 98–9, 104, 117, 118, 133–4, 139–40, 160, 169
transubstantiation 40–1
Turgot, Anne Robert Jacques 37, 94, 134–5

universal languages 14, 37–8, 77, 130–1, 139, 140–1

Vaugelas, Claude 129
Vico, Giambattista 5, 6, 16, 24–5, 26, 36, 110, 132
Viereck, Adam Otto von 69
Vitruvius 26, 84, 182
Voltaire (François-Marie Arouet) 25, 148 n. 16, 154, 155, 161
Vulgate 98

Warburton, William 5, 25–6, 36, 77, 91, 114–15, 132, 173
Webster, John 67
Webster, Noah 140
Wertheim Bible, *see* Schmidt, Johann Lorenz

Whiston, William 56
Wieland, Christoph Martin 190
Wolff, Christian 13, 46–8, 50, 51, 54, 55, 61–3, 71, 84–6, 91–2, 93, 109, 120, 126, 138, 145, 149, 158–60, 163, 166, 167, 169, 185

Wolffian philosophy 13, 39, 48, 53, 54–7, 92, 94, 96, 120, 160, 193
Wöllner, Johann Christoph 56
Wood, Robert 103–4, 109
writing 25–6, 77, 114–5, 123; *see also* Hebrew, vowel points in

Ingram Content Group UK Ltd.
Milton Keynes UK
UKHW020154090523
421445UK00005B/160